D0197721

Identity Politics and Women

Published in cooperation with
the World Institute for
Development Economics Research,
United Nations University

Identity Politics and Women

Cultural Reassertions and Feminisms in International Perspective

EDITED BY

Valentine M. Moghadam

Westview Press

BOULDER • SAN FRANCISCO • OXFORD

Typeset by Arja Jumpponen

Published in 1994 in the United States of America by Westview Press, Inc., 5500 Central Avenue, Boulder, Colorado 80301-2877, and in the United Kingdom by Westview Press, 36 Lonsdale Road, Summertown, Oxford OX2 7EW

Library of Congress Cataloging-in-Publication Data
Identity politics and women : cultural reassertions and feminisms in
    international perspective / edited by Valentine M. Moghadam.
        p.   cm.
    ISBN 0-8133-8691-8—ISBN 0-8133-8692-6 (pbk.)
    1. Women—Social conditions—Cross-cultural studies.   2. Women—
Middle East—Social conditions.   3. Women, Muslim—Social
conditions.   4. Sex role—Cross-cultural studies.   5. Identity
(Psychology)—Cross-cultural studies.   6. Feminism—Cross-cultural
studies.   7. Social change—Cross-cultural studies.   I. Moghadam,
Valentine M., 1952– .
HQ1233.I34   1994
305.42—dc20   93-28018
                                                                             CIP

Printed and bound in the United States of America

The paper used in this publication meets the requirements
of the American National Standard for Permanence of Paper
for Printed Library Materials Z39.48-1984.

10   9   8   7   6   5   4   3   2   1

Contents

PART TWO
Country Case Studies

Preface and Acknowledgments

This book is concerned with an issue that is as vexing theoretically as it is perplexing politically. "Identity politics" as used here refers to discourses and movements organized around questions of religious, ethnic, and national identity. Most of the chapters in this book deal with political-cultural movements that are making a bid for state power, for fundamental juridical changes, or for cultural hegemony. The best-known are "fundamentalist" and "communalist" movements in the Middle East, North Africa, and South Asia; the main religious groups involved are Muslim and Hindu. They are of concern because many of them have an explicit agenda for women: domesticity, control, family attachment, clearly defined gender roles. Proposals for the regulation of gender are frequently issued on the basis of cultural identity and integrity if not providence. The chapters in this book explore the relationships between culture, identity, and women, providing vivid illustrations from around the world of the compelling nature of Woman as cultural symbol and Woman as political pawn in male-directed power struggles. At the same time, the chapters provide evidence of women as active participants in these movements and women as equally active opponents of such movements. This collection provides answers to some of the pressing questions about such movements: What are the causes of these movements; who are the participants and social groups behind them; what are their objectives; why are they preoccupied with gender and the control of women?

Another type of identity politics explored in this book is movements that are more expressive than political in nature. They are not making a bid for state power or hegemony but are equally interested in issues of culture, religion, and identity. They represent the abandonment of the purely secular and the worldly for the spiritual. Among them are certain ethnic groups in Europe and the *ba'al teshuva*, or the Jewish orthodox revival in the United States. (Perhaps the New Age movement and spiritual feminism would fall into this category as well, though they are not explored in this book. There are also personalized forms of identity politics, but these, too, are not considered here.) This book contributes to our understanding of both "identity politics" as a feature of the late twentieth century and the operations of gender in political-cultural movements.

Organization and Themes of the Book

I have divided the book into three parts. Part I consists of chapters with theoretical, comparative, and historical approaches. Joan Smith discusses the relevance of world-system analysis to an understanding of gendered identities and antisystemic movements. Hanna Papanek examines the implications for women of constructions of the Ideal Society and compares Nazi Germany, Khomeini's Iran, and the anti-abortion movement in the United States. Silva Meznaric analyzes the discourse and practice of rape in two cases of ethnic rivalry in the former Yugoslavia. Mohamad Tavakoli-Targhi's historical study shows the connection between discourses about women and national Self-Other constructs.

Part II consists of 13 country case studies of women and identity politics, spanning Muslim, Christian, Jewish, and Hindu countries and communities, beginning with Ayesha Imam on Nigeria, Sondra Hale on Sudan, and Margot Badran on Egypt. Alya Baffoun compares fundamentalism in Tunisia and Algeria and Cherifa Bouatta and Doria Cherifati-Merabtine analyze representations of women in the writings of the main Algerian Islamist party.

Khawar Mumtaz examines the effects of state-sponsored fundamentalism in Pakistan. The complexity of identity politics in India is addressed in the chapters by Radha Kumar, whose focus is Indian feminism's response to Hindu-Muslim contention and the dubious role of the state, and by Sucheta Mazumdar, who criticizes the use of religious and ethnic symbols and argues for a secular and universalistic stance as an alternative to communalism.

Shahin Gerami describes her unique survey of women's attitudes to sex roles in the Islamic Republic. The fundamentalist movement in Turkey is studied by Binnaz Toprak in terms of both the search for status by marginal groups and the struggle for power. The chapter on Gush Emunim by Madeleine Tress examines both the role of women in Gush Emunim and constructions of women in religio-nationalist movements.

Debra Kaufman examines the "paradoxical gender politics" of American Jewish women who have returned to Orthodoxy. The chapter by Rebecca Klatch describes and compares concepts of family, feminism, and politics among two groups of New Right women in the United States.

Part III consists of three chapters discussing dilemmas posed by identity politics and some of the strategies designed in response. Marie-Aimée Hélie-Lucas discusses the importance of Muslim Personal Laws to the self-identity of Islamists and assesses Muslim women's responses to Islamization. Nira Yuval-Davis critically examines women and the politics of ethnicity, with attention to their complexity in contemporary Britain. The book concludes with a study by the United Nations Division for the Advancement of Women that argues that gender equality and religious freedom are not incompatible, but that fundamentalism as a political project contravenes the spirit and intent of the United Nations Convention on the Elimination of All Forms of Discrimination Against Women and as such is unacceptable.

Acknowledgments

The chapters in this book were prepared for UNU / WIDER in Helsinki. For their contributions, which could not be included in this book, and for stimulating discussions of the material herein, I am grateful to Nahla Abdo, Amrita Chhaachi, Kumari Jayawardena, Malavika Karlekar, Nassera Merah, Fatima Mernissi, Tuomo Melasuo, Sheila Rowbotham, M'hamed Sabour, Salma Sobhan, Soraya, Marja-Liisa Swantz, Nayereh Tohidi, and Judy Waters-Pasqualge. For excellent administrative and secretarial assistance with this book, I thank the WIDER staff and especially Arja Jumpponen, who has patiently gone through numerous revisions with me and shared my angst over the difficult editorial decisions.

Valentine M. Moghadam

Acronyms

AAWARD	Association of African Women for Research and Development
ANP	Awami National Party, Pakistan
APWA	All Pakistan Women's Association
AWSA	Arab Women's Solidarity Association
BJP	Bharatiya Janata Party, religio-national-chauvinist party in India
CPI	Communist Party of India
CPM	Communist Party of India-Marxist
DUP	Democratic Unionist Party, Sudan
EC	European Community (formerly EEC)
ERA	Equal Rights Amendment (a demand of the U.S. women's movement)
FLN	Front de Liberation Nationale, ruling party of Algeria
FOMWAN	A federation of Muslim women in Nigeria
GLC	Greater London Council
IDF	Israeli Defense Forces
IMF	International Monetary Fund
NCWS	Nigerian Council of Women's Societies
NEP	Northern Elements Progressive Union, Nigeria
NGO	Non-governmental organization
NIF	National Islamic Front, Sudan
NPC	Northern People's Congress, Nigeria
NWF	National Women's Front, Sudan
PPP	People's Progressive Party of Pakistan (party of Benazir Bhutto)
RCD	Rassemblement Constitutionel Démocratique, a political grouping formed in the late 1980s in Tunisia
RSS	Rashtriya Swayamsevak Sangh, national-chauvinist party in India
SS	Secret police of Nazi Germany

UNRWA	United Nations Relief and Works Agency (for Palestinian refugees)
UNU/WIDER	World Institute for Development Economics Research of the United Nations University
VHP	Vishwa Hindu Parishad, or World Hindu Congress, a major Indian fundamentalist organization
WAF	Women's Action Forum, Pakistan
WIN	Women in Nigeria

PART ONE

Theoretical, Comparative, and Historical Perspectives

1

Introduction:
Women and Identity Politics in Theoretical and Comparative Perspective

Valentine M. Moghadam

Emergence of Culture in Politics and Theory

During the 1980s, discourses and movements centered on issues of identity erupted around the world with considerable force. Questions of cultural, religious, national, linguistic, and sexual identity commanded center stage, relegating questions of economic justice, at least temporarily, to the background. Cultural revivalism, national liberation, religious "fundamentalism" and sexual affirmation all constituted some of the most vocal and visible political and social movements of recent history. The phenomenon of identity formation is not unique to a specific geographic area. The politicization of Muslim identity in the Middle East and cultural revivalism in South Asia (Hindu communalism in India and ethnic conflict in Sri Lanka) are the more "sensationalistic" of the various types of identity politics, and certainly the latter type entails more violence. But the preoccupation with national, cultural, and ethnic identity is not limited to countries of the Third World, and seems to be spreading in the 1990s. In the wake of the dismantling of Communism in Eastern Europe and the Soviet Union political-cultural movements of all types have emerged in the former socialist bloc, destroying old solidarities and redefining group identity and boundaries between groups. The tragedy in the former Yugoslavia is only the most violent. In Western Europe, the twin processes of immigration and the consolidation of the European Community have raised compelling questions about national identity. In some Western countries, issues of ethnicity, cultural rights, and sexual preference— sometimes accompanied by the rhetoric of "difference"—have motivated some states to design "multicultural" social and educational policies. These follow from the idea that people are members of different collectivities, and that the universal "we" is an imaginary construct. In some of the new discourses and movements, attention to class has been superseded by a focus on ethnicity and cultural rights. Whereas the discourse of "national character," "national psychology" and national identity used to be associated with the Right, it now spans the political spectrum. In Britain, socialists support Muslim demands for state-funded religious schools rather than insist on the secularization of the school system. Whereas the socialization of the means of production was once the dividing line between Left and Right in the West, now it is multiculturalism in the university curriculum and the school system. The workers' or labor movement is apparently a thing of the past, succeeded by a plethora of social movements, many of them organized around questions of identity.[1]

A parallel development in the social sciences and the humanities has been increased attention to questions of culture and identity. Culture, economy and polity are three essential dimensions taken into account for the appraisal of social reality. Mukherjee argues that in the 1950s and 1960s culture was treated as a dependent variable. It was presumed to change in accordance with the operation of the independent variable of economy and the concomitant variable of a democratic polity.[2] For many Marxists, too, at least other than Antonio Gramsci, theorists of the Frankfurt School, Raymond Williams and Louis Althusser, culture was considered derivative, the superstructure a reflection of the base, both of which were understood to correspond according to the dominant mode of production. However, there were alternative usages of culture. In development studies many theorists equated "culture" with "traditional society," counterposing on the one hand "modern" society with its dynamic economy and democratic polity, and on the other hand "traditional" society based largely on culture, tradition and authority, and possessing a stagnant and inert economy. In Indian anthropology, Louis Dumont compared Indian and Western values and consequently classified Indian society as "hierarchical" and Western society as "egalitarian."[3] Such a focus on values and view of culture as a coherent constant would seem to obviate contradiction and change.

In the late 1960s and through the 1970s, the modern-traditional schema underwent revision, mainly as a result of the challenge of the dependency school of development studies. Culture was no longer the province of developing societies, but a useful concept for industrialized societies as well, and began to be accorded the status of *intervening* variable. In this new view, culture is not only a product but a process. By the 1980s attention to culture assumed an acute form, and cultural analysis now pervades the disciplines. Cultural analysis is now a prominent field in sociology. There is, of course, an older cultural history associated with the sociologists Talcott Parsons and Robert Bellah, and the anthropologist Clifford Geertz. And one has only to recall earlier political science work on political culture, Max Weber's writings on Protestantism and capitalism, and Emile Durkheim's social classification schema and studies on religious life to recognize the cyclical nature of social science attention to culture. Be that as it may, sociologists who long considered culture the domain of anthropology are now turning to (or rather, returning to) cultural analysis. In the process some are reviving the Parsonian view of culture as central to the explanation of the continuity, coherence, and change of the social system. "Culture" remains a conceptually ambiguous term, difficult to operationalize, and with a number of usages (for example, culture as shared values; as popular practices; as artistic products). Further, how does one reconcile "common culture" and "multiplicity of cultures"? Still, cultural analysis as a method of social inquiry seems to be growing. As one historian has put it, it is hard not to be struck by the displacement of "society" or "economy" by "culture" in the discourse of our time. The shift is as true of historians as of sociologists and political scientists.[4]

The revival of cultural analysis reflects in part the influence of interpretive research and of discourse analysis; but it also represents the proliferation of post-modernists and post-structuralists in the academy, who have criticized "productivist bias" or "economism," especially in Marxism.[5] Post-structuralists give culture a unique role for the appraisal of social reality in their own works.[6] New areas of research include power relations, constructions of gender and ethnicity, and the multiple and competing identities of nation, ethnicity, gender, class, and race.[7] A central proposition is that identities are not shared but exist in competition. Competing loyalties may be manipulated both by the state and by social forces purporting to represent those identities. In a rejection of Marxian emphasis on economic determinants of identity formation, the new cultural analysis sees identities as historically and discursively constructed. Identities are seen as fluid and not primordial; the state may also fashion cultural identities.[8] In an interesting conceptual convergence, Western and Islamic theorists now emphasize the role of culture in shaping politics, power, and economic systems.[9] Culture may have been originally introduced to overcome some of the heavy determinism associated with social and economic analysis,[10] but since the latter half of the 1980s it has taken on a weight of its own, reified, even sacralized.

"Fundamentalism" has been widely regarded as the predominant expression of culture as an independent variable which is claimed to cut across national economies and the nation-state boundaries. Fundamentalist movements tend to emphasize cultural issues—religion, language, and ethnicity, but also gender, the family, and the position of women. Among non-Western fundamentalists, Westernization (but not necessarily modernization) is rejected as culturally alien and inappropriate. Western culture is construed as the enemy of Islamic culture and identity; certain ideas and practices associated with Western culture are strongly opposed, and a rather tendentious image of decadent Western culture is constructed based on what may be called the 3 Ps: prostitution, pornography, and promiscuity. In her contribution to this book, Ayesha Imam notes that in Nigeria, secular law is rejected by Islamists as being Christian law. Identity is at the heart of these movements.

But is cultural identity the only way to understand and explain these movements? Some analysts within the field of Middle East studies (including the present author) as well as students of South Asia have sought to refute the idea that "culture" (and its corollary, "religion") is central to the explanation of both stability and change. In their analysis, they demonstrate the salience of other theoretical "points of entry": the state, class relations, systems of production, the dynamics of the world-system.[11] In the context of the emergence of fundamentalist and communalist movements, it becomes pertinent to inquire how and why culture and group identity become problematized. Robert Wuthnow has suggested a framework for the analysis of ideological movements advocating reconstruction of a moral order that has been disrupted or changed. His framework links ideological movements to world-system dynamics, revolving around shifts in the relationship of core and periphery, and changing positions of elites in the periphery. Ideological revitalization movements occur when expansion of the world-system has given elites in peripheral areas new options that have led them to redefine their relationships with non-elites, creating among the latter uncertainty and efforts to restore the old moral order.[12] Joan Smith's chapter provides a world-systems analytic framework for the emergence of identity politics and the place of gender in the (re)construction of peoplehood. She notes that world-systems theory can account for both the universalizing project of world capitalism and the enormous differences which are produced. She then introduces the concept of *household* as a product of historical capitalism, a set of gendered relationships, and a site of opposition to the state and economic system—the "anti-systemic" movements theorized by Immanuel Wallerstein and his associates.

The world-systems perspective provides a useful theoretical starting point. The chapters in this book demonstrate that culture masks more than it reveals, making claims *on* people (especially women) as much as *for* them. The chapters also provide rich material from which to delineate the processes which seem to have resulted in enhanced attention to matters of culture and identity. A comparative assessment of the case studies suggests that the *cultural* cannot be properly understood outside of its relation to the *political* and especially the *economic*. Nor can *class conflict* be ruled out as an analytic tool and explanatory variable. I will impose on these processes a certain sequence in an attempt to tackle the macrosociological puzzle of identity formation and politicization in the late twentieth century.

1. The internationalization of capital on a world scale—the spread of industrialization to all corners of the world, international flows of labor and capital, worldwide trade and communications—has resulted in a certain homogenization of both culture and politics. On one level this is reflected in the global appeal of rock music, Coca Cola, blue jeans, and American TV. "Cultural diffusion" can also occur coercively—as in the case of the imposition of Radio Marti on Cuba.

2. Global culture and politics are also reflected in the spread and wide appeal of political discourses, movements, and institutions erroneously known as Western: human rights, women's rights, equality, self-determination, social movements, parliamentarism, socialism, democratization, privatization. These discourses and institutions, however, are not unique to a certain geographic area or a culture. Similarly, international law and various United Nations "universal declarations" are accepted and ratified—if not consistently adhered to—by the majority of member states.

3. But the economic process of globalization has been profoundly uneven as well as unequal, with some areas benefiting more from capital accumulation than others and having greater control over resources. The advantages of economic development on a world scale have not reached all societies and populations, and the distribution of resources and wealth has been extremely unequal.

During the 1970s, this gave rise to calls for the New International Economic Order; a number of United Nations conferences, and many publications, were devoted to suggesting ways of transferring some of the surplus from North to South.

4. The Iranian Revolution of 1978-79 had a profound demonstration effect: It showed that powerful states could be overthrown by united opposition—a lesson no doubt taken to heart by East Europeans. It also encouraged Islamist movements elsewhere.

5. With wealth still concentrated in the North and poverty in the South (and indeed with an inverse surplus transfer from South to North during the 1980s as a result of debt servicing), elites and intellectuals in the South turned their attention to another form of control by the North: information, communications, the media. This led to calls from developing countries for a new international information order, widely disparaged in the West. By this time, the North-South dialogue had reached an impasse.

6. Within countries, economic resources and political power are also unevenly and unequally distributed. Usually, those who own or control the economic and political resources will also determine what is the appropriate "cultural capital" and "symbolic capital." Changes in the cultural universe may come about abruptly, especially through the mass media, creating some dissonance.

7. At some point, the economic disadvantages and the cultural changes collide, leading to resentment, rejection and resistance on the part of the disadvantaged or declining groups. Struggles ensue over a more equitable distribution or for a complete shift in economic and political power.

8. Descending social groups, or disadvantaged groups, may deploy elements of the cultural repertoire or utilize cultural resources to mobilize and organize opposition and create a movement. The language of opposition may be more strongly cultural even though a motivation and cause of opposition is economic and social disadvantage.

9. Political elites may also deploy cultural resources and rhetorics to maintain their position and lend it legitimacy. They may draw on "tradition," authority, or what they claim are intrinsic values of the culture to justify their actions. They may turn to cultural questions (religion, morality, women's appearance, cultural imperialism) to divert attention from economic failures and social inequalities.

10. These activities and discourses lead to calls for cultural reassertion, and the process of identity formation is in motion.

Thus we see that the reassertion of identity and movements of cultural revival reflect the symbiosis of the economic, the cultural, and the political; they should also be seen in both the national and international context. Moreover, these types of movements reveal contention between social groups and classes over economic resources as well as political power. As Charles Tilly has noted, contenders who are in danger of losing their place in a polity are especially prone to "reactive" collective action, often taking communal forms.[13] Sometimes elites may engage in the manipulation of group identities; other times the search for status by marginal or descending groups is the motivation. Finally, the framework and sequence delineated above strongly suggest that frustration with the intractability of the world economic system and of national systems of accumulation and distribution may have something to do with the shift of focus from the economic to the cultural, and from exploitation to identity.

Mukherjee has suggested a research design in which the *world-system* as a unit of analysis is distinguished by geographic regions conforming to assumed identities of different civilizations, and that the minimal unit of study in each of these regions should be a nation-state. This is how the present book has been organized. In this spirit, I will devote the next section to a set of propositions regarding the rise of Islamist movements in the Middle East, considered here as a specific type of identity politics.[14] I would like to explain the causes of these movements in a manner consistent with the framework delineated above. At this point I will simply note the gender dimension; gender will be discussed in more depth below. As will be seen, the economic, the political and the cultural come together in this framework; historical processes as well as contemporary developments are included; and Islamist movements are situated squarely within the contemporary world-system.

The Emergence of Islamist Movements: Some Theses

1. Islamist movements have emerged in the context of a profound economic crisis in the Middle East and North Africa, which has affected oil economies and non-oil economies alike. What modernization has been achieved to date has been very lopsided because it has been the result of a single highly prized commodity. Since the late 1970s, rising indebtedness, unemployment, fluctuating oil prices, and problems arising from austerity measures in the 1980s have added to tensions in the region. These are linked to global restructuring and the worldwide socio-economic downturn of the

1980s; the falling price of oil on the world market has had an adverse effect on development and on living standards in the region.

2. Politically, the region is characterized by "neopatriarchal" state systems[15] which have silenced left-wing and liberal forces while fostering religious institutions in their search for legitimacy. Authoritarianism and development failures delegitimize existing political and economic programs. (See the references to the failures of the *parti unique* in the chapters by Baffoun and by Bouatta and Cherifati-Merabtine.)

3. Socially, capitalist relations of production are not ubiquitous in the Middle East and North Africa; as in many developing countries capitalist and precapitalist modes of production coexist. These have corresponding social and ideological forms as well as types of consciousness. There is an uneasy coexistence of modern and traditional social classes, such as the Westernized upper middle class on the one hand and the traditional petty-bourgeoisie organized around the bazaar and the mosque on the other. In many countries communal relations persist. The urban centers all have large numbers of people outside the formal wage market, among the urban poor, in the informal sector, and uneducated.

4. Increased female education and employment—while limited, it has been made possible by the expanding state—has challenged and slowly weakened the system of patriarchal gender relations. These developments have eventuated status inconsistency and anxiety on the part of the men of the petty-bourgeoisie—and to a lesser degree, the women of this class. Changes in gender relations, the structure of the family, and the position of women have resulted in contestation between modern and traditional social groups over the nature and direction of cultural and ideological institutions and practices. As such, Islamist movements represent the formation and politicization of identity informed by class.

5. The experience with European colonialism seems to have left deep and abiding tensions and grievances. The non-resolution of the Israeli-Palestinian problem, and a pervasive sense of injustice caused by Israeli and American actions also engender Islamist movements.

6. In the absence of fully-developed and articulated movements, institutions, and discourses of liberalism or socialism, "Islam" is the discursive universe—although Islam is quite variable across the various movements, and also competes with nationalism, much to the chagrin of Pan-Islamists. For some Muslims, the new ideological formation ("Islamic ideology") reduces anxiety because the ideology is able to offer a new form of assurance, and the movement offers

new forms of collective solidarity and support.[16] Islam provides a stable identity in a rapidly changing society.

7. In the context of economic, political, and ideological crisis, the vacuum can be more easily filled by Islamist-populist leaders and discourses. Most of the Islamist movements may be called populist by virtue of their social base (multi-class but mainly petty-bourgeois) and their discourses (articulation of "the people" and exhortations against foreigners). Islamist movements are political projects and are concerned with power.

8. In the new ideological formation, tradition is exalted—and frequently invented. The typical Islamist *hijab* (modest dress for women) is not at all a traditional form of dress; it is a quite novel and contemporary ensemble, deployed as a uniform.[17] And while Islamist movements are also strongly concerned with the nature of gender roles, their discourse on women is quite contradictory; different groups have differing emphases vis-à-vis gender issues.

9. Historically, the Middle East has not experienced a complete bourgeois revolution or an Enlightenment; neither has Islam completed a process similar to the Christian Reformation. Modernizing and reformist movements have been part of Islamic/Middle Eastern history, but they have not succeeded in the way such movements did in Christian/European history.[18] Islamist movements result from the process of transition (including a demographic transition) and modernization. What is unclear is whether they impede or accelerate the transition to modernity.

10. Culture, religion, and identity are thus both defense mechanisms and the means by which the new order is to be shaped. Islamist movements appear to be archaic but in fact combine modern and premodern discourses, means of communication, and even political institutions. These movements must therefore be seen as both reactive and proactive.

Fundamentalism's orgin in socio-economic crisis is also pertinent to Nigeria and South Asia. Asghar Ali Engineer's description and analysis of Indian communalism, in particular the emergence of a politicized Muslim identity, accords well with the analysis presented here.[19] But mention should be made of another factor in the growth of Islamist movements: funding by Saudi Arabian petrodollars, as discussed by Marie-Aimée Hélie-Lucas in this book. Engineer concludes that a fundamentalist or communalist movement is neither a purely religious and ethnic phenomenon nor a purely economic and political phenomenon. This applies equally well to the Gush Emunim of Israel.

Madeleine Tress observes that groups with a political agenda often justify their objectives and actions by selectively appropriating traditions and religious and historical texts.

But certainly there is such a thing as a "back to the roots" movement—people grouped together around a common identity who by reclaiming the past through myths and symbols seek to empower themselves. This would not necessarily be done at the expense of other groups, and it need not be achieved through political power. An example of this type is provided in this book by Debra Kaufman. The American Orthodox Jewish community studied by Kaufman is interested more in cultural reaffirmation than in political power. And here there is clearly more choice in the selection of identity than in cases where the political-cultural movement holds political or state power. But Nira Yuval Davis argues that ethnic groups who utilize cultural resources—and for whom multicultural policies have been designed—may in fact have political objectives. Her chapter explores theoretical relationships between individual identities, identity politics, and questions of cultural and communal representations, especially in contemporary Western politics.

There seems to be two types of political-cultural movements: (a) those which seek to *acquire* political power (oppositional movements), and (b) those which seek to *maintain* or legitimate political power by manipulating religious and cultural sentiments (state-sponsored fundamentalism). A well-known example of type (a) is the Iranian Islamist movement; a more recent example is the Algerian *Front Islamique du Salut*. An example of type (b) is Pakistan under Zia ul-Haq, discussed here by Khawar Mumtaz, who stresses the role of the state in promoting and fostering certain ideologies. In Bangladesh, too, as Salma Sobhan argues, the search for identity is essentially a political ploy by the state managers.[20] However, Ayesha Imam's paper shows how, over time and depending on the political conjuncture, movements may do either or both. Hélie-Lucas notes a striking similarity in their discourse: Islamic identity is in danger, the community must return to a fixed tradition, identity lies in the private sphere (women's behavior, dress, appearance), Muslim personal laws are necessary at the level of the state (in the case of majority Muslim societies) or the community (in the case of minority Muslim groups, as in India). In all cases, "identity," like "culture," functions to mask complex realities, to inscribe and at the same time mystify relationships. Although the quest for identity and the focus on culture is meant to differentiate one group from another, "culture," like "nation," occludes class, gender, generational, and other significant differences.

It should be clear that the causes of Islamist movements are complex—political, economic, and cultural, with social and class conflict an essential feature—and that their goals are not only cultural but frequently political. That is to say, juridical changes, upward social mobility, the acquisition of political power, and even the assumption of state power are among the objectives of many "fundamentalist" groups, facilitated through external funding. It is thus important that religious reassertion and cultural revivalism be placed in its socio-economic and political context. It is also important to understand the class and gender dynamics of these movements. Many of the chapters describe these dynamics, but an especially rich illustration of the problematics of class and gender in Islamist identity politics is the Iranian concept of *gharbzadegi* in association with the polemics surrounding hijab.

Class and Gender in Identity Politics

Variously translated as westoxication, westitis, euromania, and occidentosis, gharbzadegi denotes an illness, a virus, a "plague from the West," a phenomenon of excessive Westernization that renders members (usually those with a Western education) of the community alienated from their own culture.[21] Through those members who are "struck by the West," imperialism can penetrate the society and wreak havoc on the culture. And who are those members of the community most vulnerable to gharbzadegi? Women. It is most easily through women—by depriving women of chastity, modesty, and honor through notions of autonomy, sex appeal, and so on—that colonialists and imperialists can weaken the culture. This is said to have happened in Algeria under French colonialism, and in Iran during the rule of the pro-American Shah. And what is the main antidote to the virus of gharbzadegi? Hijab. Furthermore, veiling must be compulsory in order to protect the cultural identity and integrity of the group and of its female members. But to whom was this antidote delivered in the case of the Islamic Republic of Iran? To working class women? To peasant women? To the women of the urban poor? No. The main target was upper middle-class educated women, principally those who had had a Western-style education in high schools or in university. As far as Islamists were concerned, these women had cast off their authentic cultural identity and assumed that of a Westerner, complete with ideas about liberalism, socialism, Marxism, feminism, and sexual equality.

Such ideas were anathema to the Islamist paradigm. The persons who (quite literally) embodied these notions were the gharbzadeh women: decadent, bourgeois, cultural traitors. Thus when Ayatollah

Khomeini and his associates assumed control of the state (following violent battles with liberals, the left-Islamic Mojahedin and with the socialists), the victorious traditional petty-bourgeoisie enacted repressive legislation that was both an attack on women (gender conflict) and an attack on the upper middle class (class conflict).[22]

Bouatta and Cherifati-Merabtine describe a very similar construct of the Westernized Algerian woman. Like Baffoun, Bouatta and Cherifati-Merabtine are social-psychologists, and they bring their special analytic skills to bear on the issue of identity. The veil is now the distinguishing mark of the Islamist woman throughout the world. It is the line of demarcation between the Islamist community and other communities, distinguishing Islamist women from "Others." It is a shield against the slings and arrows of imperialists. But compulsory veiling in Iran is also a mechanism of social control: It represents the regulation of women. Moreover, it symbolizes the lack of choice in the selection of identity: identity, in the form of hijab, is imposed. As Hanna Papanek shows in her chapter, women are controlled and meant to conform to an idealized construct of womanhood and community.

In the case of Pakistan, fundamentalism and women's active participation in the fundamentalist project came in the wake of a militant women's movement. The latter movement was constituted by women of the upper middle class; predictably, the Pakistani women's movement was attacked as bourgeois, irrelevant, and culturally alien. Khawar Mumtaz reports that in the press feminists have been labeled *maghreb-zad* (the Urdu variant of gharbzadeh), and part of either the communist, red, Indian, Zionist lobby, or all of these together! One measure taken by the Zia state to prevent the spread of such women is the setting up of religious schools for girls with the intent of ensuring proper religious identity. Binnaz Toprak informs us that in Turkey, courses on religion in primary and secondary school have been mandatory since 1980—the year of the military coup. This suggests, *inter alia*, that the political use of religion can also be undertaken by pro-Western groups. Bangladesh, which began as an ostensibly secular, socialist state in 1970, now also has compulsory religious instruction. In the case of Afghanistan, secular education received by youth sent to the Soviet Union was deemed "propaganda" and "Sovietization," but the strictly religious education provided in the refugee camps somehow is "cultural" and therefore appropriate.[23] In Israel, religious instruction is pervasive, although religion is taught differently in the state-run schools from the independent religious schools.

I have been arguing that the sexual confrontation is also a class conflict. This point has also been made in this book by Gerami, Toprak,

Mumtaz, and Imam. Where upper middle-class educated women are viewed as agents of imperialist culture and are the targets of repressive legislation, class and gender conflict intersect most vividly. Alya Baffoun draws interesting parallels between the revolt of the petty-bourgeoisie in Europe in the 1930s, and that of the Islamist movements in North Africa in the 1980s. The socio-economic insecurity of a class seems to have its corresponding set of socio-psychological anxieties, often projected on women (and often on other groups: immigrants, Blacks, and Jews).

A major theoretical challenge, in terms of gender analysis, is the place of gender in the causes and outcomes of fundamentalist and communalist movements. Gender outcomes or consequences are more obvious—we know that political-cultural movements and state projects entail changes in laws, institutions, practices, attitudes to gender, and the legal status and social positions of women. Less obvious is the role of gender in *causes* of such movements. Many of the chapters in this book suggest that changes in gender relations, in particular the weakening of the traditional patriarchal family structure, the growing visibility of women, and competition between men and women in the labor market and the public sphere, may be one cause of these movements. Fatima Mernissi has made a simple but profound observation: "If fundamentalists are calling for the return to the veil, it must be because women have been taking off the veil."[24] To Mernissi the issue revolves around power: The public visibility of women terrifies and angers men. There seems to be a conflict of interest between fundamentalist men and non-fundamentalist women. Thus on one level it is a battle of the sexes, a battle between patriarchy and feminism. A number of feminists, including Amrita Chhachhi, have cited the breakdown of the patriarchal family as a principal cause of fundamentalist and communalist movements in South Asia. Indian feminist historians such as Sudesh Vaid and Kumkum Sangari have interpreted widow immolation (*sati*) as "a symbolic event which has the power to hold together all that seems to be in danger of falling apart: the extended family, female obedience to patriarchal norms, sectional group identities, Hindu tradition, Indian spirituality, and the nation itself." Further, by representing sati as definitionally opposed to modernity, Westernization and materialism, defending it is construed as combating the colonial legacy.[25] Cultural revivalists have a tendency to idealize themselves. But as Radha Kumar shows in this book, the advocates of sati are prone to a rather crass materialism and commercialism themselves.

Crisis and transition seem to bring about an exaggerated reliance on the home and family as refuge for the assaulted identity. But this is hardly unique to Islam or Hinduism, for it is present in Christian fundamentalism as well, especially in its American variety. Susan Marshall notes that American mass revivals of Christianity appear to coincide with periods of major social disruption.[26] The Second Great Awakening in the mid-nineteenth century was composed primarily of individuals uprooted by the ongoing Industrial Revolution, relocated to cities, removed from familiar traditions, and exposed to new values. The more recent "born-again" Christian movement has likewise been interpreted as a response to the turmoil of the 1960s, particularly the Civil Rights movement and the Vietnam protests, followed in the 1970s by the national crises of Watergate, the shrinking dollar, and the deterioration of American power and influence abroad. Marshall argues that these cultural crises reactivate and intensify patriarchal elements of religious traditions. In this book, Hanna Papanek's chapter includes a discussion of the patriarchal discourses of the contemporary Christian anti-abortion movement in the United States. And Rebecca Klatch's chapter shows how the profound social changes in the United States since the 1960s resulted in the growth of a religious "New Right" with a strong pro-family discourse.

The Significance of Women

We are beginning to see why women are important, and why gender is an indispensable concept in the analysis of political-cultural movements, of transition, and of social change. It is in the context of the intensification of religious, cultural, ethnic, and national identity—itself a function of uneven development and social change—that we see the politicization of gender, the family, and the position of women. Constructions of gender also seem to be inextricably tied up with constructions of the Other, as Mohammad Tavakoli-Targhi points out in his historical study of Iranian images of the West and of Western women. They are likewise tied up with national projects, as in the cases of Israel (Tress), Nazi Germany (Papanek), Nigeria (Imam), Sudan (Hale), India (Mazumdar), and the building of the Islamic Republic of Iran (Gerami). As Hanna Papanek explains, the Ideal Woman and the Ideal Society go hand in hand, although the specific status of women depends very much upon the specific vision of the ideal society.[27] For example, in the case of Afghanistan, the Marxist reformers had a proactive construction of gender, which was an integral part of their political-cultural project of development and change; the tribal-Islamist opposition had a reactive construction of gender, which was central to the maintenance of the status quo. In the refugee camps of Peshawar, women were under tighter controls than ever.[28] Sucheta Mazumdar shows that in Sanskritization—an invented tradition—Woman becomes the repository of the Hindu spirit, a symbol not to be polluted by the West. A central manifestation of fundamentalism—be it Islamic, Christian, Jewish, or Hindu—is an attempt to circumscribe women's freedom and identity. From many of the case studies in this book, and as elaborated in the chapter by Papanek, one concludes that where group identity becomes paramount, and where defensiveness and xenophobia are present, women are controlled. Alternative forms of identity, such as feminism, become suspect and unacceptable.

The imposition of identity can be in the form of attachment to religion (and its accoutrements, such as "proper dress") or it can be of a more secular type, as in nationalist movements. In her study of the Palestinian Intifada, Nahla Abdo evinces some circumspection and a certain ambivalence toward nationalist discourse. She differentiates "official-state nationalism," which can be exclusivist and racist, from "popular-national liberation movements." She problematizes the latter, identifying its gender-class oppressive moments. In a nationalist context, it becomes incumbent upon women to "produce fighters" or to reproduce more members of the community.[29] Nira Yuval-Davis has discussed this in connection with Israel.[30] In the case of the Palestinian movement for national liberation and statehood, and specifically in the context of increasing Jewish settlement in the West Bank, Palestinian women are exhorted to do their nationalist duty by producing more Palestinians. Although Abdo points to the democratic space for women that is possible in a popular struggle, there is cause for concern. Abdo has expressed some consternation with the beloved Palestinian poet, Mahmud Darwish, for the following words:

> Put it on record.
>   I am an Arab.
> And the number of my card is fifty thousands
> I have eight children
> And the ninth is due after summer.
> What's there to be angry about?[31]

Who, Abdo asked rhetorically, is supposed to look after all those children?

Because of their reproductive capacity, women are seen as the transmitters of group values and traditions and as agents of socialization of the young. When group identity becomes intensified, women are elevated to the status of symbol of the community and are compelled to assume the burden of the reproduction of the group. Their roles as wives and especially mothers are exalted, indeed fetishized. Woman's "place" in the home and in the family is lauded. It is Woman as Wife and Mother—not women as workers, students, citizens—who is ideologically constructed in the discourse and program of the movement. This is why women's dress and behavior become so important within the movement. This is why it becomes important to establish an appropriate role for women (ordained by nature or by divine will) and to put women "in their place." Women who resist this role are accused of disloyalty.

Silva Meznaric provides insights into the use to which "Woman" can be put in political battles between different cultural groups. Her chapter focuses on the contention between ethnic Serbs and Albanians in Yugoslavia in the late 1980s, and the Serbs and Muslims of Bosnia-Herzegovina in a now disintegrated Yugoslavia in 1992-1993. In the first case, rape was constructed as a political act by one group (Yugoslav Albanians) against another (Serbs). Rape as an act of violence by men against women became political and ethnic rape. In the second case, rape was a very real weapon in the hands of Serb militants to effect "ethnic cleansing" and the propagation of more Serbs. In both cases, women are pawns in the political-cultural battles between male-directed groups.

Like "fundamentalist" movements, the anti-abortion movement in the United States is preoccupied with the behavior, especially the sexual behavior, of women, as Hanna Papanek argues in her chapter. The anti-abortion movement is a legacy of the patriarchal association of womanhood with motherhood, and of the denial of sexuality for women other than for purposes of reproduction. Such patriarchal notions are powerful, widespread, and cross-cultural. An essay on the parallels between German National Socialism and Hindu communalism includes a quote from Adolf Hitler which could equally have been uttered by a right-wing anti-abortion activist in the United States, an Islamic fundamentalist in Iran or Algeria, an orthodox Jew in Israel, or an anti-communist in the Soviet Union or Poland: "The wonderful thing about nature and providence is that no conflict between the sexes can occur as long as each party performs the function prescribed for it by nature."[32] This quote exemplifies the patriarchal ideal: complementary gender roles based on innate differences; the family as the unity of these complementary roles and as keeper and practitioner of tradition; and the good wife upholding familial ideas. It is also centered on an implicit or explicit regulation of female sexuality.

For some women the designation of Woman as the carrier of culture and tradition is an onerous burden, one that they would just as soon not assume, especially as it is predicated upon control and conformity. But for other women, it is an honor and a privilege to be elevated to such a lofty and responsible position. Islamist women seem to find value and purpose in the movement's endorsement and exaltation of their domestic activities and "nature." This is why all "fundamentalist" movements have women supporters as well as women opponents. This is why feminism has its female detractors. As we know this situation is not limited to "fundamentalist" movements or the Islamic world. In the United States feminism has its female opponents, not limited to the formidable Phyllis Schlafly. But the participation of women in the anti-abortion movement in the United States, as with female support for Islamist movements in the Middle East and North Africa, may also reflect deep-seated fears among women, especially economically dependent women. Perhaps these women see the movement as a response to the normlessness of contemporary society and wish to avoid the increased pressures and demands on women. Writing about the Islamist movement in Turkey, Feride Acar has suggested that women have been exposed to contradictory, dissonant messages and practices, filled with false expectations and aspirations. This has rendered them vulnerable and receptive to an ideology that simplifies reality and promises escape from role conflict and ambiguity.[33]

Identity politics promise women security and meaning in what, from a conservative point of view, is a world gone mad. Stability lies in part in clearly defined sex roles, family life, and a religious orientation. The Orthodox Jewish women studied by Debra Kaufman report that they are psychologically alienated from sexual liberation, individualism, and the secular worldview. They have decided that their personal needs are better met in the religious community. As with Islamist women, these Jewish women fear the loss of boundaries; they celebrate gender differences and extol separatism. The American women of the New Right studied by Rebecca Klatch, especially the women she calls "social conservative," tend to see everything in religious terms (God, Christ, Man, Woman) and place the family firmly at the center. They fear the breakdown of the moral universe and blame feminists for it; narcissism and the degradation of homework are said to be the result of the feminist movement. These religious women of the New Right also fear the masculinization of the world through the blurring of gender roles.

At the same time, they evince a distrust of men for being non-committal, and support measures, such as a ban on pornography, that would "hold back man's animal nature." There are striking parallels in approaches to religion, the nature of men, and sexuality between the Sudanese women interviewed by Hale, the American Christian women discussed by Klatch, and the American Orthodox Jewish women discussed by Kaufman.[34] Ironically, some of the arguments of religious women would find resonance with (secular) cultural feminists.

One of the surprises of Islamist movements in the 1980s has been its appeal among university and educated women. One reason—apart from that provided by Acar—is that many Islamist movements exhibit a degree of flexibility in their position on women. They encourage education for women, mainly so that they can be more informed mothers but also so that they can provide teaching and medical services for other women, thus avoiding the problem of excessive male-female interaction. In an interesting twist to the preoccupation with culture and identity, pragmatism can work its way through ideology to encourage female labor force participation during wartime or a period of labor scarcity, as occurred in Iran.[35] Thus the Islamist discourse on gender combines traditional conservative ideas about "women's place," vague longings for a mythical past and golden age, and acceptance of the needs of a modern economy.

Women from traditional families in the lower middle class support these movements because they provide space for them. Women from this class can legitimately study, work, act politically and publicly, with virtue and modesty protected within the confines of the Islamist movement. Veiling becomes not only a cultural symbol and an assertion of identity but a matter of convenience—it allows women physical mobility in public spaces, free from the gaze and harrassment of men and the disapproval of family members.

What are the implications of identity politics for feminism, and for concepts of women's emancipation? What kinds of feminist strategies, or women's movements emerge in response to these movements, or within these movements? Unexpected forms of activism and consciousness are described in the chapter on Egypt by Margot Badran, Sondra Hale's study of Sudan, Imam's study of two women's organizations in Kano, the chapter on Pakistan by Mumtaz, and the chapter on Iran by Shahin Gerami. Gerami's chapter is a unique survey of Iranian women's attitudes toward their role, place and power in the Islamic Republic, and shows that although some Islamist attitudes have been internalized, middle-class Iranian women strongly object to veiling and segregation. They reject the imposition of hijab and spatial gender segregation, and strongly feel that opportunities for them should be expanded. Elsewhere, Tohidi speaks of the emergence of "Islamic feminists," or the radicalization of Islamist women previously uninterested in the advancement of women, such as the parliamentarian Maryam Gorji, who is now attempting a feminist exigesis of the Quran. Tohidi argues that this outcome is part of the evolution of the Iranian fundamentalist movement, with its mass participation of women. One might say that the new generation of Islamic feminists is "ideologically correct," and possesses the required "symbolic capital" to launch feminist-type campaigns to improve the status of women. Can they contribute to the democratization of the system? Is there a common ground between them and secular feminists? Could Islamist and non-Islamist women unite in a common movement for the betterment of women? In my view, there is common ground in matters of education, employment, family planning, and political participation. But hijab and Muslim law constitute the dividing line.

Margot Badran describes the "gender activism" of both Islamist women and secular feminists in Egypt, raising interesting questions about the "feminism" of Islamist women. Debra Kaufman argues for different types of feminism, including one that reclaims religion, where women find value, purpose, and identity in religious practices. In a recent paper, Malavika Karlekar suggested that the writings and vision of Gandhi provide an important political and cultural alternative to Indian communalism. But Sucheta Mazumdar's provocative essay warns against the use of religion or Hindu terminology by feminists, and argues for a secular discourse around which the various cultural groups in India could be expected to unite. Marie-Aimée Hélie-Lucas endorses a feminist strategy based on secularist politics, and Nira Yuval-Davis urges attention to universalist values while recognizing diversity among people.

What Is to Be Done?

In light of the emergence of political-cultural movements worldwide, given the complexities of identity politics, and considering, too, the post-modernist attention to "difference," what political responses are appropriate? What policy instrument can be effectively applied across cultures and religions to protect women from manipulation and discrimination? A good theoretical and political starting point is the United Nations Convention on the Elimination of All Forms of Discrimination Against Women, which is the note on which this book ends. In the place of a cultural relativism which would refrain from criticizing aspects of culture, the UN Convention is predicated upon the idea that there exist objective standards and universal values. As the concluding chapter from the Division for the Advancement of Women argues, the Convention is culturally neutral, but it is universal. Variance by cultural practice is not accepted as valid grounds. In Vienna's opinion, discrimination against women is not derived from culture, but from power. In this view, too, fundamentalism is politics using religion.

It is worth reminding those for whom cultures are specific, that a majority of countries are signatories to the Universal Declaration on Human Rights, the UN Convention on the Elimination of All Forms of Discrimination Against Women, and the Nairobi Forward-Looking Strategies. The latter, adopted by the General Assembly in 1986, seeks to realize the goals of equity and empowerment of women by the year 2000. Indeed, the United Nations offers a discursive framework that is very useful for political work by feminists and progressives. In the place of particularist rhetorics and exclusivist concepts of identity, the United Nations "universal declarations" on human rights and the convention on women provide a powerful rhetorical and political point of departure. I have argued in this Introduction that the causes of political-cultural movements around identity are complex, and that some of the problems from which they arise are deep and seemingly intractable. But one must begin somewhere, in politics as in theory. One answer to identity politics which seeks to control women is to disarticulate "woman" from "culture," deconstruct woman as symbol, reconstruct women as human beings, and problematize women's rights as human rights.

Notes

1. Some would interpret the preoccupation with culture and identity as reflective of the crisis of the nation-state. See Perry Anderson, "Nation-States and National Identity," *London Review of Books* (9 May 1991):3-8. It seems to me that what is in crisis is not so much the idea of a nation-state as *actually existing nation-states*. Collectivities are being reassessed and redefined, in a manner far less universal and inclusive than what has developed over the twentieth century, especially in the Second and Third Worlds. The trend seems to be toward the creation of new nation-states predicated upon more exclusivist notions of belonging and citizenship.

2. Ramkrishna Mukherjee, "Social and Cultural Components of Society and Appraisal of Social Reality," *Economic and Political Weekly* (January 26, 1991):PE-21-36.

3. Andre Béteille, "Some Observations on the Comparative Method," *Economic and Political Weekly* (October 6, 1990):2255-2263.

4. John Gillis, personal communication, April 1991. Among the many books and articles on the subject of culture and identity, see Craig Calhoun, "Introduction: Social Issues in the Study of Culture," *Comparative Social Research* 11 (1989):1-29; and Immanuel Wallerstein, "Culture as the Ideological Battleground of the Modern World-System," pp. 31-56 in Mike Featherstone (ed.), *Global Culture: Nationalism, Globalization and Modernity* (London: Sage, 1990). Apart from the UNU/WIDER conference in Helsinki from which this volume sprang, a very interesting conference exploring "rhetorics and rights of identity" was sponsored by The Center for Historical Analysis, Rutgers University (12-13 April 1991).

5. Ernesto Laclau and Chantal Mouffe, *Hegemony and Socialist Strategy* (London: Verso, 1985).

6. See especially Jean Lyotard, *The Postmodern Condition* (Minneapolis: University of Minnesota Press, 1984).

7. See György Szell, "Identities for Collective Actions: Class, Nation, Ethnicity, and Gender," paper presented at the XII World Congress of Sociology, Madrid (July 1990).

8. "Manifesto of the Center." Wilder House Working Paper no. 1. University of Chicago: Center for the Study of Politics, History and Culture (1989), p. 6.

9. See Lynn Hunt, *Politics and Culture in the French Revolution* (Berkeley: University of California Press, 1984); Michèle Lamont, "The Power-Culture Link in a Comparative Perspective," *Comparative Social Research* 11 (1989):131-150; Abol Hassan Bani Sadr, *Eqtesad-e Towhidi* [Economics of Divine Unity] (Tehran, 1978, in Persian); Seyed Mahmood Taleghani, *Islam and Ownership*, translated from the Persian by Ahmad Jabbari and Farhang Rajaee (Lexington, KY: Mazda Publishers, 1983).

10. See, for example, William Sewell's critique of Theda Skocpol's structuralism in the theory of revolution, and her response: "Ideologies and Social Revolutions: Reflections on the French Case," *Journal of Modern History* 57 (1985):57-85; "Cultural Idioms and Political Ideologies in the Revolutionary Reconstruction of State Power: A Rejoinder to Sewell," *Journal of Modern History* 57 (1985):86-96.

11. See Alan Richards and John Waterbury, *A Political Economy of the Middle East: State, Class and Economic Development* (Boulder, Co: Westview Press, 1990), Berch Berberoglu (ed.), *Power and Stability in The Middle East* (London: Zed Press, 1989), and Valentine M. Moghadam, *Modernizing Women: Gender and Social Change in the Middle East* (Boulder, CO: Lynne Rienner Publishers, 1993). On South Asia, see articles in *Economic and Political Weekly* (Bombay) and *South Asia Bulletin* (History Department, SUNY-Albany).

12. Robert Wuthnow, *Meaning and Moral Order: Exploration in Cultural Analysis* (Berkeley: University of California Press, 1987).

13. Charles Tilly, "Revolutions and Collective Violence," in F. I. Greenstein and N. W. Polsby (eds.), *Handbook of Political Science, Volume 3: Macropolitical Theory* (Reading, MA: Addison-Wesley, 1975).

14. In contrast to other types of identity politics, Islamist movements regard identities as fixed and primordial, not as social constructions. They also stress cultural uniqueness and difference. But this they have in common with other political-cultural movements, such as those mushrooming in the former socialist countries.

15. Hisham Sharabi, *Neopatriarchy: A Theory of Distorted Change in the Arab World* (New York: Oxford University Press, 1988).

16. See Diane Baxter, "A Palestinian Women's Islamic Group on the West Bank," paper presented at the Middle East Studies Association annual meeting, Toronto (November 1989). Several of the women told her that attending the meetings and hearing about Islam made them feel good. One woman put it this way: "Life is very difficult, especially during these days [referring to the Intifada]. We have many worries. Islam helps me. It teaches me what is right." Another woman said: "Islam gives me hope that the problems in our lives will end."

17. Veiling has traditionally been required of women when they appear in public, and it has taken diverse forms according to cultural setting: the tent-like Afghan *burqa*, the Iranian *chador*, the face-mask of the Gulf region, the kerchief covering the lower part of the face in North Africa. But the contemporary urban Islamist uniform is a large headscarf covering hair and shoulders, and a long-sleeved manteau over trousers or dark stockings.

18. See Philip Hitti, *A History of the Arabs* (Princeton: Princeton University Press, 1971).

19. Asghar Ali Engineer, "Remaking Indian Muslim Identity," *Economic and Political Weekly* (April 20, 1991):1036-1038.

20. Salma Sobhan, "Identity Politics and Gender: Fundamentalism and the Women's Movement in Bangladesh," paper prepared for UNU/WIDER Round Table on Women and Identity Politics.

21. The term *gharbzadegi* comes from the famous 1962 essay by the late Iranian populist writer Jalal Al-e Ahmad. The book was undergound until the late 1970s. A second, revised edition was published in Tehran in 1979. For an elaboration, see Nayereh Tohidi, "Modernity, Islamization, and the Woman Question in Iran," forthcoming in Valentine M. Moghadam (ed.), *Gender and National Identity: Women and Change in Muslim Societies* (London: Zed Books, 1994).

22. Following the political revolution, the lay and clerical leaders of the ascending new class undertook a sweeping cultural revolution, which officially began in April 1980. In addition to compulsory veiling, universities were closed for two years while all foreign elements (Western-bourgeois and Communist)

were purged from the faculty, student body, and curriculum. According to Khomeini: "When we speak of the reform of the universities, what we mean is that our universities are at present in a state of dependence; they are imperialist universities, and those whom they educate and train are infatuated with the West [*gharbzadeh*]. ... What we fear is cultural dependence and imperialist universities that propel our young people into the service of Communism." See Imam Khomeini, "The Meaning of the Cultural Revolution," pp. 295-299 in *Islam and Revolution: Writings and Declarations of Imam Khomeini,* translated and annotated by Hamid Algar (Berkeley: Mizan Press, 1981). In light of the curriculum changes in Eastern Europe since the 1989 revolutions, the political-cultural revolution of the Iranian Islamists can hardly be considered unique.

23. An example of this tendentious view of the "Sovietization" of Afghan youth in Kabul and in the Soviet Union is contained in the Helsinki Watch Report written by Jeri Laber and Barnett Rubin, *Tears, Blood and Cries: Human Rights in Afghanistan Since the Invasion 1979-1984* (New York: Helsinki Watch Committee, 1984). That girls received hardly any education at all under the "culturally authentic" Mujahidin leadership in the refugee camps seemed not to concern Laber and Rubin.

24. Fatima Mernissi, "Introduction: Muslim Women and Fundamentalism," *Beyond the Veil: Male-Female Dynamics in Modern Muslim Society* (revised edition) (Bloomington, IN: University of Indiana Press, 1987), p. xi.

25. Sudesh Vaid and Kumkum Sangari, "Institutions, Beliefs, Ideologies: Widow Immolation in Contemporary Rajasthan," *Economic and Political Weekly* (April 27, 1991):WS-2-18. See also Amrita Chhachhi, "Identity Politics in the Construction of Nationalism and the Post-Colonial State in South Asia," paper prepared for UNU/WIDER Round Table on Women and Identity Politics, and "Forced Identities: The State, Communalism, Fundamentalism and Women in India," pp. 144-175 in Deniz Kandiyoti (ed.), *Women, Islam and the State* (London: Macmillan, 1991).

26. Susan Marshall, "Paradoxes of Change: Culture Crisis, Islamic Revival, and the Reactivation of Patriarchy," *Journal of Asian and African Studies* XIX (1-2) (1984):1-17.

27. The symbolic role that women play in both identity and culture, described in the papers in this volume, has parallels in Western history. John Gillis (personal communication) notes that from the French Revolution onwards, women have been symbolically positioned as the stable, continuous, cohesive element; men have been used to represent that which is changing, progressive, disruptive.

28. See Valentine M. Moghadam, "Reform, Revolution and Reaction: The Trajectory of The Woman Question in Aghanistan," forthcoming in Moghadam (ed.), *Gender and National Identity: Women and Change in Muslim Societies.*

29. Nahla Abdo, "On Nationalism and Feminism: Palestinian Women and the *Intifada* — No Going Back?," forthcoming in Moghadam (ed.), *Gender and National Identity: Women and Change in Muslim Societies.*

30. Nira Yuval-Davis, "National Reproduction and 'the Demographic Race' in Israel," pp. 92-109 in Nira Yuval-Davis and Floya Anthias (eds.), *Woman-Nation-State* (London: Macmillan, 1989).

31. Mahmoud Darwish, "Identity Card," *The Music of Human Flesh: Poems of the Palestinian Struggle.* Selected and translated by Denys Johnson-Davies (London: Heinemann, 1989). Abdo's remarks were made at the conference in Helsinki.

32. Quoted in Charu Gupta, "Politics of Gender: Women in Nazi Germany," *Economic and Political Weekly* (April 27, 1991):WS-40-48. The quote appears on p. WS-43.

33. Feride Acar, "Women in the Ideology of Islamic Revivalism in Turkey: Three Islamic Women's Journals," paper presented at the workshop on Islam in Turkey, at the School of Oriental and African Studies, University of London (May 1988). See also Valentine M. Moghadam, *Modernizing Women: Gender and Social Change in the Middle East*, esp. Chapter 5.

34. They would probably all agree with the following statement by the late Ayatollah Mutahhari of Iran: "[H]uman love and sympathy are qualities which are attributable to a wholesome upbringing of children by really affectionate and united families. ... The solidarity between husbands and wives, often noticeable in the East, is frequently missing in the West. A significant reason can be that Westerners have come to believe in sex without love or inhibition. Sexual experimentation and diversification do not allow any specific interpersonal love to develop." See his *Sexual Ethics in Islam and in the Western World*, translated from the Persian by Muhammad Khurshid Ali (Tehran: Bonyad-e Be'that Foreign Department, 1982). Like Mutahhari, the women in the papers by Klatch, Kaufman, and Hale attach value to family, marital love, devotion to God, and complementary roles. Mutahhari's essay includes a critical assessment of Bertrand Russell's *Marriage and Morals*; Mutahhari criticizes Russell's rejection of morality and religion but lauds his endorsement of love. Will Durant's references to love and marriage in *The Pleasures of Philosophy and Our Oriental Heritage* are also cited and endorsed by Mutahhari.

35. Val Moghadam, "Women, Work and Ideology in the Islamic Republic," *International Journal of Middle East Studies* 20 (2) (May 1988):221-243.

2

The Creation of the World We Know: The World-Economy and the Re-creation of Gendered Identities

Joan Smith

Introduction

There is an implicit task set for any essay that addresses itself to the relationship between identity politics and feminism, and that is what is at stake for women in the worldwide struggles over national, racial, ethnic or religious identities. The answer to this question is elusive not because we know so little but because the question itself challenges in some very fundamental way precisely the claims of these various anti-systemic movements. In short, an answer requires an analysis that sweeps aside the very historical specifics that are at the heart of identity politics, that insist not on universalism but exactly its opposite, particularity.

The struggle over a peoples' identity is exactly a struggle to (re)kindle that which is specific to their own experience. Even more, it is a struggle to construct an "us" that is said to share a singular historical experience. Thus, the task to construct a feminist theory about this struggle is to challenge the dynamic that fuels it—historical *specificity* and a unifying *singularity*. From the point of view of women as an historical subject, the singularity of the "usness" is *absolutely* denied and the universality of the "feminine," if not asserted is at least implied as a possibility.[1]

Yet everywhere we look women are attempting to fit themselves into these struggles while at the same time understanding their unique place as women in the history of this "usness" that is being (re)constructed. It is for this reason that a general theory of identity politics that is centered on "the woman question" has become not only relevant but absolutely necessary. Certainly in the United States this struggle remains the single most important one within the women's movement. The question is simple even if a coherent answer still eludes us. How can we have a women's movement that must assume a unity in its struggles while at the same time is attuned to the most acute and fundamental contradictions between the women that constitute it?[2]

In order then to even begin a theoretical approach to feminism and identity politics, what is necessary is to grasp its subject matter—a subject matter that is simultaneously singular but as well multiple in its forms. This, of course, is exactly the conditions for theorizing that have not been met by either a Marxist approach nor one that is informed by a socio-psychological framework. Marxism recognizes a historicized but nonetheless singular class struggle and of course Freudianism has room only for the ahistorical psychodynamics of personality.

The Search for Theory

With respect to Marxism, there is no question that over the course of the last several centuries polarization has taken place—loosely knit and community based strata have been replaced by two classes, one that produces value and another that accumulates it. Obviously there are any number of factors that obscure this polarization and this is not the place to argue the point. But insofar as Marxism points to entirely new principles by which people become aware of who they are, there is little question that class consciousness is a fundamental aspect of that process. People know who they are with respect to the dominant economic processes that characterize the world-economy. That this identity is invoked so infrequently is more a measure of its potential destabilizing effects than it is evidence against its existence.

But there is as well something else going on in the world-economy that produces yet another kind of consciousness—a consciousness rooted in the personal and intimate relations of daily life. Herein lie the roots of Freudianism—though its very subject matter is a historical product.[3] What was required, as Foucault and other have now demonstrated, was the creation of a terrain that elevated the personal and the private to the status of a historical subject.[4]

Thus, we are confronted with the two possibilities of a historically situated identity: one that is formed within the market and production relations of capitalism, and another that is the product of the private and the intimate. It is precisely within the tension between the two that the question of women within identity politics actually resides. The worldwide dynamics inherent in the system we call capitalism have had a dual result.

These dynamics had the dual effect of dissolving the specific historical experiences of a people and replacing these with a universal experience derived from the system we call world-capitalism and of simultaneously constructing an institutional framework that has given new currency to oppositional identities based on the singularity of experiences. But these experiences are hardly unmediated. Instead they are constituted by that all too modern arrangement called the household.[5]

There may be some exception taken to my skipping over entirely the idea of nationality as a principal mode of identification and the state as a mechanism for transmitting identities. But I do this deliberately notwithstanding the fact that nationalism appears to be a major force in today's identity politics. First, nations as political units come and go rather more rapidly than appears to be the case at first glance. It is ironic, for example, that as I wrote this chapter a war was being waged in the Gulf region over the national sovereignty of Kuwait, an area that, at least historically speaking, only became a nation a minute ago. What is so very striking about nationality is this appearance of permanence that is belied at every step when we consider how fundamentally impermanent nations actually are.[6] It is precisely because nations and thus nationality is so impermanent that race has been so conflated with it. The latter rests, it is claimed, on the solid foundation of biology while the former clearly has its footing in the shifting sands of time.

Second, our nationality hardly flows from the pinnacles of state power. If it did, there would be little trouble from Quebecois in Canada or Native Americans in the U.S., both of whom would quickly have a national identity if it were up to the central powers. Rather, nationality is a function of communities whose historical elements are households. While it is claimed that nationality is a product of the powerful nation-state, the fact is it is the community that abrogates (or denies, as the case may be) that power unto itself.

Historical Capitalism

As feminist theory has so often pointed out, an exclusive concern with class as a way of marking boundaries leaves entirely out of account that which is so salient for women. But as we now all know, an ahistorical Freudianism has been a poor substitute. While Marxism has no specificity at all—just history, Freudianism has no history—just specificity. It is for this reason that I turn to world-systems as a theoretical foundation for constructing my own account of gender and how a gendered world fits into movements that are, if nothing else, rooted in a (re)constitution of peoplehood.[7] I will go through some of the elements of that framework quite briefly in order to get to a more extended discussion of households and their gendered character.

What is fundamental to the theory is that in today's world it is more fruitful to think of the globe not as a set of multiple systems (be they defined as nations or societies) but as a single system constituted by a single worldwide division of labor characterized by a vast multiplicity of its parts. The singularity of this system is often missed precisely because as it evolved so too (and not coincidentally) did the nation-state. Nevertheless, and as I stated above, what is so noteworthy about these nation-states is that they apparently come and go with alacrity. Here today and gone tomorrow. What has remained is a world-division of labor that not only continues but is continually being extended—how else can we read, for example, the restructuring of Eastern Europe and the USSR?

Part of the variegated character of this world-division of labor is that it has as its central feature gross imbalances—some areas are very rich and some very, very poor. There is, as we know, almost a geographical specialization whereby poor areas are induced to send a not inconsiderable portion of their wealth to better-off areas of the world (including "human resources"). But what should be kept clear is that what we are talking about here are processes and relationships and not geography *per se*. Geography is just one way these processes and relationships are expressed. There are others. Specifically, there are any number of ways in which relationships are so constituted that wealth is transferred from the poor to the wealthy. One set of these relationships is exactly what we mean by household relationships. Wealth is transferred both between various members of the household ordered by both age and gender, and between various households ordered by class and nations. *The household is the constellation of relationships that makes that transfer possible.*

What is so striking about households all over the world is that they appear to lie outside of history.[8] They are variously defined as "traditional," "patriarchal" or "precapitalist," all of which seems to denote that as social structures they are either subject to a different kind of history or no history at all![9] That a particular social formation does not look like an assembly line in Detroit is not at all evidence that it lies outside of the historical sweep of world-capitalism or is subject to another kind of dynamic.[10] Let me point to the so-called homelands in

South Africa or, earlier still, to slavery in the New World. These are novel forms of social relations but have nothing whatsoever to do with precapitalism.

Of course these are the most obvious cases since they refer to settler regions. There are, however, regions such as the Arab-Islamic world where, it could be argued, the contemporary treatment of women refers to a more historically continuous form of subordination predating capitalism. Without being an expert on the region I hesitate to offer a view and do so only to illustrate a point. Benedict Anderson uses a lovely phrase in talking about nations—the imagined community.[11] Certainly people—whether a nation or a religion—is an "imagined community," an assertion of a kind of horizontal relationship even to concrete individuals one will certainly never meet. There are in my view two reasons why the ties holding together that imagined community are strongly gendered. First, not unlike in other areas of the world, the relationship between Europeans and Arabs in the Islamic world was highly sexualized.[12] In order to construct a peoplehood in opposition to that relationship, identities had to be created not the least of which had to do with gender.

There is a second reason. This imagined community exerts its greatest pull when it is constructed out of materials that appear just in the nature of things. Skin color, one's sex, one's history all have about them a quality of the inevitable and thus without inherent motive. The very cogency of these constructs depend absolutely on the degree to which they assert connection to a past and a "nature." But both their force and their stability grow directly out of the degree to which they stand in an interdependent relationship with the ensemble of social institutions and practices of the contemporary period. It is the struggles of the present that create the myths; it is the reverence for the past that give them power and control.

Let me turn to one or two specific historical examples of the formation of the so-called patriarchal household in settler areas to make the larger point.

It is now abundantly clear that "family" (and I use quotation marks to warn us of the real problem of nominalism) tied Native Americans to both their community and their traditional economy. Participation in either was entirely unthinkable—indeed impossible—without a place in a kin-network. Family bonds defined social, political and economic relationships. However, and contrary to earlier assumptions, women were not chattel even though a brideprice was often paid. Brideprice denoted not the degradation of women—as was inferred by whites at some later period—but the value the husband's family placed on the marriage. No husband could sell his spouse; an unhappy wife on the other hand could divorce her husband.[13]

To be sure, in all Native American cultures there was a sexual division of labor. But as Joan Scott has recently warned, by itself that means nothing.[14] What is important is what the society made of that division of labor. Among any number of Native American groups, the most valued and indeed wealthy members of the group were the shamans who were not infrequently women. The gathering done by women was considerably more important in the survival of the group than was the hunting of men. Though this has only recently come to the attention of Anglo anthropologists, there is considerable evidence that the importance of women's agricultural labor was not at all lost on Native Americans groups.

Once Anglo settlers arrived in the West, a number of different Native American groups were set to work, most often forcibly, though of course the ability of the missions to "encourage" the labor of Native Americans should not be underrated. In the main by the end of the eighteenth and throughout the early period of the nineteenth century, these Native Americans were absolutely subject to commodity production for the world-market.[15] Beef, gold and furs were, if nothing else, world commodities, and their production would have made no sense without the world-market. In fact, it was changes in that world-market that led the way to the destruction of the western Native American communities that had arisen as a way of coping with their new situation. With the mechanization of agriculture, deforestation and the end of the gold rush, the labor of native peoples in the West became superfluous. Within the space of two generations Native American people first lost their traditional sources of support, the land and unrestricted access to its product, and then lost what had come to replace it. By the end of the nineteenth century unemployment and underemployment became the rule for Native American people. Of course from the vantage point of the white population this idleness was taken to be a feature of the so-called Indian personality or culture rather than something that had been imposed by developments within the world-economy itself.

But what does this have to do with gendered households? Simply this. In self-defense Native Americans organized themselves into units that were relatively small and provided support drawn from a multiplicity of sources in order to secure the well-being of its members. There was nothing "natural" or "traditional" about these units— although the missionaries took great pains to convince Native Americans to the contrary. These units were in effect the only available possibility that offered Native Americans a means of accommodating themselves to the exigencies of their circumstances—circumstances that flowed directly from the world-economy itself.

In short, market forces and state-imposed restrictions combined together to create this particular social structure that had as its deifying feature an internal hierarchy or ordering based on gender and age. On the one hand the very special circumstances of Native American peoples breathed life into these structures. On the other hand these structures were a product of a quite modern world-economy and the state machinery that was itself a feature of that world-economy. It should come, therefore, as no particular surprise that in the current struggle among Native American people, the tribe is in fact a constellation of these very modern households which are the medium within which the Native American identity is cultured.

Here then is the problem for Native American women in those struggles. The very character of the struggle over peoplehood and a viable ethnic identity requires them to embrace a set of social relations that are simultaneously mirrors of the gendered world inherited by Native Americans in their initial struggles for survival and, as well, weapons in that struggle. The very source of Native American identities is simultaneously the source of a gendered identity![16] As Wallerstein and I argue in another context, the household itself has an ethnicity—indeed in the case of intermarriage the rule of singularity of ethnic identity is imposed on households even in the face of concrete evidence to the contrary. This ethnicity constitutes a set of rules that are themselves gendered. To invoke ethnic identity as a reason for collective action—as in the case in current Native American struggles—is to invoke and to breathe new life into those rules that constitute gender.

It is within the household that the idea of a self is constructed and it is the household that is the necessary adjunct in constructing an oppositional self—a self that defies that which is generated by the "other."

Though it is clear that in the case of Native Americans there was no pre-existing patriarchy to be borrowed by capitalists—as though social relationships can be borrowed like someone's shirt—there are many cases where there is at least the appearance of a pre-existing patriarchy that becomes the appendage to world-capitalism. But this too is, in my view, more appearance than reality. Let me turn to Ireland for example.

Traditionally, Irish households spent a not inconsiderable amount of their joint time in spinning and weaving. This activity was gendered and it was hierarchical. Of that there can be no question. Yet, I would argue that the incorporation of Ireland into the world-economy spelled the absolute demise of that patriarchal household. The Irish household still continued to carry on its weaving and spinning. And men were still in charge. *But the source of that authority and what stood in its way of being exercised once Ireland was incorporated into the world-economy was utterly transformed.* This conversion of the Irish household-economy and the relationships which that economy expressed was part and parcel of the role Ireland played in the world-economy. The seeds were planted early in the seventeenth century. They were reaped by the eighteenth.

Here is the Earl of Strafford who served as the Irish viceroy during the early part of the seventeenth century describing his plans for Ireland:

> [T]here [is] little or no manufacture amongst them but some small beginnings toward a clothing trade which I had and so should still discourage all I could, unless otherwise directed by his Majesty and their lordships, in regard (it would affect) the clothing of England, being our staple commodity, so as if they should manufacture their own wools, which grew to very great quantities, we should not only lose profit we made now by ... their wools but his Majesty lose extremely by his customs. ... Yet have I endeavored another way to set them upon work and that is by bringing in the making and trade of linen cloth.[17]

By 1699 the Irish Woolen Act virtually destroyed the woolen trade in Ireland. What was substituted was the linen trade. But for that to have come about, the entire complex peasant economy had to be fundamentally reordered; responding to entirely different imperatives. Useful, of course, in that regard were the penal codes introduced and enforced by England. Under these codes no Catholic could buy land or inherit it from Protestants. Catholics could not hold life annuities or mortgages on land nor could they hold leases for more than thirty-one years. When Catholics did become renters—as they must, given restrictions on land ownership—the penal codes established that as profits from the land increased so too would the rent, thus establishing a virtual ceiling on earnings and profits from the Catholic majority.[18]

The result of the English policies were described by Arthur Young (as quoted in James):

> [Y]ou behold a whole province peopled by weavers. It is they who cultivate or rather beggar the soil as well as work the looms. Agriculture is there in ruins; it is cut up by roots, extirpated, annihilated. The whole region is the disgrace of the kingdom. As the crops you can see are

contemptible, or nothing but filth and weeds. ... But the cause of all those evils, which are absolute exceptions to everything else on the face of the globe, is easily found. A most prosperous manufacture, so contrived as to be the destruction of agriculture is certainly a spectacle for which we must go to Ireland. ... If I had an estate in the south of Ireland, I would as soon introduce pestilence and famine upon it as the linen manufacture. ... [19]

This system of production described by Young was the product of a cottage industry that had as its hallmark a strictly gendered system of production. Yet, to confuse that with what had come before would require obliterating at least one hundred years of history whereby Irish society was turned inside out in response to the demands of a world-economy in which it played out its peripheral role. That the result bears some resemblance to what had gone before is more a point about how to legitimatize such an upheaval as it is about the staying power of patriarchal forms.

The example of Ireland of course has its own unique details but the analytical point can be made about regions all around the world. Nash had called this process the "cooperation of patriarchy in the service of capitalism," but I think this is precisely to miss the point.[20] What structures gendered relationships whether in Ireland or in Iran is state policy that must be attuned to a world-economy and the state's particular position within that economy if it is to survive. In that sense what constantly reproduces these gendered relations as they are constructed by state policy is the imperative of the modern world. What makes that reconstruction work, what gives it its cogency, as I mentioned earlier, is its referential relationship to a distant past. Ironically it is the *modern* form that is invoked in movements of liberation under the cloak of traditionalism, that imagined community to use Anderson's apt phrase.

Identity Politics and Feminist Theory

Using these very few examples, let me return to the general theoretical point. As Nash has correctly argued, a good deal of the subordination of women in colonized situations where we now find new movements for cultural, religious and national identity was in fact the product of a very modern division of labor on a world-scale. Women producers were subordinated in household production that itself was a product of the world-economy. The upshot is that the so-called traditional patriarchal relationships that are said to characterize the household are in point-of-fact the very modern creations of the world-economy; subject to its dictates and interpreted by state policy.

In a recent article Candace West and Don Zimmerman advocate an approach to understanding gendered relationships they describe as "doing gender":

> Doing gender involves a complex of socially guided perceptual interactions, and micropolitical activities that cast particular pursuits as expressive of masculine and feminine "natures." [Gender is] an emergent feature of social situations: both as an outcome of and a rationale for various social arrangements and as a means of legitimating [those arrangements].[21]

While we might ponder just what it means to be gendered, for my purposes here I want to ask another question. That is, what is the *it* that is gendered? What are these emergent social arrangements that constitute a modern gendered world?

The most obvious candidate of course is the modern enterprise with its sophisticated division of labor and its bureaucratic, rational structure. But there are at least two problems with this answer. First, it is exactly the modern enterprise that is, at least normatively, not gendered at all. Second, and more important for my purposes, on closer inspection what is clear is that not only is this modern enterprise not as far flung as one would suspect, but it also directs a much smaller proportion of the world's labor than what the theory of advanced capitalism would lead us to believe. (Indeed there is some argument to be made that if the power of the enterprise to direct the world's labor force was plotted along an inverted "u" curve, we now find ourselves on the downward leg of the curve.)

The fact is that by far the vast majority of labor in the world is conducted far from the shop floor or the office desk. Once we remove the blinders that classical accounts of capitalism have offered us, it is quite clear that the single most important unit that does direct the traffic (and more rather than less of it) is the household itself. It is the imperatives of the household and place within the household that is at the helm. And of course it is within this household that gendering takes place.

In short, both the modern state and the household are two of the universal institutionalized products of historical capitalism. And their fortunes are inextricable. *It is the state that legislates the existence of households and it is within households that struggles against the state and other collectivities are conducted.*

Feminism and Anti-Systemic Movements

And here then is the historical problem presented to women by current anti-systemic movements. While these movements speak in the name of the people, their actual constituent elements are households. The numerous oppressed "people" they represent are, in fact, collectivities that understand their singularity through shared sensibilities. These shared collective sensibilities are not simply a product of the ether in which people live but of the cultural transmission lines that are families; these are households. Thus, and not surprisingly, the movements themselves have as part of their own apparatus precisely the institutional expression of the circumstances against which these movements are struggling. In this case, one would suspect that the movements would be all too ready to give up on these particular social formations, but in large measure this has not been the case. The reason is not too difficult to see. To illuminate them it is necessary to turn to what the course of events has been over the last several decades.

As Wallerstein has argued, there are actually two very different kinds of movements.[22] One expresses a universality of class and seeks wherever possible to overthrow all those structures which stand in the way of that universality. We all know the fate of those struggles. Alongside of and perhaps almost simultaneously with class struggles, what has arisen are struggles over particularity—a peoplehood that distinguishes its members from everyone else. What has happened in the recent past is that the two movements have come together.

> Labour-socialist movements have found that nationalist themes were central to their mobilization efforts and their exercise of state power. But nationalist movements have discovered the inverse. In order to mobilize effectively and govern, they had to canalize the concerns of the work force for egalitarian restructuring.[23]

There is, though, an exception to these egalitarian themes (one not mentioned by Wallerstein)—indeed almost a trade off—and that is the pervasive tendency among the movements to reassert the norms of the so-called "traditional" family that existed within a tightly gendered framework. Further, this tendency has not been an altogether ideological one. Once institutionalized, the movements had to come up with results, but results within a world-economy where the rules had not changed! New forms of oppression had to be poured into old bottles. Gender was a handy way of accomplishing this mission while at the same time laying claim to a shared and unique tradition!

(One need only listen to what Polish housewives were saying about their lives after the success of Solidarity to see how this particular aspect of the issue was getting itself played out in Eastern Europe.)

In every case regimes that have come to power via anti-systemic movements still must survive in a very modern interstate system (in spite of some of their claims to the contrary) and must continue to operate in a world-economy characterized by the uneven accumulation of capital. It is this necessity that has created the drive to preserve the household as a basic unit through which the continued exploitation of their labor forces goes on apace. In the name of a tradition that is hardly that, the vast majority of the anti-systemic movements have been at pains to reconstitute the central units through which labor power can be extracted and exploited—the gendered household.

Conclusions

I began by arguing that a theoretical understanding of women's place in anti-systemic movements is difficult in the extreme since by their very nature, these movements derive their energy from the notion of singularity. However, what I have also argued in this chapter is that anti-systemic movements themselves must be placed within a different theoretical context than that which they might claim on their own. This is the context of a world-economy that is endowed with certain features from which we can derive both the nature of contemporary struggles as well as the set of institutional arrangements that form the apparatus of those struggles.

These arrangements have not arrived on the historical stage *sui generis* but in fact were bred precisely by the circumstances against which the movements must struggle and to which they must accommodate. I have isolated the very contemporary household and the state as two of these institutional arrangements and have argued that neither is obliterated by the anti-systemic movements, but in fact is merely taken over.

The new regimes must still exist (or anticipate existing) in an interstate system and must still exploit labor power within a world-economy. In that case, the set of gendered relations that are inscribed in the household become not only part of the ideologies of the movements but premises for their successful existence in their post-revolutionary phase. It is for this reason that in spite of their vast differences, we find a common thread running throughout all of these movements, and that is the near sacredness of patriarchal forms ratified by an appeal to an imaginary precapitalist past.

Notes

1. This is simply to say that feminism has profound difficulties even with its own categories and that these difficulties must be addressed especially in the context of struggles over national, religious or racial identities.

2. This is specifically reflected in contentious events at the annual meetings of the National Women's Studies Association of the U.S. (especially that of June 1990).

3. See Michel Foucault, "Why Study Power: The Question of the Subject," in Hubert Dreyfuss and Paul Rabinow (eds.), *Bergnel Structuralism and Humanities* (Chicago: University of Chicago Press, 1983).

4. As Linda Alcoff points out, the common theme in recent theorizing is that "the self-contained, authentic subject conceived by humanism to be discoverably below a veneer of cultural and ideological overlay is in reality a construct of that very humanist discourse." The lesson for those engaged in the study of identity politics should not be lost. See Linda Alcoff, "Cultural Feminism Versus Post-Structuralism: The Identity Crisis in Feminist Theory," *Signs* 13 (3) (1988):405-436.

5. This is to argue that this modern identity is not directly a product of "humanistic discourse" but of institutional arrangements, some that were hardly humanistic. There is a profound similarity in the colonized experiences of non-Western, non-Anglo peoples and that is the degree to which they were "sexualized" by the colonizer. This creation of a "deformed" private life was the excuse par excellence for not only denigrating those subjected to colonization, but also for (re)creating a privileged terrain called the "private." Paternalism requires a private terrain within which it is exercised. See, for example, the discussion in Irvin Cemil Schick, "Representing Middle Eastern Women: Feminism and Colonial Discourse," in *Feminist Studies* 16 (2) (1990):345-380.

6. Immanuel Wallerstein, *Historical Capitalism* (London: Verso, 1983).

7. World-systems theory insists that the so-called non-Western world is no more "traditional" than the West. This insight is crucial to our discussion. When Western feminists insist on viewing the household relations of their non-Western counterpart as mired in "traditions," what they are acceding to is the totally untenable notion that the non-Western world is an historical "leftover" passed over by so-called modernity. (For a discussion of this tendency see Schick, "Representing Middle Eastern Women.")

8. In my view it is entirely Western-centric to insist that the household arrangements in the periphery and the semi-periphery are traditional while in core industrialized countries they are "modern." How can it be that "their" institutionalized relationships are so fixed while "ours" are so changing? *All*

institutional arrangements are responsive to their current circumstances and reproduced by those circumstances and responses. To argue otherwise is to come close to the kind of racism implied in current "culture of poverty" discussions and of course the infamous Moynihan report. Moynihan linked the contemporary African-American family structure to African family structure during slavery as though little of interest happened in the intervening years. Similarly, to talk of the "traditional" Muslim family as though it was forever so is to deny to that community its connectedness to the vast set of circumstances that both dictate its fate and are the product of its own ongoing struggles. To say anything less is, in my view, to deprive the Muslim community of an essential dignity.

9. This is not to say that history is not important in how people formulate themselves but only that it is *referentially* important in the ongoing struggle with the world and all of its constraints. History does not produce contemporary social relationships like a seed does a plant. But it *is* frequently invoked to protect those structures.

10. Joan Smith, "Household Labor and Labor Force Formation," in Joan Smith, Immanuel Wallerstein and Hans Dietrich Evers (eds.), *Household in the World-Economy* (Beverly Hills, California: Sage, 1982).

11. Benedict Anderson, *Imagined Communities* (London: Verso, 1983).

12. George L. Mosse, *Nationalism and Sexuality* (New York: Howard Fertig, 1985).

13. Much of what is reported here is taken from Albert L. Hurtado, *Indian Survival on the California Frontier* (New Haven: Yale University Press, 1988).

14. Joan Scott, "Gender, A Useful Category of Historical Analysis," *American Historical Review* 91 (5) (1986):1053-1075.

15. David Lamar, "From Bondage to Contract: Ethnic Labor in the American West, 1600-1890," in *The Countryside in the Age of Capitalist Transformation* (Chapel Hill: University of North Carolina Press, 1985).

16. Even when groups do not manifest the "right" kind of gendered hierarchies within the household, a whole host of pressures are brought to bear to recapture the "proper" household arrangements. See Maxine Baca Zinn, "Family, Feminism and Race in America," *Gender & Society* 4 (1) (1990):68-83. Other feminists argue that families of oppressed groups need reinforcing, not criticism!

17. D. B. Quinn, "Ireland & the 16th Century European Expansion," *Historical Studies* 1 (1958):64.

18. Francis James, *Ireland in the Empire, 1688-1770* (Cambridge: Harvard University Press, 1973).

19. *Ibid.*

20. June Nash, "Cultural Parameters of Sexism and Racism in the International Division of Labor," in Joan Smith et al. (eds.), *Racism, Sexism and the World-System* (New York: Greenwood Press, 1988).

21. Candace West and Don Zimmerman, "Doing Gender," *Gender & Society*, 1 (2) (1987).

22. Wallerstein, *Historical Capitalism*.

23. *Ibid.*

3

The Ideal Woman and the Ideal Society: Control and Autonomy in the Construction of Identity

Hanna Papanek

Introduction: Identity, Choice, and Entitlement

What do the notions of "the ideal woman and the ideal society" have to do with Identity Politics? A great deal, provided one defines "identity" in its broadest sense to include both such socially defined and often visible characteristics as race, gender, and ethnicity as well as other aspects of groups and individuals, such as belief systems, "worldviews," ideologies, and religions, that are not always considered part of identity but that increasingly form the bases of major cleavages among people. Because some of these characteristics may be hard to change while others are, at least potentially, matters of option, the question of choice plays a central role in my discussion of aspects of identity. I begin with the assumption that the extent to which individuals can choose their identity—perhaps by deciding on a particular kind of life or by giving or withholding their loyalty to a particular group—is also a measure of the *freedom of action* that people have within the larger society. By contrast, when states or other powerful institutions (such as political movements, social groups like castes or clans or domestic groups) can effectively limit identity choices by enforcing conformity to norms or ideals, individual freedom of action declines.

But because identities also represent *entitlements* to shares of a group's or a society's resources, the question of individual and group identity has also become a powerful bargaining chip in the politics of the late twentieth century. Conformity to the common identity proclaimed by social or political groups becomes increasingly important to the group's bargaining power in Identity Politics, as numbers usually become an aspect of power. Conformity pressures within the group are likely to rise as the aspirations of the group increase. The powerless within the group (often women) are most likely to suffer from these pressures for conformity.

In this chapter, I will look at these related issues through the lens of state and movement policies concerning women in three distinct yet comparable settings, following a discussion of my own views on the question of identity and some comments on the special importance of identity for women. Since sexuality and reproduction are of such central importance to women's identity, I have chosen three specific cases of state and movement policies in which sexuality and reproduction are also central, both in general terms (as related to morality, racial "purity," or religion, respectively) and with specific reference to women. I begin with a discussion of the issue of "choice" as it is being argued in the U.S. abortion debate between the "Pro-Choice" and "Pro-Life" factions, particularly in some of the law cases that embody much of the current dispute. These reveal a profound moral divide in U.S. society, concerning not only the specific issue of abortion but also, as the sociologist Kristin Luker points out, "the politics of motherhood" or differing visions of women's identity.[1] In the second part of the chapter, I examine how an ideal identity for women was imposed by two of this century's most authoritarian regimes—Hitler's Germany and Khomeini's Iran—that used the ideal of womanhood not only as one of the *symbols* of their ideal state but also as a *tool* to control and manipulate individual conformity to state policy. Here again, the manipulation of women's identity was an integral part of policies to achieve levels of control over the population that were high enough to overturn previous notions of common morality. In short, the process of shaping and using women's identities in pursuit of the broad goals of states and movements is my common focus throughout the chapter.

My decision to write about these issues and about the specific cases I have selected is both a deliberate choice on my part and an inescapable aspect of my own experience, shaped by a "multiple cultural consciousness" learned from a series of unchosen exiles and chosen places of residence in several very different societies and cultures. It is consistent with these personal inclinations that I should strongly disagree with those who claim a "primordial"—that is, fixed, ancient, and *recoverable*—source for national, ethnic, or religious allegiances. I would stress instead the responsibility of individuals and groups to determine the limits of their allegiances by acts of conscious and often hard choice, a responsibility made easier for those whose identities are somewhat fluid but one that is still arduous if taken seriously. In this, I am in full accord with the late Indonesian historian Soedjatmoko who said: "It is much more difficult to feel attracted to the insecurity of freedom than to the historical inevitability of a perfect world order from which comfort and strength can be drawn."[2] It also is in this sense that I see freedom of choice as profoundly linked to identity in the context of ideas and values that are *universally* applicable to all humanity.

By contrast, the core of Identity Politics is presented by ideas that are tied to a particular set of allegiances, usually determined by characteristics that are hard to change—race, nationality, ethnicity, gender. It is in terms of these particularities that entitlements to justice are invoked in many current conflict situations. But the notion of universal entitlements to some minimum of common rights and resources must be counterposed, again and again, to particularistic preferences. That is why the question of choice—whether of identity, appearance, or reproductive option—is central to my analysis of three distinct yet in some ways comparable twentieth-century movements and regimes.

Identity and Power: Control and Conformity

Identity—a sense of who I am—is defined by a lifetime of experience, imposed by many outside influences, and composed by the person through a unique process of growth that may not be without internal struggle.[3] It is the product of individual learning: A sense of identity develops through childhood socialization, as children learn what distinguishes them from others, those who are "not our kind"—those who belong to another group or unit in society, those who are "strangers." In other words, the core of individual identity already contains a sense of belonging to some group, defined along many different dimensions, ranging from families, kin groups, residential and ethnic groups, races, religions, and nations. Changing circumstances can lead to changes in individual identifications with particular groups as part of identity development in later life. But a sense of identity can also be shaped and reshaped—often very powerfully—by external forces bent on their own agendas of building new solidarities, new group boundaries, and new political alliances. These transformations may be experienced as a "violation of identity" but may also be embraced with enthusiasm and experienced by the person as a process of growth.

Paradoxically, therefore, one's sense of identity may be simultaneously stable in some aspects but also very volatile in terms of changing loyalties evoked in response to changing circumstances.

Questions of choice and conformity arise within a specific ethical and historical framework. In the late twentieth century, these questions recur within the context of the growing importance of group alignments and group interests in many countries around racial, religious, and ethnic commonalities. Where groups seek to build solidarity among members to increase the power and influence of the group in the wider society, the process of shaping—or reshaping—individual identities assumes special importance. Obedience to the norms of the group is one of the goals of leaders who seek strongly bounded and powerful groups of followers, especially if individuals are to be mobilized to act in ways that violate existing social norms. Heightened pressures for conformity usually exist in groups seeking to present a united front to others yet doubtful of their cohesion. The interests of the entire group in achieving conformity will then be invoked to increase control over weaker or less "obedient" members, decreasing the range of choices for individuals.

Power is a precondition for effective control; powerful states and movements are in large part defined by their ability to limit the choices of their citizens or adherents, if necessary by force. In the twentieth century, the term "totalitarian" has often been applied to movements and regimes seeking to impose maximum conformity by means of stringent control, generally including state terror. But since these goals cannot be achieved without the cooperation of at least some individuals, it is also important to look at the complicity of populations in achieving maximum conformity to the demands of a movement or regime.

Controlling Women: The Power of Identity and the Identity of Power

These ideas about identity, control, and conformity are not new—they are part of our shared understanding of the history of the twentieth century and constitute the starting assumptions I use in this chapter for a much narrower task: examining the way women are seen and used in the ideologies and practices of two regimes and one movement in order to argue for the importance of pluralism and flexibility in defining individual and group identities. In all three cases, certain ideals of womanhood are propagated as indispensable to the attainment of an ideal society. These ideals apply to women's personal behavior, dress, sexual activity, choice of partner, and reproductive options. These are all observable aspects of women's lives and, therefore, easier for coercive forces to control. How women think and feel is harder to observe and to control, yet also crucial to an understanding of the control process. I have suggested this aspect, at least in the case of Germany, by citing excerpts from an autobiographical novel.

The next step is to examine how and why certain institutions exercise control specifically over women's sexual and reproductive behavior in connection with group identity. My point of departure for this analysis is the similarity I see between the patterns of control over women's sexual and reproductive behavior exercised in those kin groups whose ideology emphasizes that their identity depends on an identifiable line of descent, and the control exercised over women in states and movements where, once again, group identity is linked to "purity"— either of race or behavior, in a concrete sense, or of ideology at the more symbolic level. In all these cases, the definition of "purity" is constructed as dependent on female sexuality and reproduction so that these aspects of women's lives become central not only to the definition of female personhood but also to group boundaries and group identity.

Control over female sexuality and reproduction requires male power, indeed enhances it, in kinship systems preoccupied with purity of descent, as has been demonstrated in studies of societies where women are segregated or secluded, where virginity tests are common and where suspected adultery by women is met with socially sanctioned punishments that may include death.[4] Although a detailed discussion of these points falls outside the scope of this chapter, I mention them here to suggest some of the deep foundations of control over women's sexual and reproductive lives to indicate the links between this control and the exercise of institutional power. In the two cases (Germany and Iran) where ideological movements became regimes, ideologically motivated norms were enforced by state power to limit or determine women's behavior in areas often thought to be intensely "private" and close to the core of an individual's sense of personal identity, that is, with whom to be friends, whom to marry, with whom (or whether) to have children. In the third case, one of the sides seeks to invoke state power in limiting reproductive choices that the other side seeks to preserve.

Control over women is also closely related to the question of identity. An *individual* sense of identity may be especially problematic for women because their societies make it so. The reasons for women's difficulties in this respect also explain why societies and movements look to changes in women's behavior as evidence for the effectiveness of social processes of control and conformity. Women are quite simply seen as normally more "exposed" to alteration by external forces. For example, in many societies women receive new names when they marry and must often live in new homes and communities. Many also experience sexual and reproductive events that change their status in the family and society, often radically. Under the circumstances, women probably need to work harder than men to sustain a sense of individual identity in the midst of change. Indeed, the preservation of women's sense of individual identity may be discouraged by particular practices, such as limitations on contact between the new bride and her natal family in some patrilineal kinship systems, as in parts of South Asia. In these cases, individual identity may be suppressed or reshaped by pressures that reflect control by others and demands for women's conformity.

Yet there is a paradox here that places women in a double bind: Many societies make women the "carriers of tradition" or "the center of the family," insisting that, especially during periods of rapid social change, their actions and appearance should alter less quickly than that of men, or should not be seen to change at all. Demands for family "stability" and an "unchanging" role for women may be especially strong when the processes of change are perceived as coming "from outside" the group and somehow alien, threatening existing patterns of life. These demands presuppose a high degree of female conformity to male controls; female compliance, in turn, provides men with a sense of mastery over events that seem to be out of control. The double bind of greater "normal" exposure to identity change and greater responsibility for maintaining group stability through their conformity contributes to women's difficulties.

The picture is often complicated by the identity crises of individuals or relatively small groups faced by societal transformations.[5] In this chapter, however, I am more concerned with the pressures exerted by organized groups—movements, regimes, and states—on individuals to conform to prescriptive norms for a *collective* identity that is seen as advancing the goals of the group. In this sense, movements promising to "restore order" to a world perceived as chaotic often restrict themselves to imposing more stringent controls on women, redefining their collective identity, rather than addressing the problems that have led to disorder.

An additional element enters the picture when the shared identity of a group is based on a presumed commonality of genetic characteristics, such as race or common ethnic descent, or simultaneously defined by both religion and descent. Here in particular, women's reproductive activities become a central issue of control where group identity is defined in terms of common descent or through fictive racial characteristics, as was the case for the "Aryans" in Nazi Germany. Belief in a "master race" opened the door wide to extreme state control over women's choices of mates, sexual partners, and whether or not to have children, in order to preserve racial "purity." More ominously, the Nazi stress on racial purity was also the central element in defining some people as "non-human" and prepared the way for their eventual murder.

With this in mind, I focus here on a central aspect of individual and group identity: the definition of the "ideal woman" in the specific context of the "ideal society" set forth in the ideology of a movement or state and the role these definitions play in establishing individual and group identities. Women are central actors in Identity Politics because they are not only thought to embody and transmit culture and tradition in a special way but also to demonstrate modernization through visible changes in their public behavior. Deniz Kandiyoti, in her historical analysis of The Woman Question in Turkey, examines the extent to which "the 'woman question' ... served as a vocabulary to debate questions of cultural and national integrity, notions of order and disorder, and finally conceptions of the indigenous relative to the foreign." And Kumari Jayawardena notes that nineteenth-century social reformers worked to improve the situation of women in their colonized countries because "the status of women in society was the popular barometer of 'civilization'."[6]

This was a major reason for the prohibition of the veil in several countries by rulers who wanted to be seen as modernizers earlier in this century. But women themselves were also eager to demonstrate that they wanted changes by publicly rejecting segregation and veiling in countries where it was practiced.[7] The reversal of these trends and the "recovering" of previously "uncovered" women has also signaled important changes in religion and ideology in a number of countries, especially in Asia, as new movements and regimes have gained power. Fatima Mernissi reminds us to see these events on two levels: the manifest, factual dimension and the unspoken latent meaning, a way of seeing that is crucial in everything to do with women.[8]

The Ideal Woman and the Ideal Society projected by a movement may be crucial to the establishment of the identity these movements promise to shape for their adherents. Some promise a return to mythical golden age—or one set forth in religious traditions as ideal—in which women and men fulfil their supposedly proper functions, a future that many women apparently find attractive, often because it differs from a situation in which they support a family without much help from men. Just how the ideals of a movement are to be achieved may remain a hidden part of a larger agenda that becomes clearer as power is gained and a regime begins to implement stated and implicit ideals. At that point, both women and men may be disappointed.

Moreover, an analysis of the place of women in Identity Politics can help to clarify more general issues of *conformity* and *obedience* for reasons related to women's social position. In many societies, for example, stringent control over women's behavior is exercised by men and other women to achieve valued attributes, such as modesty and sexual restraint, that require strict conformity to social norms. The behavior of men in the same setting is usually much less strictly controlled; indeed, restrictions on women may be rationalized by references to the dangers presented by "uncontrollable" males.[9] In the case of regimes and movements that try to achieve radical changes in the existing social order, obedience to leaders and conformity to the demands of the state or the movement become very important, first for adherents and, if the movement succeeds, for the rest of the population.

The U.S. Abortion Debate:
Women's Rights, Equality, and State Interest

Women's "right to choose" among several options in their sexual and reproductive lives is at the center of a furious debate over the limits of state control versus individual autonomy in the United States today. At issue are the limits to the choices individual women are entitled to make to determine their own sexual and reproductive fates vis-à-vis the limits that may be set by external authority, in this case state and federal governments. The contestation of these limits and the role of women's individual, private choices in this regard serve to illustrate the ideological uses of sharply contrasting visions of "the ideal woman" and "the ideal society" in the pluralistic society of the United States.

An enormous literature has developed around the abortion issue in the U.S., ranging from detailed discussions of law cases in legal journals to books and articles in the scholarly and popular media. One instructive and even-handed empirical study presents the arguments of individual activists on both sides as well as a detailed history of the development of "Pro-Choice" and "Pro-Life" movements in the state of California.[10]

The option to have an abortion—legal under specified conditions throughout the country since 1973—is the manifest heart of the debate but it owes its considerable political impact to the fact that it is an ideological "proxy" for people on both sides of a moral divide that reflects the changing position of women in U.S. society. Converging changes in labor markets, reproductive technologies, and women's own consciousness have changed the attitudes of many people toward sexuality and family life. But substantial portions of the U.S. population remain unconvinced and long for the return of a mythical "golden past" in which families were supposedly stable, women's sexuality was more tightly controlled, and men held greater power in both family and society. It is largely to these people—many of whom live in accordance with these ideals—that opponents of women's access to legal abortion have directed their appeal. But their ideological stance is often in conflict with widespread attitudes opposing state intervention and favoring "individualism." For this reason, as I note below, the abortion issue has been sharply redefined by those seeking greater state control over women's right to choose.

Mobilizational appeals have become extremely graphic on the anti-abortion side and have led to many incidents of violence, mostly fire-bombing and physical blocking of health facilities that provide abortions. A fund-raising letter sent out by the "National Right to Life Committee, Inc." in mid-1990 provides an example of anti-abortionists' stated position and of the rhetoric that is being used to mobilize certain constituencies. The letter states: "An estimated 25,000,000 babies have been slaughtered since abortion-on-demand was legalized by the Supreme Court in 1973. ... In fact, 30 percent of all babies conceived in this country are killed before they ever see the light of day. ... Where is the national outpouring of grief for these silent abortion victims? I promise you, with God as my witness, that your personal involvement will in some way contribute directly to saving an unborn baby's life."[11] In similarly inflammatory terms, Right-to-Lifers assert that abortion is much worse than the Nazi Holocaust.

Although there are many gradations of opinion on the abortion issue in the U.S., there are two major alignments: the "Pro-Choice" people, who favor retaining women's access to safe and legal abortions, as granted by a 1973 Supreme Court decision (*Roe v. Wade*), and the "Pro-Life" side that opposes abortion and works to overturn the 1973 decision. In the event of a reversal of the Court decision, regulation of abortion would revert to the legislatures of the fifty separate states, some of which were strongly opposed to abortion before 1973, although severely restrictive states were more numerous then than they are now.

The nomenclature used by the two sides reveals their definitions of the issue as well as what is likely to appeal to the American public. The side that refers to itself as "Pro-Choice" recognizes the strong individualist bias in U.S. public philosophy and knows that opinion polls show that a majority of Americans favor the right of individuals to decide among reproductive options, although actual percentages vary depending on the specific wording of questions. In a 1989 survey, for example, half of the adults polled supported the availability of abortions as specified in *Roe v. Wade* and only nine percent felt abortion should be forbidden.[12] But these polls also indicate that there is considerable ambivalence about unrestricted access to abortion and that many people favor placing some limits on the timing of abortions in the developmental cycle of the fetus, such as restricting them to the first trimester.

Those on the "Pro-Choice" side present a variety of arguments that generally stress the importance of women's own choices in the reproductive process, the dangers of death or disease from illegal abortions, and the importance of making a wide range of contraceptive options available to all, especially to those unable to pay. They may refer to the global context of the U.S. abortion debate,[13] which includes the fact that United Nations documents have, since 1968, recognized the basic right of individuals and couples "to decide freely and responsibly on the number and spacing of their children,"[14] and that, worldwide, women undergo between forty and fifty million abortions each year, of which one-fourth to one-third are illegal. These points are often part of the argument that women will continue to have abortions even if they are illegal and that making them illegal causes more women to die. Three broadly defined "moral principles" may be invoked in the discussion of "unwanted pregnancy" (a term used only by the "Pro-Choice" side): "The principle of liberty guarantees a right to freedom of action; the utilitarian principle defines moral rightness by the greatest good for the greatest number; and justice requires that everyone have equitable access to necessary goods and services."[15]

People in favor of choice are also clearly aware of the psychological and social difficulties women face when making a decision to seek an abortion. This is reflected in the widespread acceptance of laws that limit late abortions to cases where the life or health of the mother are in danger, showing that, far from favoring "baby murder," many people on the "Pro-Choice" side "view a fetus as sharing our humanity ... especially late in pregnancy."[16] In short, while there are many differences of opinion on the "Pro-Choice" side, there is a consistent tendency to emphasize individual autonomy with respect to reproductive issues. For example, it is often stated that "when the state bars abortion, it is coercing women into motherhood."[17] There is also considerable ambivalence on the question of state intervention in general—it all depends on the political climate and the substance of the intervention.

The opponents of women's rights to abortion, recognizing the importance of individual choices to the U.S. public, do not call themselves the "Pro-Control" or "Anti-Choice" faction but have a completely different definition of the issue, in part because they see their own lives as very different from those on the "Pro-Choice" side and see the issue as "a referendum on the place and meaning of motherhood."[18] "Pro-Lifers" bypass the matter of choice because they argue that the issue is very simple: abortion is murder and murder is against the law. Therefore, their goal is maximum state intervention to ban all abortions (except in a very small proportion of cases), preferably at the federal level for maximum control.

Their argument depends on two assumptions, both of which are themselves the subject of considerable public debate. First, they argue that life begins at the moment of conception, not only at birth, and that the fetus has rights as a "person." Any kind of interference with the pregnancy is therefore murder of a "baby" and not removal of an embryo. Their second assumption is that the state (in its generic sense) has an interest in protecting the fetus from the moment of conception because it is a human being that cannot protect itself.

Ironically, adherents of this movement may have conflicting views of the limits of state power: many appear simultaneously to favor the death penalty (maximum state intervention) and to oppose state regulation of the ownership of firearms by private individuals (minimum regulation). They often do not support federally funded programs to provide health care or supplementary food to poor children, for a variety of reasons ranging from opposition to "welfare state" measures and tax increases to supporting such measures only when done by voluntary organizations or local governments. In short, their support of maximum state control, preferably at the federal level, is confined to a single issue, based on a particular view of "American values," to which they want everyone to subscribe—and, if that proves impossible, to be unable to act otherwise.

A Catholic bishop, explaining why a group of bishops had hired a prominent public-relations firm to conduct anti-abortion campaigns, put it very simply: "Some organizations have lost sight of fundamental values ... they have tried to convince America that the main issue ... is the right to choose, rather than, as it really is, what is being chosen" (*New York Times,* April 6, 1990). This remark illustrates three aspects of the anti-abortion movement: the reference to "basic values," the definition of the "real" issue as murder, and the involvement of the Catholic hierarchy. Moreover, it shows the difference between a movement and a regime: if the Catholic bishops had the power of the clergy in the Iranian regime, they would not need to hire an advertising firm.

Following from the anti-abortionists' argument that the state has a "compelling interest" in preventing abortions because the fetus is "a person" that cannot protect itself against murder, much of the recent abortion debate has centered on questions of fetal viability—the point at which a fetus could theoretically survive outside the womb, using the most advanced medical technology now available in the U.S. This view implies that an impersonal institution is more reliable in protecting human life than the two persons who brought this life into being, a position not necessarily imposed in cases of children already born and badly cared for (or abused) by their parents. Moreover, a focus on fetal viability legitimates the idea of setting time limits to abortion by an external rule or agency, bypassing the person most deeply concerned, namely the pregnant woman herself.

This part of the abortion debate also illustrates the process by which a complex society negotiates the social construction of personhood because the setting of time limits may assuage the ambivalent feelings of the many people who feel uncomfortable with abortions in the late stages of pregnancy. In this process of negotiation, the deeply political nature of the controversy has also become clear as one that centers on the competing visions of women, men, children, and families held by people in an extremely pluralistic society.

In the social and political negotiations involved in the abortion debate, several institutions stand out as taking particularly strong stands, not only because their principles align them with one side or the other but also because membership adherence to shared belief systems is important to institutional self-interest. And because the abortion issue continues to be seen in terms of morality, it is not surprising to find religious denominations playing important roles in the debate, even as it becomes increasingly political. As distinct from liberal Protestant churches, the fundamentalist Protestant churches are actively involved on the anti-abortion side, both as institutions and as the ideological home of active movement leaders. Jewish denominations are similarly divided. The role of these institutions also raises issues of control and conformity. As a particularly salient example, I will briefly discuss the role of the Catholic Church.

Organizationally and ideologically, the U.S. Catholic Church plays a prominent role in the opposition to abortion even though "therapeutic abortion on medical indications was not explicitly or publicly condemned by any Roman Catholic authority before 1895."[19] On the other hand, individual Catholics (including a few religious women) have spoken out openly in favor of the need for choice. Since there is a constitutional separation of church and state in the U.S. that is generally strongly observed, the influence of the Catholic Church on non-Catholics must take a limited and indirect form. But among Catholics, the anti-abortion stand of the Catholic hierarchy, now enshrined in canon law, is closely related to the importance of believers' obedience to Catholic dogma. I have heard it said (by Catholics) on several occasions that the Church wants to be "the third person" in bed with every Catholic couple—meaning, of course, that Church teaching should be kept in mind during the act of intercourse. A Catholic who decides to use contraception—as a large number of American Catholics do—must, therefore, make a conscious decision to go against what she or he has been taught. This memorable metaphor is perhaps the most striking way to conceptualize intrusive external control over behavior most people consider intimate and deeply personal.

It also raises several crucial questions. For example, to what extent does behavior that goes against stated dogma lead to a sense of lost identity as a believer? To what extent is the abortion controversy about abortion and how much of it has to do with discipline and obedience to Church teaching? It may be that the increasingly strong public stand that the Catholic hierarchy has taken on the abortion issue in the U.S. can also be seen as a measure of the control the Church *hopes* to exercise over believers but rarely achieves. In this sense, the Catholic Church (or at least part of its leadership) is using the abortion issue to mobilize its own believers to greater conformity as well as trying to increase the influence of Catholic dogma and the Catholic hierarchy over a broad public issue, globally and not only in the U.S., probably without confining itself to the issue of abortion.

The influence of the anti-abortion movement is nevertheless limited and lacks the coercive power of the state in the presence of strong countervailing forces. But where totalitarian or authoritarian movements become regimes, as in the two examples I discuss next, coercive state power eliminates the possibility of open dissent after an initial period of struggle and the state is in a position to impose its vision on all the people within its borders.

Women as Victims, Tools, and Symbols in Hitler's Germany and Khomeini's Iran

Among the several twentieth-century regimes that attempted total transformations of their societies by extreme ideological changes enforced by extreme—and often total—state power, two stand out for the ways in which they used women as both tools and symbols of transformation. These regimes came to power in countries with very different cultures, religions, histories, social structures, political systems and economies: Germany in the early 1930s and Iran in the early 1980s. Both regimes marked the coming to power of movements that focused their ideological and mobilizational efforts on the establishment of a new identity for their adherents, an identity that would reflect the newly powerful position of their nation and would lead to their victory over those outside forces that were seen as responsible for the country's current problems. In the German case, the "Aryan" race was to be the focus of identity but it was a fraud, rooted in myth and only given reality by the control measures of the Nazi regime. In the Iranian case, a unified identity was to be achieved through a particular concept of Shia Islam developed by those members of the clergy who prepared for and eventually won power in 1979.

Both movements sought total authoritarian control over their populations—although the Nazis were apparently more successful in achieving it—and tried to mobilize both men and women through appeals to new visions of profoundly changed societies and pervasive organizations of social, economic, and political control. In neither country was there much advance planning on social and economic issues but citizens were offered the single mobilizational promise of complete change. The extent of popular adoration of the leading figures of the two movements was extraordinary. Women participated in this adoration along with men and, in both cases, many became enthusiastic adherents of the policies of the new regimes.

The global damage inflicted by Hitler and his regime in the name of national identity was enormous and began very early. Nazi racial policies are among the most effective examples of Identity Politics, based on achieving a "true" German identity through racial "purity"— the purity of the entirely spurious and mythical "Aryan" race. These policies had special implications for women because they involved ideals, attitudes, prohibitions, and special practices that affected sexual and reproductive behavior as well as women's public participation. To some extent, women were victims as well as tools of the regime. But as Rita Thalmann, Claudia Koonz and Liliane Kandel, among others, have pointed out, the willing participation of many women in Nazi activities and their complicity in many Nazi crimes raise deeply disturbing questions—questions that make it hard to argue for a separate political role that might be based on women's special "nature" or "culture."[20] Why would women support regimes that seem to promise them so little? What is it that appeals to women who give their support freely and not only out of fear? Is the promised "glory" of womanhood enough? Old images of enthusiastic crowds of women radiantly saluting Adolf Hitler come to my mind from many years ago; more recently, they have been joined by images of shrouded women in *chadors* marching enthusiastically in support of Ayatollah Khomeini. What is it that such women see to attract them, where I see only peril, fear, and suppression?

One of the more remarkable similarities between the Nazi and Khomeini regimes with respect to The Woman Question is unexpected from a purely cultural and historical perspective: both placed renewed ideological emphasis on "separate worlds" for women and men, although the starting points for this separation were different in the two nations. In both ideologies, Motherhood defines the Ideal Woman and restricts her life in the Ideal Society to home and family. Similar ideas can be found among anti-abortion activists in the U.S. This emphasis is entirely consonant with the general constrictive tendency of such movements and regimes to enhance the power of leaders and present a united facade by limiting individual choices. It serves their purposes to prevent pluralism by limiting available categories of individual identity to those based on ascribed characteristics such as race, gender, or age, and to restrict personal choices among alternatives by ideological or administrative control. Finally, both regimes at first tried strongly to discourage women from working outside the home; in both cases, this attempt was reversed when women's labor was needed for rearmament and war.[21]

"Separate Worlds" for German Women: Race, Motherhood, and Lebensraum

Adolf Hitler said almost nothing about women in *Mein Kampf*, the book in which he set down his ideas about the German past and future in the 1920s. In his single most revealing statement, however, Hitler spoke about "the masses" in terms of "woman"—using the cruder German term *das Weib* for the female—in a way strikingly paralleled by those Iranian clerics whose "allegories used ... to diagnose a general social illness found their most resonant reading onto the body of woman"[22] but that also said much about the way he planned to rule:

> Like Woman, whose sentiments are determined less by abstract intelligence than by an undefinable, emotional longing for a complementary force, and who would therefore rather submit to the strong than dominate the weak, so also the masses love the ruler more

than the supplicant, and feel themselves better satisfied by a doctrine that tolerates no rival than by the permissiveness of liberal freedom; most of the time, the masses have little use for [liberal freedom] and even feel a bit abandoned by it.[23]

In the 22-page index of the 17th edition of *Mein Kampf*, there is not a single entry that specifically mentions women or motherhood and only two entries about girls, one of these in connection with prostitution. In what Hitler wrote about education, many pages are devoted to boys— particularly to their physical training to teach them discipline, improve their physique as representatives of a superior race, and to prepare them for army duty—but only a small paragraph deals with girls. Their education is to be developed from the same point of view as that of boys: emphasizing physical training above all, then the development of emotional and, last, intellectual values. "The absolutely solid and unchangeable goal of female education must be the future mother."[24]

Hitler had been obsessed with education as a means to achieve his goals from very early on and this makes his neglect of girls even more remarkable. But perhaps not. In a speech made in June 1933, he proclaimed: "If there are still a few people among us who think they cannot change, we will take their children from them and educate them for what the German people needs."[25] Such a threat makes a mockery of the glorification of Motherhood—or rather, reduces this glorification to its essential element in the Nazi canon: women as breeders, not as educators.

Elsewhere in *Mein Kampf*, other references to girls occur repeatedly but only in connection with racial purity, always and obsessively as part of Hitler's fear and loathing of Jews: "The black-haired Jew-boy lies in wait for hours, satanic joy on his face, for the unsuspecting girl whom he will despoil with his blood and whom he will rob from her own people."[26] Hitler's obsessive anti-Semitism, which was, of course, the means by which he whipped up German sentiment for a fraudulent "Aryan" identity, here takes the form of recurrent statements that nations are always destroyed by racial "bastardization." He warns that young women must not only be prepared to choose properly "Aryan" men as mates but must be physically strong enough to resist all others in order to keep a "pure" race.

These messages reached women from many angles, once the propaganda machinery of the Nazi regime had been set up. But it is not hard to imagine the effect these kinds of statements could have on young women and their sense of themselves. If racial purity was that important—and administrative measures soon introduced by the Nazis forced all Germans to prove that their genealogies were racially "pure" and they had no Jewish ancestors even several generations back—then women had a responsibility to the nation to allow others to determine whom they could and could not marry. Sexuality and motherhood could be made to serve the interests of the state once it was understood that the fate of one's "own people" depended on making the correct choice of partner. While it is not uncommon in many groups and societies to warn young people against "intermarriage," here it is the state that issues the warning and has the power to enforce it. When the Nazi regime defined Jews as a separate "race" as distinct from "non-Aryans" in 1935, "new intermarriages and cohabitation were prohibited" to prevent the "assimilation" of Jews and the "pollution" of "Aryans."[27] And although there is some documented evidence that some partners in "mixed marriages" survived the murderous efforts of the Nazi state at extermination of "undesirables" in Germany and conquered territories, most did not.[28]

The Nazi vision of a "separate world" for women developed in a society where stringent sex segregation, as in parts of Iranian society, was culturally alien. But ideas about the natural superiority of men in family and society were firmly established and later sharply intensified by the Nazi regime by excluding women from public life "to give them back their essential honor."[29] Moreover, tendencies toward female separatism, discouraging women's political participation, also existed within the large, active, internationally oriented but internally divided German women's movement before the Hitler period.[30] For example, Gertrud Bäumer, long active in the bourgeois women's movement, wrote in her magazine (in 1932) that "the system of governance of a nation does not matter, as long as it is willing to include women."[31] Bäumer also urged women to develop their own "space" within the home and stay away from the "abrasive masculine world of business, class struggle, and high politics" so as to bring "order and humanity to public life in times of hardship and chaos."[32] Liliane Kandel argues that it was largely "thanks to this distinction ... that such a large part of German women were, in fact, rallying to and sustaining the [Nazi] regime, while thinking they were staying aloof" from politics.[33]

While ultimate control over all people in Nazi Germany rested in the hands of a small number of men within a male-dominated state bureaucracy and party apparatus, a separate bureaucracy was developed specifically concerned with women, children, youth, and motherhood.[34] It was led by a few ambitious Nazi women, yet the regime established early on that their freedom of action was to be tightly circumscribed by male officials and "even the most ambitious women Nazis knew they could never aspire to high positions in a Nazi government."[35] Those women who thought they could act independently because they openly shared Nazi goals and had achieved public influence were soon pushed aside.[36] Women were systematically excluded from higher education and responsible jobs, except for those the regime considered suitable for women's "special capacities" (social welfare, care and education of children) until some of these policies were reversed when preparations for a coming war began in earnest about 1937.

Yet in spite of all this, the solidarity of large numbers of women with the Nazi party and the regime was cemented by widespread adoration of an idealized male authority figure, the *Führer* (Leader). An enormously effective system of ideological and emotional mobilization of popular sentiment soon came into play, especially once the efficient German state bureaucracy had been enlisted to support regime efforts. The apparatus of fear and terror quickly drove dissidents into exile, death, or underground and discouraged many who might silently disagree.

How was this achieved? The German writer Christa Wolf, in her remarkable autobiographical novel *Kindheitsmuster* (Patterns of Childhood) describes the enormous impact that Nazi women teachers and youth group leaders had on her as a schoolgirl and the difficulties she faced in developing her own ideas in an overwhelmingly Nazi environment only rarely mitigated by the influence of her fearful parents. Here she describes a teacher she deeply admired and, indirectly, the Nazi ideals of personal and group identity she ("Nelly") had been taught before she was fifteen years old:

[The teacher's] greatest achievement—she never showed how much effort it cost her—must have been to bridge the deep gap that separated her own appearance from that of the Ideal German Woman, an ideal she never tired of proclaiming. Not only was she small and black-haired and had a definitely slavic facial structure, described in Biology textbooks as "flat"; beyond that, she was the only intellectual woman Nelly knew in her youth (if one did not consider Mrs L., whose husband was probably Jewish); but above all: she had not found it necessary to marry and to present the German people with children. ... In history class, she sometimes remarked that the history of Europe—resulting unfortunately in a dreadful mixture of noble and inferior bloods—had had the effect that one could find, even in persons whose appearance would not make you think so, purely Germanic thinking and feeling, in short: a Germanic soul.[37]

Women were seen primarily as breeders of a pure "Aryan" race and were controlled by the state both *because of* and *by means of* their reproductive capacities. Because German identity was to be defined in terms of a *completely fictitious* "race" defined by the Nazi regime, sexuality and reproduction became crucial to state policy. And even though women were made part of the Nazi organizational apparatus through a variety of groups, the efforts of the Nazi regime were directed primarily toward obtaining their support, obedience, and physical fitness to bear "Aryan" children. To achieve this transformation of national identity, Nazism declared a "New Morality," like the Islamist regime in Iran was to do decades later, although in different terms. As one Nazi official summarized it: "Our moral concepts of Good and Evil depend on the needs of our People (*Volk*). 'Good' is what helps our People, 'Evil' is what hurts our People."[38] Under this New Morality, issues like marriage and "illegitimacy" could not only be seen in a new light but provided crucial opportunities for state control over individuals.

A special section of the Nazi party was its *Rassenpolitisches Amt* (Bureau for Race Policy) and a key institution for carrying out those measures intended to increase the numbers of Germans of "pure" race was the *Lebensborn* ("Well of Life") organization. In effect, what were called "positive" and "negative" race policies—forcible pronatalism and mass murder, explicitly seen as two sides of the same coin—were the key features of the Nazi state's seizure of control over women's sexual and reproductive choices. The state arrogated to itself the power to dictate these choices in the name of the best interests of the German people and enforced its policies through a repressive and efficient state apparatus.

Lebensborn: The "Well of Life" and the Ideal of Racial "Purity"

Although secrecy, controversy, and denial have made it difficult to document its exact history and activities, *Lebensborn*—an organization ostensibly concerned with the welfare of women and children—came to represent the epitome of a particular kind of evil and has important implications for us even today. It began, as many Nazi policies did, from a basis in conservative ideas and culminated in extremes, as effective opposition failed to materialize. But even conservatives came to recognize that *Lebensborn* "broke through the barriers of recognized ethical norms" and it was kept out of the public eye.[39] More than twenty years after the war had ended in Germany's complete defeat, little was known publicly about *Lebensborn* and the pioneering authors of the first study of the organization faced innumerable obstacles.[40]

In the terms used by Heinrich Himmler (as the head of the elite Nazi "Security Corps," the SS, his power was second only to Hitler's) *Lebensborn* constituted the "positive" side of the development of a "pure" race, by encouraging more births of "racially pure" children to accompany the "negative selection process" already instituted.[41] The "negative" process that began with the state-mandated sterilization of the "unfit" continued with their murder and ended with the state-sponsored murder of millions with the wrong "identity" throughout Europe.

Himmler was particularly concerned with issues of race and population. He believed that Germany's low rate of population growth was due to the prevalence of homosexuality and abortion, dangerously weakening the nation.[42] He quickly implemented his ideas, with Hitler's full support, through an organization whose initial function was to dissuade unmarried pregnant women from abortion by providing all necessary services for mothers and children, ostensibly to protect them against the onus attached to "illegitimacy." In one of their first actions after coming to power, the Nazis passed legislation in February 1933 to prohibit abortion and to close family planning institutions.[43] But Jewish women were officially informed in 1939 that this law did not apply to them and any interruption of their pregnancies was in the interest of the German people.[44] And while women in the annexed countries of eastern Europe were urged to contracept and abort, a new regulation was also enacted that provided the death penalty for aborting an "Aryan" fetus.[45]

Founded in 1935 as a nominally independent "registered society," *Lebensborn* was nevertheless organizationally part of the SS and closely under Himmler's control. Group homes were set up to provide discreet shelter to mothers bearing children outside legal marriage, and attempts were made to enhance the fertility of couples by medical treatments. A high official of the organization declared "Every mother of good blood shall be sacred to us" and "we Germans cannot afford to lose a single drop of good blood." But the emphasis was always two-fold: what mattered was not only the number of births (later supplemented by kidnappings) but also the racial and medical "quality" of births. Although there is no evidence that the sex of babies was a basis for determining their survival, children born under *Lebensborn* auspices with birth defects as mild as a cleft lip were transferred to special institutions where they were killed as "unworthy to live."[46]

Within Germany, the *Lebensborn* organization was surrounded by secrecy but was the subject of persistent rumors both before and after the war. Many of its documents were systematically destroyed before its end, which only added to the speculative publicity both within and outside the country. The leadership of the SS was aware of these rumors and tried to stem them but they remained the basis for post-war publicity and some later studies. As summarized in a very revealing internal document in 1944, the so-called rumors were said to include allegations that members of the elite SS corps "had the right to impregnate the girlfriends, and even the fiancees and wives of soldiers serving at the front ... that [the women] would receive payments ... for bearing such children ... and that, if they wished to keep the birth a secret, the children would be taken over by the State for care and education."[47] These claims were denounced, in this same internal document, as "infamous enemy propaganda and conscious defamation of the entire SS by our ideological opponents" in order to undermine the morale of German troops then fighting at the front.[48]

Some interpretations of the activities of *Lebensborn* stress the extent to which the organization became a convenient "breeding institution" (*Zuchtanstalt*) or "stud farm" for the SS. Himmler "applied Hitler's obsession with race in his exhortation to SS men to father as many children as possible without marrying" and tried to speed up this program once the Nazis started the war in 1939.[49] The state was to assume financial responsibility for all the children fathered by SS men but the "unbridled behavior" of these troops produced a public outcry even from loyal Nazis, including women leaders.[50] In discussing these Nazi practices, Claudia Koonz makes an important general point: "Promiscuity within an elite movement, like chastity in a religious order, maintains men's loyalty to a masculine corps and inhibits the formation of deep ties to women and children."[51]

The writer Christa Wolf remembers *Lebensborn* in her autobiographical novel and describes the beginnings of her own conflicted revulsion this way:

> [The thirteen year old "Nelly" is reading a newspaper that her parents have forbidden her to read.] She is reading—it seems to be autumn—a report about the establishments called "Lebensborn" ... : houses where blond, tall, blue-eyed SS men are brought together with brides who look just like them, for the purpose of conceiving a child of pure race, a child— as [the newspaper] reports approvingly—who will then be given as a present by his mother to the Führer. ... The writer of the article, and [Nelly] remembers this clearly, argues sharply, ironically, against those old-fashioned prejudices that would take offence at these actions worthy of idealistic German men and women. Truthfully, it must be said that

Nelly, when she had read the article, lowered the page and thought, very clearly: No, not that. It was one of those rare precious and unexplainable occasions when Nelly found herself in conscious opposition to the convictions demanded of her, convictions that she would so gladly have shared.[52]

Iran: The "Cleansing of Society"

From the beginning, the Khomeini regime in Iran emphasized the creation of new values, a new moral order, and gave this task priority over material changes. The Islamist regime also tried hard to reverse many of the material changes accomplished by the previous regime, calling them "anti-values" that are being changed in a "new atmosphere that is conducive to [the] re-making of human beings, to the cleansing of society."[53]

Women played a central role in this process of moral transformation, a role described in especially striking terms in a 1984 editorial in the Tehran weekly women's journal *Zan-e Ruz* that deserves extended citation:

In the underdeveloped countries ... women serve as the unconscious accomplices of the powers-to-be in the destruction of indigenous culture. ... [W]oman is the best means of destroying the indigenous culture to the benefit of imperialists. ... In Islamic countries the role of woman is even more sensitive. ... Woman in these societies is armed with a shield that protects her against the conspiracies aimed at her humanity, honor and chastity. This shield is verily her veil. For this reason, in societies like ours, the most immediate and urgent task was seen to be unveiling, that is, disarming woman in the face of all the calamities against her personality and chastity. ... She was used to disfigure the Islamic culture of the society, to erase people's faith and push society in her wake toward corruption, decay and degradation. ... It is here that we realize the glory and depth of Iran's Islamic Revolution. This revolution transformed everyone, all personalities, all relations and all values. *Woman was transformed in this society so that a revolution could occur.*[54]

Much has also been written about "westitis" or "westoxication" through which some Iranian writers have used the allegory of disease to express their feelings of lost identity. Not only are these notions useful for projecting responsibility on others—in this case "the West"—but, as Afsaneh Najmabadi notes, "the allegories used by Al-e Ahmad to diagnose a general social illness *found their most resonant reading onto the body of woman,* on her public physical appearance. In its extreme expression, un-Islamicly dressed woman became the sickness itself."[55] In other words, continuing a pattern of attributing blame to women (for instance, as temptresses of men) as justification for male control of female behavior (to protect men against their own impulses), here the attribution of blame to external forces is continued by further projections onto women. This, in turn, justifies the expansion of men's control over women.

More generally, the importance given to women in social transformation also reflects a critical feature of Middle Eastern societies, in spite of important variations among them, as noted by Deniz Kandiyoti: "if an irreducible 'core' of cultural practice had to be identified I would suggest that it resides primarily in *concrete modes of control of female sexuality*."[56] These interpretations could also be applied to elements of the ideology of the anti-abortion movement: Control of female sexuality and reproductive events is essential to the recovery of an earlier moral order. This control cannot be left to individuals but must be placed in the hands of a powerful institution, leaving no room for choice. Afsaneh Najmabadi has argued that "the concept of an individual's right to choose is totally absent from Islamic thinking [and] all Islamic currents [in Iran] agree that a woman does not have the right to choose her own clothing; the Islamic community decides for her."[57] In a 1986 speech, a member of the clergy even described proper veiling as "a kind of social vaccination" to protect Muslims against the disease of society. This implies that just as vaccinations are compulsory to sustain public health, "veiling cannot be consensual" and the state does not need anyone's consent for a compulsory measure.[58]

"Guided Sexuality": Temporary Marriage in Khomeini's Iran

One of the apparently minor consequences of the Islamic Revolution has been a renewed interest in the practice of temporary marriage (*mut'a*, colloquially *sigheh*). Whereas Sunni Muslims consider it fornication and thus forbidden, the practice has the sanction of Shia law but has never been held in particularly high repute. Its revival under the Khomeini regime is not only an indication of the regime's real attitudes toward women but also a brilliant, if minor, piece of early revolutionary strategy. Regime pressures for temporary marriages increased further during the Iran-Iraq war, as a pronatalist measure to produce babies to replace the many who died in that war, but calls for a revival of the custom *preceded* the revolution and the war. Details about temporary marriage in Iran have now been provided in an exhaustive anthropological and legal study, which included field interviews in Iran before and after 1979.[59]

First, some of the legal details of temporary marriage in Iran: Like permanent marriage (*nikah*), temporary marriage (*mut'a*) is a contract. The negotiations between the adults concerned are usually private and the ceremony consists of saying a simple formula. The terms of a temporary marriage contract must include a clear statement of the length of time it will last. This may be any length the partners want— from a few hours to many years, although short of a lifetime, because that is imprecise—as long as both are aware of it. There must also be an unambiguous marriage payment, from the man to the woman. In short, although this point is often denied, the mut'a agreement resembles a simple lease.[60]

There is no limit to the number of simultaneous mut'a unions in which a Shia Muslim man can engage, in addition to the four wives legally allowed to all Muslim men (although in practice polygyny is limited). A currently unmarried Shia Muslim woman is permitted temporary marriage with only one man at a time. Mut'a marriages have always been most frequent around shrines and pilgrimage sites; indeed, pilgrims' long absences from home are usually given as the traditional justification for temporary marriages. But it is also possible to negotiate different forms of mut'a, including a specific agreement for non-sexual intimacy. After the end of each temporary marriage, regardless of its duration, a woman must undergo a period of sexual abstinence (two menstrual cycles) so that a child's legitimate father can be identified, if necessary. (The required period of abstinence [*idda*] is longer in the case of dissolution of a permanent marriage, which, of course, implies its greater social significance.)

The child of a temporary marriage is legitimate under terms of Shia law but such children "often suffer stigmatized status and are usually regarded with moral ambivalence."[61] Temporary spouses do not legally inherit from each other although, in theory, they could make this part of the contract. In actual practice for women "temporary marriages entail no rights other than that of being the man's sex object. The man is not required to pay for the upkeep of his temporary wife—not even when she is carrying his child."[62]

Haeri traces the following trajectory of the revival of mut'a. Before the 1979 revolution, temporary marriage was never widely accepted and many people stigmatized it because of its association with prostitution. Prostitution is seen as unlawful and detrimental to social welfare, whereas—at least in the view of religious scholars—temporary marriage, "while performing a similar sexual function for the individual, *symbolizes social control.*[63] Mut'a marriages were much more acceptable in religious circles, and probably more widely practiced, than among the more secular groups before the revolution.

The Khomeini regime worked hard from the beginning to encourage and educate Iranians about temporary marriage, in public gatherings, through the media, and in high schools. This was part of a deliberate campaign to "purify" and revive the institution in new terms. Indeed, the Ayatollah Murtiza Mutahhari, a leading member of the Revolutionary Council who was assassinated in 1979, had earlier written of temporary marriage as a progressive institution and "one of the brilliant laws of Islam" well suited to a modern society.[64] A crucial point repeatedly made in arguments favoring temporary marriage, both before and after the revolution, was that it would enable young people to reject foreign models of behavior while still satisfying their natural urges. In the words of Mutahhari, if young people accept the legality of temporary marriage they will be prevented from following "the decadent Western path of 'sexual communism' [which gives] liberty to the young men and young women *equally*" but will, instead, be acting legitimately.[65]

One of the variations of mut'a, trial marriage (as formulated by Mutahhari in the 1970s), was especially strongly advocated by the regime to young people in high school religious textbooks taught to students from tenth grade up.[66] But given the continuing importance of female virginity in Iranian society, the regime soon retreated from this radical proposal. A later edition of the textbook presents a type of temporary marriage "where non-intercourse is agreed upon beforehand" and suggests it could be "an interesting experience during the engagement period ... for the would-be spouses get to know each other without any feelings of sin or guilt."[67]

Mut'a and its revival need to be seen in the context of prevailing ideas of the regime about male sexuality and the social position of women. Haeri explains that in general, sexuality is perceived in Shia belief as "absolute because it is anchored in nature, it is instinctual, unchanging, and inescapable." At the same time, Shia religious scholars also view it as "dangerous and disturbing to the moral order; it must be legally contained and morally guided." And because Iranian society is based on the principle of sex segregation, strict rules and strong control measures must be brought to bear on women and men to keep them separate and acting properly. These ideas produce a certain degree of ambiguity and result in a world view that "celebrates sexuality yet tries to contain it within religiously sanctioned boundaries."[68]

The critical dimension here is the notion of *control over human impulse*, made necessary both by the strength of "natural" instincts and the importance of an orderly society. It is no coincidence that one of the arguments offered by anti-abortion forces in the United States is that "uncontrolled" sexual activity would decline if abortions ceased to be legally available. Institutional control of human impulses—because human beings alone cannot be trusted—is very important to those who hold this outlook.

In post-revolutionary Iran, it is primarily *male* sexuality that is at issue and men's sexual "needs" that must be satisfied, a view that many Shia scholars hold and one with which Ayatollah Khomeini seems to have been obsessed, according to Haleh Afshar. Khomeini saw "the Shia man ... as a highly sexed predator, easily lured by women of all ages and entitled to have sexual relations with them in marriages that could be as long or as short as he pleases."[69] As one scholar has argued, "Man's need for marriage [a euphemism for sex] is more than his need for eating and drinking."[70] There will always also be some women who support these ideas; Haeri cites the case of a woman representative in parliament who lectures Iranian women on the advantages of temporary marriage. She urges them "to put aside their selfish feelings: to be more understanding of, and attentive to, their husband's 'natural' needs if they wish to *sigheh* (temporarily marry) other women."[71]

From the point of view of mobilizing support, the encouragement of mut'a marriage could affect several constituencies and their relations to the regime, although it is unfortunate that there is no way to judge the prevalence of the practice. In this sense, they may at least partially resemble the effects that *Lebensborn* activities had in terms of bonding men through shared promiscuity and increasing their gratitude to those who made it possible. The generalizations that follow are my own interpretations and are offered here as possible starting points for further research that might confirm or refute them.

First, mut'a marriages are part of the clerical style of life in Iran and may be seen by clergy themselves as part of their perquisites, even though they tend to refer to the religious merit of temporary marriage. As in other regimes that follow a revolution, those new to power try to make sure that their own preferences become both clear and desirable to their followers. Relatively easy sexual access to women carries immediate rewards, especially for those young men on whom revolutionary leaders depend for support.

Second, it is clear that special efforts were made to convince young adults of the advantages of mut'a "as opposed to the middle-aged population, who have been traditionally the most frequent practitioners."[72] If parents continue to be concerned with their daughters' virginity as a prerequisite to a conventional marriage, the possibility of a temporary marriage undoubtedly results in quarrels and perhaps a permanent break between the generations. Being able to start sexual activity "without any feelings of sin or guilt" can be very attractive to young people and provides an immediate reward for revolutionary commitment. It also reinforces the generational discontinuities necessary for continued support of new ideas by young people.

Third, Haeri's field work in Iran in 1978 and 1981 (facilitated by family connections), especially around the pilgrimage centers of Mashhad and Qom, revealed that the men—many of them religious officials—involved in mut'a marriages were very satisfied with their personal situations although they stressed the religious merit of the practice. But the women, with few exceptions, were deeply unhappy and often felt betrayed.

Finally, even if it is not widespread, the very existence of mut'a reinforces the already strong cultural and psychic boundaries against much of the rest of the world that the Khomeini regime developed— and it does so along two fronts: "the West" and Sunni Islam. Shia Muslims stress that "temporary marriage is said to gain God's reward because it directly challenges ... the ban on its practice" imposed in the mid-seventh century by a supreme religious leader (the Second Caliph) whom Sunnis venerate but Shia Muslims reject.[73] Like the other mobilizational tactics mentioned earlier, this boundary maintenance on two fronts served the purposes of the regime by emphasizing the isolated position that revolutionary Iran occupied in the world, leaving those who lived there with few choices between conformity (or at least quiescence) and exile.

The encouragement of mut'a marriages by the Khomeini regime, in short, shows another aspect of this regime's view of women, no matter what the official rhetoric about women's central role in the transformation of society might be. From this viewpoint, the very existence of mut'a and the official encouragement given to the practice show to what limits the regime is willing to go for ideological reasons and, perhaps, in line with the self-interest of the newly powerful clergy. The Ideal Woman as a central symbol in the achievement of the Ideal Society is shown by the Iranian case to be an example of profound inequality in which the deepening of male-female distinctions is used not only to alter the position of women and men in society but also makes women's resistance to change subversive, an attempt to weaken the state itself.[74]

Conclusions: Limits and Consequences
of Identity Enforcement

Notwithstanding the pluralism of our world, attempts by movements and regimes to enforce single identities in the service of their cause are increasingly common occurrences, perhaps in barely conscious recognition of a pluralistic world, but more explicitly in search of particularistic entitlements to power and resources. I have argued for the importance of choice, both in identity and in some of its aspects, such as among sexual and reproductive options, because the ability to choose among alternative world views is one of the hallmarks of genuine pluralism. However, when one considers the discussion of the legal bases on which "Pro-Choice" cases are being argued in the U.S., it matters a great deal how choices are conceptualized and sustained. The "privacy" defense of women's right to choose among reproductive options in the U.S. protects the individual from the intrusion of the state but says little about gender equality. The "equality" argument, on the other hand, points to the consequence *for women* of having restricted choices among sexual and reproductive options.[75]

Throughout the complexities of the three comparative examples, I have also tried to emphasize the general point that individual choices are inevitably reduced by groups and institutions whose search for power is grounded in the promise of greater entitlements for their members on the basis of a single, shared identity. This reduction of choice is entirely consonant with the general constrictive tendency of such movements and regimes to enhance the power of leaders and present a united facade to the outside world. It serves their purposes to prevent pluralism by limiting available categories of individual identity to those based on ascribed characteristics such as race, gender, or age, and to restrict personal choices among alternatives by ideological or administrative control.

The California "Pro-Life" activists studied by Kristin Luker in the late 1970s and early 1980s were largely housewives who saw themselves as defending a vision of women and of motherhood that they proudly embodied in their own lives. But the "Pro-Life" movement has increasingly come to be dominated by men in the leadership and among the activists who participate in violent demonstrations, even issuing death threats to those who try to limit their movement's passion to prevent the deaths of fetuses. By contrast, the "Pro-Choice" movement is led largely by women activists and, although it has the public and private support of many men, its demonstrations are largely composed of women. This difference suggests that at least some men find the views of the "Pro-Choice" movement sufficiently threatening to involve them passionately and often violently in a movement initially started largely by women. Such men, as well as the powerful figures in political, religious, and judicial institutions that openly support the anti-abortion cause, are clearly intent on enforcing a particular female identity and to do so through the power of the state. The supporters of the "Pro-Choice" movement reject both this particular vision and the use of state power to enforce it, believing—as I do—that decisions about sexuality and reproduction are best made by women themselves, wherever possible in conjunction with others who care about them.

In short, Identity Politics offers women a two-edged sword because so many of the "identities" being offered as ostensibly new points for popular mobilization are, in fact, selective reincarnations of particular visions of the past. These visions, usually called "traditions," are no such thing: They embody the hopes for future power and domination by those who manufacture them against the perceived threats of a pluralistic world that requires accommodation and compromise. Yet these "traditions" generally have one thing in common: the subservient status of women and often the restriction of women's lives to a rosy vision of domesticity and motherhood.

Claims to establish (or restore) a "pure" identity have brought great harm to women and men alike. The story of these three often violent attempts to do so demonstrates the catastrophic consequences of a denial of choice in women's sexual and reproductive decisions, not only for women but for everyone because these decisions are inseparable from broader political, social, and ethical concerns. Freedom of choice based on ethical frameworks that apply to everyone is not only most desirable in terms of outcomes but also reflects the specific reality of the twentieth century that a "pure" identity is an unattainable illusion and is not effective, even in the short run, to gain greater entitlements to a share of the world's resources. Claims for more equal entitlements must be framed within an acknowledgement of our common humanity and of the rights due universally to all of us. Given the complexities of human history, perhaps we are all "bastard children of history"[76] and must take responsibility for actively shaping our own sense of identity within a pluralistic world order.

Notes

Many influences, events, friends, and colleagues should be acknowledged but there is room for only a few. I owe particular thanks to Val Moghadam for providing the stimulus of a fascinating WIDER Conference, and to Vina

Mazumdar and Kumari Jayawardena for encouraging me to focus on the dangers presented by fundamentalist and revivalist movements. For comments and suggestions on the paper, I owe special thanks to Ruth Dixon-Mueller, Karen Paige Ericksen, Helen Fein, Adrienne Germain, Shahla Haeri, Liliane Kandel, Malavika Karlekar, David Kettler, Kristin Luker, Diane Margolis, Val Moghadam, Afsaneh Najmabadi, Frances Olsen and Rita Thalmann.

1. Kristin Luker, *Abortion and the Politics of Motherhood* (Berkeley: University of California Press, 1984).

2. Soedjatmoko, Dyason Memorial Lectures: I. "Indonesia: Problems and Opportunities," and II. "Indonesia and The World," East Melbourne, Australian Institute of International Affairs: *The Australian Outlook* (December 1967), pp. 288-289.

3. For an early discussion of the concept in psychological terms, see Erik H. Erikson, *Childhood and Society* (New York: Norton, 1950).

4. See, for example, Hanna Papanek and Gail Minault (eds.), *Separate Worlds: Studies of Purdah in South Asia* (Columbia, MO: South Asia Books, and Delhi: Chanakya Publishers, 1982); Karen Ericksen Paige and J. M. Paige, *The Politics of Reproductive Ritual* (Berkeley: University of California Press, 1981); K. E. Paige, "Virginity Rituals and Chastity Control during Puberty: Cross-Cultural Patterns," pp. 155-174 in Sharon Golub (ed.), *Menarche* (New York: Heath, 1983); K. E. Paige, "Female Genital Mutilations in Africa," *Behavior Science Research* 23 (1-4) (1989):182-204.

5. See, for example, Malavika Karlekar, *Voices from Within: Early Personal Narratives of Bengali Women* (New Delhi: Oxford University Press, 1991); Hanna Papanek, "Afterword: Caging The Lion — A Fable For Our Time," pp. 58-85 in *Sultana's Dream* by Rokeya Sakhawat Hossain (New York: The Feminist Press of the City University of New York, 1988).

6. Deniz A. Kandiyoti, "Slave Girls, Temptresses and Comrades: Images of Women in the Turkish Novel," *Feminist Issues* 8 (1) (1988), p. 35; Kandiyoti, "Emancipated but Unliberated? Reflections on the Turkish Case," *Feminist Studies* 13 (2) (Summer, 1987):317-338; Kumari Jayawardena, *Feminism and Nationalism in the Third World* (London: Zed Books Ltd., 1986), p. 12. See also Nira Yuval-Davis, "Fundamentalism, Multi-Culturalism and Women in Britain," paper presented at the XII World Congress of Sociology (Madrid, July 1990).

7. For an early Egyptian example, see Huda Sharawi, *Harem Years: The Memoirs of an Egyptian Feminist*, translated and introduced by Margot Badran (New York: The Feminist Press at the City University of New York, 1987). For an early Indian Muslim experience, see Gail Minault, "The Extended Family as Metaphor and the Expansion of Women's Realm," pp. 3-18 in Gail Minault

(ed.), *The Extended Family: Women and Political Participation in India and Pakistan* (Columbia, MO: South Asia Books, 1981), pp. 11-13.

8. Fatima Mernissi, *Beyond the Veil: Male-Female Dynamics in Modern Muslim Society*, revised edition (Bloomington: Indiana University Press, 1987), p. xv. See also Fatna A. Sabbah, *Woman in the Muslim Unconscious* (New York: Pergamon, 1984).

9. See Papanek, "Afterword: Caging The Lion."

10. Luker, *Abortion and the Politics of Motherhood.*

11. John C. Willke, MD, Fund-raising letter headed "ABC, CBS & NBC Declare War on the Pro-Life Movement," National Right-to-Life Committee, Inc., Washington, D.C. (1990: dated only "Friday afternoon" but circulated mid-year).

12. Jodi L. Jacobson, *The Global Politics of Abortion*, Worldwatch Paper 97 (Washington, D.C.: Worldwatch Institute, 1990), p. 45.

13. *Ibid.*, pp. 7-12.

14. Cited in Ruth Dixon-Mueller, "Abortion Policy and Women's Health in Developing Countries," *International Journal of Health Services* 20 (2) (1990), p. 307.

15. Ruth Macklin, "Liberty, Utility, and Justice: An Ethical Approach to Unwanted Pregnancy," *International Journal of Gynecology & Obstetrics*, Supplement 3 (1989), p. 37.

16. Frances Olsen, "Unraveling Compromise," *Harvard Law Review* 103 (1) (November 1989) , p. 131.

17. *Ibid.*, p. 120.

18. Luker, *Abortion and the Politics of Motherhood*, p. 193.

19. Jacobson, *The Global Politics of Abortion*, p. 46.

20. Rita Thalmann, *Frausein im Dritten Reich* (Frankfurt: Ullstein, 1987 [1982]); Claudia Koonz, *Mothers in the Fatherland: Women, the Family and Nazi Politics* (New York: St. Martin's Press, 1987); Liliane Kandel, "Le Mouvement Feministe Aujourd'hui et le National-Socialisme," *Les Temps Modernes* (524) (March 1990):17-53.

21. For Germany, see Thalmann, *Frausein im Dritten Reich*, pp. 157-188; for Iran, see Haleh Afshar, "Women in the Work and Poverty Trap in Iran," pp. 43-67 in Haleh Afshar and Bina Agarwal (eds.), *Women, Poverty and Ideology in Asia* (London: Macmillan, 1989) and Val Moghadam, "Women, Work and Ideology in the Islamic Republic," *International Journal of Middle East Studies* 20 (2) (May 1988):221-243.

22. Afsaneh Najmabadi, "Hazards of Modernity and Morality: Women in the Contemporary Middle East." Text of talk at the Harvard Divinity School (April 6, 1989), p. 15.

23. Adolf Hitler, *Mein Kampf* (München: Zentralverlag der NSDAP, Frz. Eher Nachf., 17th Edition, 1943 [1925, 1927]), p. 44, author's translation.

24. *Ibid.*, p. 460, author's translation.

25. Quoted in Alexander Stein, *Adolf Hitler: Schüler der "Weisen von Zion"* (Karlsbad: Graphia, 1936), author's translation, p. 83.

26. Hitler, *Mein Kampf*, p. 357, author's translation.

27. Helen Fein, *Accounting for Genocide: National Responses and Jewish Victimization during the Holocaust* (Chicago: University of Chicago Press, 1979), p. 21.

28. See, for example, Thalmann, *Frausein im Dritten Reich*, pp. 259-264.

29. Propaganda Minister Goebbels, cited in Thalmann, *Frausein im Dritten Reich*, p. 81, author's translation.

30. *Ibid.*, pp. 17-72.

31. *Ibid.*, p. 89, author's translation.

32. Koonz, *Mothers in the Fatherland*, p. 107.

33. Kandel, "Le Mouvement Feministe Aujourd'hui," author's translation, p. 20.

34. NSDAP [National Socialist German Workers' Party], *Organisationsbuch der NSDAP* (München: Zentralverlag der NSDAP, Franz Eher Nachf., 1943, 7th Edition), pp. 266-273.

35. Koonz, *Mothers in the Fatherland*, p. 59.

36. Thalmann, *Frausein im Dritten Reich*, pp. 89-110.

37. Christa Wolf, *Kindheitsmuster* (Darmstadt: Sammlung Luchterhand, 1986 [1976]), 14th Edition, paperback), author's translation, p. 205.

38. Georg Lilienthal, *Der "Lebensborn e.V.": Ein Instrument national-sozialistischer Rassenpolitik* (Stuttgart, New York: Gustav Fischer Verlag, 1985, Akademie der Wissenschaften und der Literatur, Mainz), author's translation, p. 43.

39. *Ibid.*, p. 165.

40. Clarissa Henry and Marc Hillel, *Of Pure Blood* (New York: McGraw-Hill, 1976), pp. 11-21.

41. Lilienthal, *Der "Lebensborn e.V.,"* p. 23.

42. *Ibid.*, p. 20.

43. Thalmann, *Frausein im Dritten Reich*, p. 137.

44. *Ibid.*, p. 123.

45. *Ibid.*, p. 153.

46. Refer to Lilienthal, *Der "Lebensborn e.V.,"* pp. 38, 41, 43, 84-100.

47. Cited in *ibid.*, p. 153, author's translation.

48. *Ibid.*, author's translation.

49. Koonz, *Mothers in the Fatherland*, p. 398.

50. *Ibid.*, p. 399.

51. *Ibid.*, p. 399.

52. Wolf, *Kindheitsmuster*, p. 208, author's translation.

53. 1986 speech by Rafsanjani, quoted in Afsaneh Najmabadi, "Iran's Turn to Islam: From Modernism to a Moral Order" *Middle East Journal* 41 (2) (Spring, 1987), p. 216.

54. Cited in Afsaneh Najmabadi, "Power, Morality, and the New Muslim Womanhood." Paper presented at workshop on "Women and the State in Afghanistan, Iran and Pakistan," Cambridge, Mass., MIT Center for International Studies (March 20, 1989), pp. 9-11, emphasis added. Forthcoming in Myron Weiner and Ali Banuazizi (eds.), *The State and the Restructuring of Society in Afghanistan, Iran, and Pakistan* (Syracuse: Syracuse University Press).

55. Afsaneh Najmabadi, "Hazards of Modernity and Morality," p. 15, emphasis added.

56. Kandiyoti, "Emancipated but Unliberated?" p. 335, emphasis added.

57. Azar Tabari, [Afsaneh Najmabadi], "Islam and the Struggle for Emancipation of Iranian Women," pp. 5-25 in Azar Tabari and Nahid Yeganeh (eds.), *In the Shadow of Islam: The Women's Movement in Iran* (London: Zed Press, 1982), p. 23.

58. Najmabadi, "Hazards of Modernity and Morality," p. 16.

59. Shahla Haeri, *Law of Desire: Temporary Marriage in Shi'i Iran* (Syracuse: Syracuse University Press, 1989); see also Haleh Afshar, "Khomeini's Teachings and their Implications for Iranian Women," pp. 75-90 in Azar Tabari and Nahid Yeganeh (eds.), *In the Shadow of Islam*, pp. 82-83; Afshar, "Behind the Veil: The Public and Private Faces of Khomeini's Policies on Iranian Women," pp. 228-47 in Bina Agarwal (ed.), *Structures of Patriarchy: State, Community and Household in Modernising Asia* (New Delhi: Kali for Women and London: Zed Books, 1988), and Afshar, "Women in the Work and Poverty Trap in Iran."

60. Haeri, *Law of Desire*, p. 52.

61. *Ibid.*, p. 35.

62. Afshar, "Khomeini's Teachings," p. 83.

63. Haeri, *Law of Desire*, p. 6, emphasis added.

64. *Ibid.*, p. 96.

65. *Ibid.*, p. 97, emphasis added.

66. *Ibid.*, pp. 96-97.

67. Bahunar et al., quoted in Haeri, *ibid.*, p. 98.

68. Haeri, *Law of Desire*, p. 5.

69. Afshar, "Khomeini's Teachings," pp. 82-83.

70. Makki, quoted in Haeri, *Law of Desire*, p. 64.

71. Haeri, *Law of Desire*, p. 8.

72. *Ibid.*, p. 96.

73. *Ibid.*, p. 7.

74. See Afshar "Khomeini's Teachings," and Val Moghadam, "The Reproduction of Gender Inequality in Islamic Societies: A Case Study of Iran in the 1980s," *World Development* 19 (10) (1991):1335-1349.

75. For an elaboration, see Olsen, "Unraveling Compromise," and Frances Olsen, "Liberal Rights and Critical Legal Theory," pp. 241-54 in Christian Joerges and David M. Trubek (eds.), *Critical Legal Thought: An American-German Debate* (Baden-Baden: Nomos Verlagsgesellschaft, 1989).

76. Salman Rushdie, "In Good Faith," pp. 393-414 in *Imaginary Homelands: Essays and Criticism 1981-1991* (London: Granta Books), p. 394.

4

Gender as an Ethno-Marker: Rape, War, and Identity Politics in the Former Yugoslavia

Silva Meznaric

Introduction

This chapter examines two cases wherein women and their bodies have been pawns in male-directed battles over ethnic identity. Rape as politics in the Serbian aggression in Bosnia in 1992-1993 has roots in the Kosovo conflict of the late 1980s. In both cases gender, ethnic identity, and political competition intersected, with tragic consequences.

Women are the special victims of nationalist ideologies and quests for ethnic purity. As with every nationalism, conservative Balkan nationalisms (Albanian, Serbian, Croatian) reassert the theme of the "home and hearth" as women's natural location. Nationalist exhortations disguise the opposition between men and women that inevitably accompanies the entrance of women into the public domain in traditional societies. In one case considered in this chapter (Kosovo), the fear instilled in women of entering into the public domain because of the rape which awaits them there masked the power struggles among the men themselves. In another case (Bosnia), rape became an all too real instrument of ethnic cleansing.

In May 1990, I completed a study of the "discourse of rape" in the Serbian-Albanian conflict in Kosovo, illustrating the uses and abuses of gender in ethnic conflicts. An early paper pointed out that the Serbian use of the discourse of rape and the media campaign against Albanians as rape perpetrators sharpened the ethnic border between Kosovo Serbs and Kosovo Albanians.[1] Two developments ensued: Serbian criminal law was partially amended to include the category "ethnic rape";[2] and Kosovo ceased to exist as a multiethnic region. Kosovo became a deeply divided society, with Albanians discriminated against in all vital areas of public life: in schooling, health services, public administration. The "rape campaign" succeeded thoroughly and realized the unspoken goal: to separate, by disseminating fear, two vital channels within the ethnic social network — working women (mostly Serbian) and Albanian men. I did not envisage the possibility that the rape campaign would escalate into rape policy via ethnic cleansing. It took only one year (summer 1990-summer 1991) for the first incidences of ethnic rape to appear during the Serbian-Croatian war; and it took only a few months for systematic rape in Bosnia to become the world's nightmare. According to one report: "All sides have committed abuses, but Muslim women have been the chief victims and the main perpetrators have been members of Serbian armed forces."[3] Ironically, the Serbian state which promulgated its criminal law with the "ethnic rape" article in it initially targeted at Kosovo Albanians was soon engaged in a war with the Muslim civilian population where its own soldiers or paratroopers engaged in massive and systematic rape as part of the ethnic cleansing strategy.

Thus the lesser-known media campaign and discourse of rape in Kosovo in the late 1980s was the prelude to rape as a strategy in ethnic cleansing in Bosnia. In Bosnia, the earlier war of words over rape graduated into systematic rape whose aim was forced pregnancy. *Rodit ces cetnika* (You will give birth to a *chetnik* soldier) was the slogan of Serbs raping Muslim women.

There have been many attempts to analyze the causes behind the massive rapes in Bosnia. Some have suggested that rapes in Bosnia are messages of intimidation from one adversary to another; or that rape in war is a continuation of masculinist politics by other means. The Bosnian Muslim anthropologist Sokolovic argues that rape of Muslim women in Bosnia is a "fateful consequence of the clash of two fundamentally different patriarchal cultures, and within that, a clash of two totally different approaches towards women."[4] The analysis in this chapter rests on a developmental framework that includes socio-economic and demographic variables, and a feminist explanation of patriarchal cultures in which "... violence was endowed with legitimacy, and legitimacy with violence."[5]

The relationship between gender, violence and "controlled sociability" has been addressed by early feminist writers among others.[6] The analysis developed by Maynard provides a good theoretical basis for the treatment of the use of gender and violence as a means of social control:

> The fear of violence, it has been shown, limits women's freedom of movement. It constrains what they can do, where they can go and with whom they can socialize. In other words, both the reality and the fear of violence act as a form of social control.[7]

Various theories of rape have been formulated to explain the incidence of actual rape. As summarized by Baron and Straus, these are gender inequality, pornography, social disorganization, and legitimate violence.[8] Their analysis of the cultural support for violence and the cultural spillover theory of rape could be used as the theoretical framework for the case of Kosovo. According to them, cultural spillover theory is based on the idea that

> [R]ape may be influenced by the implicit or explicit approval of violence in various areas of life such as education, the mass media, or sports. Cultural spillover theory predicts a carryover or diffusion from social contexts in which the use of violence is socially approved to social contexts in which the use of violence is considered illegitimate or criminal.[9]

Another useful framework for understanding events in the former Yugoslavia is provided by Barth, who argues that when groups compete over the same niche, the consequences may be either accommodation or displacement of one group by the other.[10] Socio-economic variables, and especially the unevenness of development, are also a part of the explanation. With this framework in mind, we now turn to an examination of the rape campaign in Kosovo, which preceded the breakdown of Yugoslavia and the horrors of Bosnia.

Prelude to Bosnia's Rapes:
The Rape Campaign in Kosovo

In 1981, the autonomous province of Kosovo constituted 4.2 percent of Yugoslavia's territory and 7.8 percent of the total population of the former Yugoslavia. Within Kosovo, the Albanian majority comprised 77.4 percent of the population. (See Table 4.1.) Beginning in that year, and continuing since, conflict emerged between the Albanian majority and the Serbian and Montenegrin minorities. The conflict between the majority and minority ethnic groups created divisions in the economy, in property, in culture and communications (especially the mass media), in the definition of traditions, in the labor market, and in the spheres of political power and popular mobilization. By the end of 1991, Serbia's new constitution exempted from Kosovo's competency important areas of autonomous rule, such as representative institutions, public administration, and police. The Serbian government, which assumed political control in the province, deployed various approaches to hamper communication between the two ethnic groups. Some of these strategies include the use of gender as a means to control communication and to sharpen the boundaries between two opposed ethnicities. These gender strategies may be classified in two groups: the "hardline" approach and the "soft" approach. In Kosovo, the hardline approach employed the discourse of violence, especially rape, with the aim of spreading fear of interaction and communication among the ethnic collectivities. The soft approach used the discourse of the need to control the birthrate of the growing Albanian population.

My focus here is the hardline approach, that is, the discourse of rape which constructed Serbian women as victims and Albanian men as perpetrators. This discourse developed as a means to establish control over interaction and communication between "targeted" actors among the ethnic groups in conflict. The targets were actors in the region whose behavior was least predictable, who were most liable to non-institutionalized networks of the local community or whose social role was the most stable. In the patriarchal and underdeveloped Kosovo region these were Albanian men and Serbian and Albanian women. Spreading fear of interaction and communication among them enhanced the central authorities' social control in the multiethnic community.

The culture of violence — explicit and implicit approval of violence toward women in Kosovo — allowed the Serbian government to extend the discourse of rape in order to disseminate fear of communication among ethnicities. Moreover, socially approved legitimate violence within the family and within conjugal relations was carried over to the broader social context in which the use of violence is considered illegitimate. In the Criminal Code of the Republic of Serbia, "political rape" is distinguished from "ordinary rape." The violence of "ordinary rape" is less severely punished because victims and perpetrators are presumably not of different nationalities, whereas when a victim is of Serbian nationality, rape is qualified as a political act and penalized more severely.

TABLE 4.1　Population According to Nationality in the Province of Kosovo and in the Republic of Bosnia-Herzegovina, 1981

	Province of Kosovo		Republic of Bosnia-Herzegovina	
Nationality	N	%	N	%
Albanians	1,226,736	77.4	4,396	0.1
Croats	8,718	0.6	458,140	18.4
Macedonians	1,056	0.1	1,892	0.2
Montenegrins	27,028	1.7	14,144	0.3
Muslims	58,562	3.7	1,630,033	39.5
Romanies	34,126	2.2	7,251	0.2
Serbs	209,497	13.0	1,320,738	32.0
Turks	12,513	0.8	277	0.0
Others	6,204	0.4	67,069	1.6
"Yugoslavs"	2,676	0.1	320,316	7.7
TOTAL	1,584,440	100.0	4,124,256	100.0

Source:　*Jugoslavija 1918-1988; Statisticki Godisnjak* (1984), p. 439.

The first overt signs of the Albanian-Serbian conflict appeared with the phenomenon of Serbian emigration from Kosovo. Emigration from Kosovo had always been a typical feature of Kosovo as an underdeveloped region; but political problems emerged as more Serbs and Montenegrins left Kosovo than did Albanians. For both ethnic groups the crucial question was how to live in a region in which demographic and economic indicators of underdevelopment are overwhelming. The mortality rate of live-born infants in Kosovo was the highest in Europe (in 1987, 50.7 per 1000 live births), twice as high as in Yugoslavia as a whole and more than two times higher than in Serbia proper. Again, in 1987 the birth rate per 100 was 24.8, which in relation to 1950 decreased only 5.3 points, while in the whole of Yugoslavia the birth rate has decreased 11.1 points. In Kosovo, unlike anywhere else in Yugoslavia and probably anywhere else in Europe, the number of individuals per household grew in this century, from 5.71 per household in 1921 to 6.92 in 1981. Population density increased from 67.3 per square kilometre in 1948 to 163.3 per square kilometre in 1986.[11] In 1988, 40 percent of all employed persons in the former Yugoslavia were women, whereas in Kosovo, only 22 percent were women. Only

9.6 percent of the female active population were employed in Kosovo, against 32.7 percent for the country as a whole. Albanian women were five times less active than Serbian women.[12]

According to the World Bank, Kosovo in 1987 had a gross domestic product per capita of $800. As a result, Kosovo would be classified as at the bottom of semi-developed countries.[13] Between 1948 and 1986, Kosovo underwent urbanization and industrialization, resulting in a decline of the farming population from 81 percent to 25 percent. In the same period, every 100 dinars of investments in Yugoslavia produced an average 15.2 dinars of GDP growth whereas in Kosovo it resulted in only 10 dinars. The Yugoslav state tried to close this gap by financing Kosovo's growing needs through special federal funds for underdeveloped regions. In 1987, 44 percent of the Fund was channelled to Kosovo. According to economists, such distribution policies did not succeed in closing the gap because they were not accompanied by development strategies.[14] Relative to the former Yugoslavia's average, GDP per capita in Kosovo in 1987 represented only 28 percent, the employment rate only 44 percent, and capital assets per capita 37 percent.

Cultural and Spatial Aspects
of the Conflict in Kosovo

Demographically, if there is to be any chance of a complementary and adaptable life in a common niche-territory, a great imbalance in numbers of among ethnic groups should not exist. Barth writes:

> Whenever a population is dependent on its exploitation of a niche in nature, this implies an upper limit on the size it may attain. ... If, on the other hand, two populations are ecologically interdependent ... this means that any variation in the size of one must have important effects on the other.[15]

These effects need not always be struggles, and in Kosovo historical accounts attest to the fact that for centuries the population developed a system of mutual adjustments.[16] However, migration began to upset this, especially when large numbers of Serbs began to migrate out of Kosovo in the 1980s.

Resettlement emigration and population growth were always mechanisms of adjustment for ethnic groups in Kosovo. But since the 1970s, their mutual balancing was disturbed by high emigration of Serbs and high social costs of the natural growth of the Albanian population.

Research findings from both Serbian and Albanian sides showed that Albanians had a low degree of territorial mobility: 68 percent of Albanians in Kosovo live in their place of birth.[17] In the period 1971-1981 Serbian emigration from Kosovo represented 84.1 percent of the overall negative net migration of Kosovo, while the Albanian share of it was only 2.7 percent.[18]

The conflict between the two ethnic communities led to an emphasis on the need for renewed definitions of Serbs and Albanians, and identification of those objective markers which most effectively show "who is who," who belongs where, and what belongs to whom. The redefinition of Serbs and Albanians as *ascriptive* and *exclusive* ethnic groups was necessary because it restored the outlines of ethnic groups, outlines which had become blurred. Above all, this redefinition introduced continuity and tradition, not only for the ethnic groups involved but also for those outside the region. In the 1980s, both groups spent enormous amounts of money, energy and ideas on defining tradition and continuity. They discovered ancient states and territorial rights, cradles of national identity, monuments, battles from the 15th century, friends and enemies dating from the Middle Ages, and so on.

Identification of ethnic markers frequently entails recognition of ethnic identifiers such as language, dress, lifestyle, and housing — these are customary for every ethnic group. What happens when these identifiers are similar and cannot easily distinguish the groups? In the case of Serbs and Albanians, not only did they demarcate themselves in terms of language, dress, and housing, but they also insisted on separation of schools, instruction, literature, history, and so on. Even so, overt signals and signs for defining boundaries were not enough. Sharpness of boundaries demanded additional differentiation in the field of the "standards of morality and excellence by which performance of persons is judged."[19] This was accomplished by the power structure of the time — the Serbian minority in Kosovo, and Serbians and Albanians within the Party. The defining field of differentiation was found in the "culture of violence." Under this category, "rape" and other kinds of sexual abuse were selected as the field for constructing boundaries between ethnic groups. The manner of construction entailed the stigmatization of Albanian men as rapists of Serbian women (and men). This is the sense in which gender became an ethno-marker. Classic markers of ethnic differences (language, religion, housing, territory) were insufficient because they could be erased or blurred by the modernization of life. But by constructing ethnic difference on the basis of one group's cultural proclivity to violence and rape, the boundary between the two groups became fixed. This new ethnic differentiation was particularly compelling as an ethnic marker because it locates itself in the sphere of everyday life. Within the sphere of everyday life the bearers of "everyday sociability" were defined: Albanian men and Serbian women. As the most active in everyday life, they can be treated as "gatekeepers"[20] who control access to various forms of sociability, interaction and communication. Therefore, in order that boundaries between them be most sharply defined and maintained, they must be confined to the area that will register fear and frustrate any future contact: this is the field of rape.

Sharpening the Ethnic Boundary: Gender and Rape as Ethno-Markers

The media campaign around rape in Kosovo emerged and reached its peak in the summer of 1987. When the issue of rape first emerged, the views of both sides, Albanian and Serbian, could be expressed and heard. But when the rape crisis peaked in the summer of 1988, the Serbian press uniformly stigmatized Albanians as rapists. In Kosovo rape not only became a traumatic experience for the woman involved — carrying with it the stigma, fear, and anxiety that it does all over the world — but it became politicized and manipulated for ethno-political gain. In my own field research in Kosova, and after interviews with both Albanians and Serbs, I found that stories of rape were very often invented because for women and men in Kosovo and Serbia, sexual intercourse outside of marriage is still considered shameful; according to some sources, a few girls, after losing their virginity, would invent stories of rape and, to prove it, would injure themselves.[21] Such cases seemed to be equally distributed among the Albanian and Serbian population.

In 1986 a discussion emerged which sought a differentiation between attempted and actual rape within criminal law. An article in the Belgrade press offered the following information:

> In the period from 1982 to 1986, the Kosovo police reported 114 arrests for criminal rape and 128 for attempted rape. The majority of cases were Albanian men raping Albanian women ... 15 rapes and 14 attempted rapes were by Albanian men on Serbian women. Among Serbian and Montenegrin men there were 5 rapes and 19 attempted rapes on women of the same nationality. Montenegrin and Serbian men attempted rape on Albanian women in three cases, and one of the attempts was realized. This summer in Kosovo one rape and two attempted rapes of Serbian women have taken place.[22]

A discussion opened on the legal qualifications for rape, introduced by detailed analysis of attempted rape. After stating that "pressure of the hands, touching legs or breasts" can qualify as attempted rape according to local culture, the press accorded attempted rape the same status as actual rape. In 1987 legal qualification of attempted rape acquired the meaning of actual rape. In many cases, even before an investigation began, the press would publish details of the alleged rapist's workplace and residence, including initials of names and family description of the mostly juvenile suspects, making it easy to identify the alleged rapists. Names of adult perpetrators, Serbs and Albanians alike, appeared in the press even before criminal charges were brought against them, let alone the sentence passed. In public meetings and ethnic rallies following news of attempted rape of Serbian women or girls, data on the family of the Albanian perpetrators were published. The press began to echo the rallies' demands; attempted and actual rape both received the same treatment in public and criminal law. Public reaction in Kosovo and Serbia was beginning to be described as "lynching." According to one article:

> Several tumultuous meetings have been held recently in the village of M. [following the attempted rape of a 16-year-old girl of Serbian nationality] ... at town meetings, in the presence of the commune leadership, the oppressive actions of juvenile XY [initials] was condemned unanimously and with great disgust. Also, the meeting condemned the attempts of his father, who is currently working in Switzerland, to bribe the police to conceal the whole matter ... . This and previous attempts to rape Serbian girls by young Albanian boys in village M. was characterized by the meeting of the village as a conscious and perfidious tactic of Albanian irredentists and separatists, with the aim of disturbing the consolidation of relationships between the Serbian and Albanian population of this area.[23]

In 1988 the self-organization of Serbs against ethnic violence turned to paramilitary organization. Another press account described the attempted rape in the following way:

> [I]n the center of a tourist settlement, a ... juvenile Albanian XY [initials] tried to rape a housewife (20 years old) of Serbian nationality who a little after 11 am returned home from the post office. This attempt failed because the housewife succeeded in tearing herself away and calling the neighbors for help. After this, a meeting was held in B. of the Committee for National Defence and Protection (a paramilitary formation). At this

meeting it was decided that this disgusting act was another attempt by Albanian nationalists and separatists to frighten Serbs living in this area and force them to move away.[24]

In 1986-90 an affair labelled by the press "Fadilgate" appeared. Fadil Hoxha, an Albanian and prominent Kosovo political personality, became a symbol of the perversity of Albanian sexual culture ("rapist with a smile"). Allegedly, his proposed solution to rape was "organized prostitution" in Kosovo. The press interpreted his idea as basically free entrepreneurship, where non-Muslim prostitutes would serve frustrated Albanian clients. The "Fadilgate" affair began with a gathering of the society of war veterans and reserve army officers of Kosovo at the beginning of October 1986 in Kosovo town. Fadil Hoxha was the Albanian member of the Yugoslav presidency representing Kosovo. In his talk Hoxha referred to current relations between ethnic groups. He reportedly "emphasized the problem of the rape phenomenon, but in connection with this he smiled and said he earlier told some comrades that it might be better to behave more tolerantly toward the phenomenon of some immoral behavior in some cafes ... toward girls who work as waitresses and on the side favor these immoral phenomena."[25]

According to the interpretation of the audience, Fadil Hoxha's prescription for fighting rape was the following:

> There are some examples of rape in Kosovo; I think that it is necessary to allow women from other parts of Yugoslavia to come to private coffee-houses in Kosovo so that those who would rape women of other nationalities can indulge themselves. Albanian women won't do this but Serbian and other women would like to, so why not let them?[26]

Hoxha later apologized to non-Albanian women saying that he intended only to "relativize" the problem of rape so as to emphasize that one of the sources of rape in Kosovo "could be sexual frustration."[27]

An initiative began for criminal proceedings against Hoxha by the war veterans association, the women's association, and individuals. They wished to sue not only the author of the statement but also the top leadership of the province. The initiative was advanced because of reasonable evidence that the leadership had "inflamed national hatred and undermined the constitutional order of Yugoslavia." Hoxha was even accused of the murder of certain famous Serbian partisan leaders. Eventually, Fadil Hoxha resigned his government post. He was indicted for "expressing national, religious and race hatred, discord and intolerance."

The Rape Controversy:
Data and Their Meaning

How did feminists respond to the Kosovo rape phenomenon? There were two fundamentally different feminist responses to rape in Kosovo, both of which derive from the culturalist discourse of rape. Sklevicky calls these two responses the "patriarchal" and the "pseudo-feminist" models of rape.[28] The patriarchal model explains rape on the basis of the statement that rape "damages the honour of a woman, that is, her strength, the faithfulness of her husband and her virginity." In this way the sacred society is tarnished, and the victim is the group — the ethnic group — and not the individual. The pseudo-feminist model explains rape by criticizing the patriarchal model, "but inconsistently."

> The feminist thesis that rape cannot be interpreted by means of numbers and statistics but as a problem is repeated. They insist on understanding rape as a political act, as a means of revenge between conflicting groups (of men), but only as inter-national, when the rapist is Albanian. ... The act of rape is characterized in harmony with feminist analyses which are much wider than legal enactments and include every form of aggression of men against women. In this is included "grabbing hand and breasts," love calls and profanity thrown from buses to the street or the fields. ... Stronger punishment is sought by feminists for "ethnic" rape than for the ordinary one.[29]

Sklevicky argued that feminists, and especially the most radical feminists who justifiably called for solidarity of all women of Yugoslavia against inter-national rapes, missed the opportunity to denounce the manipulation of rape in inter-ethnic conflict. Her critique of both models is that the patriarchal model "is buried in the contradictions of the logic of the functioning of the patriarchy itself, while the pseudo-feminist model selectively accepts radical theses."[30] Drakulic thinks along similar lines when she discusses the codification of rape in the Serbian legal system as "pure violence." The "rapes" in Kosovo led the Republic of Serbia to modify its penal code, introducing in 1986 a new criminal offense, "sexual assault on citizens of different nationality." Until then rape was punishable with no reference to nationality, since the law treated all citizens equally. The incrimination of the ethnicity of the victim or perpetrator introduced the category of ethnicity as a possible aggravating circumstance in the occurrence of rape or attempted rape. Thus rape has become a political act. Taking into account the circumstances surrounding the codification of rape as a political act it can be safely assumed that the incrimination of the perpetrator was established with a particular ethnicity in mind. Political rape was introduced into the penal code with Albanian men as presumed rapists and Serbian women and men as presumed victims. Rapes within ethnic communities are not treated as political acts by the legislator, and as such do not merit harsher sentences. From the point of view of the rape victim, however, Drakulic asks: "Could it be possible that political rapes are more offensive to women than an 'ordinary' rape — after all, for a woman being raped the fact that the rapist is a Serb, an Albanian, a Croat or a Bosnian makes no difference."[31]

Belgrade feminist Mladjenovic correctly notes that "in Serbia, rape acquired race, nationality, and history." She maintains that "violent sex underlines the social organization; passion is based on violence that women have to suffer."[32] In a research study conducted by the feminist group *Zena i drustvo* (Woman and Society) in Belgrade, March 1988, 35 percent of women "explicitly talked about being forced to make love against their will and when asked if they had ever been hit by a man, only 17 percent of the interviewees answered negatively. Sexual violence, then, is just one form of violence that a majority of women have to bear in order to survive."[33]

How the women in Kosovo, Serbia and Albania reacted to such a use of their bodies is largely undocumented; only the protests of Serbian women against "Fadilgate" were made public. There is little or no data available on protests of Albanian men or women; accounts of these are most likely confined to their inner walls or their private communications and will probably emerge as subtle protest in new national myths or even in an epic form. As Slapsak shows in her deconstruction of the Serbian national myth of the battle of Kosovo — the historical defeat of Serbs by the Turkish armies in the 14th century — the role of the Serbian woman is to clean up after the battle; she either collects the pieces of dismembered warriors or dedicates her life to the continuation of the family. In the first case, the woman is "a victim. ... She is the final evidence of the crime against life, the crime of war and epic consciousness."[34] The woman accepts the sacrifice, but before that she "catalogs" the fragments of the male world, of their bodies, and thus, by bearing evidence to the crime in a naturalistic description of the slaughtering of the Serbs, she denounces the epic system of power. In the other case, accepting the role of carrier of tradition and family, she does not accept the system; she rather destroys it radically. "The female victim openly refuses to play the designated role and realizes her life project, the development of family and social prosperity, unrepentantly."[35]

In 1990, new evidence put the Kosovo rape phenomenon in an entirely new light. The Independent Commission of the Yugoslav Forum for Human Rights and the Association of the Yugoslav Democratic Initiative, issued their report on rape in Belgrade in 1990. The report disclosed the findings that there were no reliable data on the nationality of those committing criminal acts in Yugoslavia in general and in Kosovo in particular. Rape which is considered a separate criminal act is hidden under an act "against the human survival and morals."[36]

The findings of the Yugoslav Forum for Human Rights were based on examination of police data about reported rape and attempted rape committed by Albanians on Serbs and Montenegrins. For the period 1979-1988 they disclosed the following figures: there were 2.5 times fewer rapes in Kosovo than in Yugoslavia as a whole. Moreover, the proportion of Albanians who perpetuated rape was less than their proportion in the total Yugoslav population; Serbs and Muslims perpetrated a greater share of total rapes than their share in the total population. (For example, Albanians in Kosovo were 7 percent of the total Yugoslav population; Albanians convicted of rape were 6 percent of the total of convicted rapists in the former Yugoslavia.) Of the total number of criminal proceedings in Kosovo for rape and attempted rape in the years between 1982 and 1988 (N=323), 9.6 percent or 31 rapes were committed by Albanians on Serbs. After 1982 the trend falls, and in the three years from 1987 to 1989 there was not one case of rape of a Serb by an Albanian. The report argued that the almost non-existent inter-ethnic rape in Kosovo could be a sign of the total breakdown in communication between ethnic groups. The data showed that intra-ethnic rape was over-represented and all inter-ethnic indices were negative (see Table 4.2). The index of association for Albanian-Serbian rate (-22.8) means that the ethnic factor "acts in the direction opposite to that proliferated in public opinion and political propaganda."[37]

Less than a year after the rape controversy in Kosovo, the multiethnic fabric of the former Yugoslavia unravelled. Central to this process was gender violence.

TABLE 4.2 Perpetrators and Victims of Rape in Kosovo by Nationality (1982-1989); Indices of Association

Victims (women) by Nationality	Perpetrators			
	Albanians	Serbs	Others	Total
Albanians	33.5	-24.4	-9.1	239
Serbs	-22.8	25.3	-0.9	101
Others	-10.7	-0.3	10.1	33
TOTAL	302	49	22	373

Source: S. Popovic, D. Janca, and T. Petovar, eds., *Kosovski cvor: dresiti ili seci?* (Belgrade: Izvestaj nezavisne komisije, 1990), p. 45.

Bosnia-Herzegovina: A Developmental Framework

Although gender violence and ethnic conflict in Bosnia are of a different order from the earlier events in Kosovo, understanding and explaining their emergence is best accomplished by a similar developmental framework.

Economic and demographic findings in the late 1980s disclosed a wide gap in the development of specific regions in Bosnia. Key variables in such analysis have been: net-migration, population dynamics and the participation of local communes in the GNP of the republic. Impasses found in communal (regional) development could hardly be explained solely by national/ethnic diversity or the composition of the local community. There were well-to-do local communities and regions with mosaic ethnic composition, and poor communities with homogenous populations. Nonetheless, the data support at least one rather well-established assumption: that in the last two decades, ethnic/national diversity has been associated with higher migration rates.

In the 42 years between 1948 and 1991 the total population of Bosnia-Herzegovina grew by over 41 percent; this substantial growth was due mainly to the transition from high vital rates to low ones, and from a low to higher standard of living. Once the most fertile Yugoslav region, Bosnia-Herzegovina began its demographic transition in the 1950s, and in the 1980s reached a rate of natural growth close to 1 percent per annum and a fertility rate of 1.9 per annum. The latter was significantly lower than the Yugoslav average at the time (2.14) and was under the threshold of population reproduction. This downward trend was more dramatic and took a shorter period of time than in other Yugoslav republics. Hence in the late eighties demographers were arguing that "some serious turbulences occurred in the population reproduction in Bosnia-Herzegovina." In particular, they were referring to the differences in the birthrates found among national groups in Bosnia-Herzegovina (1981): rates were 15.8 for Croats, 14.8 for Serbs, and 21.0 for Muslims. Consequently, the "nationality" structure of newborn babies in 1981 was significantly different from the structure of the total population. Concurrently, the demographic transition being almost completed, the birthrate decreased from 26.2 (1950-1954) to 10.7 per million (1980-1983). The population grew older: in forty years, the proportion of people over 65 years in the total population almost doubled, from 3.2 percent to 6.1 percent. The urban population grew from 15 percent (1953) to 36 percent (1981).

In 1981, Bosnia-Herzegovina had 106 administrative units (communes); in 67 of them the population diminished, in some cases drastically, with a more than 30 percent reduction in the period between 1963-1981. The majority of them were communes with a Serbian majority, part of today's "Krajina" and eastern Herzegovina. Such a shrinking of local populations diminished their fertile and productive segments. A similar pattern occurred in communes with Croatian majority.

Pre-war analysis which combined population dynamics in communes (population growth/decline) and their participation in the republic's Gross National Product (rise or fall) between 1963-1981, suggested four types of development in pre-war Bosnia-Herzegovina. Among the 67 communes where population growth declined, as we noted earlier, only seven increased their participation in the republic's GNP. All of them were ethnically mixed; five of them are situated in what is nowadays called the "Serbian corridor" in Krajina and two of them are in the "Croatian corridor" in western Herzegovina. Four of these communes (Bijeljina, Bosanska Gradiska, Celinac and Derventa) were among the first targets of Serbian aggression and cleansing. Central Bosnia (nowadays known as the Muslim region) presents the type of development which has combined substantial population growth and considerably decreased participation in the republic's GNP.

The ethnic composition of Bosnia-Herzegovina has been rather stable, although in comparing groups one should bear in mind administrative changes and changes in categories (such as the statistical introduction of dummies like "nationality not declared", "Muslims as an ethnic group,"

"Yugoslavs").[38] Nonetheless, it would be quite safe to say that nationally/ethnically mixed areas were, to a certain degree, going through more significant changes than ethnically homogeneous ones.

Figures for Serbs particularly show a significant drop in their proportion of the population, both in Bosnia-Herzegovina as a whole and in the regions.[39] This may be due to the shift in self-identification from Serbian (1971) to Yugoslav nationality (1981). This appears to be the case in both Krajina and Herzegovina. In Krajina, for instance, the proportion of Serbs decreased by 7.8 points between 1971-1981, while that of Yugoslavs increased by 8.2 points.

A typical citizen of Bosnia-Herzegovina, irrespective of whether he/she was Croat, Serb or Muslim, was young (50 percent under 31 years; Serbs are slightly older than others); married to a spouse of the same group (curiously enough, even Yugoslavs marry "Yugoslav"), had about 8 years of education (though for women, fully 38 percent had less than 4 years of education); owned a house or an apartment or shared one with her/his parents; was not living on a farm and had no arable land; and did not move anywhere during her/his lifespan.[40] He or she lived in a rural or semi-rural area, in a settlement with a population of less than 2,000 inhabitants (58 percent of respondents).

One could find an equal distribution of conservatism, ethno-centricism, and authoritarianism throughout the population; Croats, Muslims and Serbs view changes more or less cautiously. They were equally for strong government and central decision-making. The majority were "egalitarianists" ("same needs — same earnings"), and they tended to prefer a "strong hand" government (Serbs more than others).

Attitudes towards mixed-marriages have at least two interesting features: first, the decisive negative expressed by 50 percent of the total population referred only to the Albanian choice; opposition to marriage with other groups (Croat, Muslim, Serb) was around 21 percent. Secondly, those opposed had significant variations among particular groups: thus Muslims were significantly against choosing a Croat as a spouse; Croats and Serbs had the same feelings about Muslims. In short, regarding marital preferences, the cleavages between Muslims and others seem much deeper than those between Serbs and Croats. If these preferences are taken as indicators of the processes of exclusion/inclusion in particular ethnic communities we might say that, judging from our data, in pre-war Bosnia, such processes mainly concerned the Muslim community.

Rape and War in Bosnia-Herzegovina

Although it is true that in the Balkans, rape was always a part of military campaigns, events in Bosnia appear to be unprecedented in that mass rape with pregnancy and reproduction as the goal was key to the ethnic cleansing strategy. Numerous sources mention rapes committed by Serbian soldiers on women of Muslim nationality. At this writing (March 1993), it was not possible to completely verify the data, and control of the findings was possible only by comparing information from various sources and by checking the statements of victims and witnesses.[41]

The report of the Coordinative group of women's organizations of Bosnia and Herzegovina estimate that 20,000 to 50,000 women had been raped. On September 29, 1992 the daily paper *Vecernji list* (Zagreb) reported that the Serbian Orthodox bishop of Bosnia, Nikolaj, stated on the independent Belgrade TV station "Studio B" that 30,000 Muslim women had become pregnant by rape. According to the European Community's Investigative Mission an estimated 20,000 Muslim women have been raped. Although there is not general agreement as to the number of victims, one could say that there is agreement in the sources concerning several important points: (1) mass rape has had at least several thousand victims; (2) there have been many rapes of young girls between the ages of seven and fourteen (3) rape is often committed in the presence of the victim's parents/children and generally the rape victim is raped by several assailants.

Many eyewitnesses have reported on the brutality of the rapes. Frequently, when families are arrested the men are separated from the women and children. Young, more educated and more affluent males are practically always killed, and the women are then raped. Rape victims are both women and girls, regardless of age. Consecutive raping of girls younger than 15 years of age result in a high death rate or else in permanent invalidity.[42] Daughters are often raped in the presence of their parents, mothers in the presence of their children, and wives in the presence of their husbands.[43] Women victims are led away from camps to trenches on the front lines for the satisfaction of the warriors. Women suffered rape because Serbian soldiers threatened the lives of their loved ones. However, often they could not save their relatives or themselves. Some did not even want to remain alive.[44]

Furthermore, descriptions of witnesses and of the very rape victims, as well as the official reports indicate the existence of a large number of "public houses" into which Muslim and Croat women are brought, of "special areas" in known concentration camps where Serb soldiers sexually abuse women, and there are also indications of "specialized" camps in which young girls and women are raped. Often those women who survived and became pregnant were held by Serb soldiers in the camps until they were close to the end of the pregnancy term, after which they were replaced by other victims or allowed to escape. According to the EC report, there was no proof that rapes were conducted on command, but all indicators suggested that there were no attempts to prevent them (and that they were perhaps encouraged).[45]

If one compares the ethnic picture of Bosnia and Herzegovina with the available data and locations of camps, that is, "public houses" and information on rapes, one can notice that massive rapes occur in areas where Serbs are a minority, and Muslims are in relative or absolute majority (Brcko, Rogatica, Foca, Zvornik, Visegrad, Prijedor, Tuzla, Sarajevo, Bihac, Bosanska Krupa, Sanski Most), or else in areas where Serbs are in a majority position but where there are significant Muslim and/or Croat minorities (Kalinovik, Kotor Varos, Banja Luka, Bijelijina, Nevesinje).

Conclusions

This chapter has examined the complex relations between identity politics, ethnic rivalry, and gender violence in the former Yugoslavia. In particular, I have tried to show that gender is an ethno-marker in boundary maintenance and in conflicts between groups. In Kosovo, the discourse of rape blocked interaction between two ethnic groups. A new category of rape emerged — "inter-national rape with political consequences" — and this aided the mobilization of Serbs against Albanians. The actors in rape, Kosovo Albanian men (assailants) and Serbian women (victims), were prevented from any kind of daily communication. They were confined to functioning within the enclosures of their respective ethnic groups. The manipulation of rape for political ends, and the construction of Albanian men as rapists, created fear among women, Albanian and Serb, and restricted their mobility. This relegates to some undetermined future the time when women will have the ability to constitute themselves as citizens. The discourse of rape in the case of Kosovo evolved into the practice of rape in Bosnia. In both cases, rape was embedded in the gender dynamics of ethnic rivalry and identity formation. These phenomena are rooted in the patriarchal nature of Balkan society and of nationalist movements.

In the manifesto of Young Belgrade Feminists issued in March 1990, an important point was made concerning the implications for women of ethnic rivalry and national ambitions of the leaders. According to "The Woman Question and the Nation: Points of Discussion":

> Nationalism produces and promotes a set of conservative ideas and values, and threatens basic human rights, especially women's rights. Woman as a public and private being is subordinated to the alleged national interest. ... Instead of channelling the social energy released during the process of the social pluralization into emancipation of men and women ... the role of woman and man is being instrumentalized. At a time of national segregations, and due to the quick impoverishment of the whole society, woman is regarded as "reproductive machine."

Similarly, one can only agree with Sklevicky's conclusion that:

> It is necessary to face the fact that ... rape victims are our sisters and our symbols. As long as women cannot find their own voice to express their own experiences of "little" and "big" everyday rape, they will remain pawns in political conflicts whose actors use women's experience for their own aims.[46]

Notes

I wish to extend many thanks to Val Moghadam for her encouragement and fine editing of this chapter.

1. Silva Meznaric, "Gender and Ethnic Violence." Paper prepared for the XII World Congress of Sociology, Madrid, July 1990.

2. "Zakon o izmenama i dopunama Krivicnog zakona SR Srbije," *Sluzbeni glasnik SRS* 39 (1986):2739-2740. In a new article 61b, sexual assault or rape as an "ethnic crime" has been introduced. If perpetrator and victim are of different ethnic origin, the criminal law recognizes this fact as aggravating. In spite of criticisms from lawyers' guild jurisprudence, the law passed in the Serbian parliament. (See N. Memedovic, *Krivicno delo silovanja u jugoslovenskom pravu,* Beograd, 1988, pp. 300-303.)

3. Amnesty International, "Bosnia-Herzegovina: Rape and Sexual Abuse by Armed Forces" (London: International Secretariat, 1993), p. 3.

4. Dj. Sokolovic, "Matriarhat pred zmago," *Republica,* January 10, 1993, p. 8.

5. D. Apter, *Rethinking Development* (London: Sage, 1987), p. 237.

6. In *Against Our Will* (New York, 1975), p. 15, S. Brownmiller stressed that rape could possibly function as an instrument of social control. See also I. Baron and A. L. Straus, *Four Theories of Rape in American Society* (New Haven: Yale University Press, 1989), and A. Brittain, *Masculinity and Power* (Oxford, 1989).

7. M. Maynard, "The Reshaping of Sociology? Trends in the Study of Gender," *Sociology* 2 (1990):269-290, quote on p. 270.

8. See Baron and Straus, *Four Theories of Rape*, pp. 61-146.

9. *Ibid.*, p. 9. To the culture of violence as the prolific environment in the Balkans for ethnic policies refers also J. Stojanovic, *Silovanje* (Niksic, 1988), p. 268.

10. F. Barth, ed., *Ethnic Groups and Boundaries* (Boston, 1969), p. 209.

11. *Statisticki godisnjak SFRJ* (Belgrade, 1988), p. 420.

12. B. Maxharraj, "Potreba za populacionom politikom na Kosovu", *Pogledi* 2 (1988 or 1989), p. 183.

13. K. Mihajlovic, "Privredni razvoj Kosova," in M. Milenkovic and M. Komatina, eds., *Kosovo; proslost i sadasnjost* (Belgrade, 1989), p. 172-178.

14. *Ibid.*, p. 177.

15. Barth, *Ethnic Groups and Boundaries*, p. 209.

16. Historical accounts about the coexistence of various ethnicities in the region of Kosovo and Metohija during recent centuries are controversial and ethnically biased. Modern Serbian and Albanian historiography is not doing any better. We choose to rely on S. Cirkovic, "Kolevka Srbije," pp. 19-30 in M. Milenkovic and M. Komatina, eds., *Kosovo; proslost i sadasnjost*, especially pp. 19-20.

17. Davidovic and Petrovic, "Migracije u Jugoslaviji i etnicki aspekti,", p. 200. See also M. Petrovic and M. Blagojevic, *Seobe Srba i Crnogoraca sa Kosova i Metohije* (Belgrade, 1989), who provide a detailed account of the forced emigration of the Serbian minority from Kosovo. They found that "being threatened" and various discriminatory Albanian policies were the main push factors for Serbian emigration (p. 334).

18. M. Macura, "Razvojni, socijalni i demografski problemi Kosova," *Pogledi* 2 (1988), p. 399.

19. Barth, *Ethnic Groups and Boundaries*, p. 203.

20. A. Brittan, *Masculinity and Power*, (Oxford, 1989).

21. Lj. Bulatovic, "Napad na dostojanstvo," *Intervju*, 10 December 1986, p. 37.

22. P. Nesic and D. Rajh, "Silovanja na Kosovu," *Intervju*, 29 August 1986, pp. 5-9.

23. S. Markovic, "Istraga je u toku," *Politika ekspres*, 25 May 1986.

24. D. Mrkic, "Pritvoren maloletni napasnik," *Politika* 27, March 1987.

25. TANJUG, "Tzjava kroz smijeh," *Borba*, 10 October 1987. OR "Naknadno uvrstena doskocica," *Vjesnik*, 18 October 1987.

26. P. Zivancevic, "Zene nece cutati," *Ilustrovana politika*, 13 October 1987, p. 17.

27. TANJUG (1987).

28. Sklevicky, "Silovanja na Kosovu," p. 12.

29. *Ibid.*

30. *Ibid.*

31. Drakulic, "Silovanje kao politicki ispad," p. 61.

32. Mladjenovic, "Zensko seksualno ropstvo," *Svijet* no. 35 (1988), p. 61.

33. *Ibid.* Bette Denich also refers to domestic violence as a norm of conjugal relations: "In all these societies women not behaving in the properly submissive manner are liable to beating by their husbands," Denich, "Sex and Power in the Balkans" M. Z. Rosaldo and L. Lamphere, eds., *Woman, Culture, and Society* (Stanford, California: Stanford University Press, 1974), p. 255. For an account of how women in the Balkans learned over centuries how to deal with the culture of violence see the study of Slapsak, "Zenska knjiga, zensko pismo, zenske studije," *Izraz* nos. 2-3 (1990): 220-30.

34. Slapsak, *ibid.*, p. 221.

35. *Ibid.*, p. 223.

36. S. Popovic, D. Janca, and T. Petovar, eds., *Kosovski cvor: dresiti ili seci?* (Belgrade: Izvestaj nezavisne komisije, 1990), pp. 27-59.

37. *Ibid.*, p. 46.

38. Most sensitive data, those on Muslim and "Yugoslav" nationality, are hardly comparable through time; their definition varied significantly. Thus, in declaring their ethnicity, Muslims had the following options: Nationality not declared — Muslims (1948); Nationality not declared — Yugoslavs (1953); Ethnic group — Muslims, and Nationality not declared — Yugoslavs (1961); Nationality — Muslims (1971).

39. This was particularly the case in communes: Sanski Most, Bosanska Gradiska, Bosanska Dubica, Bosanski Novi, Bosanska Krupa. There, proportion of Serbs in local population decreased between 1971-1981 (on average) for 9 percent. S. Zuljic, *Narodnosna struktura Jugoslavije i tokovi promjena* (Zagreb: EI), p. 54.

40. *The Class Composition of the Contemporary Yugoslav Societies — Bosnia-Herzegovina: A Survey* (Ljubljana: Research Institute of the Faculty of Social Sciences, University of Ljubljana, 1988).

41. In this chapter we used: (1) Information from the government of Bosnia and Herzegovina as presented in the mass media; (2) Specific reports (i.e. from the Direction for Humanitarian Aid of the Office of Bosnia and Herzegovina in Croatia, the Coordinative Group of Women's Organizations of the Bosnian-Herzegovinian government and the *Riyasat* of the Islamic community, the EC Investigative Mission for the treatment of Muslim women in the former Yugoslavia, January 29, 1993, "Bosnia-Herzegovina: Rape and Sexual Abuse by Armed Forces" (Amnesty International, 1993); (3) Statements of witnesses and rape victims in the archives of the Office of Bosnia and Herzegovina in the Republic of Croatia, archives of the Croatian Information Centre, Department for collecting documentation and processing data on the liberation war, and personal documents and collected statement in Ibrahim Kajan's book

Muslimanski danak u krvi (which have been partially cited in the following text); (4) Reports and articles in the daily and weekly press.

42. For instance, one woman from the village of Kozarac (Prijedor commune) reported: "They take girls younger than thirteen to the camp, and then young women, and then take them to be raped several times." A man from Kozarac stated: "One day they led away five girls of thirteen years of age from M.'s house and the day after they returned them in such a state that the doctor S.P. barely managed to 'sew' them to make up to whole beings, while three were sent to the Prijedor hospital, where they had been taken away to in the first place."

43. A.L. from Brcko (northern Bosnia) claimed: "That Ranko raped a woman — the mother of two children, and her mother was also present." According to one informant from Doboj (central Bosnia): "H.R., Salih's son, hung himself after his wife Ramza had been violated by several Chetnisk who raped her before his eyes." Another man from Kozarac gave the testimony: "Through the open window I heard the cry of women from a distance of about twenty metres away. One of them was crying as she said, 'People, I was operated only a month ago!', 'Do you have a mother?' they asked, and brought before this girl her mother and father. They raped her mother before her father's eyes."

44. In the words of one woman from Miljevina: "They were all our neighbors. And, they forced me from my house and took me to the house of that (neighbor) who had been shot, killed. And there were four young girls there, young wives, and they led each one of them, one by one, into some room and there was nothing that they did not do to us. They beat us, abused us, raped us, they did everything they wanted. They threatened us that if we would say anything, they would come the next day and slaughter us and the children. A.L. from Brcko testified: " ... they raped the two daughters of R.H., who made use of an opportunity, he let the gas out and caused an explosion in which all were burned. R.H. was in in the Bosnian Territorial Defense in the village of Rajic."

45. There have been statements made by rape victims that suggest commander officer involvement. For instance, one victimized Muslim woman states: "This same commander knew what was happening because he was one of them."

46. I. Sklevicky, "Silovanja na Kosovu," *Svijet*, no. 35 (1988), p. 11.

5

Women of the West Imagined: The *Farangi* Other and the Emergence of the Woman Question in Iran

Mohamad Tavakoli-Targhi

Introduction

Since the early nineteenth century, the image of European women has been integrated into Iranian political discourse and has served as a point of reference for modernists and traditionalists, secularists and Islamists, monarchists and anti-monarchists. In the writings on European women, the female body served as a terrain of political and cultural contestations and as an important metaphor for delineating self and "Other," Iran and Europe, Islam and Christianity. In these contestations, women of the West were often a displacement and a simulacrum for Iranian women. The focus and reflection on European women resulted in the production of the veil as a woman's uniform and as a marker of cultural, political, and religious difference and identity. What was perceived to be an Islamic dress for women was a product of the cultural and political encounter with the West. These encounters transformed the notion of femininity (*zananigi*) from a polar opposite of masculinity (*mardanigi*) into signifier of Western-mediated gender identity, a transformation which began with the Persian voyagers' curiosity about the exotic women of the West.[1]

Beginning in the eighteenth century, an increasing number of Persians from India and Iran traveled to Europe (*Farang/Farangistan*). By exploring the "Otherness" they found there, the Persian voyagers constituted Europe as an object of analysis and gaze and authored important texts for the production and dissemination of knowledge about the Farangi-Other. In their texts, the Persian Occidentalists discovered and imagined similarities and differences, concord and conflict, intrinsic and extrinsic.

With increased European penetration into India and Iran in the nineteenth century, the images of the Western adversary entered into political contestations and influenced the formation of new political discourses and identity politics. The emerging discourses were as much reflections on the powerful new Other (Europe) as of the self in formation. By giving meanings to the observed/imagined Farangi-Other, the Persian Occidentalists constructed the boundaries of self-identification and -alteration and influenced the emergence of diverse orders of politics, economics, cultures, literatures, and gender relations.

In this chapter, I will demonstrate that women were the loci of observation and gaze for many of the early Persian travelers. By constituting woman as the point of radical *différence*, the female body served as a terrain of political and cultural contestation,[2] and as an important metaphor delineating self and Other, Iran and Europe, Islam and Christianity. I will contend that woman's veil was constituted as a marker of identity and that it was a product of cultural and political encounters among the Iranian traditionalists, reformists, and revolutionaries. These contestations led to the Constitutional Revolution of 1905-1909 and the emergence of Islamist (*Mashru'ahkhvah*) and Secular-nationalist (*Mashrutahkhvah*) camps. These antagonistic camps had as their sub-text two conflicting images of the West. One viewed the West as *Farang-i ba Farhang* (the cultured Farang) and the other as *Kufristan* (the land of the infidels). One was grounded in a positive notion of freedom (*azadi*) anchored to the memories of the French Revolution and called for the educating and unveiling of Iranian women. The other was grounded in a negative notion of freedom constructed on the indecency and corruption of European women and sought to protect Iranian women and the nation of Islam from the malady of the deviant gaze (*mafasid-i harzah chashmi*) which would result in fornication (*zina*), sedition (*fitnah*), bloodshed (*khunrizi*), syphilis, and the discontinuation of the human race.[3] These antagonistic articulations of European women have remained the organizing elements of twentieth-century Iranian modernist and Islamicist political discourses. The Islamization of Iran since 1979 was grounded in the rejection and condemnation of unveiled women as European dolls (*'Arusak-i Farangi*).[4]

The Persian Gaze and Women of the West

Persians traveled to Europe as early as 1599 and kept records of their encounters with the Farangi-Other.[5] Among the individuals who traveled to Europe in that period, three converted to Christianity and adopted the names Don Juan, Don Philip and Don Diego. Don Juan wrote a memoir which was first published in Castilian, but no trace of the original Persian manuscript has been found.[6] A few other Persians traveled and/or migrated to Europe in the seventeenth and eighteenth centuries. Among these travelers, Muhammad Riza Bayk, who traveled to France in 1714, appears to have inspired Montesquieu to write *The Persian Letters*.[7] Although the eighteenth century Persian travelers included some women who settled in England, unfortunately their names have been lost. In 1765 I'tisam al-Din, an Indian-Persian, traveled to Europe; his account of his trip, *Shigirf Namah Vilayat* (The Book of Wonder Land), is the earliest available Persian travelogue.[8] Among individuals who traveled to Europe in the early nineteenth century were Mirza Abu-Talib Khan (1752-1806), Mirza Abu al-Hasan Ilchi (1780-1860),[9] Mirza Salih Shirazi, Riza Quli Mirza, Mirza Yusuf Khan, Iqbal al-Dawlah, and Mirza Fattah Garmrudi (d. 1843 or 1844). For these early Persian voyagers Europe was a new text in need of reading, comprehension, and interpretation. Being unfamiliar with European languages, they could not easily decode the cultural meanings of observed scenes and incidents. Consequently, they often interpreted an observed scene by displacing it onto their familiar cultural environment. These culturally translated readings and interpretations, like the Orientalists' readings and interpretations of the East, were deeply immersed in the power and politics of self-perception.[10] What travelers uttered about the Other, in other words, were also utterances about Self.

When traveling in Europe, the "exotic" Persians were occasionally invited to ballrooms, theaters, concerts and masquerade parties sponsored by the nobility and the upper class European ladies and gentlemen. In such gatherings, the Persian observers found the level of male-female intimacy to be radically different from male-female intimacy in the public spheres in India and Iran. Unable to inquire through the medium of language and uninformed about the differences in class and social practices, the Persian travelers translated their observations into their own cultural language. Through such cultural translations, the Persian travelers (re)invented and (re)discovered Europe. To an observer who was used to seeing women veiled in public gatherings, male-female relations in ballrooms and masquerade parties where women not only appeared unveiled but danced with many men signified to the Persian travelers a reality radically different from the experienced reality of the observed Europeans. In Europe, a Persian traveler witnessed/imagined the obliteration of cultural distinctions between the interior and the exterior, the private and the public, the moral and the immoral, the decent and the indecent, the violable and the inviolable. The observed/imagined irregularities and differences of female social space provided the loci for imagining the life and power of Farangi women.

For the Persian travelers Europe was a text lending itself to multiple readings and interpretations. Mirza I'tisam al-Din traveling to Europe in 1760 viewed Europe as a wonderland, an emporium of beauty (*vilayat-i zibayi*), and a heaven on earth (*firdawsî bar rû-yi zamîn*). He viewed European women as fairy-faced (*parî tamsâl*) ravishers of hearts who moved with blandishment and coquetry.[11] Mirza Abd al-Latif, writing in 1799, described the unveiling of women (*bî pardigi-i zanan*), their participation in ballrooms (*khanah-'i raqs*) and pleasure houses (*bayt al-surur*) and their high social status.[12] Mirza Abu Talib, who had traveled to Europe in 1801-1803, found many female admirers. He referred to his beloveds using terms such as *kharam raftar* (graceful), *zulal lab* (limpid-lip), *nadarah-'i sihrkar* (rare magician), *kasir al-muhibat* (full of affection), *masih asa* (messiah-like), *raqiq al-qalb* (soft-hearted), *niku gamat* (well-postured), and *qamar sima* (moon-faced).[13] Mirza Abu al-Hasan Ilchi, writing in Persian-English praised British women: "This very good country—English ladies handsome; very beautiful—I travel great deal; I go Arabia, I go Calcutta, Hyderabad, Poonah, Bombay, Georgia, Armenia, Constantinople, Malta, Gibraltar, I see best Georgian, Circassian, Turkish, Greek ladies, but nothing not so beautiful as English ladies—all very clever—speak French, speak English, speak Italian, play music very well, sing very good—very glad for me if Persian Ladies like. ..."[14] Mirza Salih, who studied in London between 1815-1819, viewed England as a land of freedom (*vilayat-i azadi*)[15] and praised the decency and intelligence of European women. Riza Quli Mirza, a Qajar Prince, who along with two of his brothers took refuge in England in 1837, on a few occasions met with the future Queen Victoria and was attracted to the moon-faced (*mah ruy*) and bare-headed (*birihnah sar*) women whom he viewed as the "plunderers of heart and religion" (*gharat kun-i dil va din*).[16] Mirza Fattah, who traveled on a diplomatic mission in 1839, referred to European women using signifiers such as *khushgil* (beautiful), *dilruba* (heart-ravisher), and *dahan mu'atar* (perfumed-mouth) and noted that they are "appreciative of freedom and proud of self-reliance."[17] Lutf-Allah (1802-1874), while viewing the English women as "nymphs of paradise," noted that "the freedom granted to womankind in this country is great, and mischief arising from this unreasonable toleration is most deplorable."[18] Sahhafbashi, a late nineteenth century traveler, reported that in Farang women and men could kiss under a tree and no one would bother them. He further noted that in Farang "virgin women are rare and womanizing is like eating bread and yogurt in Iran and is not offensive."[19]

These and other travelers, while constructing and reconstructing new knowledge about Europe, focused their attention on women because for them, the public appearance and behavior of European women symbolized a different order of politics and gender relations. Although they recognized a familiar male hegemony in politics, they found eccentric the politics of gender relations. The Persian observers, by focusing on women, decoded different sets of bio-power relations.[20] Some found that bio-power relation desirable and hoped to recode gender relations in Iran and India. Others viewed it as deplorable and sought to maintain the prevalent gender relation. To demonstrate these two different articulations, I will focus on *Shigirf Namah* (*The Wonder Book*) of I'tisam al-Din and *Shab Namah* (*The Night Report*) of Mirza Fattah Garmrudi.

The Wonder Book *of I'tisam al-Din*

Mirza I'tisam al-Din traveled to England in 1865 A.D./1180 H. Like other travelers to strange places, he constructed his own England. He made sense of the observed scenes through other texts and by comparing England with his homeland. His comparison of England and India enabled him to reflect on government, gender, education, and legislative differences.

The spectacle of male-female intimacy in public parks was among the scenes which attracted the attentions of I'tisam al-Din and many other Persian travelers. For example, recalling the observed scenes of a public park near the Queen's Palace in London I'tisam al-Din wrote:

> On Sunday, men, women, and youths, poor and rich, travellers and natives, resort here. This park enlivens the heart, and people overcome with sorrow, repairing thither, are entertained in a heavenly manner; and grieved hearts, from seeing that place of amusement, are gladdened against their will. On every side females with silver forms, resembling peacocks, walk about, and at every corner fairy-faced ravishers of hearts move with a thousand blandishments and coquetries; the plain of the earth becomes a paradise from the resplendent foreheads, and heaven

(itself) hangs down its head for shame at seeing the beauty of the loves. There lovers meet their fairy-resembling sweethearts: they attain their end without fear of the police or of rivals, and gallants obtain a sight of rosy cheeks without restraint. When I viewed this heavenly place I involuntarily exclaimed:

> If there is a heaven on the face of the earth,
> It is here! It is here! It is here!
> (*Agar firdawsi bar ru-yi zamin ast*
> *hamin ast, hamin ast, hamin ast!*)[21]

Observing women unveiled in the public sphere, the Muslim travelers recalled the male-constructed promised heaven where all earthly limitations were to be obliterated. For example, Mirza Abu Talib, who articulated a position similar to that of I'tisam al-Din, abandoned his cherished goal of learning "English Sciences" (*'Ilm-i Ingilish*) in favor of "love and gaiety."[22] On this change of heart he wrote:

> Henceforth we will devote our lives to London
> and its heart-alluring Damsels:
> Our hearts are satiated with viewing fields,
> gardens, rivers, palaces.
> Fill the goblet with wine! if by this I am
> prevented from returning
> To my old religion, I care not,
> nay I am the better pleased
> If the prime of my life has been spent in the
> service of an Indian Cupid,
> It matters not: I am now rewarded by the
> smiles of the British Fair.[23]

The observations of Persian travelers did not stop with such exotic fantasies in heavenly Europe. They were also conscious of the legal order that might make women's participation in the public sphere less restrictive. I'tisam al-Din explained the relative sexual liberty of Europeans with a recourse to legal differences:

The courts have nothing to do with cases of simple fornication, unless a woman complains that she was forcibly violated. ... If a man and woman commit fornication in a retired house, or even in any place whatever, they may do so with impunity, and neither the *cutwal* nor the censor [*muhtasib*] can take any notice of it; for it is a common saying, 'what business has the superintendent inside a house?' [*Muhtasib ra dar durun-i khanah chah kar?*] In England it is completely the reverse of what it is in this country, for there the cutwal and the censor have little or nothing to do, and don't have the power of seizing either a fornicator or a fornicatress, what ever the people may say.[24]

I'tisam al-Din further observed that "the King of England is not independent in matters of government ... and can do nothing without first consulting and advising with his ministers and nobles and a few selected men."[25] By focusing on the relative freedom of women and the restriction on the power of the sovereign, he shifted the meaning of freedom (azadi) into a new field of signification:

In England every one is free [*azad*]; no one can lord it over another, and there is no such thing known as master and slave, which is totally different from other countries, in which all are slaves of the king. In England, both great and small would be greatly ashamed at the term slave.[26]

The new understanding of power and class relations compelled I'tisam al-Din to study the components of gender identity. He recognized that school is an important site for the construction of diverse gender relations. Comparing the British educational system with that of his homeland, he noted:

In England it is usual for the people of rank to send both their sons and daughters to a distant place of education. ... The people of wealth in England, commencing at the age of four years, keep their sons and daughters constantly employed in writing, reading, and acquiring knowledge; they never permit them to be idle. If a man or woman not be acquainted with the musical art, be unable to dance or ride, he or she is accounted by people of substance as descended from a mean parentage, and taunts and reproaches are not spared. ... The ladies, particularly, who can neither dance nor sing, are considered in a very inferior light; they will never get well married.[27]

I'tisam al-Din reprimanded his own people for retaining teachers as house servants.[28] Such observations on the education of women became important elements in the formation of the modern political "imaginary" in Iran. For example, Sahhafbashi, praising the education of women in Europe, noted, "We raise our girls in a cage and would not teach them anything besides eating and sleeping. ... Unfortunately we comprehend the enjoyment of eating and intercourse more than progress and education."[29]

Mirza I'tisam al-Din, like many nineteenth century reformers, praised the European devotion to the search for knowledge and compared it to the Persian-Indian quest for the beloved:

> They are not like the people of this country, who repeat Hindi and Persian poems in praise of a mistress's face, or descriptive of the qualities of the wine, of the goblet, and of the cup-bearer, and who pretend to be in love.[30]

Like Mirza I'tisam al-Din, Mirza Abu Talib was also attracted to the European educational system, especially the education of women. Commenting on the "apparent freedom" (*azadi-i zahiri*) and education of British women, Mirza Abu Talib noted that the British have "cleverly controlled them [women]" (*bih danayi nisvan ra muqayad kardahand*). But to him the Muslim women, "regardless of *pardah* which is a kind of bondage, are instigators of sedition and corruption."[31] A century later, with the emergence of the "woman question," such a comparison became central to the call for educating and unveiling of women. The early twentieth century Iranian modernists tied the progress and moral strength of the nation (*millat*) to educating and unveiling of women, and encouraging their participation in the public sphere.[32]

While praising the order of things in England, I'tisam al-Din appears to have turned down the offer of teaching Persian at Cambridge. In response to the suggestion of marrying an English woman and settling down there in England, he replied, "Poverty in my own country is much better than wealth in this, and I consider the dark complexioned women of Hindoostan far preferable to the fairy-faced damsels of England."[33] After two years and nine months, I'tisam al-Din returned to India in 1769/1183. His *Shigirf Namah* is an important source for the study of the language of modernity and anxieties of "westoxication"[34] in Iran.

The Night Report *of Mirza Fattah Garmrudi*

Among the numerous reports and travelogues written by Persian travelers to Europe, the *Shab Namah* (*The Night Report*) of Mirza Fattah Garmrudi deserves special attention. Unlike many earlier Persian travelers, he developed a distaste for European manners and characteristics and warned against closer contacts with them. He called upon the *ulama* (senior clergy) and the political elite to distance themselves from the "wicked group" of Europeans. He warned that the people of the West should not be trusted because in an opportune time they will "damage the religion and the state and will destroy the *Sharia* traditions."[35] He referred to Europe as the land of the infidels (Kufristan) and concluded his text by noting that "due to the emotional depression and immensity of regret and sorrow that resulted from my observation of the state of affairs in Kufristan, I have been able to narrate no more than a seed from a donkey's burden and a drop in a sea about the obscene acts and indecent behaviors of this malevolent people."[36]

Mirza Fattah was a member of an Iranian delegation which was dispatched to Europe in 1838 and traveled to Vienna, Paris and London. The main objective of the mission, which was led by Mirza Husayn Khan Ajudanbashi (Adjutant General), was to offer condolences to Queen Victoria on the death of her father, George IV, to offer congratulations on her accession to power, and to ask the British government to recall John McNeil, its Minister Plenipotentiary, for being unsympathetic to Iran's political claim on Afghanistan.

This delegation, arriving in London in April 1839, faced a most discourteous reception. Queen Victoria refused to see them. The British government refused to receive them as governmental guests. Lord Palmerston pointed out that "The Persian Ambassador must be Europeanized" by making him pay for all of his expenses.[37] The Iranian delegate was asked to revise the Shah's letter to the Queen, changing her title from *Malikah* to *Padshah,* for, according to Palmerston "we have no sexual distinction for our sovereign," a distinction which is implied in the concept *malikah* but not in *padshah.*[38] This hostility, instead of the expected hospitality, shaped the Iranian delegates' image of Farangistan and perception of Farangis. This is clearly illustrated in Mirza Fattah's *The Night Report.*

In *The Night Report* Mirza Fattah narrated approximately twenty events and incidents which he claimed either to have witnessed himself or to have collected from his newly found Persian-Indian friends who were in England at that time. Through the narration of these events, Mirza Fattah constructed an image of the West centered on women and their sexuality. This image, contrary to Europeans' self-perception, portrayed the Europeans, both men and women, as irrational, immoral, and aberrant.

After the introduction discussing the source of his narratives, Mirza Fattah noted that he would "briefly explain some of the conditions and characteristics of the women and their husbands." He then wrote:

In this land of diverse ideologies, women and girls are generally pantsless and without a veil [*chador*] and have a constant desire for able pummelers. Covered women are rare and unacceptable. Women are masterful in the realization of the wishes of men. They are addicted to pleasure and play, and are free from suffering and toil. In actualization of the demands of their partners, they are always daring and exquisite, while in preservation of their own honor they are incompetent and frail.[39]

According to Mirza Fattah, "A common characteristic of [European] women is their extreme desire for sexual intercourse." In his view,

They have escaped from the trap of chastity into freedom and have masterly leapt from the snare of purity. They have extreme desire for union with men and are endlessly coquettish and flirtatious. They glorify freedom and appreciate self-reliance.[40]

Women and men, Mirza Fattah says, are united nights and days in ballrooms, theaters, coffee-houses, and whorehouses. To highlight this point, he told a story of how he was surrounded by women at a party while an old woman in a wheelchair was gaining satisfaction by making sure that everyone had a partner.

After narrating this episode, Mirza Fattah offers a graphic description of how some women satisfied their sexual desires by keeping dogs at home.[41] Mirza Fattah explained that this practice was accepted and appreciated by the husbands:

In this land, due to the enormity of women's lust, a man does not have the strength to satisfy and realize their wishes promptly. Consequently, if a woman has an affair with another man and receives from him a payment, or due to her nobility and magnanimity, doesn't receive anything, according to the law of the nation the poor husband has no right to punish her. Under such a condition the zealous husband is thankful that the dog has done the job for her instead of a neighbor or an ignorant rogue in the street. To be just and fair, the poor husband cannot be blamed.[42]

This story was followed by the narration of a case of adultery of a European wife who was "ugly and bad looking, and singularly ill-created and ill-humoured."[43] In this narrative, the husband had become impatient and preferred "living in a cave with a snake" to the companionship of his wife:

But since in their nation it is established that a man cannot have more than one wife, he was compelled to give in to his destiny and persevere, always praying to God for mercy and his liberation from his yoke of damnation.[44]

One day the husband came home to find his wife with another man. He asked the adulterer why he was not looking for a better woman. The adulterer replied, "I do not have such bad taste. I am laboring and getting paid for it."[45] Because of the incompetency of European men and the voracious sexual appetite of European women, Mirza Fattah explained that the women relied on extra-marital relations and used instruments resembling the male phallus to satisfy themselves.

The question of why Mirza Fattah focused on such incidents deserves attention. Besides the obvious fact that the special mission for which Mirza Fattah served as a secretary was ill-treated by the British government, there are a number of other factors which may illuminate his motivation for the writing of *Shab namah*. The text itself provides a few clues for a search of such factors. For example, he wrote:

> With all these destructive conditions and deplorable actions, if a person in the nations of Farangistan, especially in England, unintentionally (which is the necessary nature, meaning that it is the second nature of human beings) names chest and breast, or vagina and phallus, or the like among women, they will immediately print and register them in the newspapers and will disseminate it around the world that so and so in such and such gathering, had no shame and talked about such and such in front of women.[46]

This statement indicates that Mirza Fattah and his friends might well have been victims of such journalistic intrigues, which capitalized on the Persian travelers' unfamiliarity with European norms, mocked them, and portrayed them as indecent and strange. This might also explain Mirza Fattah's rather negative view of newspapers which were highly valued by earlier Persian travelers. He wrote:

> Since the majority of newspapers print pure lies and they lie thoroughly, then it is clever of them to clean their posteriors with these papers. There is no better use for them. They believe that with these papers the feces is cleaned from their rears, but this is neither clear nor obvious. It is not clear whether in reality their rears are cleaned by the papers, or whether the newsprint is actually purified by the excrement.[47]

Because the members of the special mission had become an object of gaze for both the general public and journalists, they became extremely sensitive to and angry with journalists who seemed to have reported on all that seemed irregular and unfamiliar to their readers. It should be noted that it was such glaring harassments of the Persian-Other which might have led Montesquieu to write his celebrated line, "How can one be Persian?" (Comment peut-on être Persan?)[48] In order to explain Mirza Fattah's negative perception of the European newspapers, which had gained the highest admirations of earlier Persian travelers, one would need to study the coverage of this special envoy in various British newspapers.

Besides possibly being an object of journalistic gaze and harassment, one can find other explanations for Mirza Fattah's attempt to construct a negative image of Europeans. As the text itself suggests, it also seems possible that Mirza Fattah was responding to a particular Orientalist exposition on Iran. After narrating a number of stories, he remarked:

With all these desolate affairs and deplorable conditions, they [Europeans] have written some books to reproach and reprimand Iran. Especially the Englishman [James Baillie] Fraser has denigrated Iran and has gone to extremes in this regard. Among his charges is that the men of Iran have excessive desire for beardless teenagers and some men commit obscene acts with them. ... Yes, in the midst of all nations of the world, some fools, due to the predominance of lascivious spirit and temptations of Satan, commit some unacceptable acts. It is far from just that the people of Farangistan, with all of their imperfect attributes and obscene behaviors for which they are characterized and are particularly famous, i.e. the establishment of eunuch- and whore-houses, where they go at all times and pay money and commit obscene acts, that they characterize the people of Iran with such qualities and write about them in their books.[49]

After discussing his disapproval of Fraser's generalizations about and condemnation of Iranians, Mirza Fattah narrated the story of an Italian lord who had sex with the son of an English gentleman after gaining the consent of the boy's father. After narrating that incident, he concludes:

The above incident, besides signifying injustice and the engagement [of Europeans] in demeaning behavior, is also an indication of the stupidity and foolishness of this people, because they had left alone occurrences between themselves and attached their own characteristics to others.[50]

Reflecting on the changing image of Iran in Europe, Mirza Fattah recognized the importance of power in determining the type of relations with other countries.

Apparently, they always interact on an appropriate and humane basis with strong states and never initiate opposition. With a state which appears weaker, however, they constantly search for excuses, make downright illogical statements and resist listening to logical views.[51]

He did not fail to comment on praiseworthy European political institutions. He wrote, for example,

Individually, the people of Farangistan are not very wise or mature nor are they endowed with much eloquence or intelligence; but the parliament and the house of consultation that they have established apparently conceal these shortcomings. When the interests of the government and the country are at issue, a number of selected wise-men (*'uqala*) and governmental trustees (*umana'*), through consulting and advising each other, reach the depth of an issue and evaluate the good and bad of a claim and, finally, from the views of the wise-men, a thoroughly considered position is adopted and used. Accordingly, it is clear that mistakes and errors are reduced and affairs are based on an expedient conscience. ... Most often they strongly believe in deceit and falsity. Even in regards to their honest friends, at necessary occasions, they will not restrain themselves. Indeed, any government whose trustees are addicted to such habits are not considered to belong to the ranks of the wise and the advanced, but are amongst the two-faced and ignorant.[52]

As was indicated earlier, the text ends with a warning that the Iranian governmental elite should distance themselves from the "wicked group" of Europeans, for they would damage the foundation of the state and the religion. In the course of the nineteenth century, such views and images of Europe provided the ammunition for an intensified struggle against the reformists who were idealizing the West. Such negative construction of Europe entered into the Islamic discourses on the danger of unveiling in the twenties, women's suffrage in 1950s and 1960s, and the protest against the moral corruption brought about by the Iranian "Farangi dolls." In all these cases unveiledness and sexual liberty of women were viewed as the cause of corruption and moral degeneration of Europe. Such arguments have been central to the Islamic Republican discourse in Iran since the 1979 revolution. In what follows a few examples of such articulations will be offered.

The Farangi Other in the Iranian Political Discourse

With the emergence of a new class of intellectuals educated in Europe and in European style schools, the Farangi ways of life became a serious threat to the position of the ulama. Consequently, the image of Europe became an important component of political contestations in Iran. While the positive image of the West entered into the reformist and revolutionary discourses, the negative image of the West was constituted as the organizing element of anti-reformist and Islamic discourses.

One of the earliest clerical tracts on the "new malady" of Europeanization, of what Jalal Al Ahmad calls Westoxication almost a century later, was written by Hajj Muhammad Karim Khan Kirmani (1810-1871), leading Shaykhi theologian.[53] In his account of the new malady which was viewed to be a result of the efforts of "pleasure-seeking individuals, who refuse to associate with the ulama, and would no longer abide by religious principles,"[54] Muhammad Karim Khan relied on the eyewitness account of Europe narrated to him by "a leading Iranian notable" who had taken refuge in England.[55] Elaborating on the dangers of European domination over the Islamic lands, he notes:

Can any Muslim allow the incompetent women to have the affairs in their hands so that they could go wherever they choose, sit with whomever they desire, leave the house whenever they wish? They [Europeans] have not yet gained control of Iran but they are already ordering our women not to cover themselves from men. Would any Muslim consent to women wearing makeup, sitting in the squares and at shops, and going to theaters? Can any Muslim consent to the independence and beautification of his wife and allow her to go to the bazaar and buy wine and drink it and get intoxicated ... and sit with rogues and ruffians [*alwat va awbash*] and do whatever she chooses? God forbid! Would anyone consent to allowing freedom and losing charge of one's daughter, wife, slave and housekeeper? And allow them to go wherever they please and do whatever they like and sit with whomever they choose and have available in their gatherings any kind of wine they desire and mingle with rogues, and not be able to protest because an unbeliever has ordered that Iran should be the land of freedom (*vilayat-i azadi*)?[56]

Kirmani described his antagonists as "ignorant, conceited youth who, upon hearing the call of freedom, immediately make themselves look like Europeans, adopting European customs and betraying Islam and Islamic values."[57] He warned:

When they hear the call to freedom they would shape themselves like the Farangis, organize their assemblies and associations patterned after Europeans, model their behaviors on the bases of European customs, and turn away from Islam and Islamic traditions.[58]

[T]hen if your wife abstains from you, if she chose to convert to Armenianism, she would go to a church and after she is baptized in public, she would enter the Christian religion. ... If the deviant women wish to become apostates no one can protest. Due to freedom a large number of people would become apostates and the ulama and others would have no power to speak out. In conclusion, they would establish schools, and classes would be taught by European teachers ... and then the simple-minded people would send their children to European schools and they would become totally Christianized.[59]

He further warned that if Iranian women mingled with European women, they would be tempted to dress like Europeans, dance in public celebrations and gatherings like them, drink wine just like them, and sit with men on benches and chairs and joke with strangers just like them.[60] Concluding his essay, Karim Khan Kirmani declared that "anyone who befriends a European would be considered a European himself ... and thus has apostatized and adopted the religion of the Europeans."[61] This line of argument was later followed by Shaykh Fazl Allah Nuri in his pronouncements against the constitutionalists of 1905-1909 whom he viewed as "Paris worshippers" (*parisparastha*).[62] Indeed, these concerns became an important component of the anti-Constitutionalist discourse of 1905-1909. Shaykh Fazl Allah Nuri, a leading cleric of Tehran and the intellectual leader of the anti-constitutionalist camp, expressed many of the concerns of Muhammad Karim Khan in his pamphlets and leaflets produced in the course of the Iranian Constitutional Revolution (1905-1909).

The social cleavages that developed as a result of the encounter with Farang provided the terrain for the emergence of a new type of poetics and politics in Iran. To express the aspirations of a new class of intellectuals, who had either traveled to Europe or were educated in European schools and to air the desperation of the traditional religious intellectuals, a new literature of *munazirah* or dialogics emerged. In this type of literature, a professor of the seminary school encountered a student of Dar al-funun (Iran's first modern college); an Iranian traditionalist encountered an Indian familiar with the secrets of the West; a Prince Kamal al-Dawlah from British-India corresponded with a Prince Jalal al-Dawlah from Iran; and a Muslim debated a Faranagi, who attributed the achievements of the Europeans to their adaptation of Islamic sciences.[63] These debates, which personified Iran and Farang, tradition and modernity, touched on all social, political and economic problems of the nation, and at the end a blueprint was offered for the salvation of Iran and Iranians from poverty, misery and ignorance. The blueprint often outlined an Iranian modernist's image of the West. Contrary to the view of the theoretician of *gharbzadegi* (westitis or westoxication), fascination with the West did not result in the loss of self-identity and cultural alienation. The fascination with the West provided the discursive terrain for the imagining of a "glorious," "prosperous," and "victorious" pre-Islamic Iranian past, a past which could match the glory land the prosperity of the contemporary Farangi-Other.

What was before imagined to originate in Europe now became identified as having a basis in Iranian past—a past which was, however, as much an imaginary construct as was this Europe. Although the political and military self-alterations in nineteenth century Iran were modeled after the West, they were discursively connected to an *imaginary* Iranian past. Muhammad Shah, in a proclamation calling for the adaptation of Western-style military uniform, argued that the new uniform was a re-adaptation of what the ancient Iranians used to wear. He authenticated his claim by pointing to the similarities between the new uniform and the uniform of the soldiers engraved on the walls of Persepolis. Mirza Abd Al-Latif Shushtari, writing in 1798, also discovered a Persian origin for the European custom of dining at a table. He argued that the term *mizban* (host) was etymologically connected to the word *miz* (table). Accordingly, the term mizban constituted a trace of a forgotten Persian custom adopted by Europeans.

Mirza Aqa Khan Kirmani, a late nineteenth century political modernist, attributing the progress of Europe to the ideas of liberty and equality, argued that those ideas were first introduced in Iran by Mazdak fourteen centuries earlier.[64] The ideals of the French Revolution, merging with the nineteenth century movements for the revitalization of pre-Islamic Iranian history and simplification of Persian prose, changed the signification of millat from the "people of Shia religion" to the "people of Iran." The former meaning of millat had come from a paradigm in which God was viewed as the source of sovereignty, the state and religion were articulated as twin brothers, and social images and ideals were drawn from Islamic history. The new meaning of "the people," however, emerged with the nostalgia for pre-Islamic Iran and devotion to the ideals of liberty (*azadi/hurriyat*), equality (*barabari/musavvat*), and fraternity (*baradari/ukhuvvat*).

Consequently, the people of Iran (*millat-i Iran*) discursively replaced the Divine and the Shadow of God (*Zill Allah*) as the source of sovereignty and made possible the emergence of democratic popular politics, a new era in which the term *siyasat* no longer meant execution and punishment but instead the carrying out of national decision making.

Nineteenth century Iranian Occidentalism, while institutionalized in the process of self-alteration, was never confined to universities, scholarly journals and conferences. The Iranian Occidentalists' interpretations of the West were as diverse as the Orientalists' interpretations of the East. While many of the nineteenth century Iranian observers of the West were fascinated by Europeans, others were disgusted and outraged by them. These conflicting responses were anchored to two diverse patterns of Iranian self-identity. The former looked back to the lost utopia of pre-Islamic Iran and the latter looked back to the golden age of Islam. The commentaries on the Farangi Other were as much about the self, self-identity, and self-image as about the West. The cultural and political contestations leading to the Constitutional revolution and the emergence of *Marshru'ahkhvah* (Shariatis) and *Mashruahkhvah* (Constitutionalist) poles had as their subtext two conflicting images of the West. One was grounded on a positive notion of freedom anchored to the memories of the French Revolution, the other grounded on a negative notion of freedom constructed around the indecency of European women.

Shaykh Fazl Allah Nuri, the intellectual leader of the anti-constitutionalist movement, arguing against the idea of equality as articulated by the Constitutionalists, wrote:

> Oh you who lack integrity and honor, the founder of the Sharia has granted you integrity and privileges because you belong to the [community of] Islam! But you disenfrancise yourself, and demand to be brother and equal with Zoroastrians, Armenians, and Jews?"[65]

Arguing against the conception of freedom (azadi) which was a key element in the Constitutionalist discourse, Shaykh Fazl Allah stated that, "the strength of Islam is due to obedience and not freedom. The basis of its legislation is the segregation of groups and summation of differences, and not equality."[66] Arguing against the "Paris worshippers" he wrote:

> Oh, you God worshippers, this National Assembly (*shura-yi milli*), liberty (*hurriyat va azadi*), equality (*musavat va barabari*), and the principles of the present Constitutional law (*asas-i qanun-i mashrutah-i haliyah*) is a dress

sown for the body of Farangistan, and is predominantly of the naturalist school (*tabi'i mazhab*) and transgresses the Divine law and the holy book.[67]

He asked the Constitutionalists why, among "so many banners of long live, long live, long live equality! Equality, Fraternity! why don't you once write: long live the Sharia, long live the Quran, long live Islam?"[68] In his sincere protestations Shaykh Nuri clearly understood that the new conception of politics, or, if I am allowed to put words in his mouth, the new "political imaginary," would alter the traditional order of the society and establish something which owes more to the parliament of Paris than to Islam. It was quite clearly so. And when Shaykh Fazl Allah Nuri was condemned to execution by the revolutionary tribunal in 1909, the guiding principle was the French Revolution and Robespierre. Like the execution of Louis XVI, the execution of Shaykh Fazl Allah, the most learned of the ulama of Tehran, marked a radical rejection of the previous social and symbolic order.[69] It also inaugurated a new age of popular national politics. For Iranian modernists, women's education, unveiling, and participation in the public sphere became a marker of civilization and national progress. In contrast, the Islamic forces viewed such relaxations as heretical, anti-Islamic and a marker of Christian domination over Iran.

Conclusions

As I have shown, then, there was a link between the politics of gender and identity and the Iranian encounter with Europe at its formative stages. In both views articulated in this early period, gender is at the center of identification with or against the West, and woman's body is the site on which such constructions are made. In the twentieth century, the narratives of European women have been anchored to diverse textual, sexual, and political strategies. For modernists, women of the West provided an ideal model for the education and unveiling of Iranian women and their participation in the public sphere. In contrast, for the Islamic forces European woman was a metaphor for corruption, immorality, pornography, secularization, and deviation from the straight path of Islam. For them and for many other anti-imperialist/anti-Shah activists of 1960s and 1970s, the "European doll" ('*arusak-i Farangi*), the simulacrum of Iranian woman mindlessly imitating Europeans, became a symbolic condensation of all social and political evils brought about by the Shah's regime. To eradicate the Shah and the Western influence on Iran, the post-revolutionary Islamic government set itself the task of eradicating the "European dolls" of Iran by establishing the veil as a compulsory uniform, removing the makeup from women's faces, and closing night clubs and all other institutions modeled on an imagined Europe. In short, the nineteenth and twentieth centuries' "political imaginary" was constructed on the image of European Woman—the European woman as imagined by Iranian male travelers.

Notes

In developing this project, I have received critical and editorial comments from many friends and colleagues including Palmira Brummett, Bruce Craig, Diane McQueen, Afsaneh Najmabadi, Catherine Peaden, Zohreh Sullivan, and Julie Shaffer. My special thanks to Valentine Moghadam who placed this project in the center of my scholarly endeavor.

1. For a further elaboration of the themes of this chapter see my book, *Women of the West Imagined: Occidentalism and Exotic Europeans* (Berkeley: University of California Press, 1992).

2. On this point, see Farzaneh Milani, "Hijab va Kafsh-i Chini" (Woman's Body as Sign and Symbol: On Veiling and Footbinding), *Iran Nameh: A Persian Journal of Iranian Studies* 2 (1990): 246-260.

3. In the first three decades of the 20th century a new Islamic genre focusing on the dangers of unveiling appeared in Iran. For example see: Zabih Allah Mahallati, *Kashf al-ghurur ya mafasid-i Sufur*, 2nd ed. (Tehran: hapkhanah-' 'Asgari, 1338/1959 [originally published in 1933/1352]); Muhammad Sadiq Sadr al-Islam, *Vujub-i niqab va hurmat-i sharab* (Tehran: Ustad Mirza 'Ali Asghar, 1329/1911).

4. Such condemnations were also to be found in the statements and declarations of Iranian feminists and women organizations in 1979-1980. For a selection of these documents see: Mohamad Tavakoli-Targhi, "Archive," *Nimeh-i Digar* no. 10 (Winter 1989):167-197, and no. 11 (Spring 1990):96-157.

5. The delegation included Husayn Quli Bayk, 'Ali Guli Bayk, Uruj Bayk and fourteen other individuals. For further information see: Najafquli Hissam Mu'izzi, *Tarikh-i Ravabit-i Siyasi* (Tehran: Nashr-i 'Ilm, 1366/1987), pp. 181-187.

6. Don Juan, *Don Juan of Persia: A Shi'ah Catholic, 1560-1604*, trans. by Guy Le Strange (New York: Harper & Brothers, 1926).

7. The first edition of *The Persian Letters* was published in 1721. In Letter 92, writing about the Muhammad Riza Bayk who commited suicide on September 1, 1714, Montesquieu noted: "There has appeared a personage got up as a Persian ambassador, who has insolently played a trick on the two greatest kings in the world." (*Persian Letters*. New York: Penguin, 1973, p. 172.) For an interesting interpretation of *Persian Letters* see: Josué V. Harari, *Scenarios of the Imaginary: Theorizing the French Enlightenment* (Ithaca: Cornell University Press,

1987), pp. 67-101. Also see: Adam Vartanian, "Eroticism and the Politics in the *Lettres persanes,*" *Romantic Review* LX:1 (February 1969): 23-33.

8. Mirza I'tisam al-Din, *Shigirf Namah-'i Vilayt* (Excellent Intelligence Concerning Europe being the Travels of Mirza Itesa Modeen in Great Britain and France) translated from the original Persian manuscript into Hindoostanee, with an English version and notes by James Edward Alexander (London: Parbury, Allen, and Co., 1827).

9. For the English translation of Mirza Abu al-Hasan's travelogue see: Mirza Abul Hasan Khan, *A Persian at the Court of King George: The Journal of Mirza Abul Hasan Khan, 1809-10,* trans. by Margaret Morris Cloake (London: Barrie & Jenkins, 1988).

10. On Orientalism and Orientalists' self-perceptions see: Edward W. Said, *Orientalism* (New York, Vintage Books, 1979); Rana Kabbani, *Europe's Myths of Orient* (Bloomington: Indiana University Press, 1986); G.S. Rousseau and Roy Porter, *Exoticism in the Enlightenment* (Manchester: Manchester University Press, 1990).

11. Mirza I'tisam al-Dawlah = Mirza Itesa Modeen, *Shigirf namah-i Valayat = Shigurf Namah-i Velaet* (London: Parbury, Allen and Co., 1827).

12. Mir 'Abd al-Latif Shushtari, *Tuhfat al-'Alam,* edited by Samad Muvahid (Tehran: Kitabkhanah-'i Tahuri, 1363 [1984]), p. 251.

13. Mirza Abu Talib Isfahani, *Misir-i Talibi ya Safrnamah-'i Mirza Abu Talib Khan* (Tehran: Sazman-i Intisharat va Amuzish-i Inqilab-i Islami, 1363 [1984], pp. 130-131, 134, 143, 144.

14. Abul Hasan, "The Persian Ambassador," *The Morning Post* (May 29, 1810), reprinted in Denis Wright, *The Persians Amongst the English* (London: I.B. Tauris, 1985).

15. Mirza Salih Shirazi, *Guzarish-i Safar-i Mirza Salih Shirazi,* edited by Humayun Shahidi (Tehran: Rah-i Naw, 1362 [1983]), p. 205.

16. Riza Quli Qajar, *Safar Namah-'i Riza Quli Mirza Nayib al-Saltanah,* edited by Asghar Farmanfarma'i Qajar (Tehran: Intisharat Asatir, 1361/[1982[), p. 361.

17. Mirza Fattah Garmrudi, "Shab Namah," in *Safar namah-'i Mirza Fattah Khan Garmrudi bih urupa dar zaman-i Muhammad Shah Qajar shamil-i sah risalah: Chahar Fasl, Shab Nasmah va Safarnamah-'i Mamasani,* edited by Fath al-Din Fatahi (Tehran: Bank-i Bazargani Iran, 1347/[1968[), p. 951.

18. Lutfullah, *Autobiography of Lutfullah: An Indian's Perception of the West,* 2nd edition (New Delhi: International Writers' Emporium, 1985), p. 433.

19. Ibrahim Sahafbashi Tihrani, *Safar Namah-i'i Ibrahim Sahafbashi Tihrani,* edited by Muhammad Mushiri (Tehran: Shirkat-i Muäallifan va Mutarjiman-i Iran, 1357 [1978]), p. 62.

20. On the notion of "bio-power", see Michael Foucault, *The History of Sexuality,* pp. 24-26, 122-27, 139-45.

21. Mirza I'tisam al-Dawlah = Mirza Itesa Modeen, *Shigirf namah-i Valayat* = *Shigurf Namah-i Valaet*, pp. 45-46; when necessary, all translated materials have been modified. For my modifications I have consulted the Urdu translation of *Shigirf Namah*. Henceforth references to translations will be noted by E for English and U for Urdu.

22. Mirza Abu Talib Isfahani, *Misir-i Talibi ya Safrnamah-'i Mirza Abu Talib Khan* (Tehran: Sazman-i Intisharat va Amuzish-i Inqilab-i Islami, 1363 [1984]), pp. 107-108. For the English translation of this travelogue see: Mirza Abu Taleb Khan, *Travels of Mirza Abu Taleb Khan in Asia, Africa, and Europe During the Years 1799 to 1803*, trans. from Persian by Charles Stewart, reprint edition (New Delhi: Sona Publications, 1972); originally published in 1814.

23. Wright, *The Persians Amongst the English*, p. 49. For the Persian original see: Mirza Abu Talib Isfahani, *Misir-i Talibi*, p. 128.

24. I'tisam al-Din, *Shigirf Namah*, pp. 149-150 E, 131 U.

25. *Ibid.*, p. 137 E.

26. *Ibid.*, pp. 138 E, 120-121 U.

27. *Ibid.*, pp. 157-159 E.

28. *Ibid.*, p. 159 E.

29. Sahhafbashi, *Safar Namah*, p. 81.

30. I'tisam al-Din, *Shigirf Namah*, p. 168 E.

31. Mirza Abu Talib Isfahani, *Misir-i Talibi*, p. 226.

32. On this point, see the "woman section" of newspapers and journals such as *Tajaddud, Iran-i Naw, Iranshahr, Farangistan* and *Nahid*.

33. I'tisam al-Din, *Shigirf Namah*, pp. 195 E, 175-176 U.

34. Westoxication (*gharbzadegi*) is the title of an influential essay by Jalal essay by Jalal Al-Ahmad. Written in 1961/62, Al-Ahmad's essay provided an important component of the anti-Shah popular movement. Westoxication, which came to express the increasing adaptation and imitation of European values and patterns of behavior, was viewed by Al-Ahmad as "a sickness, a disease imported from abroad, and developed in an environment receptive to it." (*Plagued by the West: Gharbzadegi*, trans. Paul Sprachman. New York: Caravan Books, 1982, p. 3).

35. Garmrudi, *Shab namah*, p. 983. All translations are mine.

36. *Ibid.*

37. Denis Wright, *The Persians Amongst the English*, p. 49.

38. Palmerston to Ajudanbashi, 11 July 1839 (Iranian Foreign Ministry Archive, document #500). This document was made available to me by the Iranian Ministry of Foreign Affairs. My special thanks to Ahmad Hajhosseini of the Iranian Interest Section, Washington D.C., who made possible the acquisition of this document in 1989.

39. Garmrudi, *Shab namah*, p. 951.

40. *Ibid.*

41. *Ibid.*, pp. 955-956.
42. *Ibid.*, p. 956.
43. *Ibid.*
44. *Ibid.*
45. *Ibid.*
46. *Ibid.*, p. 959.
47. *Ibid.*, p. 961.
48. Montesquieu, *Persian Letters*, trans. by C. Betts (London: Penguin Books, 1973), letter no. 30, p. 83.
49. Garmrudi, *Shab namah*, p. 962.
50. *Ibid.*, p. 964.
51. *Ibid.*, p. 982.
52. *Ibid.*
53. For a detailed study of Karim Khan's thought see: Mangol Bayat, *Mysticism and Dissent: Socioreligious Thought in Qajar Iran* (Syracus: Syracus University Press, 1982), pp. 63-86. Also see Abbas Amanat, *Resurrection and Renewal: The Making of the Babi Movement in Iran, 1844-1850* (Ithaca: Cornell University Press, 1989), pp. 286-294.
54. Quoted in M. Bayat, *Mysticism and Dissent*, p. 85.
55. The above mentioned individual appears to be either Riza Quli Mirza or his brother Najaf Quli who settled in Iraq where Hajj Muhammad Karim Khan was attending seminars offered by his master Sayyid Kazim Rashti.
56. *Risalah-i Nasiriyah*, pp. 388-389. For an alternative rendering see Bayat's *Mysticism and Dissent*, pp. 388-389.
57. Bayat, *Mysticism and Dissent*, p. 85.
58. Kirmani, *Risalah Nasiriyah*, p. 389.
59. *Ibid.*, p. 390.
60. *Ibid.*, p. 391.
61. Bayat, *Mysticism and Dissent*, p. 86.
62. Shaykh Fazl Allah Nuri, *Lavayih-i Aqa Shaykh Fazl'allah Nuri*, edited by Huma Rizvani (Tehran: Nashr-i Tarikh-i Iran, 1362/[1983]), p. 62.
63. For example see: Fitrat Bukharayi, *Munazirah-'i mudarris-i Bukharayi ba yik nafar Farangi dar Hindustan* (Istanbul: Hikmat, 1327/[1909]); Anonymous, *Mukalimah-'i sayyah-i Irani ba shakhs-i Hindi* (n.l.: Paradis Press, n.s.); Anonymous, *Shukh va Shaykh* (Unpublished manuscript, Ayat'allah Mar'ashi Library, Qum, Iran).
64. Mirza Aga Kan Kirmani, *Ayinah-'i Sikandari*, pp. 522-523.
65. Muhammad Turkuman, *Majmu'ah-yi az rasayil, i'lamiyah'ha, maktubat, ... va ruznamah-'i Shaykh-i Shahid Fazl'allah Nuri* (Tehran: Khadamat-i Farhangi-i Rasa, 1362/[1983]), 1:108.
66. Turkman, *Majmu'ah*, p. 320.
67. Nuri, *Lavayih*, p. 62.

68. *Ibid.*

69. On the use of the French Revolution in Iranian revolutionary discourse see: Mohamad Tavakoli-Targhi, "Ta'sir-i Inqilab-i Faransah," *Iran Namah* 3 (Summer 1990):411-439.

PART TWO

Country Case Studies

6

Politics, Islam, and Women in Kano, Northern Nigeria

Ayesha M. Imam

Introduction

In this chapter the term identity politics refers to forces organizing and appealing to a group defined by specific ascriptive characteristics, and mobilizing this group identity as a means of gaining access to power. These characteristics are usually, but not exclusively, those ascribed by virtue of birth—to parents of a particular religion or ethnic group, par excellence. Power here may be either control of or influence in the state or access to control over resources. As I use the term, fundamentalism is a particular form of identity politics which claims an exclusive (usually God-given and eternal) truth and which seeks state power in order to impose this view of the "natural" moral and/or social order, whether on dissenting members of "their" group or on others. These definitions imply a distinction between identity politics, group identity (where people acknowledge themselves via these characteristics to be part of a group or community) and identity formation or change (where definitions, values and discourses associated with characterizing a group are adopted, adapted or created). Identity politics and identity formation or change may develop simultaneously, but this is not necessarily so.

In northern Nigeria the bases of identity politics have been particular definitions of ethnicity (Hausa/Fulani) and religion, specifically Islam. Islam has been associated with state power in northern Nigeria since the fifteenth century. Ironically, secular British colonial rule effectively gave Islam renewed impetus, and the northern political parties which emerged in the run-up to independence (both populist and conservative) drew heavily on Islamic discourses. Significantly the more conservative party also mobilized a regional-ethnic identity. Since independence in 1960 Nigeria has been a secular, federal state. Nonetheless, the creation and maintenance of a northern/Islamic bloc has remained important. With the increase in fundamentalism (Islamic, Christian and political), and the proposed return to civilian rule in 1992, these linkages between politics and religious faith have taken on a new sense of urgency and power.

Throughout these periods the corporate and individual actors involved have had varying views as to the nature of gender relations and particularly of women's relationship to political power, participation and authority. These views, their effects in the past and implications for the future are considered. This is particularly salient because until recently Kano women did not organize as women to promote their interests. However, in the 1980s branches of two groups were formed in Kano: Women in Nigeria (WIN), which aims to promote women's interests on secular grounds; and a federation of Muslim women (FOMWAN), which attempts to redefine Islamic discourses on women while maintaining legitimacy with existing religious and state authorities.

The issues are examined through a case study of Kano women, which is discussed through a focus on two themes. One is seclusion, as expressing a gamut of concerns about gender relations and the proper role of Muslim women which include: husbands' decision-making and the control of women as wives by husbands, physical mobility/public invisibility (which is related also to dress codes), the non-mingling of the sexes, and the primacy of the wife/mother role for women. The second theme is women's direct political participation and authority.

Pre-Islamic Hausaland and the Coming of Islam

The area known as Hausaland lies mostly within the northern part of what is now the Federal Republic of Nigeria. There have been contacts with Islam since about the eleventh century, by way of traders and itinerant preachers through the medium of the trans-Sahara caravan trade. About the fifteenth century, during the reign of Muhammadu Rumfa (1463-1499), Islamic influence and political power came to be strongly associated. Rumfa corresponded with Al-Maghili and invited him to come to Kano, where he wrote a treatise on Islamic statecraft. According to *The Kano Chronicle* it was also Muhammadu Rumfa who "began the custom of *kulle* [seclusion]."[1]

Nonetheless, despite the injunction to break with animism, the seventeenth and eighteenth centuries were periods of transaction between Islam and *Bori* for most of those nominally Muslim.[2] Thus Hausa identity gradually incorporated being Muslim as part of itself, over a period of four hundred years or so. During this time Islam spread gradually and largely affected only the ruling groups (*masu sarauta*) and rich merchants. The *talakawa* (common people) were little affected. However, from the fifteenth century on, when Islam was a major discourse of rulers, women's formal roles began to lack recognition. The beginning of the practice of seclusion also occurred at this point, but this affected only very high ranking women and took a very strict form.

By the late eighteenth century Islam had become an important ground of ideological legitimation in the struggle for political power which resulted in the establishment of the Sokoto Caliphate around 1807.[3] The rallying call was the promise of a social order based on Islamic principles as had been realized in Mecca under the "rightly guided caliphate,"[4] with justice, fair taxation and moral purity. There were frequent references in the denunciations of the *jihadists* (holy warriors) to lewdness, promiscuity and "free women" (a euphemism for courtesans, as neither under husbands' control nor that of their fathers). The moral purity of Muslim women was one of the markers used to legitimate and set off the distinction between the "reformer" Muslims on the one hand, and the "lapsed, corrupt" emirate Muslims (and, in a minor key, the practitioners of indigenous religions), on the other.

During the Sokoto Caliphate (around a hundred years) there was an extension of the prestige of Muslim identity, as it had a direct association with power and patronage via the distribution of office, in a period of an expanding economy.[5] The desirability of being Muslim was not only felt among the ruling elites. Mai Gashin Baki, a nineteenth century caravan leader, described the way that even minimalist Muslims, barely able to recite the *al-Fatiha* (the first *sura*, or Quranic verse, every child learns), could claim to be a brother and fellow believer "and be received by the Hausa with general friendship and kindness."[6] It is most probable that as the authority of Islamic discourses grew, the ideal of seclusion, associated with both high status and piety, became more widespread. Along with the public performance of the five daily prayers by men, the seclusion of women and the Islamic code of dressing constitute the most visible everyday markers of Islamic practice. From Mai Gashin Baki again, there is an indication that the use of the *mayafi* (cloth used to drape the head and/or shoulders) had become general—he describes meeting his future wife and not being able to see her face as "following the custom of the country she knelt, wholly covered by her cloth."[7]

Thus by the end of the nineteenth century Islamic discourses were imbricated in temporal authority and a definer of identity and solidarity in the emirates that paid tribute to the Sultan of Sokoto, whose other title was Sarkin Musulmi (ruler of the Muslims). Women had, by this time, virtually ceased to have political office and formal authority. And, although most women were not secluded, the ideal of seclusion was widespread and there was the development of an increasingly specialized gender division of labor, in which many of the tasks allocated to women could be carried out within the compound.

The Colonial Period

Ironically, the conquest of Northern Nigeria by the British (Christians basing their authority on secular grounds) resulted in a new impetus for Islam. An Islamic cultural identity (including the practice of seclusion) became a means of resistance to British rule, and the effects of colonial rule, particularly through increasingly heavy taxation, did nothing to mitigate the appeal of harking back to the Golden Age of the early Caliphate. Thus again there was a basis for an identity politics around Islam. But this was in a changed context.

Islam's introduction to Hausaland had been through peaceful means, via contact with Muslims through trade and conversion. It had spread gradually over several centuries. Its adaptability to local customs and the syncretism between Islam, Bori and custom during most of this time[8] had meant that being Muslim gradually became adopted as part of a Hausa identity. Since the fifteenth century, Islam had been a significant discourse of all rulers. Again, although most of the Jihad leaders had been ethnic Fulani,[9] they were Fulani who had been living in Hausaland over several generations at least and who spoke Hausa. Furthermore, the Jihad had the support, because of economic grievances, of the Hausa rural *talakawa* "who had not smelt the scent of Islam."[10] In fact, without their support the guerrilla war of the Jihadists could neither have been fought nor won. None of these factors applied to British colonial rule. The proselytization of Islam (and of seclusion as an identifier and symbol of Islam) became a call to pre-colonial tradition vis-à-vis the ways of the colonizers, and perhaps a way of coping with the ignominies and difficulties of being a colonized people.

British colonial administrative policy inadvertently helped to promote Islamization among the Maguzawa (non-Muslim Hausa) and non-Hausa peoples in northern Nigeria, as well as among nominally

Muslim Hausa. The factors which have often been associated with this are the ending of warfare and the improvement in transport and communication networks which gave rise to increased physical security, enabling Muslims to travel and preach in Muslim areas and to penetrate new territories, while the colonial state largely excluded Christian missionaries from the north.[11] However, the issue of increased physical security—one of the planks of legitimation of British colonial imposition—has been over-stressed.[12]

There were a number of other factors which were also influential in promoting Islamization. Cultural resistance and the effects of an ever-increasing burden of taxation have been mentioned. The establishment of *Sharia* courts throughout the Protectorate of Northern Nigeria legitimated and gave authority to Muslim law (which discriminates against non-Muslims) at the expense of indigenous systems of practice. The expansion of the *mallamai* (Muslim literati) as clerks for the colonial administration meant that devout Muslim men were sent all over the Protectorate, with both the opportunity to preach, and (in representing the authority of the colonial state) the power to coerce people into Islam. Since the Anti-Slavery Proclamations did not abolish slave status but merely prohibited the creation of new slaves, slaves often deserted, turning up elsewhere claiming to be free-born Muslims.[13] The lack of a policy of mass secular education and restriction of missionary education in the north meant that the religious fellowships had a virtual monopoly in the provision of mass education. This they undertook increasingly as a means of acquiring a mass base of membership. As Paden says, "the dramatic increase in religious writing in Kano is a reflection of the desire to read and write."[14]

The cumulative and combined effect of all these factors, therefore, was to expand the numbers of those identifying themselves as Muslim and to make Islam an issue in political consciousness. This was to have particular implications in the struggle over state power that led to the end of formal colonialism and thereafter. Both then and later it also had consequences for women. By the end of the Caliphate where office-holding positions for women still existed, although the personal influence of the incumbents might not be insignificant, the offices themselves had only a residue of their former authority.[15] However, the possibility of office-holding only ever applied to a small minority of upper-class women. And, until the colonial period, so too did the practice of seclusion.

It is clear that during the colonial period the practice of seclusion increased and became general among the population.[16] As with Islamization, there were economic and administrative factors which influenced the generalization of seclusion. These include: withdrawal from field labor (or a non-acknowledgement of women's working on field labor) in order to reduce the number of those counted as tax-payers in the household; concentration on spinning cotton and processing groundnuts (both women's tasks in the division of labor, and both in demand as they were increasingly cash cropped in the colonial economy); and, the increasing pressure on land and hence diminishing of bush which made it difficult for women to continue with those occupations which depend on foraging.[17]

Nonetheless, withdrawal from public economic activities like farmwork or foraging was neither solely an economic response, nor is it the exact equivalent of seclusion. What converted this withdrawal into seclusion was the ideological context in which it took place. The boost given to Islamic fervor as a means of resistance to colonial domination, and the increased proselytization in rural areas meant that women's proper place in Islam also became an issue preached about to rural communities (as were the anti-Islamic nature of singing and drumming at funerals or of the chewing of mildly narcotic leaves). Whereas formerly seclusion had been almost wholly a phenomenon of the urban officeholders and wealthy, it now became a topic of concern in rural areas also.

It is still a moot point as to whether seclusion is a mandatory part of Islam.[18] Dan Fodio, a century earlier, had argued that it was preferred rather than obligatory.[19] But seclusion is historically associated with Islam in Hausaland, and it was associated with high status, wealth and respectability, as well as with piety. Up to this point the dominant discourse on seclusion had been of the most restrictive variety, whereby secluded women emerged not at all or extremely rarely from their homes. However, this form of seclusion is less feasible for small-scale cultivating households than for the wealthy. Although there were impulses for the withdrawal of women's labor from public space, there were also impetuses to continue—the fetching of water, fuel and wild plants for food and the harvesting of cotton and groundnuts were also women's tasks in the gender division of labor. Indeed the increased production of groundnuts and cotton meant a continued (and heavy) demand for women's labor at harvesting periods and women did continue to harvest these crops. For the *talakawa* being evangelized, there was a contradiction between their labor needs and the requirements of being good Muslims presented to them. It seems likely that this is what led to the development of the *tsari* form of seclusion, where women may leave their compounds for specific purposes but still be considered secluded.

During early colonialism the politics of identity was directed largely against the British as Christian overlords. But from the late 1940s on nationalist agitation, originating in the south and spreading north, coupled with the particular administrative structures of British colonialism in Nigeria, resulted in the politics of identity taking on a particular cast, with profound implications for Nigeria's future.

The Run-up to Political Independence

Up to this point the colonial administration of Nigeria was not centralized,[20] but consisted of the Northern, Eastern and Western Regions. The guiding principle behind the tripartite federation was that each region had a "majority ethnic group" which was to play the role of the leading actor—in the Northern Region, the Hausa/Fulani. The challenge posed by the rise of nationalism in the south precipitated the formation of a pan-northern party, the Northern Peoples Congress (NPC). This was also partly to fight the challenge of the Northern Elements Progressive Union (NEPU). NEPU had won twice as many seats as Native Authority candidates in the regional elections,[21] and with its strong anti-feudal posture this was clearly disturbing for the *masu sarauta*. In Kano the political field was dominated by these two parties. One was based on the *masu sarauta* who had allied with the colonial administration, thus retaining many of their privileges and control of government. The other was based on independent artisans, small traders and farmers, with visions of universal franchise in a secular democratic state.[22]

One of the issues over which these two parties contested was that of women's rights in Islam and how this should be interpreted in contemporary society. NEPU was the only party in the north of Nigeria to make the position of women a concern of its platform at that time, arguing for women's enfranchisement and rights to education. This was couched in the language of Islamic rights, quoting, for example, sura *Ash-shura* (42:38) that Muslims are those "whose rule [in all matters of common concern] is consultation among themselves" and the surahs specifying the religious rights and duties of all Muslims (which specifically include women), to argue that this meant that all, regardless of rank or sex, should have a direct say in a democracy.

However, it was the more conservative NPC which, with the aid of election manipulation by the colonial administration and the use of state instruments like the police to intimidate NEPU activists and supporters,[23] won the elections and held power from the end of the colonial period until 1966. One of the concerns of NPC was to build up a power base in the north by stressing differences in culture and religion between the north (largely Muslim) and the south (by this time largely Christian, but with sizeable Muslim communities). Women's position was one of the *points de capiton* in this discourse. The NPC also couched its language in Islamic discourse. They argued that women's seclusion was not only legitimate in Islam but obligatory and drew upon appeals to tradition also (arguing that seclusion was traditional in Hausaland). Speaking for the NPC, as well as himself, the Northern Region Premier stated that "female suffrage is inimical to the customs and feelings of the great part of the men of this region."[24] Northern women did not then get the vote.

Ironically, despite Hausaland's long history of association with Islam of at least five centuries, it was during the five decades or so of colonialism that seclusion became extensively practiced. By the end of direct colonial rule, the practice of seclusion in northern Nigeria had changed dramatically from an urban and high status group phenomenon, to being widespread in rural areas and among the largest and poorest group of the population, the *talakawa*.[25] This development was related both to the economic changes consequent on the way in which northern Nigeria was incorporated into the world capitalist economy as a producer of certain primary commodities for export, and the way in which British colonial rule resulted in the promotion of Islam as a self-conscious ideology, a source of group identity and resistance, and, as a power base for control of the federal state. This was to such an extent that even NEPU, a party wanting a secular state, couched their appeal in Islamic terms.

During the colonial period the religious-political ideologies on seclusion had also changed. At least since the time of Dan Fodio there had been a subordinate discourse in which, while seclusion was recommended, it was permitted for women to leave their homes in circumstances of necessity, which were quite widely defined. In this discourse it was even occassionally admirable for women to be out of their compounds. The dominant discourse, however, had been that seclusion was mandatory for true Muslims and that going out, for whatever purpose, was antithetical to the proper practice of seclusion and was reprehensible if not forbidden. This dominant discourse, over the course of the colonial period, shifted to include concepts of group identity and tradition. Seclusion became assimilated in political rhetoric (regardless of actual historical accuracy) as tradition and custom, which identified and set off the Muslim north of Nigeria first from the British colonialists and later also from southern Nigerians. In this way to argue against seclusion became characterized as anti-Muslim and anti-

Hausa/northern. Thus, *tsari* seclusion, despite its extensiveness, remained religiously and ideologically unjustified. Furthermore, to argue for women's political rights or possibilities of leadership, was similarly characterized as anti-tradition (despite Amina of Zazzau or the queens of Daura), un-Islamic (despite Aisha, the Prophet's wife who was certainly an influential political figure), and anti-northern (as aping the "black whiteman," as Ahmadu Bello characterized Christian and Western-educated southern Nigerians).

Independence

At independence Nigeria became a federal secular republic. But the inherited regional structure meant that the north had a permanent majority at the federal level. The NPC, the party of the *masu sarauta* (turned bourgeoisie) therefore had an interest in maintaining a northern (Hausa-Fulani)/Muslim bloc as their identity and power base. Part of NPC's strategy for this included defending and maintaining the right of men in the north to control "their" women. Hence there was a continuation and repetition of the hegemonic myth that Muslim women are traditionally secluded and content. Thus, for example, as late as 1965 it was stated in the National Assembly that

> We in the North are perfectly happy: our women are happy about their condition and I appeal to other members of the republic to please leave us in peace. There is not a single Northern woman who has told anyone that she is unhappy. We know what is right for women and our men know what is right for themselves. [26]

This statement ignored the existence of women like Gambo Sawaba— imprisoned sixteen times by the British and the Native Authority for her role in anti-colonial and anti-feudal protest and a strong supporter of women's rights—or Ladi Shehu, who was the NEPU Women's Wing General Secretary. Likewise it ignored the various resolutions and memoranda of the NEPU Women's Wing, which included a call for the right to vote, a minimum age of marriage, an end to forced marriage, improved access to education and jobs for women, and a call to the Sultan of Sokoto, the Emirs of Katsina, Kano and Kafanchan, the Shehu of Borno and Sarkin Shanu to "stop oppressing women in their emirates."[27]

Following the coup of 1966 and the Civil War, a policy of reconciliation and the promotion of nationalist identity and patriotism was instituted. It was in this same period that women in the northern states gained the right to vote and that a policy of universal primary education was adopted. However, the institution of such policies as that of Federal Character[28] meant that there remained a basis for organizing around sub-national identities, or ethnicity.

Over the past few years, the salience of identity politics has again revived in Kano, as in the rest of Nigeria. The development of three factors can be identified as responsible for this. The first is the huge increase in federal revenue from petroleum. Three-quarters of the federal budget is derived from this single source, so that those in control of the federal state control the distribution of very large sums. Second, from the January 1984 coup on, as in all military regimes the local states have less autonomy and are increasingly directed from the central federal government. Thus influencing developments within the local state means also influencing those in center government and tactical alliances and maneuvers have resulted with the aim of achieving this. Third, the evident failure of development and modernization promises and of "democratic" party politics have given rise to increasing pessimism and cynicism and a recourse to religion.[29] This latter, as far as Islam is concerned, is fueled by developments in Iran and by money from Saudi Arabia, Libya and Iran. Added to this is President Babangida's imposition of a two-party policy for the proposed return to civil rule, which has given rise to fears of North/South or Christian/Muslim split. The fear of being in whichever group which does not succeed in gaining central state power in 1992, and of consequently being left out of the division of the spoils, has added impetus to identity and fundamentalist politics.

Contemporary Islamic identity politics in Nigeria has two quite distinct class bases and projects. One draws its support largely from the elites and its project is related to political control of the state. This has been called the Northern Oligarchy or "the Kaduna mafia."[30] The other originated within the ranks of the increasingly destitute urban poor, although it also has wide rural support. This would include the Maitatsine and Izala groups as well as the renewed mass-based activities of the Jamaat Nasril Islam and other religious groups. Although these latter have economic concerns their project is more focussed about the minutiae of everyday life—such as the prohibition of exorbitant marriage payments, correct rituals for prayer and fasting, abstention from drugs including alcohol and cigarettes, and proper behavior of women.

However, the need for mass support has drawn the former group (which might be referred to as the political Islamists) into the more fundamentalist position of the latter. Thus, for example, the agitation for a Federal Sharia Court of Appeal equally ranked with the Federal Court of Appeal has been increasingly argued, not simply as for those who wish to apply to it, but for "the Muslim communities of Nigeria." And not only the Common Law and Statutes inherited from colonialism, but also decrees and legislation enacted since then, have been decried as "Christian Law," although the heads of state for 20 of Nigeria's 30 years of independence and the majority of legislators throughout have been Muslim. Nonetheless, the worldviews and objectives of the political and the fundamentalist Islamists have not become wholly identical and there are lines of tension between them. One of these concerns women's rights and ideal gender relations.

Both groups of Islamists are broadly in agreement that women, although having equal souls before Allah, are under the jurisdiction of men as fathers and husbands on earth. Both groups also see women as having a different physiology and psychology from men, which fits them essentially for the role of mother and wife. In this role, however, the fundamentalists stress the importance of physical seclusion, while the political Islamists are more willing to concede that women may venture out of the home, if only they will dress decently and avoid "unnecessary" interactions with men. Furthermore, the fundamentalists support education of women primarily in order to enable them to be better teachers to their children and to proselytize among women. The political Islamists accept this objective but also see roles for women in the wider economy—mostly, in sex-stereotyped jobs. Fundamentalists defend the right of men to marry barely pubertal girls, political Islamists often advise waiting a little. These lines of tension are evident in, for example, the report of the Kano State Committee for Women Affairs. The Committee stated on the one hand, that women have no better place than as wives and mothers and are unsuited to any occupation unrelated to weaning and household duties. On the other hand, they also recommended a minimum age of marriage, education and jobs for women and said that women may work outside the home "in order to contribute to the development of [their] society."[31]

Nonetheless, the position of both groups has shifted to a more liberal position since the heyday of the NPC—most markedly on the issue of women's role in political activity. This is in part a reluctant recognition of contemporary realities. Women do have the vote. Their support or lack of it can be decisive as the PRP election success in Kano in 1979 showed.[32] Thus the fear that non-Muslims will win the federal government has meant that, since non-Muslim women have the vote and are unlikely to give it up, Islamists no longer insist that "their" women should not vote. Furthermore, in order for women to be mobilized to vote, some women must be able to go and address them—and therefore cannot be physically secluded. In addition, since non-Muslim women will run for office, Muslim women in office are needed to counteract them, although not in "sensitive" posts requiring "maximum rationality and minimum emotionality." These concessions are made on the principle that women's political activity is the lesser of two evils—the greater being non-Muslim control of the state. Notwithstanding this, the dominant view is explicit that Muslim women's political activity should be to ensure that Muslim men get state control, after which matters can be safely left where they should be, in the hands of men.[33]

The position of Islamists in the 1980s has thus allowed women more rights than that of the 1950s. It has meant that women have increased access to basic literacy and ideological sanction not to be wholly restricted to seclusion. Increasing numbers of women have been enthusiastically taking advantage of these opportunities. Even so, in the 1980s the Islamists' advocacy of women's rights to education, to remunerated work, and to vote and be voted for, still falls far short of Wali's relatively radical position four decades earlier. Women's subordination to men and control by men is emphatically a part of the Islamist program.

Women, as a category, have never been merely passive victims in these struggles. However, in Kano, it is mainly in the last decade that women have started organizing in groups "for themselves" and with definite political ends. Of these, the two most significant groups are WIN (Women in Nigeria) and FOMWAN (Federation of Muslim Women's Associations in Nigeria). The next section focusses on the ways in which WIN and FOMWAN define the boundaries of their respective gender group identities, their views of gender relations, the tactics and strategies each group uses and the implications of these for their own objectives and for Nigerian women.

Kano Women Mobilized

Unlike some other ethnic groups in Nigeria, Muslim Hausa women have very little history of autonomous women's associations or organizations with some power and influence over both their own members and wider aspects of society, compared to (for example) Igbo village women's associations.[34] Some women's groups did exist however. The first of these appears to be the *'Yan Taru*, a religious study group, started in the early Caliphate period by Nana Asama'u, the daughter of the Jihad leader.[35] In the pre-independence period both the NPC and the PRP had women's wings. The NPC Women's Wing was largely of "free women" to entertain the male crowd at rallies, as women did not then have the vote nor did the NPC support female franchise. Although the NEPU Women's Wing were more than mere entertainers and did discuss political issues, it (like that of the NPC) was not autonomous from the main party, whether in defining issues and priorities or policy-making or activities.[36] Nor were the women's wings of any of the political parties after independence. Similarly, the claim to autonomy of the contemporary Nigerian Council of Women's Societies (NCWS) is debatable. Since it was recognized by the state as the "umbrella body" for all women's groups, it has been largely funded by and supportive of the state. In addition to these, some women's clubs exist, like Jamiyar Matan Arewa but these confine themselves to charitable works.

Nonetheless, the lack of women's organizations does not mean that women were not active in the restructuring and conflicts over gender relations within identity politics. Islamist positions cannot be seen merely as one of imposition on women. For instance, women were also active in the religious fellowships.[37] In the colonial period there were Maguzawa women choosing to convert to Islam in order to retain their marriage gifts on divorce. Many Muslim women actively sought (and still seek) seclusion, making a trade-off between autonomy over their mobility and effective economic autonomy in increased time for their own household-based remunerated occupations, material security where the husband is relatively well-off, respectability and status. Women might also resist through refusal to marry secluding husbands, through *yawo* (returning to her natal home or relatives and forcing her husband to negotiate with them for her return) by running away, or simply through a refusal to be secluded.[38] However, either their activity was within a male dominated organization or was individual, though often supported by networks of women and men. Only relatively recently have women in Kano organized themselves into associations over which they have control and which include the specific aim of furthering women's rights in society.

Formed in 1985, FOMWAN was the first national organization for Muslim women with a strong branch in Kano. FOMWAN sees its priorities as promoting the Islamic and general education of Muslim women, the recognition and enforcement of women's rights in Sharia, the family and upbringing of children, and the rights of Muslims in general. Within the second priority FOMWAN is attempting to shift some of the negative currently hegemonic discourses on women to ones more favorable to women (posed as "enlightening ignorance" about Islam and removing the influence of custom over religion).

Drawing on the legitimacy of the recent revival of interest in Islam and concern with how to live as good Muslims within Nigeria, their strategy has been to draw on selected statements from accepted religious authorities and try to weld these into a coherent interpretation of Islam. Hence Dan Fodio is often quoted (both regarding his support for women's education and his condemnation of men for telling women that their happiness lies in being obedient to men and doing domestic tasks).[39]

Thus, Zainab Kabir argues that women are restricted in the name of Islam because Islam has been adulterated with tradition and that it is tradition which is responsible for many aspects of Muslim women's subordination. She states that Muslim women can and should participate in every aspect of human endeavor. Women are free to go out as long as they dress modestly, that is, wearing loose and non-transparent garments that cover all but the face, hands and feet. For Kabir, what Islam requires of women (and men) is not restriction to the house and kin, but the avoidance of immoral behavior and decent dressing.[40] She argues that the injunction that a woman is under the authority of her husband (*Surah Al-Baquarah* 2:228), must be interpreted in the light of later revelations, to wit that men and women are defined as protectors and caring companions one of the other equally (*Surah At-Tawbah* 9:71).

Furthermore, she points out that most of the authority cited for women's subordinate position are hadith and Sharia, not suras. While the verses of the Quran itself are sacrosanct, hadiths must be evaluated in the light of the circumstances in which they were said and according to the authority of citation. Similarly, the various schools of Islamic law (Hanafi, Hambali, Maliki and Sha'afi) are not to be accepted without question either, as each person must act according to their own conscience. She notes that almost all practitioners of *tafsir* (exegesis) have been men who interpreted suras and hadiths without regard for women's interests and says it is necessary for women to become scholars and make their own interpretations. Nonetheless, given the unambiguous statements in the Quran regarding women's roles as wives and mothers, Kabir (like other members of FOMWAN) finds it necessary to argue both for women's liberation and that women are primarily wives and mothers.[41] And it is this tension that lead to the contradictions in the Kano State Committee on Women Affairs.

However, even to shift the discourses in the limited sense that FOMWAN has so far chosen has theological difficulties. On the issue of seclusion the main contradiction is between accepting that women can go out for their lawful needs, and the issue of who decides what those lawful needs are. Additionally there is the problem of with whom Muslim women may decently interact; there are no suras on this, other than those which are addressed to the Prophet's wives, and the reported well-known hadiths are not helpful. It will certainly take a sustained effort by committed Muslim scholars to seek plausible theological arguments on these and other gender issues in Islam.

But for the short term at least the obstacle to establishing this discourse is power—or rather the lack of it. Thus far FOMWAN's tactics have been to seek support from liberal but influential Muslim scholars and judges. But, although the boundaries in the discourses on seclusion have shifted over time, even these sympathetic scholars are restrictive and reserve the possibility of returning women to physical seclusion (unlike FOMWAN itself). And, since the loosening of the boundaries have to do with the fear that Muslim men will not dominate the Third Republic, so that the political support of Muslim women is needed, it seems quite likely that even this limited support for a more liberal discourse may be withdrawn should the ulama decide that women's support is no longer necessary. Secondly, Kabir argues for the need for women to do *tafsir*, but she does not address the important question of how those interpretations can gain legitimacy. It has not been the case that woman-sympathetic discourses have been entirely lacking in the history of Islam after all, but that they have not been able to attain authority. It does not seem likely that FOMWAN will fare better, despite its relatively high legitimacy in the eyes of the ulama, compared to other more radical and secular groups such as Women in Nigeria (WIN).

Unlike FOMWAN, WIN (which was formed two years earlier in 1983) is a secular organization and one which allows men with feminist principles to join, although they may not take the leadership. WIN has an explicit commitment to the necessity of both women's emancipation and the elimination of class oppression. Furthermore it has a nationalist orientation, promoting the interests of Nigerian women rather than of women of particular religions or ethnicities. WIN thus disavows identity based on ethnicity or religion in favor of a gender identity informed by class and national in orientation. As a result WIN has nationally a more widespread appeal than FOMWAN.

In Kano, however, it suffers from the allegations of being "Western," too radical, and non-Muslim oriented. This is despite the fact that WIN has been careful not to attack religious sentiments directly (though its denunciation of ethnic chauvinism is uncategorical). Rather WIN focuses on fighting for the economic and political conditions for women's autonomy. Vis-à-vis religion per se WIN, like FOMWAN, argues for the implementation of the rights women have in Islam or Christianity. However, WIN members do this with a rather more consistently radical interpretation of women's rights in religion and a stronger critique of men's gender interests in maintaining the status quo.[42] At the same time, WIN maintains that as a secular state with a multi-religious population, religious sentiments should not be used to define gender (or other) roles and rights in Nigeria.[43] Furthermore, WIN is at pains to stress that poor women (and men) regardless of religious and ethnic affiliation are in the same structural situation.

WIN's attempts to forge an identity of women as a gender group while recognizing that women in different classes can and do have divergent interests over specific issues have met with some success. This was most notable in the debate over the Nigeria's political and socio-economic structure in 1985-86. By holding workshops throughout Nigeria with thousands of ordinary women and in indigenous languages (hence, in Kano in Hausa, rather than solely in English), WIN was both able to solicit views and perhaps influence them. In this mobilization process WIN found that across Nigeria many women could and did identify themselves in this way.[44]

Unlike FOMWAN or the NCWS, WIN deliberately rejects affiliation to or identification with the state, religious bodies or political parties. This, as well as its more radical worldview, means that WIN suffers from a chronic shortage of resources, being funded neither by the state nor by religious bodies. In addition, there is often a deliberate policy of hindering WIN's access to the mass media—an important factor in a country the size of Nigeria. Furthermore, the state has so far refused to register the organization. However, surprisingly frequently, elements of WIN's critiques of state gender policies are taken up at various levels of the state (especially at the federal level), if not often in ways WIN would like (as in the Better Life for Rural Women Programme).

Nonetheless, although politics is about access to power and influence, it is also about the visions of what to construct with that power and influence. In the long run, the group identity WIN aims for, which refuses to place limits on the extent to which women may exercise autonomy and which focuses on improving the economic and political conditions of all Nigerian women, is more likely to result in improving women's positions in Nigeria than FOMWAN's exclusively Islamic project.

Conclusions

I have argued that certainly up to the fifteenth century and most likely into the seventeenth century, Islamic ideologies were gradually being incorporated as part of the identity of the Hausa—although this is not to say there were no political linkages within the ruling class. With the Jihad, there was a distinct period of identity politics between the Hausa emirate rulers, and the millenial Islamists of the Jihad (Fulani and Hausa). This was followed by a period of consolidation of Islam as Hausa and its generalization among the people as a process of identity formation rather than as identity politics. Colonial conquest and rule then resulted in two forms of identity politics: as Muslim Hausa versus colonial British, as Muslim northerners (dominantly but not exclusively Hausa-Fulani) versus Christian southern Nigerians—both organized round custom/tradition, religion, and ethnicity. Politics in Nigeria continued to be influenced by this colonial experience—a formally secular federal state with ruling groups mobilizing identity politics to create power-bases. Following the civil war there was some shift to the construction of one national rather than several regional identities. In the 1980s and 1990s, as fundamentalisms of all kinds are increasing worldwide, again a period of attempts to capture the state through the creation and/or mobilization of oppositional group identities has arisen.

This summary exposition should make it clear that identity is dynamic rather than static. The construction, form and maintenance of group identity and of identity politics are analytically only stages in process. Those periods in which identity politics is dominant are precisely the periods in which identity mobilization is a political project over state power, markedly in the Jihad and in the pre-independence period. Identity unites and calls together people, but simultaneously distinguishes them from other people. In the periods of conflict the lines are most clearly drawn, as Muslim versus Christian, or Hausa/Northern versus Southern, for example. Identity construction becomes a way of mobilizing larger groups of people in the struggle for political power.

Constructions around identity do not depend only on ideological representations and power struggles. The changes in northern Nigeria's economy—especially the economic changes that permitted women's large-scale withdrawal from field labor—affected the nature of the discourses and vice versa. This is the context in which the practice of seclusion was generalized. Furthermore, both the advocacy and the varying practices of seclusion have specific class associations, as can be seen between the political and the fundamentalist Islamists, for example, or in the development of the distinctions between full *kulle* and partial tsari.

Despite the changes in content and context of the ideological representations, there are features common to all the identity politics discourses. The first is the claim to revival of tradition or a better past vis-à-vis the corrupt present. During the Jihad, the past referred to was the Meccan community during the time of the Prophet and the "rightly guided caliphate." Since then to this has been added the early Sokoto Caliphate. However, as the analysis of the discourses around seclusion shows, this past is at least partly invented (re-ordering and construction of representations). Quite apart from the debates over their doctrinal basis, neither seclusion nor *hijab* was generalized in either period. However, the appeal is both to realize again the ideal community, based on the unchangeable law of Allah and the *sunna* of the Prophet, and for a return to roots. This appeal is simultaneously a claim to legitimacy and also has the effect of naturalizing the demands of these discourses. In so doing, it obscures the process of invention and makes illegitimate counter-acting arguments which reveal the material interests or socio-economic groupings of those advocating fundamentalist discourses, forcing the ideological conflict to take place on their chosen terrain and within the terms of their discourse. Hence, the democratic secular and anti-aristocratic vision of NEPU, for example, was couched in Islamic language. Similarly, FOMWAN finds it necessary to argue for a purification of gender relations based on an appeal to relatively liberal interpretations, rather than their transformation. This is, however, a path fraught with difficulties. Although those who are defined as the constituency of the identified group may thus not be immediately alienated, it also means that the debate is priorly circumscribed and constrained.

Gender relations have in every period been consistently used as one of the markers of the identity politics discourse, in a way that the worshipping of idols, or eating improperly slaughtered meat, or paying taxes, or singing and dancing have not. This is the case in conflicts internal to the identified community (such as between NPC and NEPU) or external to it, (such as between those claiming to represent the North against the South). This makes it the more surprising that many analysts have managed to ignore the issue of gender relations altogether, or, at best, mention it only in passing, and points to the need to re-evaluate the analyses of identity politics in a way which takes account of the issue of gender relations.

Notes

I am grateful to Zenebework Tadesse, Ann Whitehead, Morag Simpson, Tiyembe Zeleza, Amina Mama and Mamadou Diouf for their pungent comments on various drafts. However, since I have not always been influenced by them, all deficiencies remain mine.

1. Herbert Palmer (transl. and commentary), The Kano Chronicle *Journal of the Anthropological Institute* 38 (1908):57-98.

2. Muhammed Ahmed Al-Hajj, "The Mahdist Tradition in Northern Nigeria." Ph.D. Thesis, Ado Bayero College of Ahmadu Bello University, Zaria, 1973; Yusuf Usman, *The Transformation of Katsina (1400-1883): The Emergence and Overthrow of the Sarauta System and the Establishment of the Emirate System* (Zaria: Ahmadu Bello University Press, 1981); Abdullahi Mahadi, "The State and the Economy: The Sarauta System and its Role in Shaping the Society and Economy of Kano Emirate with Particular Reference to the 18th and 19th Centuries." Ph.D. Thesis, Ahmadu Bello University, 1982.

3. Murray Last, *The Sokoto Caliphate* (London: Longmans, 1967); Usman, *The Transformation of Katsina.*

4. John Ralph Willis, *"Jihad fi Sabil Allah:* Its Doctrinal Basis in Islam and Some Aspects of its Evolution in Nineteenth Century West Africa," *Journal of African History* 7 (3) (1967):395-415.

5. This is not to say there was a single Muslim identity but that identity was circumscribed in terms of being Muslim.

6. M. B. Duffil, "A Translation and Annotation of E. R. Flegel (1885), *Biography of Madugu Mohamman Mai Gashin Baki.*" Paper to Fourth Seminar on the Economic History of the Central Savanna of West Africa, Ahmadu Bello University, Zaria, 1976), p. 9.

7. *Ibid.,* p. 18.

8. Cf. Dean Stuart Gilliland, "African Traditional Religion in Transition: The Influence of African Traditional Religion In Northern Nigeria," Ph.D. Thesis, Hartford, 1971; Ahmed Beita Yusuf, "Legal Pluralism in the Northern States of Nigeria: Conflict of Laws in a Multi-Ethnic Environment." Ph.D. Thesis, University of Buffalo, 1976.

9. Usman, *The Transformation of Katsina.*

10. Al-Hajj, "The Mahdist Tradition in Northern Nigeria," Usman, *ibid.*

11. See C. N. Ubah, "The Administration of Kano Emirate Under the British, 1900-1930," Ph.D. Thesis, University of Ibadan, 1973; Mansur Ibrahim Mukhtar, "The Impact of British Colonial Domination on the Social and Economic Structures of the Society of Kano, 1903-1950." M.A. Thesis, Ahmadu Bello University, 1985.

12. See Imam, "The Development of Women's Seclusion in Northern Nigeria," in *Women Living Under Muslim Law Dossier*, forthcoming.

13. Zuwaqu Abungwon Bonat, *The Colonial Phase of the Underdevelopment of Zaria Province, 1902-1945*. M.A. Thesis, Ahmadu Bello University, 1985; Mukhtar, "The Impact of British Colonial Domination."

14. John Paden, *Religion and Political Culture in Kano* (Berkeley: University of California Press, 1973), p. 139. For a more detailed treatment of these arguments, see Ayesha Imam, "The Development of Women's Seclusion in Northern Nigeria,"

15. Renee Pittin, "Marriage and Alternative Strategies: Career Patterns of Hausa Women in Katsina City." Ph.D. Thesis, University of London, 1979.

16. Michael G. Smith, "Introduction" in *Baba of Karo: A Woman of the Muslim Hausa* by Mary F. Smith, (Yale: Faber, 1981); Polly Hill, *Rural Hausa: A Village and a Setting* (Cambridge: Cambridge University Press, 1972), and *Population, Prosperity and Poverty: Rural Kano 1900 and 1970* (Cambridge: Cambridge University Press, 1977).

17. See Imam, "The Development of Women's Seclusion in Northern Nigeria."

18. Isa Wali, "The True Position of Women in Islam," *Nigerian Citizen* (a series of 5 articles between July 18 and August 4, 1956); Imam, "The Development of Women's Seclusion"; Balaraba B. M. Sule and Priscilla Starrat, "Islamic Leadership Roles for Women in Contemporary Kano Society," pp. 29-49 in Catherine Coles and Beverley Mack (eds.), *Hausa Women in the Twentieth Century* (Madison: University of Wisconsin Press, 1991).

19. Usman dan Fodio, *Nur-al-Abab*, extracts in T. Hodgkin (ed.), *Nigerian Perspectives: An Historical Anthropology* (Suffolk: Chaucer Press, 1975).

20. Much of the analysis in this section is taken from Jibrin Ibrahim, "The State, Accumulation, and Democratic Forces in Nigeria." Seminar Paper to C.E.A.N., Université de Bordeaux I, 1989.

21. Rima Shawalu, *The Story of Gambo Sawaba* (Jos, Nigeria: Echo Communications Ltd, 1990).

22. Ibrahim, "The State, Accumulation, and Democratic Forces in Nigeria." See also Shawalu, *ibid.*

23. Shawalu, *ibid.*

24. Ahmadu Bello, *My Life* (Cambridge: Cambridge University Press, 1962), p. 223.

25. Seclusion was generalized but was not then, nor is it now, universal in Kano, despite the tendency for non-secluded women to be ignored in rhetoric, policy-making or research.

26. Waziri Ibrahim quoted from the *Sunday Times*, 27 May 1979.

27. Shawalu, *The Story of Gambo Sawaba*, p. 105.

28. This was an attempt to avoid having members of some ethnic groups being prominently visible in state structures (as had been Ibos in the First Republic because of their higher levels of "Western" education) by appointing people of the various ethnicities to governmental offices, the civil service, parastatals and the like, in ratio to the proportion of the said ethnic groups in the total population of Nigeria.

29. The link between the contemporary rise in fundamentalism and deteriorating economic conditions is particularly clear in Nigeria. Fundamentalist politics took off after the oil price crash and the beginning of the Austerity and Structural Adjustment Programmes. Although, for example, the Maitatsine group had exisited for several decades, only at this period did it begin gaining mass support.

30. Ibrahim, "The State, Accumulation, and Democratic Forces in Nigeria;" Adebayo Olukoshi, "Bourgeois Social Movements and the Struggle for Democracy in Nigeria: An Inquiry into the Origins, Growth, Nature and Activities of the 'Kaduna Mafia'." CODESRIA Workshop on Social Movements, Social Transformation and the Democratization of Development, Algiers, 1990.

31. Kano State Committee for Women's Affairs, *Report of the Kano State Committee for Women Affairs* (1987), p. 147.

32. Barbara Callaway, "Women and Political Participation in Kano City," *Comparative Politics* 19 (4) (1987):379-393.

33. See interviews in *The Muslim Woman* 1 (1) (July 1988), FOMWAN (Federation of Muslim Women's Associations in Nigeria).

34. Nina Mba, *Nigerian Women Mobilised: Women's Political Activity in Southern Nigeria 1900-1965* (Berkeley: University of California Press, 1982).

35. Jean Boyd, *The Caliph's Sister, Nana Asamau (1793-1865): Teacher, Poet and Islamic Leader* (London: Frank Cass, 1989).

36. Shawalu, *The Story of Gambo Sawaba*; Callaway, "Women and Political Participation in Kano City."

37. Paden, *Religion and Political Culture*; Sule and Starrat, "Islamic Leadership Roles."

38. See Ayesha Imam, "Dependence and Autonomy: Hausa Women in Diribo and Gangur." Paper to the Symposium on Muslim Women in Nigeria, Lehrstuhl für Islamwissenschaft, Universität Bayreuth, May 19, 1990.

39. Fodio, *Nur-al-Abab*.

40. Zainab Kabir, "Women's Liberation: Myth or Reality," in *The Muslim Woman in the Fourteenth Hijra*, FOMWAN, 1989.

41. *Ibid.*

42. Contrast, for example, Ayesha Imam, "Women's Liberation: Myth or Reality" (Paper to Muslim Sisters' Organisation Conference, Kano, 1985), pp. 68-73 in *Women's Struggles and Strategies: Third World Perspectives* (Rome: ISIS, 1986), with Kabir, "Women's Liberation."

43. WIN (Women in Nigeria), *The Conditions of Women in Nigeria and Policy Recommendations to 2,000 AD* (WIN, 1985).

44. WIN, n.d., *WIN Pamphlet on the Role of Women in Politics.*

7

Gender, Religious Identity, and Political Mobilization in Sudan

Sondra Hale

Introduction

This chapter examines the politicization of gender and its manifestation in identity politics in Sudan. The causes of this politicization can be traced to the relationship of the state and its apparatuses to religion, to the particular expression of gender in Islam, to the politicization of Islam itself, and to forces outside the Middle East in the form of international capital and its accompanying culture.

In raising questions about the relationship of the state to issues of gender, ethnicity, class, and religion, I have attempted to isolate the mechanisms that the state and/or party employ for achieving both political and cultural hegemony.[1] In Sudan, this has meant an examination of the identity politics that may be a strategy of, an effect of, or a reaction to state or party hegemonic processes. Among the Islamists, these strategies include (1) the manipulation of religious ideology toward a more "native"/"authentic" culture; (2) the representation or reiteration of the centrality of women in this process; (3) the attempt to create a new trend in the gender division of labor or to stem recent changes within that labor system; and (4) the goal to purge women's culture of particular "negative customs" such as the *zaar*.[2]

Among many of the secularists, such as the Sudanese Communist Party and its Women's Union affiliate, the strategy may look different, but there are underlying similarities: (1) in political oppositional work, the relegation of Islam to the "private sphere" of party members, coexistence with Islam, or efforts to work within an Islamic framework, perhaps seen as the "authentic" culture of northern Sudan's "working class" and peasantry; (2) the centrality of women in the political process, as half of Sudan's population, and therefore, a potential political force and also as the mothers of the future population (the workforce); (3) a view of Sudanese women as potentially significant in the workforce, i.e., as workers; and (4) activism toward purging women's culture of particular "negative customs" (such as the zaar).

In contemporary northern Sudan, therefore, as in many other areas of the Middle East, we are seeing two seemingly contradictory or antagonistic processes in juxtaposition—the "secular" forces, usually associated with a nationalist era and/or a contemporary Left movement, and Islamic forces, having older historical roots. Correspondingly, there are two types of women's movements, one represented by the secular Left of the Sudanese Women's Union and the other by the cultural nationalists, the women of the National Islamic Front (NIF). Both claim to elevate the position and status of women, the former by placing the "woman question" and the emancipation of women at the forefront of the political struggle, the latter by placing women and the family at the center of the culture.

Characteristic of both of these perspectives, however, is a class-interested politics of "authenticity." These groups address such questions as: What *is* Sudan's authentic culture? What is Sudan's "correct" history? Who is a "real Sudanese" and who are the "masses?" What are the authentic roots of Sudan's Islam? In a search for authenticity, for an identity which is "uniquely" Sudanese in the face of international interlopers, a tendency to essentialize has emerged in the rhetoric and in the testimonies of many Sudanese. This new essentialism, which is also a part of state ideology, is most evident in the attempts to characterize women and women's roles in Sudan's past and future. The identity politics which result from the search for authenticity are proactive so that, like women elsewhere, Sudanese may be ideologically manipulated by male-controlled religio-political and secular political institutions to engage in or disengage from particular cultural practices or economic activities—all in the name of the ideal woman, an essentialized category.[3]

The theoretical framework outlined above has generated hypotheses to account for (1) the Sudanese state's manipulation of religious ideology and the nature of identity politics; (2) the centrality of gender in this process; and (3) the impact on the gender division of labor and gender arrangements. With regard to women, I am exploring the paradoxical forces in post-colonial Sudan that have produced, on the one hand, an apparent secularization of societal institutions and a concomitant rise in the legal status and social positions of women, and on the other, the rise of Islamism. The subversive Islamism, the recent "Islamic Trend," is the product of a class which seeks to meet the needs of international capital with its liberal window-dressing (a "modern" look), without being culturally imperialized, as well as to answer the continuing crisis of Sudan's economy. Women and the family unit are among the nexi of these processes, which also require domestic and wage labor and political participation by women.

The State, Gender, and Religion in Northern Sudan

It may be helpful to begin by enumerating the most salient characteristics of Sudanese society: (1) It is a Muslim society that is still steeped in other indigenous and oftentimes contradictory traditions; (2) The Sufi/Sunni interaction has been highly complex, and the sectarian ethnic identity politics that emanate from this religious history remain active; (3) In terms of ethnicity, Sudan is Arab, Nubian, and African; (4) It has had a pluralistic legal system in which *Sharia* (Islamic canon law), civil, and customary law are said to co-exist; (5) Women's rights had been fairly well-developed; (6) There is a strong and vibrant women's culture; (7) There is a well-developed Left and a socialist tradition which was among the strongest in the Middle East and Africa and from which originated a strong women's movement; (8) There is today a vigorous Islamist movement; (9) The "urban" labor movement is only quasi-urban in that it is shored up mainly by the very small town and village workers on the railways and ports; (10) Peasant class formation is highly complex, and recent ethnic/regional power realignments have changed Sudan's class structure; (11) There has been a variety of state formations within the last two centuries: various colonial regimes (Ottoman and "Anglo-Egyptian"), Islamic states (Funj, Mahdist), parliamentary democracy (1956-1958, 1964-1969, and 1985-1989), diverse military regimes, and now an incipient military theocracy; (12) Since 1972 there has been a pronounced influx of multinational corporations, non-governmental organizations, and foreign aid projects (Arab, European, and American) that have dominated Sudan's economy, altered its class structure, and are seen by many Sudanese as challenging their gender arrangements and culture; (13) Sudan is one of the poorest 25 countries in the world and endures a persistent civil war which has had a profound impact on the conditions of women's lives and the nature of their activism.

Let us begin with an overview of political developments, and the relationship between the state and Islam in Sudan. The boundary between politics and religion has always been ambiguous and the basis of much of twentieth-century Sudanese politics has been sectarian. Two parties have dominated: the Umma Party, the political wing of the Ansar (followers of the Mahdi who combine Sufism and Sunni fundamentalism), and the Democratic Unionist Party (DUP, formerly the National Unionist Party), the political wing of the *Khatmiyya* (or *Mirghaniyya*) sect. The late 1980s saw the emergence of a very different Islamic polity, first a civil government's "New Islamic Trend," followed by a military government's "National Salvation Revolution." The military has ruled Sudan for most of the period since independence in 1956. For many of those years the Sudan, a political entity whose boundaries were the creation of colonialism, has also been split by a civil war between the north and the south, often simplistically categorized as the "Christian African" South versus "Muslim Arab" North, but in actuality a result of uneven regional and cultural development.[4]

From 1969 to 1985 the Sudanese state was headed by military dictator Jaafar Nimeiri. During that period, not only did Nimeiri introduce strict application of Sharia, but Sudan's economic situation was adversely affected by the influx of international corporations and agencies which served to perpetuate underdevelopment and dependency.[5] A civilian coalition overthrew the Nimeiri regime in 1985 and elections were held in 1986. The new government was initially dominated by the Ansar sect, led by Saddig al-Mahdi, head of the Umma Party, but ultimately established an Islamic Trend government, inspired by elements of the *Ikhwan* (Muslim Brotherhood), in the form of the National Islamic Front (NIF). In June 1989, a "National Salvation Revolution," another military *coup d'etat*, ousted the civilian government and, in essence, installed an NIF government. It also continued Islamization.

As for civil liberties, despite the strength of sectarian politics, Sudanese had been relatively relaxed about Islam, the dominant religion (for 70 percent in the country as a whole, and some 90 percent in the north), displaying some tolerance for diversity. Prior to 1983, civil and customary legal codes were dominant, although the Sharia was part of the legal system.[6] Northern Sudanese women wore a body covering called a *tobe*—a thin, cotton, full-body wrap-around—which was more a kind of national dress than a "veil." Although they practiced genital surgeries (both clitoridectomy and infibulation), they were considered by some to be among the more "emancipated" women of the Muslim world. This was especially true after 1965, when women earned suffrage, and in 1973 when the Permanent Constitution offered women as well as men a number of civil rights and freedoms and singled out women for specific protections.

The situation changed in 1983 when Nimeiri imposed and attempted to enforce strict Sharia and set mechanisms in motion for developing an Islamic state. He also invited Islamists into his government, namely Hassan al-Turabi, then leader of Sudan's Muslim Brotherhood. Since then there has been an intensified struggle between, on the one hand, secular forces, who see the non-Muslim Southern Sudan and women as potentially adversely affected by the implementation of Sharia, and, on the other hand, cultural nationalist religious forces, who see a "pure" and authentic Islam as Sudan's only defense and cultural salvation against an invading West, and the only answer to Sudan's dismal economic situation. This is not an unfamiliar pattern in the Muslim world.

Why did Nimeiri intensify Islamization? The spiralling national debt resulted in pressure from the World Bank and the International Monetary Fund (IMF) to prune the civil service and raise food prices—which caused riots in 1979 and 1982. Nimeiri was also faced by an increasingly successful insurrection in the south, and growing political opposition from the National Front. By then Nimeiri had run out of supporters. A parallel development was the growing visibility of women in the labor force, in particular in the context of male labor out-migration.[7] Nimeiri's "opportunistic Islamization," derived in part from Sudan's reliance on oil-rich Arab states (mainly Saudi Arabia) and the advantage of being able to co-opt some of the National Front's Islamic themes. But it also served to pave the way for the NIF to gain ascendence, in line with the ascendence of a new middle-class.[8]

Thus, on September 8, 1983, Nimeiri passed the notorious September Laws, declaring Sudan an Islamic republic and enforcing strict adherence to Sharia. Subsequently Sudanese saw the establishment of "decisive justice courts," the application of harsh *hadud* (Islamic criminal punishments), replacement of income tax by *zakat*, an alms tax, and the attempt to Islamize all the banks, banning interest. Self-appointed moral guardians harassed women in the streets about their conduct or dress. The Evidence Act applied conservative laws of evidence to women and non-Muslims, whereby the testimony of women in major crimes is inadmissible, and two women witnesses are needed to offset the testimony of one man.

Although it was mainly poor women (such as prostitutes and vendors of local brew) who bore the brunt of the moral guards, this period also offered an ominous hint of things to come for middle-class and professional women. More significantly, national debates were occurring about whether or not too many women were being trained in certain professions. I will return to the employment debates below.

The uprising of April 1985, which overthrew Nimeiri, left much of the Islamization project incomplete. However, as a Mahdist (Saddig al-Mahdi) was elected to office not long after—the Mahdists representing the land-owning and commercial ruling class as well as a special Sudanese combination of Sufism and fundamentalism—it was unlikely that this process would be aborted. In the summer of 1988 Prime Minister Saddig formed the "Government of Consensus" which invited the NIF into the official ranks of government. But NIF fundamentalism has a modern look. Even the use of the word "trend" suggests something forward-looking, a process which is keeping abreast of contemporary behavior. Modern Islamization concerns itself with "secular" matters, such as Islamic banking, Islamic insurance companies, appeals to potential constituencies through the media, use of television for proselytizing, and recruiting women—if donned in *hijab*, Islamic dress—for political organizing.

Why do Sudanese leaders call religion into play during crises? Many popular and academic writings suggest that people embrace religion during periods of extreme deprivation or oppression, and that the "masses" accept a religious regime in the context of economic difficulties. But what of leadership motivation? Many people I interviewed stated simply that Nimeiri used Sharia in 1983 as a last resort ("opportunistic Islamism"), as his final power play. I would suggest instead that Islam is an integral part of the political culture and of popular culture, even though in Sudan, as elsewhere, religion may be manipulated by elites.

In the section below, I discuss some of the class and gender dynamics of the shift to Islamism.

Gender, Class, and Islam

In the years just after independence the state's expression of gender ideology usually took the form that a "developing" Sudan needed emancipated women. At that time, with the expressed need to build up the urban workforce, the term "emancipated" was thought of as synonymous with wage-earner. State apparatuses, such as Government media, civil service recruitment, and school curriculum urged the necessity for male-female partnership in developing Sudan. Media images presented the new Sudanese woman as sophisticated consumer or respectable civil servant (earlier as nurse or teacher and later sometimes as doctors). By the early 1960s the state could point proudly to the first women doctors. During the 1970s, however, capital-intensive economic schemes, the appearance of multinational corporations and agencies, uneven regional development, labor migration, ethnic power realignments, and developments in cultural imperialism led to socio-political and economic crises.[9] The unemployment rate rose and salaries did not keep up with inflation. One of the results was an enormous increase in male labor out-migration. This affected gender arrangements, although initially not so profoundly because the out-migration was of working class or minor civil service personnel. But soon a "brain drain" set in of intellectuals and middle to senior level personnel. This coincided with World Bank and IMF pressure to prune the overburdened civil service. At the same time, women began to move into better jobs, ones perceived by some to be the preserve of men.[10]

In Sudan, as elsewhere, the class base of Islamism is the middle-class. Islamic fundamentalism, at least in the form of the Muslim Brotherhood of Sudan, and now including the Islamism of Sudan's NIF, mainly recruits from the urban professional middle-class. There is some evidence that Islamic ideology is suited to middle-class interests, and especially to the commercial class. According to Jay Spaulding, commercial capitalism began to replace feudalism in the Nile Valley about 1800, a process which was accelerated after the Turco-Egyptian conquest of 1821. Aristocracy gave way to a new middle class which, consisting mainly of merchants, needed a more sophisticated legal and commercial code. Islam was the obvious choice.[11] This relationship between Islam and the middle class and Islam and capitalist activity is on the rise today. That is, Islam, as an ideology, is often a reflection of these commercial class interests. Although the Brotherhoods of both Egypt and Sudan are interested in the commercial aspect of Islam, it is with Sudan's NIF that we see a highly sophisticated rationalization and articulation of Islam and commerce—especially banking and insurance.

If Sudanese Islamism appeals to the modern middle class and recruits from among professionals, what of its stance toward women? Islamists often promote an atavistic and essentialist image of women—the family upholding the moral fabric of society—which they regard as functional for the movement. In a context of high unemployment, the romanticizing of reproduction could pressure women out of the labor force or steer them into "appropriate" jobs. Islamism appears to discriminate against women in the spheres of law and employment.

And yet, the case of Sudan presents some unexpected anomalies, for the NIF also claims "equal participation" for women.

Women's participation in the formal workforce increased at a regular, if somewhat slow pace during the years following independence. In the 1970s the liberal ideology of capitalism had been effectively disseminated throughout urban Sudanese society; a woman with a wage was seen as an important element in the society, and legal and constitutional apparatuses seemed to support that idea. Moreover, many women *have to* work for wages outside the home, although this is rarely acknowledged. Throughout, women have received contradictory legal and constitutional messages. On the one hand, they achieved the vote in 1965; later they were given equal pay for equal work; and in 1975 they won the right to pensions. Public Service Regulations also give women special benefits such as paid maternity leaves. The same Permanent Constitution of 1973 that paved the way for a more Islamized Sudan also provided equality for women in a number of areas: Part III, which deals with human rights and duties, makes no gender distinction, and does not exclude women. In fact, Article 38 provides that "The Sudanese have equal rights and duties irrespective of origin, race, locality, *sex*, language or religion."[12]

Article 56 is a workforce anti-discrimination clause which covers gender. Women are given equal education rights, the right to hold public office, freedom of association and unionization, and freedom of speech and *movement*. Women and children are even accorded *special* protection by the state in Article 55. On the other hand, there is little doubt that the rules of civil and criminal law, procedure and evidence, now discriminate against women, and that other agencies of the state ignore some constitutional rights. For instance, despite freedom of movement guarantees in the Constitution, a relatively new (1987) Women's Committee (consisting of one man) was formed in the Department of Passports, Immigration and Nationality for the purpose of assuring that any woman who is traveling alone abroad has the permission of a male relative—her father, husband, son—before she is issued an exit visa. Although University of Khartoum anthropologist Zeinab el-Bakri criticized this committee in a 1988 newspaper article, the committee and the requirement stand.

By the 1980s a national debate had emerged (which continues) around whether or not there were too many women being allowed to study medicine—notwithstanding the fact that over 80 percent of male medical graduates go abroad for more lucrative positions. Conservatives, underpinned by Ikhwan and later NIF ideas, mainly took the position that women doctors are needed, but that they should be directed into *appropriate* fields of medicine. The fields which are inappropriate for women are surgery and obstetrics; these are both seen as too physically strenuous for women, especially for women with families, as they may be called away from their family duties at any time of the day or night. Women had begun to invade these fields, which are, incidentally, the most lucrative in Sudanese medicine. Many well-known women doctors with impeccable credentials are deprived of senior positions in certain areas of medicine. There is an attempt by the Ministry of Health to channel women into Mother and Child Health clinics, into Public Health positions (which is still undeveloped in Sudan in terms of the power in policy-making that public health can mean in other areas), and, more significantly, into general medicine.[13] NIF women doctors have organized themselves extensively within the field of general medicine and act as apologists for the channelling of women into this sphere.

This is the modern approach of the NIF. Women should only work if they do not have children and only if their income is needed by the family. This means that Islam and Sharia make allowances for working-class women who need to work. But there are limits. The jobs women have should not threaten the power structure and should be appropriate, that is, they should be extensions of their domestic labor and reflect the "essence" of woman.

In a study of Iranian women in the post-revolutionary workforce, Val Moghadam examined the effectiveness of the initial state rhetoric discouraging women's employment and imposing an ideology of domesticity and found a "discrepancy between ideological prescriptions and economic imperatives."[14] There are similar contradictions in the NIF's ideological prescriptions and the society's economic imperatives, as for example, in the cases of female participation in medicine and agriculture. However, there is a less ambiguous response to jobs in the informal sector of the economy held by lower class women, such as vendors of local brew, prostitutes, and some entertainers; these are under attack as affronts to Islam.[15]

Public Debates on the Ideal Islamic Woman

In my interviews in 1988, I asked a series of questions about the changes respondents anticipated in their daily lives once Sharia is implemented. Some of these were "experts" in the field: two judges (one a woman Sharia judge, another a southerner), several lawyers and doctors, some religious figures, a number of educators. Others were uneducated, non-literate and working-class women whose lives had been disrupted by the 1983 September Laws; others described themselves as "ordinary women" (middle-class "housewives," clerks in government offices, and the like). The interviewees also spanned the political spectrum.

Through these interviews, both formal and informal, and by studying the popular press (which was very active at the time, with over forty newspapers in existence), I was privy to an active public debate in the summer of 1988 about the potential impact on various groups if Hassan al-Turabi and Saddig al-Mahdi, under the Islamic Trend banner, succeeded in consummating the Islamization process through strict application of Sharia. Although for years the secularist Women's Union (Sudan Communist Party affiliate) had been the major voice in debates about women, for complex reasons of politics and personnel, by 1988 it had lost a great deal of influence in this "democratic" era (1985-1989).[16] Instead, the debate on women's rights was coopted by the activist voices of the Islamists and conservative wings of old sectarian parties— such organizations as *al-Jabha al-Nisa'iyya al-Wataniyya* (the National Women's Front or NWF), the women's wing of the *Ikhwan* and NIF, the women's wing of the Umma Party (led by Sara al-Fadl, Saddig al-Mahdi's wife) and even earlier by the women's organization of the Sudan Socialist Union. In a cooptation of the left discourse, the NWF spoke of helping working women, fighting sex discrimination in employment, extending maternity leave, offering free transportation for women workers, and organizing women in the informal sector. But the main goal was expressed in familiar essentialist language: to build an image of the "ideal Muslim woman." This image was both reactive and proactive. Much of the organizing was clearly directed toward designing the ideal Islamic woman and family. Goals were to educate women about Islam, "make women aware of their rights according to the Quran and Sunni and to tell them about the values of religion ... to educate her with the values and beliefs of the religion." With the establishment of kindergartens, the "children should be brought up in an Islamic way."[17]

By 1988 Islamic welfare work was certainly a dominant function listed for the women's organizations registered under the Ministry of Social Welfare, and virtually all the organizations (about twenty) aimed to create nurseries; work on childrearing, health and nutrition; build awareness; and "eradicate bad customs." The Association of Sudanese Women Believers stated as its objectives that they want "the whole of Sudan together in one group as God wishes; [to] teach correct childrearing, Islamic Studies, and patriotism ... [and to] make people aware of Islam." The Charity Union of Worshippers of God aimed "to give importance to Muslim women ... [and] encourage Islamic instructions." The Charity Association of Imam el-Mahdi for Women (Ansar sect) aimed "To encourage a modern Islamic society and make a link between individual behavior and the behavior of a person in Islam and to encourage Mahdist culture under Islamic culture."[18]

One of the more active moral welfare groups was the Association of Leading Reformers that militated against illicit unions by performing televized free mass wedding ceremonies for the poor in the football stadium, *zowag el-kora* (reference to putting all the people in a bowl and marrying them). Because marriage and wedding expenses had become prohibitive for most of the poor, this *Jumaya Raidat el-Nahda* was an effective organizing strategy and spread to other Islamist political parties such as Umma.

Even Islamic economic institutions have been active in creating the ideal Islamic woman and her family. A Development Cooperative Islamic Bank was established in 1983 "to enable women who have training in home economics to purchase their work requirements; the bank strives to establish family production societies."[19] However, a more reactive approach was taken to interaction between the sexes. The Chair of the SSU Women's Union, Nafissa Ahmed el-Amin, was barred from chairing a session in Khartoum on "Women's Rights under Islam" at the First International Islamic Conference on the Implementation of Sharia. A protest had been filed by the Saudi delegation that it was not Islamic to permit a woman to chair a meeting where men were present.[20]

These attempts to remold Sudanese women to fit an ideal image of the Muslim women were not totally accepted. There were outcries in 1988 from very religious working-class women. Nurses and workers from Abu Anja Hospital in Omdurman expressed defiance against attempts to shape their lives through Sharia. One very old Arab Muslim said she would "take to the streets again" if Sharia were re-implemented. Another, a Muslim woman from the Nuba Mountains, said:

> I am just a Muslim. ... I'm not fanatic, but I am religious. ... What they say about the equality of men and women in Sharia is false. They [women] are not equal in the eyes of Sharia—even if they do the same job their wages are not equal; the way they are viewed is not equal. There is discrimination. ... I want absolute equality with men. ... I'm doing the same job, so why not?[21]

A senior male doctor at another hospital, an activist in the now-banned Doctors Union, criticized impending segregated schooling which would result in inferior resources for women and less effective medical care for women patients. He was already not being allowed by his women patients to examine them from the neck down.[22]

Taha Ibrahim, a lawyer and vocal critic of implementation of Sharia, argued that Islamization was religious manipulation by Nimeiri, Saddig, and Turabi to save the Islamic banks, a common thread throughout my interviews. Ibrahim also described women under Sharia as deprivation of capacity and legitimacy as a legal entity. He stressed:

> Islam knows two sorts of male/female relationships (1) buying her—as a slave—and he can do anything with her he likes—violate her in any way ... he also owns his own children and can sell them ... (2) marriage: in Islam the relationship is based solely on buying and selling ... he owns her ... he owns her sexual parts ... to such an extent that, if she is ill and cannot give him what he wants at any time he wants, she cannot collect alimony. So, with the dower [*mahr*] he buys her sexuality.[23]

To Ibrahim, the onset of Sharia would have an adverse effect on the lives of everyone, but especially women and non-Muslims.

Republican activist Batoul Mukhtar Mohamed Taha wrote a series of provocative newspaper articles in 1988, one of them challenging the right of the two NIF women representatives in the People's Assembly to represent all women. Claiming that society needs to value women as human beings, "not as a mere type, the 'female'," she argued that the two NIF women accept traditionalist assumptions that men are the custodians of women, agree with the marriage of four women to one man, the woman's "house of obedience," with the beating of women, and concede the exclusive and unilateral right of divorce to men.[24]

Other women, reassessing themselves in relation to society, expressed uncertainties and were clearly affected by the activism of the Islamist women. One told me:

> There are elements in society—mainly women—who are creating a revolution—and because it is coming from women considered conservative or traditional, it is very confusing to women like me— educated, liberal women.[25]

It was clear too that, by 1988, NIF ideology about the nature of woman and the ideal role of women had permeated middle-class urban society. Five students I interviewed at the University of Khartoum, members of the Democratic Unionist Party (the DUP's base is the *Khatmiyya* sect), Umma, and "secularist" Baath, expressed views of women strikingly similar to those of the NIF. One hijab-wearing woman, whose family is DUP, stressed the importance of women's place in the home: "She has something more important to do at home— looking after the children, teaching them properly—their norms, their values." Another woman, not wearing a hijab or tobe, and from an umma family, said that although women get equal pay in Sudan, they have a poor work record. To a male student who is self-described Sufist from a DUP family, the traditional role of woman was valorized: "She has babies and she deals with the three stages of the human being. She has a wide experience. This job cannot be done by a man. It is the most important job, more so than engineers or architects." All of the students agreed that it was the man's *responsibility* to work outside the home, but the woman's *duty* to be at home.[26]

During my 1988 stay in Sudan, the most visible Islamist woman activist was Suad al-Fatih al-Badawi, one of the only two women representatives in the People's Assembly, both of them NIF members. In her statements to the press, she took great effort to be forward-looking and open, stating, for example, that, "We [NIF] are not opposed to corrections and changes [in the current Sharia laws] so long as ... [they do not] take us back to the English laws." Moreover,

> I do believe in separate roles [for men and women] in the construction of the nation. Men and women complete and perfect each other. ... It was an obligation for women [to make] the representation of women *authentic* and *real.* ... Those women who have attained a high level of consciousness which is *progressive* and *untainted* by blind imitation of both the East and the West must not be stingy with their intellectual effort. ... This era is marked by issues of development which the *enlightened vanguard* must struggle to solve in a fundamental way.[27]

The second woman NIF representative, Hikmat Sid Ahmed, whom I interviewed, echoed Suad al-Fatih's statements and also presented woman as responsible for the education of the new generations. In an *Al-Sahaafa* article and in our interview she presented a "correct model" for teaching that is the same for home, school, and work. She expressed concern for women who are gainfully employed as "partners" in the construction of the nation. She made a plea for good Islamic childcare institutions, but also for technical training in the use of local raw materials to substitute for foreign imports.[28]

It was clear from Hikmat Sid Ahmed that only women who *have* to work should work, and only if they have "appropriate" childcare (preferably a close relative).[29] When I pressed the issue, it became apparent that Islamic nurseries were to be constructed for working-class women whose abilities to raise their children in an "Islamic way" are seen by the NIF as limited. The state, then, would substitute its Islamic teachings. In the interim, intense missionary work was being carried out by NIF women in existing nurseries.

Of the five Islamist women I interviewed more than once and in different settings, three of them—well-educated, professional, and upper middle to upper class—gave me the fullest explanation of the *ideal Muslim woman.* Nagwa Kamal Farid who is no longer active in public politics, was Sudan's first woman Sharia judge; Wisal al-Mahdi is a lawyer, wife of Hassan al-Turabi, sister of Saddig al-Mahdi, and an NIF activist; and Hikmat Sid-Ahmed, mentioned above, was an NIF representative in the government and is an Arabic teacher. Prior to a group interview, judge Nagwa Kamal had explained to me women's many rights in Sharia and what she described as the "differences in small detail" in the everyday life of men and women. Concerning going to the mosque, she said:

> Men get 27 percent more benefit from praying at the mosque. Going in a group gives more benefit than if you pray alone ... it is better for women to pray at home and not go to the mosque at all. She has duties at home. But if she prays at home, she has the same benefits as men. Men are compelled to go [that is, for women it is voluntary].

About polygamy, she commented:

> The reason for this [men being allowed to have four wives] is that for some men one wife is not enough. Instead of playing around with other women, he should get married. ... If the first wife does not have kids, this gives him a better excuse. But even if there is not an excuse, he has the right for another wife—just because we want him to be a good Muslim. ... Maybe the first wife was not one he wanted, [or] maybe his first wife got old, and men do not get old as quickly as women, so he thinks of having another wife. Why not? It is better than having him look around outside of marriage.

As for inequities in inheritance, Nagwa took the strong position that Sharia protects women so that they never have to support themselves. In her words:

If Sharia were implemented here in Sudan, life would be very different and people would be much happier. No woman would be needing anything. ... People keep asking why in Sharia women get less [inheritance] than men. But the situation is that she is not supposed to support herself; that burden falls on men, so they need more inheritance.

All of the interviewees agreed that Sharia permits a woman to work, but Nagwa added, with the others, that:

There is one condition in Islam [in allowing a woman to go out to work]. It says that the first ... message for the woman ... is to raise her children and take care of her house. So, if she wants to go to work she should be well-dressed, not too much perfume so as not to attract attention. ... She has to go out respectably ... to cover her hair, all of her face and hands should be inside, not too colourful. ... When a man stands beside her, he should remember work and nothing else.

She continued by saying that some women workers set very bad examples: lack of punctuality, too many sick days, and the like: "She's there; her effect is there, but she's not there working." Also on the subject of work, Wisal al-Mahdi claimed that, "there is no program as such of the NIF to take women out of the workforce." And Hikmat added that they need women to work.

The three narrators of this interview also commented on the *nature of woman* and the inherent differences between men and women, especially related to the dictate in Sharia that during criminal proceedings, two women witnesses are required to offset the testimony of one man. Hikmat explained:

We know that women are different from men ... women, by their *nature*, sometimes forget. Sometimes they sympathize with somebody. Perhaps he may be a criminal ... when one of them [woman witness] forgets, the other will remind her, and if one of them sympathized with the criminal, the other could correct her. ... I don't think it is a problem for women to find themselves treated differently in the court ... because it is *natural* ... the entire principle [in Sharia] is in accord with the way women are *created*, since women are *naturally empathetic* (italics mine).

Wisal gave en example of a murder trial:

[I]n a situation of somebody taking a ... knife and stabbing another, a woman would be so much *excited* that she would not recognize exactly what happened, because after all, a *woman is weaker than a man* and all her *nervous system* is made different [from a man's] ... so she may say something that she believes ... happened, not what she saw happen. ... Women are more *sentimental,* because they are the mothers who breed children. ... That is why, in Sharia law we guard against the sentimentality ['*aatifiyya*', 'empathy', 'compassion', 'sympathy'] of *womankind* (italics mine).

Wisal al-Mahdi maintained that women have a broad range of options under Islam and Sharia and that, if there are differences spelled out in the law, it is because women are different by nature—and that they should want it that way: "We are *women* after all. ... I am *not* like a man." But she went on to say that a woman can be anything or do anything.

All three women agreed that men oppress women, that Arabs have a low opinion of women, and that Arab men try to give a false idea to women about their rights under Sharia. Nagwa commented, "Sudan is still a man's society ... the man is the boss." Wisal, in commenting on a very conservative group, *Ansar al-Sunna,* which opposed any public activity by women, said, "They are against women. ... They think a woman's voice is like woman's breasts showing." She repeated it in Arabic, "*Sawt al-mar'a 'awra,* a woman's voice is a private part that must be concealed."

Wisal al-Mahdi was the main feminist commentator in her defiant statements against male oppression of women:

They [Arab men] are against women, and that is why *we are much against them.* We know our rights; we have learned the Quran and Sharia; we know what Sharia gives us. ... We think that *women are better human beings* than they think. ... And ... *we are standing up for our sex.* We are working in the NIF *to praise women* and to make women have a better status and to tell the world that we are as equal as men and are as efficient as men and we are as educated as men and we are as good as men and as great as men (italics mine).

Wisal reminded me that, "We are Muslims *by nature,*" and that the NIF is not doing anything different except to give more emphasis to the Islamic nature of society.

We want Islam to be practiced in everyday life, not just inside the house. ... We don't want it to be only a corner of the life of the family. We want it to be the *core* of life ... [for] the whole society and the whole Sudan and the whole Muslim world.

The devotion and commitment to the NIF on the part of women was striking, as was their militancy and defiance. Nonetheless, their language was contradictory. This reflected, on the one hand, an internalized view of women as weak, emotional, and sentimental, and as having as their primary duty the domestic sphere; on the other hand, these women are defiant and are actively pursuing a change in the status of women in a sea of male hostility. That they seek this change in an Islamist framework is why I see at least one of them, Wisal al-Mahdi, not as "feminist," but as what Margot Badran in this volume calls a "gender activist." This is not to overlook the fact that these women—the leaders—also have class interests.

Women are among the most active and *visible* organizers. The strong appeal that the party has for women is, at least superficially, manifested in the fact that at the universities over 50 percent of the students are wearing the hijab.[30] I would estimate that at the University of Khartoum this represents an increase of over 40 percent in less than a decade. At the level of the state—and within political movements related to state formation—there are requirements for maintaining the gender ideology while balancing labor needs. Within the NIF, for example, there are contradictions in terms of the availability of human resources and the imperatives of the organizational strategies of such a small group. That is, despite some ideological prohibitions, women are needed by the NIF for many political tasks.

Women are, of course, relied on to socialize the young with the Islamic values and to carry out this job at such locations as the nursery schools that the NIF is establishing in mosques all over Sudan. But this socialization duty is also actively carried out in the schools where the NIF has been organizing since the 1950s and where there are mainly women teachers. The NIF can point to this *public* activity of NIF women in answering the clichéd charge that if the party were to come to power, it would send women back into home. Likewise, to defend against their critics' charge that the only tasks women are given are but extensions of their domestic labor and part of their essentialized view of women, the party at that time was able to point to the fact that the only two women elected to the People's Assembly were NIF representatives. These two politicians, Suad al-Fathi and Hikmat Sid Ahmed, have high public visibility—even though the People's Assembly itself was abolished by the 1989 military junta. Furthermore, the wives of NIF politicians are known to be active behind the scenes and in public.

Wisal al-Mahdi is a good example because, although her house is segregated into women's and men's quarters, she adheres to the hijab, and her lifestyle is one that follows strict Islamic dictates about the roles of men and women, she considers herself a powerful force "behind" her husband and an activist in her own right.

Conclusions

This chapter has examined identity politics as a strategy of and reaction to state and/or party hegemonic processes. I have examined one party, the NIF, Sudan's modern Islamists, to analyze the manipulation of religious ideology toward a more "native" culture, and have explored the centrality of women in this process. We have seen that there is an attempt by the Islamists to create a new trend in the gender division of labor whereby women are active in the workforce, but only under the conditions that fulfill the requirements of the party/state. Islamist women, at least the activists, are complicit in both of these processes.

While current Islamists argue that men and women are regarded in Sharia as complementary, for reasons of the need for state control over the gender division of labor and the necessity to abrogate Western values and deny Western imported goods, particular representations are now being conflated: woman/family and sometimes woman/ family/Islamic community (*umma*). The modern Islamist woman is the *embodiment* of the Islamic nation and the reproducer of its culture. But she must also carry out some of the other significant tasks of nation-building. These expectations, then, often require that she earn wages, that she hold office, drive a car, get an education, educate the children, and the like. She becomes, then, the *modern Islamic woman*, in line with NIF ideology.

There is every indication that the various Islamic groups—and at this point the NIF is the most influential and powerful—will *not* assault the numbers of women in working-class or traditional occupations, but that there will be selective control over women's access to power and privilege, both private and public. I expect an intensification of the representation of Sudanese women as *ideal Muslim women* in the media, in the school curricula, and in family ideology.

The National Islamic Front is now a dynamic component of the state. The state constructs gender matrices to control human resources. When economic crises have to be addressed, they are rarely ever articulated in secular terms, but are often rationalized along religious lines. Religions, because of their fundamentally moralist, normative, and prescriptive core regarding sexuality, reproduction, the sexual division of labor, and the family, are useful in protecting class interests and in obscuring secular/economic interests.

Notes

The fieldwork for this chapter, part of a larger project on northern Sudan, was carried out in 1988 in Greater Khartoum. Thanks are due to my Khartoum field assistants, Amal Abdel Rahman and Sunita Pitamber, to my UCLA research assistant, William Young, for his excellent translations, to Sherifa Zuhur, and to Val Moghadam for her careful editing.

1. My approach to the state is inspired by Antonio Gramsci, *Selections from the Prison Notebooks* (London: Lawrence and Wishart, 1971), and on women and the state by Carole Pateman, *The Sexual Contract* (Stanford: Stanford University Press, 1988); *The Disorder of Women* (Stanford: Stanford University Press, 1989).

2. The zaar, usually referred to as a spirit possession cult, is a women's ritual in which a possessed woman is the focus of a gathering of her friends and zaar functionaries who, through various mechanisms of self-help and solidarity address the woman's grievances (usually against a male relative).

3. Some women's potentially liberatory cultural identity and practices (for example, the zaar) may be consciously thwarted by both secular and Islamist interest groups, while other aspects of culture with problematic emancipatory aspects for women may be either consciously encouraged (or coerced), viewed with acquiescence, or rationalized. See my "Transforming Culture or Fostering Second-Hand Consciousness? Women's Front Organizations and Revolutionary Parties — the Sudan Case," in Judith Tucker (ed.), *Women in Arab Society* (Bloomington: Indiana University Press, 1993).

4. For a historical background on Islam in Sudan and religious sects, see J. S. Trimingham, *Islam in the Sudan* (London: Oxford University Press, 1949); for politics in the modern period, see, inter alia, Tim Niblock, *Class and Power: The Dynamics of Sudanese Politics, 1898-1985* (New York: State University of New York Press, 1987); Gabriel Warburg, *Islam, Nationalism and Communism in a Traditional Society: The Case of Sudan* (London: Frank Cass, 1978); Peter Woodward, *Sudan, 1898-1989: The Unstable State* (Boulder, Colorado: Lynne Rienner Publishers, 1990); Afaf Abu Hasabu, *Factional Conflict in the Sudanese Nationalist Movement* (Khartoum: Graduate College Publications No. 12, University of Khartoum, 1985). For an analysis of Sudan's civil war see Sondra Hale, "Sudan Civil War: Religion, Colonialism, and the World System," in Suad Joseph and Barbara Pillsbury (eds.), *Muslim-Christian Conflicts: Economic, Political, and Social Origins* (Boulder, Colorado: Westview, 1978).

5. Most of these projects were focussed on rural development, such as the Kennana Sugar Scheme, a partnership of the Sudanese government, Kuwait,

Lonrho, the Arab Investment Company, a Japanese company, and Gulf International Corporation. Mahmoud asserts that the policy weakened the state and increased the dependency of the bourgeoisie on the metropolitan centers. Fatima Babiker Mahmoud, *The Sudanese Bourgeoisie: Vanguard of Development?* (London: Zed Press, 1984), pp. 70-72.

6. Dina Sheikh el-Din Osman, "The Legal Status of Muslim Women in Sudan," *Journal of Eastern African Research and Development* 15 (1985):124-142; and Carolyn Fluehr-Lobban, *Islamic Law and Society in the Sudan* (London: Frank Cass, 1987).

7. A number of sources document the "brain drain," but only in my interviews were the phenomena linked. Interviews in Khartoum with Dr. Afaf Abu Hasabu, United Nations Development Programmes, July 19, 1998; Dr. Nahid Toubia, July 22, 1988; and Fawzia Hammour, Women's Studies Coordinator, University of Khartoum, June 16, 1988.

8. See John Esposito, *Islam and Politics*. Revised 2nd edition (Syracuse: Syracuse University Press, 1987), especially pp. 283-284. See also Khalid Duran, "The Centrifugal Forces of Religion in Sudanese Politics," *Orient* 26 (1985):572-600, and John Esposito, "Sudan," in Shireen T. Hunter (ed.), *The Politics of Islamic Revivalism* (Bloomington: Indiana University Press, 1988).

9. For useful analyses of Sudan's crisis, see Tony Barnett, "Introduction: The Sudanese Crisis and the Future," in Tony Barnett and Abbas Abdelkarim (eds.), *Sudan: State, Capital, and Transformation* (London: Croom Helm, 1988) and Norman O'Neill and Jay O'Brien, *Economy and Class in Sudan* (Aldershot, Hants: Gower [Avebury], 1988).

10. See Nur el-Tayib Abdel Gadir, *Al-Ma'a al-Amila fi es-Sudan* [The Working Woman in Sudan] (Khartoum: Department of Labour and Social Security, Division of Research, Information, and Media, 1984) and Samia El-Nagar, *Patterns of Women* [sic] *Participation in the Labour Force in Khartoum* (Unpublished Ph.D. Thesis, Sociology, University of Khartoum, 1985). Information also based on the interviews with Abu Hasabu, Toubia, and Hammour cited in Note 7.

11. Jay Spaulding, *The Heroic Age in Sinnar* (East Lansing: Michigan State University Press, 1985).

12. Osman, "The Legal Status of Muslim Women", p. 126 (italics in original).

13. Information based on an interview with Dr. Nahid Toubia, Khartoum, July 22, 1988. She took part in the debates and is an ex-member of the Council of Surgeons and former Head of Pediatric Surgery, Khartoum Hospital. The same debate arose around the increased numbers of women being admitted to the prestigious Faculty of Agriculture, University of Khartoum, long an exclusively male bastion. Allowing women into the field means gender power-sharing in an agricultural society where women perform a higher percentage of

agricultural labor. Part of the debate was captured in *SudanNow*, "Letters" (October 1979 and January 1980).

14. See Val Moghadam, "Women, Work, and Ideology in the Islamic Republic," *International Journal of Middle East Studies* 20 (1988):221-243. Moghadam found that government employment for women was somewhat higher in the mid-1980s than before the revolution (p. 221), but that there was a class difference, that is, the rates for lower middle class women had actually increased, but "Thus far, educated, Western-oriented, upper-middle-class women have borne the brunt of the regime's most retrograde policies ..." (p. 239).

15. See Batoul Taha's critique in the local press, Batoul Mukhtar Taha, "Today, No Guardian," *SudanNow* 13 (January-February 1987).

16. See Sondra Hale, "Feminist Method, Process, and Self-Criticism: Interviewing Sudanese Women," in Sherna Gluck and Daphne Patai (eds.), *Women's Worlds: The Feminist Practice of Women's Oral History* (London: Routledge, 1991).

17. Sudan Socialist Union, *Summary of Working Plans for the Offices of the Executive Office of the Union of Sudanese Women* (Khartoum: Sudan Socialist Union, Section for Political and Organization Affairs, n.d.).

18. All quotes from Ministry of Social Welfare, *Women's Organizations Registered under the Ministry of Social Welfare* (Khartoum: Ministry of Social Welfare, n.d.), pp. 4-5.

19. See *SudanNow* (10 September 1985), p. 14.

20. See *SudanNow* (9 November 1984), p. 12.

21. A series of interviews with doctors, nurses, and workers at Abu Anja Hospital were carried out on June 20, 1988. Because of the repressiveness of the current regime, I have not named anyone in this essay who is still in the country, whose views were not already written or well-known, or who said anything self-incriminating against Sharia, Islam, the Islamization process, or particular political parties.

22. Interview in Khartoum at the headquarters of the Doctors Union, June 18, 1988.

23. Interview in Khartoum North, July 10, 1988. His view was echoed by a number of women interviewees.

24. See Batoul Mukhtar Taha, *SudanNow* (May 16, 1988), p. 8. The Republicans [formerly Republican Brothers] have spent years in court trying to prove the unconstitutionality of Sharia. Additional information from my written interview with Taha, August 3, 1988.

25. Interview in Khartoum, July 14, 1988, with a professional woman with a Ph.D. in Public Administration.

26. The quotes from the University of Khartoum students are all from a June 30, 1988 group interview.

27. Both quotes are from *Al-Sahaafa* (May 3, 1986), p. 10, italics by the author.
28. *Ibid.*

29. The following statements by Hikmat Sid Ahmed or Wisal al-Mahdi are from an interview at the home of the latter and her husband, Hassan al-Turabi, July 12, 1988. Nagwa Kamal Farid participated in that interview, but was also interviewed alone on July 4, 1988, in Khartoum. Statements are taken from both interviews.

30. Information from a July 17, 1988 interview with University of Khartoum, Anthropology Honors student, Mohamed Osman, who had taken a sample of students for his unpublished paper on "The Social and Political Aspects of the Veil."

8

Feminism and Muslim Fundamentalism: The Tunisian and Algerian Cases

Alya Baffoun

Introduction:
The Usurpation of the "Feminine" by
the "Masculine" in the Arab Hemisphere

Throughout the varied social structures in the Arab World, feminism is as difficult to be articulated to socialism (consider the Algerian case) as it is to economic liberalism (consider Tunisia or petro-dollar Kuwait). Paradoxically, women who have massively contributed in the nationalist movements of liberation have been relegated to political back scenes and inferior economic sectors, once the Nation-State has been established. In the Algerian case this outcome invalidated the optimistic hypotheses of Frantz Fanon. Thus, notwithstanding internal differences of many types, the Arab hemisphere seems to draw its homogeneity and its common cultural background from the superstructures whose most outstanding markers are a static and ahistorical view of women.

In social practice, resistance to changes in the situation of women is expressed in a markedly unequal struggle between the sexes where women are denied—no matter what their abilities and scopes—access to power, prime responsibility, and decision-making. The infantilization of women and the denial of their maturity are generators of scorn and the very sources of contradictions. Conflicts, disorders and violence in human relationships, damaging family life and society alike, have been examined in a multitude of surveys.

How are we to interpret patriarchy's exasperating vigilance and the attempt at the "confinement" of Arab women in spite of historical developments?[1] The reason may be a refusal to divide power among two different sex categories, but further than that, there is the unconscious desire in Arab society to preserve its identity in quasi obsessional modes in the face of a reality it fails to comprehend and with which it hardly identifies. Indeed, these regions of conquest and noble civilizations, whose very identity has been mitigated by the trials of history and the hazards of colonialism have determined to desperately safeguard the last signposts and bastions of their collective ego. The female as the ultimate reference matrix bears within her deepest being those very notions through which societies identify and by which they name themselves.

The most aggressive speeches and acts (I refer here to relentless acts of violence against Arab women, reported daily by newspapers and in courts) unveil the gripping fear that "women too might join in the flight" notwithstanding the alienation and the state of absolute dependence of the Arab societies induced by their insertion in the international division of labor. Everything echoes with "if they slip out of our hands ... who else will acknowledge us? Let us subdue them." Arab women play the role of a lifebuoy to which one holds on in an turbulent ocean. In fact the lifebuoy is far from being satisfactory. The desire to confine the Arab woman in the position of a guardian of a lost identity is a blind attitude of negation of an estranged ungraspable social reality that might devastate us if we do not foster our creative spirit. Freedom would then surge from the abysses of ourselves but also from the real and actual needs of those societies where, as noted by Berque, the "masculine in various respects blocks off and unsurpates the feminine."

The remainder of this section offers preliminary remarks to the study of the strategies used in the unequal sexual order and its aggravation in times of social upheaval, beginning with a historical perspective on the oppression of women.

Throughout human history, and notwithstanding the mode of production and the stage of evolution of any given society, the position of women is distinguished with very rare exceptions by social inequality in comparison with men's. The ubiquity of such a state of subjection and domination remains the most striking fundamental constant in the development of humanity. Engels observed that the oppression of women was the first of all forms of oppression and that "it marked, along with slavery and private property, the beginnings of that very era continuing to our present times in which each stage of progress is a relative regressive step, as the well-being and the development of some are achieved through the misery and the repression of others."[2] Of all these human phenomena, inequality between the sexes is observed consistently and its obsessional perpetuation is sustained and reproduced throughout successive generations as one of the most complex and interesting issues. Likewise, it is, in our view, one of the most paradoxical and aberrant inequalities, as this subordination is initiated by men against the one being that is closest to them and to whom they relate through blood and quasi-organic ties: mothers, sisters, wives, and so on.[3]

Such inequality, continued most irrationally in human history, delivers its tragedies to the daily lives of peoples and orchestrates their pathologies and reactionary comportment. It is indeed in these very existential daily realities of women, their subjection and subordination by the male category and their devastating implications, that any humanist reflection should be grounded. The highly male-saturated field of social sciences lacks concern in the psycho-social significance of the state of women and their subjection in terms of social pathology for both sex categories, as well as in terms of basic social injustices. Our precociously manipulated subconsciousness fails to consider this as the most urgent human issue to examine and the most difficult to abolish.

Today, totalling half the population of the earth, and due to mere genetic chance upon which a tremendously humiliating superstructure has been built, women perform two-thirds of the work made in the world in utter exploitation and oppression, receive one-tenth of the income and own less than one-hundredth of the planet's riches.[4] This compels us to urgently examine the mechanisms set up to perpetuate the ancient subjection of women and the alarming female poverty throughout the globe in order to denounce the strategies contrived to reproduce such injustices dressed in insidious modes whether symbolic or ideological and impaired with complacency. The modern feminist movement, with its critique launched against a six-thousand-year-old male order, bears the seeds of the greatest cultural revolution to come. This is a revolution that does not aim to supplant an exclusive female order for an exclusive male order, but one that will substitute structures and a culture emanating from humanity as a whole with its female as well as male components.[5]

Social Crisis and Reductionist Ideology:
Theoretical Framework

The rise of ideologies militating against the liberation of women is not specific to Muslim societies (for example, Iran, Pakistan, Algeria, Sudan), but manifests itself in other religious and national communities, as the chapters in this book reveal so well. Nor is it a novel phenomenon in the history of humanity. In all cases, anti-feminist ideologists coincide with or result from social and economic upheavals. A well-known European example is the perverse effects of the thirties' depression and the succeeding fascist movements: German Nazism with its notorious slogan about women "Kinder, Kirche, Küche." Fascism in Italy, sexism in Belgium, and Stalin's conservatism on women—all have attempted and sometimes contrived successfully to set laws destined to diminish the freedom gained by women, to maintain the status quo, or to confine women in the home. In this context their procreative role was magnified to the detriment of their political and civil rights.

The fundamental principles of this view of women may be thus delineated:

- Housework is more appropriate to women than are other professions.
- Morbidity and mortality rates are higher among working women than among household women.
- Juvenile delinquency originates in disrupted families; conversely, the family is disrupted because of women's work.
- Female employment induces male unemployment; moreover, employment is a personal and family matter and should not be a matter of national planning.
- Working women's morality is dubious.

In the 1930s the Belgian Christian Democrats drafted laws that only the employers' need for cheap female labor was able to discourage.[6] Moreover, an actual return to the fertility and maternity cult, drawing on a mystical and mythological conception of women served to reinforce the pseudo-scientific procreative trend professing that "Doctors know that four to six child births are necessary for normal woman to avoid disorders. They know that these must be complete, in that they must comprise both child delivery and breast feeding ... ."[7] The Belgian sexist movement went further in the sense as it advocated capital punishment for women who would practice abortion. As the

Belgian left offered no viable alternative to this anti-feminist campaign, women were compelled to adhere to the fascist movement. Not until 1948 could Belgian women vote. This fascist vision and confiscation from women of a great part of their historical gains also served to displace social conflict. It functioned to manipulate social actors by giving them the illusion that evil had been identified and that difficulties had been smoothed out.

It should be clear by now that the present resurgence of custom, tradition and religion, with its negative implications for women, is not a novelty in the history of humanity. Ayesha Imam has noted that "With the wave of religious fundamentalism that has been sweeping the world recently, new religious groups and organizations have been springing up all over Africa. ... These ideologies, both traditionalist and religious, provide support for regimes by identifying a concern and reassuring people that something is being done. At the same time, they focus attention away from general question of exploitation or maldistribution of resources as well as from the specific issues of women's oppression. Not only do they rationalize it, but they legitimize measures to reinforce it. Thus for example, the bill to ban wife-beating was defeated because Kenyan MPs regard it as a traditional right of men to beat their wives. ... The Family Code is restructured in such a way that women would lose the right to divorce and become legal minors needing men to represent them. Similarly in Nigeria, non-married women were evicted by their landlords and denied access to public housing estates on the ground that this would promote immorality."[8]

Such ideologies aim to give more legitimacy to the authority of men over wives and sisters. They inculcate a sense of guilt in women who end up feeling that they are responsible for the ills of the society and at the same time flatter men's archaic, narcissistic and pre-genital tendencies.[9] These ideologies legitimize all forms of constraints on women and violence exercised against women, such as the " ... destruction of market women's stalls and beatings in Ghana in 1989, or in Zimbabwe in 1983, with the arrest of prostitutes and single women, or in Sokoto, Nigeria when prostitutes were arrested and released only if men paid fines and married them."[10]

The present fundamentalist ideology is a dangerous totalitarian product as it contrives to enslave symbolically and physically half of humanity, especially in the African and Arab Islamic regions. In the following, we shall discuss the salient features of this ideology, its complex relationship to the state, and its impact on women in society by focussing on two countries that share a cultural background and a colonial past, Tunisia and Algeria.

Muslim Women in Two Societies: Similarities

Until the recent upheavals in Iran, Islam was not perceived as a force of mobilization in the Islamic world (as was the case with anti-colonial struggles). Even so, the Orientalist Bernard Lewis observed that Muslim opposition movements have always drawn on the theological register in the same spontaneous fashion as Europeans drew on the register of ideology. More recently, Islam has proved to be an extremely important factor for political mobilization.

Today there is a patent dichotomy between two types of Islam. On the one hand, there is a more or less reformed official Islam and a modernized Islam. Examples are Tunisia under Bourguiba and Egypt under Nasser, where Kamal Ataturk's secular model had been adopted. Here secularization is a direct consequence of the autonomy of a civil society and the need to protect people of different beliefs by making religion a personal matter. On the other hand, there is a more popular and less scholastic Islam. The latter may espouse more radical activist pan-Islamic forms, often backed up by local or foreign financial aid; such movements are set against secular societies and the West which, it is believed, bear a harmful and a debasing influence. Today, the woman question according to fundamentalist Islamic trends is at the very center of this secularization and westernization.

Fundamentalist Islam's claims are to purge, regenerate, and return to the source. Such notions are in fact ambiguous and ill-defined when it comes to relating them to social actors and to quotidian life. They aim to drive back the Islamic nation to the right path by practicing an authentic Islam whose benefits they will enjoy. This fundamentalist Islam has witnessed two spectacular successful events during the last decade: the overthrow of the state and the massive popularity of the Ayatollah Khomeini in Iran, and the assassination of President Sadat in Egypt.

Yet a study of the social program embedded in this Islam, in spite of its being popular among certain social categories, reveals that it rests on a theoretical assemblage rather than on a systematic and an actual understanding of social issues. This form of activist Islam is not a lucid adaptation to modern times as it fails to comprehend that the autonomy of a civil society is a fundamental feature in a modern society based on the separation of political and economic life, regulated by laws that are independent and extrinsic to men's intents. Such, indeed, was advocated by Ibn Khaldoun as early as the fourteenth century in his Arab Maghreb Social Theory.

Today this attempt to return to the sources and to the Islamic golden age is ambiguous, in the sense that it is both the expression of a project aiming at transforming a reality felt to be unbearable and at the same time an impasse in the transformation of that reality. Nevertheless, such calls unveil the total absence of an alternative discourse, and this prohibits a genuine understanding of this unbearable reality. As a result injustices remain the same, and Arab-Islamic thought is trapped in the vicious circle of a moralizing discourse. It is "a pathetic form of thinking."[11]

The Islamist resurgence in Algeria and in Tunisia is best examined in the light of the following three factors: (1) the national system of government, (2) the cultural duality of the elite (comprised mainly of the petite bourgeoisie), and (3) the deficiencies of "modernization" in this part of the world, the economic depression, and its negative social and cultural consequences. The nation-state in Algeria and in Tunisia is characterized by a one-party system which leaves little space for other forms of political expression or association; it is an authoritarian and an anti-democratic state based on clientelism. These Maghrebian regimes draw their legitimacy from anti-colonial liberation movements (FLN in Algeria, Bourguiba and the Neo-Destour in Tunisia) and the independence movements of their countries dating back to the 1960s.

A mere generation after independence, these regimes found themselves with half of their population made up of young people aged under twenty who were confronted with vital problems obstructing their future, notably a high cost of living and high unemployment. These youth continue to search for a "social program" that would address the problems of daily life. But, the petite bourgeoisie, an important political fraction without the homogeneity of a social class, exercises domination over the nation-state. This class has never elaborated a social program that would involve the rest of social actors who find themselves marginalized and excluded from the mainstream of development even though they constitute large sections of the society: peasants, youth, women, workers, emigrant workers. Moreover, this petite bourgeoisie is distinguished by a cultural dualism that serves its own interests. On the one hand, it benefits from a modern culture that it assimilates to its native tongue in order to consolidate its economic power; on the other hand, it benefits from an attachment to traditional culture as a legitimation of its authority. The educational policy seems to reinforce such dualism by training a bureaucratic elite cut off the population.[12] The modern culture sustained by the petite bourgeoisie remains subordinated to a traditional culture established as an intangible value, and Laroui further adds that no one would want to see any modern rationalization go beyond the limits of the factory and the office, and to extend to either the socio-political domain or the household.

The persistence of traditional thought and the inability of the political elite to impose a pattern of a society based on a modern rationale are the ways by which the irrational and the mythical become a form of social organization and management. In the meantime any liberal or secular thought appears as a Western trick, especially within an Islamic fundamentalist milieu.

The failure of the development policies, and the position of the Maghreb in the international division of labor with its increasing dependence vis-à-vis overseas markets, brought about serious tensions in the region. Tunisia and Morocco were most threatened by the enlargement of the European Community (EC) and its protectionist stance, especially when the EC increased to 12 members with the participation of Spain and Portugal. This market absorbed up to 50 percent of Moroccan exports and up to 70 percent of Tunisian exports. Hence, the danger of a greater economic and political instability with the closing up of the European market looms large. In Algeria the decade following independence was one of triumph and optimism as it was characterized by "the Algerian model and the national path of development." But during the 1980s, the economic depression stirred up a profound political malaise—the result of which was the totally unexpected October 1988 upheaval, in which thousands of Algerians, mainly young people, took to the streets to demand political and economic changes.

The indebtness of these countries is enormous. In 1984, the Tunisian debt amounted to 3,707 million dollars; in 1990 it was 7,700 million dollars (military debt included). In Algeria, debts amounted to 22.2 million dollars. This state of affairs induced the intervention of the International Monetary Fund (IMF) and the World Bank, which predictably suggested a policy of structural adjustment. Unfortunately the proposed measures lack attention to specificity as the same remedy is applied to all countries. These policy measures are (1) a massive deflation of the currency, (2) reduction of the state budget, (3) reduction of salaries, (4) elimination of subsidies for basic products and goods, and (5) the liberalization of trade and of external payments. As was the case for Egypt in 1977, Sudan, Zambia and Morocco in 1984, and the Ivory Coast in 1990, such measures had a serious impact on the social situation: bread riots in Tunisia in 1984, street riots in Algeria in 1988. Thus, the measures that were destined to settle the balance of payments proved not only politically inconclusive, but also economically damaging.[13]

The response of external sectors to such measures was marginal and it aggravated inflation and unemployment, damaged the system of production, and widened the gaps between incomes. The crisis situation can thus be described as the following: weakening and lack of credibility of the government; monopolizing of the economic and political sphere by the petit-bourgeois elite, a social group alienated and dependant; an unsatisfactory insertion of these societies in the world market and the failure of development policies. These elements combined to precipitate an Islamic revival, reactive patriarchal laws and sentiments, and restore dependency on Islamic symbols. As one commentator notes: "Given the centrality of women and family (the private sphere) to the Muslim identity structure, increased constraints on female mobility are a common result of religious resurgence."[14]

Without entering into the debate on the status of women in the Quran and the *Hadith*, suffice it to say that a feminist vein seems to run through the Quranic text, whereas the most hostile passages to women were selected and interpreted in a very misogynistic way by the *Sharia*, thereby imposing male supremacy.[15]

Women and Islam in Algeria
and in Tunisia: Dissimilarities

We have already noted that the reactivation and politicization of religion is present in both societies with its totalitarian and pro-fascist aspect, and that its function is to insure in times of crises the displacement of social conflict. It is important to emphasize that this is done by taking away from women, who are strategic social actors as to their number and their responsibilities, a substantial part of their social rights.[16] The remainder of the social actors, faced with the absence of social alternatives, are easily manipulated since they have nothing to lose and believe that their problems are almost solved.

It is interesting to note that the Iranian Revolution had a great impact on Algerians, especially through the mass media, Khomeini becoming a model of reference for the youngsters.[17] The situation was utterly different in the Tunisian case, for the mass media never adhered to the Iranian cause. The Tunisian Embassy in Iran was closed during the first months of the year 1980; Khomeini was not glorified but rather ignored. In Tunisia a large audience is faithful to two foreign television stations, the Italian (Rai Uno) and the French (Antenne Deux) which counteract the sacro-irrational spirit that a population not always educated and easily manipulated could carry along. These TV stations broadcast very interesting programs on the objective, the rational and the universal.

Fundamentalist Islam in Tunisia may still be qualified as "underground," and submissive to a strong and resistant state as well as to other different authorities representing it in civil society. This situation of control and of resistance to fundamentalist Islam is backed up by a legal, secular and associative network. It counteracts the Islam of those who are fanatics, through the women's associations created recently, and through the very active role of the National Union of Tunisian Women. The latter is close to the ruling party but its positions are genuinely feminist.[18] We should also note the strong support of the League of Human Rights as well as its section "Women Rights."

Despite their fragmentary and sometimes competitive character, which gives an impression of dispersion and wastefulness of energies, all these associations militate in the same direction. They serve to safeguard the rights acquired by women, the result mainly of former President Bourguiba's visionary project. Tunisia's Personal Status Code of 1956 is unique in the Muslim world as it applies a very modernistic vision of Islam (applying the notion of *Ijtihad*), and a very daring interpretation of the traditional Sharia in a feminist way. The earlier reforms of Kamal Ataturk apparently served as a model to the Government and legislators of Tunisia under President Bourguiba.

In order to understand the difficulties faced by Tunisian Islam at the level of the State and of civil society, let us examine more thoroughly the reforms which positively affected women. The present role of women in Tunisian society and their insertion in the production system resulted from the determined action of a deeply feminist legislature, which immediately after independence served as a counter-current to customary and social practices. The promulgation in 1956 of the Personal Status Code immediately put an end to the intervention of the Quranic law in one inegalitarian interpretation, that is, the double moral standard (what is good for men is not for women). Despite the opposition of conservative and traditional forces, these considerable legislative gains, which are of prime importance to the social future of these regions, protected women from arbitrary and unilateral male actions and ensured them with dignity, respect and equality of rights, mainly in the following fields:

- Marriage: Freedom to choose a husband and the abolition of polygamy.
- Divorce: Could now be initiated by women.
- Children: Women have the right of custody and since 1981, in case of the death of the father, the mother automatically acquires the guardianship of the children.

- Right to Education and Work: This new development, supported by a policy of family planning, allowed women to have access to the "outside"; the street, the school, the office, the factory.

A few words about family planning policy are in order. As with most countries of the Third World, Tunisia is characterized by "a runaway increase in population" (about 2.6 percent annual increase). Consequently, it has a large young population; 45 percent of this population is under the age of 15 and are thus outside the sphere of productive activities. Tunisia also has a higher female life expectancy rate and a lower infant death rate.[19] If current trends continue the total population in the year 2000 will reach 12 million people. Thus state policy in family planning is to encourage the "limitation of reproduction" through setting a legal minimum age of marriage (20 for men and 18 for women), restricting family allowances (only the first 4 children can benefit from them), and the availability of birth control devices in pharmacies.

One aspect of state policy seems to have succeeded. The median age of marriage was 26 for men and 20 for women in 1977; in 1988 it was 23 for women. However, the effects of family planning have been less successful, especially in rural areas. This may be explained by noting that the introduction of family planning is relatively recent. But it can also be explained in terms of a cultural preference for large families, especially in the countryside and in regions such as Kairouan. Nonetheless, despite its deficiencies, the policy of family planning is rich in positive repercussions, notably in the possibilities it opens up to women concerning the way they deal with their bodies.

The role of associations in Tunisia must also be mentioned, for they are important to the application of the Code, and to its continuing legitimacy. Jurisprudence is mainly made up of men who try to modify the law and orient it towards an inegalitarian and patriarchal direction. The legislature seems to be more feminist than are the customs and mores. These associations try to effect a strict application of the international conventions ratified by Tunisia but which are unfortunately not always respected or enforced. In most cases these associations are composed of educated women who are members of the professional network. Their task is to record the blatant injustices that women endure daily, document the physical and symbolic aggressions in Muslim countries, and build solidarity among women. Tunisian periodicals engage in campaigns to publicize the critical situation of Algerian women.

In this context and unlike in Algeria, fundamentalist Islam is forbidden in Tunisia and is deprived of any legal status. The official reason for this is that Islam is a religion which belongs to all Tunisians; no one can monopolize Islam as a party or an association. This policy undermines the ability of a "totalitarian" party to decree who is a good Muslim and who is not. In this spirit an important part of the political and intellectual class believes that the law is neither a believer nor an atheist, but for the good of everybody it must be secular. Pluralism and democracy are the best shield against fanaticism and irrationality.

Let us now turn to Algeria.

In Algeria, the 1989 law introducing a multi-party system benefited the fundamentalists who had a runaway success in the June 1990 elections. This victory was regarded by some people as a political catastrophe, a phenomenon as disastrous as AIDS, devoid of an antidote. Such characterizations were widespread in the sensationalist popular press in 1990. The fundamentalist victory was made possible by the abstentionism of the other political parties opposing the ruling FLN, which they wanted to undermine. The absence of any social alternative to the FLN as well as the existence of a *parti unique* in most Third World countries discourage and destroy any initiative which does not emanate from this very party. Going "back to the roots" often remains the only way to crystalize energies. Some studies claim that rich oil-producing countries such as Iran and Algeria experienced the most extremist resurgence of Islam because they had undergone a too rapid and profound change. This may be true but it does not explain the case of Pakistan or Sudan, which are not oil-producing countries but have undergone the same extremist revival of Islam. It seems that in order to understand the extremist revival and reactivation of Islam and its present impact on women, especially in a country like Algeria, we must examine the following essential factors: the condition of the economy, the nature of the state, and the position of women in the production system. In Algeria, neither advanced technology and industrialization nor the "Green Revolution" could solve the problem of unemployment. Moreover, the female share of the labor force is one of the lowest in the world (5 percent in 1989). This fact has contributed to strengthening the oppressive vision of women and its perpetuation as a reference model. Thus, access to employment (and all the outside sectors of social life) which liberates women was neglected in the Algerian development model. This is the contrast with Tunisia, a non-oil-producing country but where women's labor is relatively important, especially in the manufacturing sector.

Despite her contribution to the national liberation struggle, the Algerian woman was expelled right after independence from the political, social and employment spheres. This situation was then ratified in 1984 by one of the most reactionary family codes which so diminishes woman's political status that it authorizes a man to vote by proxy for three women. The Algerian "socialist State" has hardly done anything to improve women's status. As in many Third World countries the State has considerable power, and it can either contribute to the emancipation of social actors or on the contrary oppress and marginalize them. "The unevenness of development and the weakness of class structure and conciousness explain the centrality of the State in the Third World. Decisive historical action does not lay in the hands of a bourgeoisie, a proletariat, or landowners, but rather in the State."[20]

Women's inequality is presented as an inequality of rights for which the Algerian government is to a large part responsible. An Algerian woman militant has noted that under the FLN it was a struggle to find a job, and that it is common to refuse accommodation to women living alone. Thus it is in a productivist society with a technological economic model disturbing the social order, but not creating new jobs, and where women's labor is not believed necessary since the State is deeply patriarchal and male-oriented, that the Algerian Muslim movement could move along. The resistance at the level of the society was badly organized and quite recent. In the Islamist program, women are their first target. Despite the reassuring declarations of the FIS, it seems that this movement applies the policy of the "stick and the carrot." The carrot is offered to the poor and the marginals to whom they provide philanthropic support. For example, during the last earthquake the FIS was on the spot, trying to assist the victims. The policy of the stick is used against the secular groups and women. A sort of "morality brigade" is in charge of intimidating women in order to secure their virtue. Cases include that of a widow whose flat was burned down, along with her baby, just because a man had visited her; women students beaten up because they stayed out late. It may be that the FIS is digging its own grave because of its fanaticism, intolerance and its somewhat adventurist Islam. For the time being the FIS social project with its obsessional misogyny compel the civil society to reorganize in a more conscious way. The temporary victory of the FIS is destined to mobilize the lucid energies of the Algerian nation to fight for democracy, freedom and the safeguarding of universal ideals. Already the Algerians are channeling their sentiments into a protest front against inquisition and intolerance.

Conclusions

The failure of the model of development (high technology for Algeria and free economy for Tunisia) is the context in which primordial forms of traditional solidarities re-emerge in society. Meanwhile there is no creation of new jobs; unemployment increases; and the international crisis whose repercussions are acute leads to a state of social tension and of psychological insecurity. When this happens, women are the main victims. The result of this model of development and the changes in attitudes and behaviors is frequently a crisis of identity. This crisis of identity is a dual one corresponding to the main cleavage in a society: (a) alienation and cultural dependence of the elite due to the consumption model, channelled by the modern sector of the society; (b) breakdown of traditional values and a resulting "return to the sources" and to a mythical golden age that we observe in the resurgence of tradition and religion. The resurgence of tradition is the sign of incompetence of the Government in attempting to propel, right after independence, a social "project guide," capable of crystallizing the poorest social actors. The weight of frustrations and alienation that it brought about as well as the big inequalities between the privileged elite and the underprivileged bulk of the society gave rise to alternative ideologies feeding themselves with tradition and Muslim identity. This reference to identity would be legitimate if it did not put into question the social gains of secularity, the offspring of the popular struggle. Instead, they wish to impose laws adaptable to an outdated social dynamic. This seemingly magical discourse crystallizes around itself many energies and attracts many people, men and women, young and old, educated and illiterate, to its sacro-mythical mode. Not being necessarily rhetorical or symbolic, "fundamentalist Islam" calls upon the entire reality, exercising pressure on the institutions and intimidating civil society. In Tunisia, creeping Islamization tackles the body of feminist laws, and tries to discourage the application of international conventions, even though ratified.[21] In any case the revival and the vitality of the Islamist movement feeds itself with diseases from which the Maghreb Muslim society suffer: corruption, authoritarianism, lack of democracy, social problems such as high unemployment and blatant injustices such as the ostentatious wealth of a minority and an excessive westernization. For this reason fundamentalist Islam is a symptom of a crisis and not a credible and effective response to it.

Notes

1. See Juliette Minces, *The House of Obedience* (London: Zed, 1980). In a reinterpretation of René Habachi, Jacques Berque ("Les arabes d'hier à demain," Ch. 9, p. 155) defines women in Islam as an integral essence and a broken existence "doomed to clandestine life, as formidable taboos cripple their self accomplishment from one generation to the next, their life reverts back to a standstill."

2. Frederick Engels, *Origin of the Family, Private Property and the State* (NY: International Publisher, 1972 [Original 1882]).

3. See Alya Baffoun, "Les stratégies de reproduction de l'ordre sexuel inégalitaire." Paper presented to AAWARD, Dakar, 1989.

4. United Nations Decade for Women, Nairobi, 1985.

5. This comes from Roger Garaudy, *Pour l'avénement de la femme* (Paris: Albin Michel, 1981).

6. See the essay by H. Peemans in M. A. Macciochi (ed.), *Les femmes et leurs maitres* (Paris: C. Bourgeois, 1976).

7. *Ibid.*

8. Ayesha Imam, stated in Nairobi, 1985.

9. See the works of the Freudo-Marxist Wilhelm Reich, especially his work on fascist mass psychology, "L'irruption de la morale sexuelle."

10. Ayesha Imam, stated in Nairobi, 1985.

11. See the essay by Samir Amin, "Le dévéloppement et la question culturelle — quelques réfléxions sur la question arabo-islamique." Presented at the Forum du Tiers-Monde, Nations-Unies, Dakar, 1987.

12. This argument has been made by Abdallah Laroui, *L'idéologie arabe contemporaine* et *La crise des intellectuels arabes* (Paris: Maspero, 1973).

13. See *African Development* 10 (1985).

14. Susan Marshall, "Paradox of Change: Culture Crisis, Islamic Revival and the Réactivation of Patriarchy," *Journal of Asian and African Studies* XIX, I (2) (1984), p. 2.

15. See the various works by Nawal El Saadawi; see also Fatima Mernissi, "Le Harem politique ou le Prophète et les femmes" (Paris: Arbin Michel, 1990).

16. We should not forget that we are dealing with societies where the rate of emigration is high and where, as a consequence, the number of women as heads of households is also very high. Some surveys reveal that in certain areas 4 heads of families out of 7 are women.

17. N. Chellig, *La femme musulmane algérienne vue par les lycéens* (CRESM: Annuaire de l'Afrique du Nord, 1979).

18. The dominant political grouping in Tunisia is called the Rassemblement Constitutionel Démocratic (RCD).

19. Whereas in 1960 the infant fertility rate was 50%, in 1982 it was 32.9%. Infant death rate in 1960 was 16%, in 1982 it was 7.6%.

20. Alain Touraine, in E. Hermassi, *The Third World Reassessed* (Berkeley: University of California Press, 1980).

21. For instance a recent action of the Education Minister to modernize school curricular materials by omitting texts that express negative attitudes to women and condone violence, has been strongly opposed by fundamentalists.

9

The Social Representation of Women in Algeria's Islamist Movement

Cherifa Bouatta and Doria Cherifati-Merabtine

Introduction

An everyday observation of Algerian society reveals the impact of the Islamist movement on behaviors, attitudes, and opinions of individuals and groups. One example is the new clothing men and women are adopting: the *khamis* for men and the *hijab* for women. Another example are the new rites and customs that govern ordinary relationships and discourses. These new forms of behavior result from the fact that young people have espoused and joined the Islamist movement. The older generation now sees that its morality, values, religion, and ancestral roots are questioned by its own children.[1] Indeed, youngsters enter into open conflict with their parents because the latter do not follow "the righteous path." Young girls, as well, are calling their fathers and mothers to order, to the Islamist order.

On the political level, the elections of 12 June 1990, which resulted in an electoral victory for the Front Islamique du Salut (FIS), showed the sociological root of the Islamist movement and the discourse it generates. One has to keep this in mind to better understand their importance in the socio-symbolic and political structures. Indeed, the Islamist current and discourse affect politics, families and individuals. The present authors are both active members in a women's association. As students in the 1970s, we looked to the ideal of universal values of equality and rights. The "Moudjahidates model" in particular reinforced this ideal. Women believed in the birth of a modern and socialist Algeria. On the political level, the socialistic conception dominated.

And those with an evolutionist and linear vision believed that with access to education and work all women would adopt this female example, the Moudjahidates model.

A scientific perspective contributed to this understanding. In previous research on the social representations of women, we found egalitarian principles present at the level of aspirations and at the level of experience.[2] These egalitarian principles, underlying the elaboration of the representations of women, are today regressing. They seem to have little impact on young people who reject them because these values are apparently alien to them. All these reasons, then, have led us to deepen our interest, integrating a new dimension to it, the Islamist one. The Islamist movement is a comprehensive social phenomenon.[3] We have chosen to restrict this study to the Islamist conception of women. What is the Islamist approach to The Woman Question? Which features of the female model are suggested or denied? These are the main questions addressed in this study, through an examination of the position of *El Mounquid* towards women.

Why *El Mounquid*?

With the emergence of the multi-party system on the political scene, the different political parties focus on the question of women as part of the quest for identity. For them, it has become the vehicle to cultural identity. They are bound, in one way or another, to take a stand: in other words, they must define their position on women's role and status in society. The discourse on the question of women, then, is placed in a context with highly antagonistic conceptions. This is the reason why, for practical and methodological needs, we can set out two categories, Islamist and modernist.

The official institutionalization of the FIS has been followed by the appearance of its newspaper *El Mounquid*. The latter appears twice a month in Arabic and in some issues inserts appear in French. *El Mounquid*, which means "Savior," is a newspaper that relies on Quranic verses and words of the Prophet. A motto at the head of each issue ends with a recommendation; one is requested to take it to heart. Beginning with the second issue of *El Mounquid*, readers' letters or notices addressed to women denounce "the affair of the Islamic scarf."[4] With issue number six, a new page was added called "the woman's corner."

Our concern is to infer the female models which structure the representation of "women" as it appears in the vision of one formation of the FIS. This organization dominates the field of production of symbolic assets. The first level of analysis consisted of the study of the writings on women in *El Mounquid*. Our starting postulate was a corpus of texts dealing with the female question and producing female images. This was followed by wider representations which Islamist women make of themselves.

The sources of the newspaper, from the start, grant to its content an authority of truth, even of sacredness. This dimension adds to the difficulty of our field of study. With the secular and the sacred conjoined, subjectivity might interfere in our analysis. Moreover, research and theoretical formalization on this topic are rare in Algeria, most notably in the field of social psychology. For this reason, and for the purposes of this article, we emphasize the secular aspect of the discourse. The sacred aspect is omitted. The corpus discussed here is composed of 21 articles from 21 issues.

Our corpus originally consisted of 42 texts (articles and notices) of unequal length. The authors' identity is unclear: we do not know whether they are journalists or readers. The repeated signature of certain names leads us to think that are linked to the newspaper; and the names are male and female. The other signatures, either single or in groups, suggest to us that they are readers. These are both men and women, though female signatures prevail. This group is characterized by its youth, mainly students, pupils and youngsters. This population comes from the populous neighbourhoods of Algiers or from schools and campuses.

Because of the richness of the corpus, we limit ourselves, on a methodological aspect, to a thematic and structural analysis. We initially wanted to draw a comparison between female writings and male writings. But we soon discovered a homogeneity in the writings and the non-relevance of the sex criterion. Moreover, women's articles are more important than men's articles. We thus take into consideration the corpus as a whole.

Methodology

Our research design was based on several elements: (1) a repeated reading of the articles in order to expose the contents that are developed, (2) singling out the major themes, then the recurrent ones which launch the different discourses and which are part of our categories of analysis, and (3) locating qualifiers and key words in the different articles.

These data become meaningful in the identity quest that is going on in Algeria among the different female groups. Indeed, one witnesses the construction of ego images as well as various collective images. Their symbolic referent either coincides with or rejects the proposed model by either one or the other category. We considered it interesting to investigate the social representations women draw upon themselves in an environment characterized by the rivalry between and inadequacy of the proposed models. This approach allowed us to avoid a quantitative examination because the same terms can be found in most of the texts studied. On the one hand, we have identified and singled them out. On the other hand, among the key words some have to be considered separately because of the newness of their use in the common language. Next, these words seem to bear a meaning of their own. They accumulate a set of meanings that make them function in an autonomous way.

The theoretical background of our approach stems from social psychology. The social representations under investigation are tackled in terms of both the content and process, as the content depends upon culture and gives its meaning and social rootedness to the social representation. These processes demonstrate the conditions of the ordering and structuring of this content. Its result is the creation of female patterns that reflect and obscure any symbolic relations between the groups. This approach, because of its incursions in culture, steps into cultural anthropology. The dynamics of each of the emerging female models, their novelty, and the strategies they set in motion deserve particular attention.[5]

A Brief Presentation of the Islamist Movement in Algeria

The paucity of studies on the Islamist movement in Algeria compels us to present some of its aspects. This might help the reader to situate it in the socio-political and cultural context of contemporary Algeria. Islamic thinking as a social and political reality cannot be denied. It emerges under different circumstances through religious and socio-cultural associations as well as political organizations. The Islamist movement is not monolithic. It seems to be composed of several groups and formations, but the following dominate the political scene: *El Irchad oua el Islah, Rabitat Eddawa, El Islamya, El Oumma*, and the FIS. These organizations pervade the society. They recruit from different social classes and socio-cultural milieux. One can find, for example, intellectuals, unemployed, businessmen, clerks, men, and women. They differ on the organizational level, but they share a common field of inquiry on the ideological level: "The struggle against depravity, decadence, and the implementation of the *Sharia* is the panacea to all evils."[6] Their methods of action and objectives range from the call for Islamization of society to the assertion of the will for power.

Today, this movement defines an identity which is rooted in the pan-Arab history of the Nahda period.[7] The movement also strives to be the alternative to, the answer to, the failure of the nationalist, modernist, socialistic, and secular regimes of the post-independence era of the Arab world. The FIS must therefore be understood as an Islamic political party, the bearer of a political and civilizing mission. It seeks political power. This party sprang out of the combination of four groups: *Ahl Attalia* (the avant-garde people), *Jamaat El Tabligh* (the society of the message), and *Jamaat El Jihad* (the society of the holy war). The FIS was officially recognized on September 6, 1989. It claims to have, according to its spokesman, three million members. The preamble of its program is as follows:

> While the present governing party is incapable of curing the multi-dimensional crises that shake the country, the Algerian people wonder how to revive a civilizational type that would lead, after a democratic and pluralistic confrontation, to the building of an authentic Islamic society. The failure of the different Western and oriental ideologies impels us to use our religion in order to safeguard as an opposition to external and internal threats, our historical and civilizational acquisitions, our human and natural resources. ... The birth of the Islamic Front of Salvation (FIS) responds to the need to lead the Islamic call and to organize the believers.[8]

The municipal elections of June 12, 1990 revealed the FIS as the leading political party, way ahead of the FLN, the party in power. The latter had lost its one-party status after October 1988.[9] This compels us to have a closer look at the discourse the FIS develops towards women and its approach to the woman question.

Analysis of the Corpus: Three Female Patterns

Is there a woman question in the Islamist discourse as developed by *El Mounquid*? The answer can be affirmative if one considers its special column dealing with women's problems as well as the number of articles on women. However, the majority of authors who treat it refuse to consider the woman question as being of any interest, thus justifying a particular treatment. For example: "There is no need for a Woman Question since Islam has provided all rights to the woman for 14 centuries."[10] To refer to it, to mention it, and to make an issue of it would mean "to imitate the West." "It is a Western creation," and "a plot fomented by Marxism, the Jews ... ." This question in itself is dangerous. Its objectives are "to attack Islam." Its claims are neither real, legitimate, nor acceptable. They are instead "phantasmatic, imaginary."

Thus we observe, in one sense, plain denial of the female problem. Even though most copies of *El Mounquid* do address it, the newspaper refutes it. Rights, equality, and liberation are the central and founding themes developed around the Woman Question. But in the Islamist perspective, from the start, the Muslim woman is a privileged woman, she is endowed with rights, and she is the equal of the man. This is "the right of the feminine Muslim."[11] Thus, she has the right to education, primarily religious education; she has the right to respect, and to inheritance; she has the right to free opinion and the right to vote; she has the right to refuse an imposed husband; she has the right to spread the Muslim gospel—the *Dawa*; and she has the right to fight in the name of God.

These rights are found in all the articles consulted. Some authors add the right to divorce, and the right to work. A woman has the right to sue for divorce only if she can "prove" and "show" that she is living in an "unhealthy relation" which is "damaging" to her. A woman has the right to work because it is legal. Nevertheless, this right undergoes several changes in reality. First, work is restricted: a woman is not suited for all kinds of jobs. Next, it takes a reversed meaning. Employment becomes forbidden because it is incompatible with femininity and morals.

A comparative approach in the Islamist discourse aims at establishing the superiority of the female Muslim. It consists, on one hand, of evaluating her status before the *Jahilia* (pre-Islamic "era of ignorance" in Arabia). This era "oppressed," "humiliated," "buried alive," and "rejected" women. They were also "disinherited," and "used for men's lust." That was Woman's fate during the pre-Islamic Arab period. With the dawn of Islam, the woman became a human being. Another comparative approach is vis-à-vis the West, where the latter symbolizes "depravation of morals," "decay," and "decadence." In fact, because of the contents they cover, the Jahilia and the West match and are synonymous. This comparative outlook becomes a polemical strategy. Arguments and reasoning are elaborated to face and oppose other standpoints which result from another different logic.

Nature, Culture

Once these rights are claimed, the next attempt is to make clearer and to legitimate the taboos imposed on women. Thus, a woman cannot be a political leader; a woman cannot work (keeping in mind the qualifications we have seen earlier); a woman must refuse mixed company: a woman must wear the hijab. She must avoid all kinds of exhibitionism and "showing off": wearing make-up, wearing perfume, wearing clothes that reveal the shapes of her body.

What is the explanatory paradigm of this set of taboos? In all cases, two kinds of reasons are given. The first concerns divine order. That is, the taboos are divine prescriptions. Being sacred, they are beyond the human will and have an undisputed and inviolable character. The second reason relies on a profane thinking to throw light on the restrictions imposed on the woman. It relies on the biological and psychological differences between the sexes. The feminine nature is understood in terms of "its natural features," "its physical constitution," "its physiology," "its functional change," and "its feminine nature." All these features characterize a female nature in opposition to a male nature. The obvious and single dimension of biological difference is added to notions of psychological difference. A linear relation is drawn, then, between both orders of reality, biology and psychology.

In this paradigm the man is physically and psychologically superior: he has "force and authority." As a consequence, he is "the bread-winning head of the family." The man is also different because of his "strong sexual appetite," his "avidity." The "yearnings" and "temptations" of men are often referred to. A series of regulating mechanisms therefore exist. Polygamy is one of them (others will be seen later in this chapter). Two articles are devoted to polygamy and their author is a man. Polygamy is justified from a biological point of view: the man naturally tends to polygamy because of his strong "sexual appetite." His "inner predispositions" allow him to father several children with different women. Polygamy, satisfying and regulating the male's natural needs, permits a major social function: It weakens the burden of single women on society and confers to them a certain number of considerable psychological and social benefits: like "to be kept." The woman is endowed with the respectable and honorable status of mother and wife.

On the other hand, "polygamy is unthinkable for a woman." Her nature, and "her innate predispositions" imply that she "can be expecting only once a year," and "that she belongs to one man, and to one man only." Polygamy for women is also "impossible because of children's blood relation." As a conclusion, polygamy is moral and humane in Islam.[12] Polygamy in the West, by comparison, is a reality, even though not institutionalized. But there it is "inhuman and immoral." The Western man has several "sexual affairs" but this proves his "selfishness" and "irresponsibility." Seduced and abandoned, the Western woman is left alone, "shamed," "dishonored," an accusing finger pointed at her, and most of the time compelled to carry alone the burden of an illegitimate maternity.

The women's articles are numerous, and they do not differ much from those written by the men, except for polygamy. Interestingly, they never mention it. Whether these women writers support polygamy or not is unclear and requires further evidence. However, these women vehemently oppose one of the claims of the women's movements: the abolition of the Family Code. They accuse Algerian feminists of "going against God's will" and thus of leading the Muslim world into the dark age of the Jahilia.

The woman's psychology emerges out of the dichotomy established between masculinity and femininity. Psychologically, masculinity—as we have seen above—is "force" and "authority." Femininity would rather side with emotions, relations, and maternity. These "personality features" find their best expression in the domestic sphere.

Motherhood

The procreating function is praised and symbolizes honor and dignity. Thanks to the mother's religious education, her offspring—"the future generations"—will follow the Islamic path. This task remains the most noble one Islam ordered her to pursue. The woman is the first Islamic school. Thanks to this mission, she is the mother of society. She becomes the cornerstone of a type of society, the Muslim type, that would establish a perennial Islamic order. In this perspective, marriage is not a contract between two individuals. It is a sacred union in which (and through which) sexual difference entails a distinction of the roles. The man is the head of the family. A woman must obey her husband. She must also confide in him, give him her opinion, and be nice to him because she is the man's mate. Beside this role based on sexual division, the Dawa (proselytizing) is another female function.

Reference to the Dawa rarely appears in the articles. However, in an interview by a group of Islamic women published in *El-Mounquid* (no. 19), this function is claimed as a female mission of the first order. It must be recognized by all the advocates of the Islamist movement. Indeed, with the women's Dawa, homes can be reached, housewives enlightened, and the Islamic society built (also through mothering). Consequently, its reinforcement and improvement would show "others" that the Islamist movement, far from ostracizing women, invests them with a civilizational mission. They become, as it were, the makers of history.

The dual biological and psychological determinism orients and predisposes her to bring up children, to found a family, and to belong to one man. Thus, the biological and psychological characteristics intermingle to define her status and forbid her to earn a living, especially if the work requires force and/or authority. A woman cannot wish nor claim tasks or activities which might alter her femininity, keep her away from her original function and eventually disturb the social order. The social order establishes the dichotomy and the hierarchy between the sexes. It gives them differentiated status and roles. This order is legitimated: it complies with divine prescriptions, hence its sacred character beside its biological and psychological differences.

The Taboo on the Body

The taboo on the body is related to a certain number of founding themes of the discourse studied. They have to do with the hijab, mixed society, female employment, and the practice of sport. In one way or another, these themes fit the relation between the sexes, lust and taboos, order and disorder, and in the last instance refer to sexuality. The themes are: The hijab is compulsory for the Muslim woman; mixed society must be forbidden; female jobs, only when necessary, must occur in sex-segregated areas; the practice of sporting games should be avoided.

The hijab is the cloth of honor and purity. It is an "atomic weapon," destroying what comes in its way. It is an extraordinary and invincible weapon. A woman must cover her body, the symbol of her femininity. She must avoid exhibitionism by hiding her body. There is an orthodox hijab, strictly regulated. Yet, if the hijab today is a social fact, it is far from being uniform. Women play with colors, fabrics, and design. The *khimar* is an example: it has bright colors, it is worn with a twisted string, and it is finely embroidered. In short, the hijab shows the *moutahajiba*'s elegance. It becomes the expression of one's own identity; it emphasizes difference; it loses its original purpose: standardization in order to limit "yearnings and temptations."

Some sharp voices denounce these heterodox practices to remind women of the canonical example. The hijab must be a cover; if not austere, certainly not an ornament. The Muslim woman must comply with the principles which institutionalize it. She must also convince other women to wear it.

Whatever the kind of hijab, its characteristic is ambiguity. Its aim is to hide and segregate. In this way, it establishes the distinction between masculinity and femininity. Wearing it gives access to public places, reminding people that a woman belongs to private spaces. In all cases, it informs about the relation to the other and recognizes the lust of the other.[13] In the Islamist discourse, a mixed environment is inconceivable. A man and a woman, whatever their age, cannot share the same space. The integration of the sexes seems terrifying: it is the dissolution of morals, and the destroyer of dignity. It is a means to get to prostitution and to men's sexual avidity and desire. In short, it is the return to the Jahilia. The meeting of the two sexes is always threatening. It may end up with savagery or the uncontrollable; in other words, to sexual satisfaction.

Female employment is rejected. It diverts a woman from her natural and sacred function. It is impossible indeed to reconcile the family duties with work duties. As proof, writings in *El Mounquid* mention the lack of affection children suffer when their mothers work. It is said that mothers even forget to pick them up at the kindergarten. Working also means that a woman ends up in inappropriate places or integrated places. Only the widow can earn a living. The divorcee is nowhere mentioned.

El Mounquid disapproves of sports. The reasons given are the following: It is incompatible with our religion. It obliges the woman to take off her clothes of decency and to exhibit herself in outfits that hides only the object of her virtue. To oppose the practice of sport is to fight ignorance and illiteracy. In fact, sports make the woman aware of her body. Practicing may signify a privileged relation to the body. It means, in a certain way, to display it, to take care of it, to pay attention to its shapes, and to feel its needs. It is also a means to blossom, to be desired, and to realize one's ability to please. If sports are not banned, taboos will disappear.

All this is unthinkable for a mind obsessed with the female body. The meeting of both sexes may only lead to the free expression of sexual needs. In this discourse the book *Au-delà de toute pudeur* must be banned simply because it deals with sexuality: "This is a danger to our society and values." Hence, the woman must confirm to a strict spatial segregation, hold to her "natural" functions, and wear the orthodox hijab. This is to allow the social order to be built. If these rules and taboos are transgressed, the result will be decivilization—"law and order are utterances of sex."[14] Everything happens as if men's desires exist in a rough state. It should be noted, though, that if a woman is a desirable object, she is not a desiring subject.

Cultural anthropology teaches us that all social groups impose a certain number of sex taboos to their members. Everywhere sexuality is controlled and formalized. At an early age, the child's desire is confronted with the paternal taboos. Having understood the impossibility to satisfy their desires, children use other means to realize themselves. Sublimation replaces sexuality to enter into the world of art and culture. The desire, law, sublimation and culture come first. This is to say that sexuality results from a psychic elaboration and from culture. Human sexuality is a psychosexuality and a formalized one. It could not mingle with animal life.

The Muslim female pattern which emerges from this presentation is strongly valued. It is based on reference and values, particularly Arabo-Muslim, and on the relation with a well-determined historical era: the rising of Islam. The model is *the* model, the only one possible. It is proposed—imposed to a specific reader: "my Muslim Sister, my Sister in Islam." This suggested pattern is addressed only to this particular group of women. To agree with it suggests a participation in purity, innocence, and transcending materialistic preoccupations and things. It is access to power. It embraces individuality/identity/formalization. The Muslim woman must be singled out from other women, the impious. Moreover, she builds up her identity through social relations by way of interiorizations of the rules that make up the model.

This model must be defended against another pattern, and against her adversaries who are numerous. And the warnings are constant. All authors enjoin her to be vigilant, to pay attention, and to be on her guard with those who use a sugary language. These in reality want to destroy society via the woman. In this vision of the woman, and the world, evil is everywhere and threatens society and civilization at any time. A society is ordered, harmonious, and healthy only if the woman obeys the proposed model. In contrast, if a woman violates the ideal conventional pattern, society as whole falls into decay (*el fassad*).

The state of being of a society depends, then, on woman. If other sources of social pathology exist, the woman would be the cause. The equation gets established between the three terms that form the social order: woman = family = society; hence the role she is given and the taboos that are imposed.

Conceptualizing the Other: The Western Woman

What happens in case of transgression and who transgresses? The Western world, people, and the feminist movements do not confirm to the conventional model and refute it. These speak only of women's liberation and equality. They constitute a threat to Islam and civilization. Their purpose is to ostracize the Muslim woman, to make her lose her honor, dignity, femininity. Her enemies are in the West but also in the Muslim countries.

The Western Woman is a sexual object, a piece of merchandise, subject to men's desire, a show-off object, ornamented, and exhibited for the satisfaction of men's lust and sexual hungers. The ideas of equality, rights, women's liberation—according to the author's approach—cover several meanings. They have a positive connotation when their frame of reference is Islam. Their meaning change when their context changes. The Western woman's liberation is a mystification. She has been freed from her home, her family, and duties to her children; she has been thrown in the world of employment where she is exposed to repeated constraints and to sexual aggressions. The title of one article in *El Mounquid* alludes to the meaning of liberation when it distances itself from the Islamist perspective: "They say you have been liberated, yet you have been betrayed." Employment not only destroys family and femininity, it is also oppression. Compelled to earn a living, the woman must do any kind of jobs; the hardest, and sometimes the vilest.

The sexual disorder established by the Western social system tends sometimes to the confusion of sexual identities. One can no more distinguish men from women. This is unbearable to a vision obsessed with sexual difference and the clear-cut separation of both sexes. The Western woman is exploited on two levels, sexually and socially. All this in daring contradiction with morals, and feminine and psychological nature. It can only produce social pathology. It induces despair, anguish, mental sickness, even suicide. Yet the Western woman is not responsible for that. Her behavior stems from a social order which has not respected the founding rules of order. She is a victim and a poor thing. She is the token, however, of the anti-pattern, the bad object. Because of the cause-and-effect relationship between the woman and society, the West has gone the wrong path by betraying its women. One must denounce it and reject it.

Yet, a way to salvation exists. Some Western women recognize that the system they live in is the route to exploitation, oppression, and alienation. They choose to break with the Western degrading heritage and to submit to the rules and prescriptions commanding the Muslim woman's pattern. They, then, set themselves free from the evils which burden them and acquire peace of mind and serenity. They have chosen the right way. They become symbols. They are presented as an example to dismantle the West and to argue that salvation cannot be but in the

Islamist answer. An Englishwoman is cited who opposes mixed society which causes the birth of illegitimate children. An American woman is also cited who believes that family crises and crimes have an origin in the breaking up of homes, and she defends the housewife status.

The Turncoat Model

The authors identify a third female type, the Westernized Algerian woman. But in opposition to the ideal pattern and the anti-pattern, the third type is not autonomous. It is in close link with both models, it betrays the first and cheaply imitates the second. It is also the most vilified model. If the Western woman is the victim of her own society, nothing can justify or excuse those women living in a land of Islam. They are imitators and parrots. Their ideas and claims are imported, they come from the West. These women are odd because of their clothes, their language, and their thinking.

But what do they want and what are they searching for? To abandon the female tasks, natural and sacred. To dominate the man, to marry him when she wants and divorce him when she wants. To go in and out when she wants. To travel without a chaperon (*Moharem*). To deny man's tutoring, authority, and force. To abolish the Family Code, the only legal text based on the Sharia. To create a conflict (*fitna*) between men and women. The rights they claim are unacceptable, inconceivable. They are fictitious rights. They show off with indecent clothes. They are ornamented and their face is made up. Their behavior is contrary to morals and to the legitimate and legal rules of the Sharia. They display their flesh to men. They are soulless bodies and souls whose bodies give course to baseness. They are the offspring of France. They want to transgress what is sacred and based in nature and culture. Through the ideas they defend and the behaviors they adopt, their aims are "hidden," and they foment plots with the help of "Marxism, Zionism, the Jews, the West, the Freemasons, laymen ... ."

Though the Muslim woman is endowed with all her rights today, this is due to Islam which put an end to the era of trouble and chaos, symbolized by the Jahilia. Yet, the very existence of Westernized Algerian women and their way of life is a serious threat. They endanger morals, culture and humanity. In this perspective, the Jahilia is not a historical step integrated in the general history of Arabs and thus belonging to a dead past. The Jahilia interferes with the present. The social order is so fragile and vulnerable that one may step into the Jahilia. It acts as terrifying phantasm. It mobilizes ontological effects and fears that haunt the collective memory.

The regression to pre-history, to the primitive, to the absence of rules is dreadful, it signifies the sinking of the Muslim world. Salvation is ensued only in a return to origins and roots. Islam—and the Muslim woman's pattern that springs from it—is the starting point out of which law is enunciated and the world order is established.[15] Hence, two patterns are outlined: (1) Both the Muslim woman and the converted Westerner share the same symbolic environment, (2) The Western woman—evil object—who delivered a turncoat offspring, the Westernized Algerian woman.

Both models share dichotomy, antagonism and exclusiveness. They are defined according to a manichean conception, right/wrong, virtue/vice, human/non-human, order/disorder, morality/Jahilia. The list can be longer.

The first model is situated in well-defined categories, all having a positive connotation, the good, virtue, the human, and so on. The second model, however, has negative connotations, the bad, vice, the unhuman. This apprehension of the female fact and the construction of these social representations are instances of a restricted view of the world. The other, or the different, is adversity and fear. It must, thus, be wiped out, at least on a symbolic level.

Representations of Women:
A Reconstruction of the Real

To oppose the ideal woman—the Muslim woman—to the bad woman, one has to appeal to a series of operations to render this opposition possible. Concealment, negation, denial, and blanking out are used in the re-construction of a real in so far as it lies within the representations of women one wants to inculcate. These representations are rooted neither sociologically nor historically and present no psychological density.

First concealment: the daily life of women with its ups and downs—the problems of school failures that mothers face, unemployment, overcrowded apartments, consuming problems—is ignored. But also ignored are the dreams and desires they cannot realize, but that they wish for their daughters. The rites and customs that punctuate their lives, the Turkish bath, the visits, the parties, their poems, and songs express their desires, loves and frustrations. All this is concealed. The fact also is that in Algeria the female world is not homogeneous. Women are socially rooted in different arrangements—whereas the women presented in the corpus are an abstract character. The only real problems the authors mention are those of the women students in conflict with blind university authorities. The latter impose the practice of sports and mixed groups at the university.

Second concealment: the participation of women in the War of Independence was a decisive turn in the life of the Algerian woman. Keeper of home and traditions, she played an active role in one of the greatest gambles the country has ever taken, liberation and national independence. In the collective memory, the *moudjahidates'* role is still alive. They are a symbol with which a whole generation of women has identified. They are today a landmark for the women's associations. But all this is denied in the Islamist discourse. The only references worth mentioning, to the authors, are those related to the origin of Islamic history.

Third concealment: the multidimensional changes that occurred in the country since independence have led to social, cultural, and political transformations—their impact on the family and on the female status and role is never tackled. The phenomena dealt with are morals, and the deprivation of manners, consequences of the imitation of the perverse West which threatens the Islamist order. Universal history, the glory of Arab nationalism, the women's participation in anti-colonial struggles, the history of employment in the world and in Algeria are simply wiped out. We notice, however, three events that we consider as incursions in contemporary history. Saik Zeghoul, the leader of the Egyptian nationalist movement, once back from exile uncovered Huda Sharawi, the feminist. This gesture was considered bad because it incited a Muslim woman to abandon her decent clothes to imitate the West. Zeghoul becomes the enemy of Islam. Zenab El Ghazali, famous Egyptian Daiya (an advocate of faith) considers March 8 as a Jewish Day which does not concern the Muslim woman. The Afghan woman is the ideal/model because she resists and fights atheism to preserve her Muslim identity. Yet these three events do not make history. They remain minor events and anecdotes. They change nothing to the ahistorical vision of oneself and of the other.

Being ahistorical by the mechanisms it uses, this vision of the world of women is surely static and stiff. Beside, it is based on the invariable, the unchanged, the constant. Only one change is seen and accepted, the passage from Jahilia to Islam, from the pre-human to the human. Links are established between these two historical steps and the described female patterns, the ideal-female. The Muslim woman is linked to the origins of history whereas the anti-model is linked to pre-history, to the Jahilia. The conflict is also integrated in individual and collective history. Yet, the proposed representations of women, even though the result of antagonistic social relations, refuse any conflicting dimension.

For a woman, the acceptance of the conventional pattern puts an end to contradiction, to inter-psychic and inter-individual conflict.

On a collective level, when the Islamic society will be in place, the conflict will disappear from social life. There will be no reason for it to exist. The very idea of a conflict is rejected. The women's movement is reproached for the instigation of dissension between men and women. The notion of social classes is rejected, the "woman question" is claimed to be a Western creation and an imported product. The opposition between social classes and class interests could not structure the social and political environment of the Islamic order.

The dialectic of social representation-real is shown through the constitutive cultural items of the representative content and the elements at work for its structuration. We stress that in the light of our previous analyses the social representations are not an internal retaking of an external reality. They are an original construction, a re-construction of a real. Produced by mental activity and social interaction, it is a knowledge they diffuse. A knowledge most certainly different from the scientific knowledge, but its study is nonetheless important. These social representations are a knowledge whose aims are practical and functional. They are knowledge in the sense that they allow the individuals in the group to organize the world they live in, to understand it and take a stand. They are also an expression of personal and social identity. The Muslim woman knows where and on what her identity rests. Knowledge allows her argumentative resources and ideas, it designates the enemy to figure out the identical and the different in order to resist it and oppose it.

Social Representations and Communications

When one gets away from the analytical approach developed above and considers the discourse as a whole, *El Mounquid* as a means of communication has several salient features. It has a well-organized and well-structured vision of the object of representation. Nawal Saadawi is said to want to take women away from their roots by spreading terrifying ideas. In the view of *El Mounquid*, a discourse that diffuses the divine law and its explanatory paradigm remains essentially a divine order. The pattern of the Muslim woman answers a divine order. All other arguments, biological or psychological, are secondary. By sanctifying the Muslim woman pattern, it becomes transcendent, indisputable, invariable, a feminine eternal. From that, all difference, alternatives, and compromise become transgression of the religious order and are forbidden. The social representations of women are the stakes of identity struggles. One has to fight on a symbolic and the ideal levels by transmitting, teaching the ideal and unique model. One has to fight also so that it becomes the dominant model. One has also to fight in the literal sense.

The Jihad is present and some authors threaten the women who initiate trouble not of divine wrath but of material sanctions. The reader addressed is well identified. The discourse about the object of representation, the woman, rejects all kinds of definition of the difference. These are the characteristics of communication, propaganda is propaganda device.

The discourse diffused by *El Mounquia* is based on the exaltation of attributes and peculiarities of its religious group. It has an absolutist thinking which admits neither compromise nor alternative. On the contrary, all that is external to the Muslim female ideal must be excluded. The presence of The Other is considered for the sake of argumentation. It is the proof that imposes the superiority of the Muslim woman and the Islamic order. The discourse is a recurrent one out of which certain words and terms are used, as we have already seen. Concepts such as Jahilia are, semantically speaking, rich. They cover several meanings and function in autonomous ways. They are in themselves the representations of women. Uttering them is evoking a symbolic universe, is evoking female types, and female models. They allow a classification and a reduction of female diversity. The model Muslim woman is also constructed, on its principles and functioning, on the traditional conception of sex relations. The representation of sexes is always ranked, asymmetrical. The sexual division establishes a segregation of work and space. The woman belongs to the inside space, to the world of procreation and maternity. Public spaces, streets, even employment are male attributes. We can then speak of perpetuating the traditional female pattern. However, the rupture is in several ways. Tradition was kept by mothers and was transmitted orally. Then traditions proceed to combinations and establish a compromise with the other term present in the cultural field, modernity. In this analyzed discourse, tradition leaves home, yet sanctified. Young female students write to other women and present them the pattern of the Muslim woman, a tradition whose elements change. Ancestors are no more relied upon but the first women of Islam.

Another difference is that this presentation is instituted and does not admit compromise. The pattern of the Muslim woman is also in breach with the official discourse which existed before the coming of the Islamist Movement. Indeed, the official discourse in its apprehension of the female issue tried to articulate tradition and modernity, to introduce novelty in conventional thoughts. In addition to creating a new tradition the Islamist discourse eliminates, by refusing modernity, all form of bipolarity. It is homogenous and coherent.[16]

Conclusions

The corpus we have analyzed shows that the discourse on women as developed in *El Mounquid* is a propaganda discourse that aims to promote the female ideal type, what we call the Muslim woman pattern. This model is sacred because it applies divine prescriptions. The biological and psychological explanations for the necessity of this model remain secondary or are idealized to draw the merit of the religious order. In another step, the Muslim woman is established in nature and culture. This model, the only possible and conceivable one, excludes a whole series of data, the female participation in real life but also in contemporary history, universal history. The historical dimension is present only under the form of anecdotes or distorted form. It excludes also the Western woman and the westernized Algerian woman, seen as the instigators of disorder, conflict and backwardness. In this light, the discourse works as a discourse of non-recognition. At the same time, the construction and identification of these female models suggest to specific women readers arguments, values and emotional connotations to build a specific identity in opposition to other identities.

Notes

1. Cherifa Bouatta, "Attitudes et représentations sociales des femmes concernant les rôles sociaux," Thèse de 3ème cycle, Paris, 1986.

2. See *ibid.*, and Doria Cherifati-Merabtine, *Les représentations sociales chez un groupe d'ouvrière* (Alger: Magistère, 1987).

3. See, for example, M. Yared, "Radioscopie du courant islamiste," *Rev. Arabies* 43-44, (Juillet-Août 1990):23-25.

4. A number of Muslim schoolgirls, living in France, began to attend school wearing the Islamic headscarf. The school authorities banned its wearing. In the light of this affair Islamic associations in France and Algeria denounced the pseudo-tolerance of laicization (secularism).

5. See, for example, D. Jodelet, *Fou et folie dans un milieu rural francais: une approche monographique, l'étude des représentations sociales* (Paris: Debachaux et Nieste, 1986), and S. Moscovici, *La psychanalyse, son image et son public* (Paris: PUF, 1976).

6. B. Etienne, *L'Islamisme radical* (Paris: Hachette, 1987).

7. M. Arkoun, "De la Jahilia au bricolage religieux," *Algérie Actualité* 16 (22) (August 1990):2-23.

8. *El Mounquid,* March 7, 1989.

9. In October 1988 a violent rebellion put an end to the one-party system. It gave birth to multi-party politics and to the recognition of the rights of citizens. See, for example, A. Djeghloul, "Le Multipartisme à l'algérienne," *Revue Maghreb-Mashrek* (Jan- fev-mars 1990):194-210.

10. The quotations in this paper refer to the articles of the authors in *El Mounquid.*

11. We are indebted for this term to N. Saadi, *La loi au féminin algérien.* See also F. Mernissi, *Sexe, Ideologie, Islam* (Paris: Tierce, 1983).

12. Most women's associations demand the abolition of the Family Code of 1984. Some want its revision, the abrogation of certain provisions such as the one authorizing polygamy. The Islamist movement claims these women really want polyandry.

13. M. Chebel, *L'esprit de Sérail* (Paris: Lieu commun, 1988).

14. G. Balandier, *Anthropologiques* (Paris: Le livre de poche, 1985), 2ème éd.

15. *Ibid.*

16. For a scholarly view quite different from that of *El Mounquid,* see A. Bouhdiba, *La sexualité en Islam* (Paris: PUF, 3ème éd., 1982).

10

Gender Activism:
Feminists and Islamists in Egypt

Margot Badran

Introduction

In Egypt, and among a number of intellectual women across the ideological spectrum, one detects a kind of "feminism" or public activist mode without a name. This activism transcends ideological boundaries of politically articulated feminism and Islamism. I shall refer to it as gender activism. It is a response by women deciding for themselves how to conduct their lives in society. Thus many women whom I shall refer to in this chapter as feminist, pro-feminist, and Islamist women are taking similar positions on women's societal roles and engaging in common forms of activism. In periodizing Egyptian women's activism, I call this the third wave of feminism and Islamism. The second wave, from the late 1960s to the late 1980s, was characterized by polarization expressed in ideological combat with women lined up on opposing sides.[1] The first wave occurred from the 1920s to the 1950s; organized feminism emerged in the 1920s and women began to participate in the Islamic movement in the 1930s. Although the first wave women made choices between two movements, the period was not marked by adversarialism. The present third wave constitutes a new configuration of female forces and has collapsed some of the hard-drawn lines that emerged during the second wave. This is not to suggest that the grounding of women's gender activism in divergent ideologies is insignificant. On the contrary, the ideological context of gender activism is crucial as ultimately it separates the basic agendas of the feminist and Islamist women. The term gender activism intends to capture women's common "feminist" modes of thinking and behavior in the public sphere without denying the reality of distinct feminist and Islamist "movements" and the separate experience of uncommitted (pro-feminist) women.

Feminists include women who publicly declare their (feminist) identity and those who admit to being feminists in private but do not make public affirmation of this. Pro-feminists are those who take various stands that can be understood as feminist but who reject being identified as feminists. Islamist women publicly declare themselves by wearing a head veil (*hijab*) and are called *muhajjabat*, or wear a face veil (*niqab*) and are known as *munaqqabat*. These women represent a wide range from those who accommodate themselves to veiling as part of a general social current to those with a profound commitment to Islam. Our concern in this chapter is with the latter. Contemporary feminists and pro-feminists are mainly from the middle and upper middle class while Islamist women come from a broad background ranging from the lower middle class to the upper middle class. The class base of feminists of the second and third waves has remained consistent for the most part while the class background of Islamist women has expanded over the past two decades encompassing more women from the upper strata of the middle class. The Islamist intellectual women, however, are from the more privileged strata of the middle class, as are their feminist and pro-feminist counterparts.

Many women who are pro-feminist shy away from the feminist label for pragmatic reasons, saying they find it too confining or misleading. Others among the Leftists find feminism incompatible with their socialist ideology yet have various pro-feminist leanings. Islamist women in Egypt reject the notion of feminism as superfluous or heretical and accordingly preclude the possibility of an "Islamic feminism." The exception so far has proven the rule. Even many feminist and pro-feminist women have problems with the term feminism, largely because of Western associations, even though they concede that this belief is misguided. Egyptian feminists and Islamists alike have difficulties with the stereotype of feminism prevailing in Egypt—which Islamists believe to be true and feminists reject—as aggressively anti-men and in conflict with the culture's moral code, and do not wish to be associated with such views of gender and culture.

The gender activism which I describe is for the most part not a social movement but mainly involves individuals or a few loosely structured groupings. It is mainly pragmatic rather than political in the more highly-organized or self-conscious sense, and low-profile and subtle rather than public and confrontational. The exception to the above characterization is the Arab Women's Solidarity Association (to be discussed below), which has suffered from government suppression. Feminist women would regard this as feminist activism, pro-feminist women might, but Islamist women would not.

What is the significance of gender activism? It means that many women across a broad spectrum insist on maintaining or increasing their own roles in society and promoting a public presence of women in general. It means that many women insist on their own growth, productivity, and creativity in diverse spheres. It means that women are fighting back against retrogressive forces that wish to push them to the margins of society. It means some erosion of a bifurcation among women and some lessening of the tensions arising from ideological polarization within the Muslim community and among Egyptians more generally. It means a certain freeing of women from patriarchal dominance in the family. It does not mean a lessening of women's concern for the family. Finally, it indicates a certain opening out within the Islamist movement.

This chapter draws on numerous interviews as well as more informal conversations and debates in Egypt from 1988 to 1990 with women of different ages who are feminists, pro-feminists, and Islamists. These women are intellectuals, writers, and professionals mainly from the middle class. I also conducted interviews with a number of men who would be designated as pro-feminist or Islamist. I chose to interview persons who were active in society and concerned with the issue of women's public roles. Although I have included writers I also wanted to obtain the views of those who do not express themselves in print or public speaking. As I was eager to be oriented toward what people thought were important aspects of the subjects under discussion, the interviews were conducted in an interactive fashion. As a result, lively debates ensued and broader comparisons were made. It was out of these encounters, my research, and in the course of daily living that I developed my understanding of what I came to call gender activism. What I learned through previous historical investigation about what I have termed the "gender politics" of women in Egypt early this century has had compelling echoes which also helped focus my thinking on the subject.[2]

The Contemporary Context

Since the 1970s there has been a growing Islamist climate in Egypt with critical implications for women. Until recently, the Islamist movement was mainly associated with populist ideologues and militants who focused on the issue of an Islamic state and who stressed female morality and expected women in the movement to be passive followers.[3] Recently, the circumference of the Islamist sphere has been broadening so that now more mainstream and liberal male religious writers and speakers are becoming part of the movement. At the same time, there are efforts to attract more women who are now encouraged to play active roles in the movement.[4]

Historically there has been room in Egypt for the competing discourses of the state, Islamists, and feminists on the Woman Question. This continues into the 1990s.[5] The state and the feminists have had to take into account Islamist social and political sensibilities; indeed Islamist forces have tempered the agendas and public discourses of the state and many feminists. At the same time, the state has curtailed the movements and public expression of Islamists who are themselves hostile towards the state and feminists. Yet, while alternative or competing discourses may have co-existed in Egypt, they have occurred in different historical climates. At the moment the broad conservative atmosphere in Egypt permeated by populist Islamist influences tempers public and explicit feminist expression.

Since the 1970s conservative social ideology articulated by Islamists has been clashing with imperatives created by economic need, producing strains and tensions exacerbated still more by the ostentation of a small strata of the new inordinately wealthy. During the 1980s economic conditions continued to deteriorate. Many middle and lower class families came to require the income of more than one working member. Households have had to draw on the income-generating capacities of women as well as men who often hold down more than one job. This poor economic situation does not show signs of abating in the foreseeable future.

This is the broad context in which we must locate the current gender activism. Since the end of the 1980s there has been some liberalization on gender issues within Islamist ranks, or possibly political expediency concerning women, to which I shall return. I do not, however, see gender activism as springing from these socio-economic phenomena. I do believe, on the other hand, that gender activism may help spawn an Islamic "feminist" activism in Egypt during the decade of the 1990s.

Identity: Going Public and Remaining Private

The prevailing conservative Islamist climate in Egypt influences what may be called the politics of disclosure or concealment. Is one's identity to be publicly proclaimed or to be disguised?

Islamist women insist upon public identification of themselves as committed Muslims with the hijab or, less frequently, the niqab being the most obvious sign of their commitment. While the hijab is usually understood to be an Islamic requirement the niqab is seen as being excessive and not prescribed by religion.[6] Without the external symbol of the veil they believe that women cannot be true and committed Muslims. Veiling is seen not only as a religious requirement but as a symbol of cultural authenticity. Kamila al-'Arabi, a television announcer fired for donning the veil says, "The hijab is ... a matter of identity and self-discovery after a long fall and being lost in Westernization when colonialism imposed its clothes on us ... that is why the hijab was and must be a national issue of great importance ... ."[7] Islamist women, including religiously observant Muslims as well as purely nominal Muslims, call Muslim women who do not veil secularists, often implying much more. Islamists, however, make distinctions between *alamaniyya bila din*, or secularism without religion, and *alamaniyya*, or a secularism within religion. Non-Islamist women often resent being labelled as secularists and negatively judged by (Islamist) co-religionists, which they do not see as befitting a Muslim.

It is striking that many contemporary women who identify with feminism are reluctant to publicly affirm this, in contrast to the practice of feminists earlier in this century. The reasons for this contemporary behavior seem to be pragmatic and political. Feminists today feel freer both personally and professionally by being less explicit. Some shrink from taking a public stand because of family and/or societal pressures in today's conservative atmosphere. Over and over, many feminist and pro-feminist women with whom I talked expressed their difficulty with the feminist label, saying that it was confining. Development specialist Sumaiya Ibrahim Huber recalled her reactions a few years ago, "I didn't want to be put in a corner. ... I think I had a problem with labels. ... I think people use the term badly and I thought that a feminist was like a fanatic." She added, "I [still] wouldn't call myself a feminist but I don't react as strongly as before."[8] Publisher Eva Elias said succinctly, "I think labels limit you."[9]

Many also fear the negative consequences of being associated with feminism. Even when women reject public perceptions of feminism as stridently anti-male and in defiance of moral norms, they are anxious about being associated with such thinking. In Egypt, feminism is also widely branded as Western. This notion is re-enforced in part because the term itself is a Western coinage, and so far no word for feminism has been minted in Arabic. Heba al-Khouly, a development specialist and a feminist, says, "I think there is a real problem with the term feminist because it is a Western term. I think it is a fear about loss of identity. It is not so much that it [feminism] is radical."[10] Hala Halim, a graduate student in comparative literature, confessed, "There seems to be something mutually exclusive about being a feminist and being an Egyptian, as if you reject your bonds to your own country."[11] Historian Huda Lutfy admits, "We are made to feel guilty [if we are feminists] about [allegedly] being Western, as you know."[12]

Other ideological problems inhibit women. Pro-feminist women confess to being unclear about what feminism means. Some equate feminism with activism and believe they cannot be feminists if they are not activists. Socialist women and current or past members of the Taggamu Party hold that women's causes must be furthered within the framework of socialism broadly speaking, or more specifically within the context of the Taggamu Party. Although they may take positions similar to those of feminists on particular issues, their ideological and political orientation precludes their coming out as feminists. For these women feminism is not a comprehensive analysis dealing with the whole of society but a partial approach which they see as privileging women and as a luxury in a Third World country like Egypt. Writer and professor of literature Radwa Ashur asserted, "To talk about women's rights as such seems to the majority of Egyptians a kind of luxury."[13] Similarly, writer Latifa Zayyat, a member of the Taggamu Party, said, "We cannot afford the luxury of a feminist movement."[14]

While many people convey a sense of a monolithic feminism in Egypt, some speak of a plurality of feminisms. Hala Halim said, "This may be taking things too far but I think there is a feminism for every woman."[15] For her this means until she has worked out her own version of feminism she eschews the feminist identity, a position which seems common among a number of pro-feminists.

Today's feminists in Egypt are women with layered identities, only one of which is feminist. By publicly asserting one identity they might be seen as giving priority to that identity over others, and this most are unwilling to do. In contrast to feminists and pro-feminists, Islamist women claim a single paramount identity which according to their ideology must be publicly asserted.

Unlike the case for the Islamists there is no ready external symbol for the feminists signalling to others who they are. More fully committed feminists make public declaration of their identity and stand. They are known through their words and actions. Feminists are largely identified through their affiliation with the *Jam'iyyat Tadamun al-Mar'a al-'Arabiyya* (The Arab Women's Solidarity Association), or with collectives producing journals such as *Majallat al-Mar'a al-Jadida* (The New Woman

Magazine) and *Majallat Bint al-'Ard* (The Daughter of the Earth Magazine), published in Mansura in the Delta. Similarly, the group of professional women who published *al-Huquq al-Qanuniyya li al-Mar'a al-Misriyya bain al-'Nadhariyya wa al-Tatbiq* (The Legal Rights of the Egyptian Woman in Theory and Practice) have made their feminism known. For women from the afore-mentioned groups, taking a public stand is integral to their feminism. Other committed feminists—and this applies to pro-feminists as well—who are not formally involved with a group might acknowledge their position when the occasion calls for it but otherwise their stand would not necessarily be known.

Essentializing Culture and Forgetting History

Islamist women are seen as having cultural norms on their side while feminist women appear to be challenging indigenous culture. The burden of proof of authenticity, or correctness, is on feminists. They have to show that they are not tainted by alien, mainly Western, influences. This is a problem feminists have virtually everywhere in the Arab and Islamic worlds, if not everywhere in the Third World. As Algerian feminist Nassera Merah notes about Islamists vis-à-vis feminists in Algeria, "their supreme reproach [to the feminists] is their association with the West." Islamists, on the other hand, are *ipso facto* indigenous and authentic.[16]

In the current popular Islamist discourse in Egypt there is an essentializing of culture, an allocation to women of timeless attributes. The Muslim woman is first and foremost, if not only, a good daughter, wife, and mother, ideally spending her life in the home ministering to her family. This is an ageless model for women exhorted by Islamist men and, to a lesser degree, by Islamist women.[17]

Quite different was the Islamic modernist movement of the late nineteenth century led by Shaikh Muhammad 'Abduh. He called for renewal and reform, advocating the practice of *ijtihad*, individual inquiry into religion and its interpretation in the light of new socio-economic needs. Ushering in a liberal era when innovation in various areas of life was regarded as Islamic, this brand of Islam prepared the ground for the rise of Egyptian feminism elaborated within a religious framework. During this period, too, Egyptian feminism drew support from liberal Egyptian nationalists.[18] At the turn of the twentieth century, women with a feminist consciousness and activist agendas such as Nabawiyya Musa and Bahithat al-Badiya articulated their programs in the discourses of Islam and of nationalism.[19] Equally, the early organized feminist movements led by Huda Sha'rawi and Duriyya Shafiq operated within an Islamic framework.[20]

Feminist movements in Egypt in the first half of the century and public policy under Nasser's program of Arab socialism assisted women in making vast inroads into all aspects of society. Today they are found in virtually every sector of the economy and at all levels, although generally not heavily clustered at the top.[21] In the 1970s, with the state-encouraged shift away from Arab socialism during Sadat's rule, Islam was used as a counter ideology which fed the rise of social conservatism. Only at the end of the twentieth century, with the ascendancy of a conservative popular Islamic culture, did feminism come to be widely branded as anti-Islamic.[22]

With the Islamist wave unfolding from the late 1960s and accelerating in the 1970s there was some reversal of previous gender trends in society. The second Islamist wave idealized women's family and domestic roles re-assigning women to the home and urging them out of the workplace.[23] The movement among women to re-veil set some Muslim women apart from others in a political as well as religious statement. This fed a discourse of modesty that further endangered women's public roles even though some women argued that the veil facilitated their presence in public.[24] Segregation of the sexes and a return to the home were part of this rising discourse of modesty articulated in the name of Islam.[25] In Egypt the move to the veil has been widespread among educated women.[26] Whereas the conservative Islamic discourse in Egypt was mainly articulated by men, there have been some women who have contributed to it as well. Prominent among them are Zainab al-Ghazali, the founder of the Muslim Women's Association in 1936 (which in 1948 became the Society of the Muslim Sisters when it allied with the state-supressed Muslim Brothers) and Safinaz Kazim, theatre critic for *al-Musawwar*, a columnist for the Islamic paper, *al-Hilal al-Dawli* (published in London) and mainstream Egyptian papers, and author of several books. Both have extolled women's conventional roles. But they have also spoken out in support of women's roles in society. Moreover, both have insisted upon playing active roles in society themselves.

Al-Ghazali and Kazim have been antagonistic to feminism. Before leaving to form the Muslim Women's Society, Al-Ghazali was briefly a member (in 1935) of *al-Ittihad al-Nisa'i al-Misri*, the Egyptian Feminist Union, founded and headed by Huda Sha'rawi. She told me recently, "The Egyptian Feminist Union wanted to establish the civilization of the Western woman in Egypt, the Arab world, and the Islamic world."[27] Kazim agrees with this view. In *Mas'alat al-Sufur wa al-Hijab* (The

Question of Unveiling and Veiling, published in 1982), she argued that the feminist movement led by Sha'rawi pulled women away from Islam. Sixty years after Sha'rawi publicly unveiled her face—leading to the final removal of veils by women of the middle and upper class—Kazim asserted that women's unveiling was the aberration not the norm.[28]

Second Wave Feminism

Coincident with the ascendancy of conservative Islam was the rise of second wave feminism associated with Nawal al-Saadawi whose writings took feminism in a new direction. Her feminism calling for social, economic, and cultural revolution was not initially articulated within an Islamic framework although she drew on certain Islamic arguments. A medical doctor, her 1972 book *al-Mar'a wa al-Jins* (Woman and Sex), focused on sexual oppressions of women resulting in physical and psychological disease. She likewise attacked the sexual double standard. She enlightened many women in Egypt and helped to raise the consciousness of a whole generation of women students in the democratic movement.[29] However, because she entered an area of taboo she also evoked intense popular criticism. Often misunderstood, her feminism was associated with encouraging the immorality of women and violating religion. Indeed, feminism *per se* came to be widely seen in this light. Just as al-Saadawi put the spotlight on sexual abuses, the nascent Islamist movement by advocating a return to the veil heightened awareness of women as (vulnerable) sexual beings. Islamists and others associated feminism with sexual freedom and the link has yet to be broken.[30]

Organized feminism resurfaced in Egypt in the early 1980s—three decades after the Egyptian Feminist Union and other feminist associations had been suppressed—with the creation of the Arab Women's Solidarity Association headed by Nawal al-Saadawi.[31] In 1984, some young women who as students had been part of the democratic movement of the 1970s formed a study group. They investigated the history of feminist movements in Egypt led by Sha'rawi and others. In the face of the growing Islamist movement they wanted to recover some of the gains of the Nasser period but rejected state authoritarianism and felt women should identify their own needs. Two years later, the group created *The New Woman Magazine* to reach out to other women. Another collective effort emerged in Mansura where a group of women who had organized with others in public protest over the Israeli invasion of Lebanon in 1982 went on to form *Jam'iyyat Bint al-'Ard*, the Society of the Daughters of the Earth, to continue their activism along feminist lines. They encouraged girls in this Delta city and surrounding rural areas to develop their minds and take part in the life of their communities. In an effort to make wider contact, they started *The Daughter of the Earth Magazine* in 1984. The first issue addressed the problem of women being pushed back into the home. The problem was examined again in the sixth issue in 1990. At the same time, the editorial collective proposed a debate in print between two veteran activists, the feminist Amina Sa'id, and the Islamist Zainab al-Ghazali, but the latter did not agree.[32]

The crisis provoked in 1985 by the rescinding of the liberally revised personal status law of 1979 led to the formation of a broad feminist coalition called *Lajnat al-Difa'i 'an Huquq al-Mar'a wa al-Usra*, the Committee for the Defense of the Rights of the Woman and the Family, to fight back. On the eve of the Egyptian delegation's departure for the Nairobi conference marking the end of the United Nations Decade for Women, the coalition succeeded in obtaining the re-instatement of the law, albeit in truncated form.[33] Later, disagreements among feminists split the united front and the coalition fragmented.

Gender Activism

The gender activism of the end of the 1980s and beginning of the 1990s signals a pragmatic moment for Islamist, feminist, and pro-feminist women. Committed feminists proceed with their projects: seminars, conferences and publications. They maintain high visibility while working to achieve their feminist goals—as do Islamist intellectual women in advancing their causes. Pro-feminist women advance women's causes within the framework of their professions but keep their feminism largely out of sight. Non-association feminists talk more about their activism and less about their ideology while association feminists and Islamists are oppositely inclined. Feminists and pro-feminists are presumed to advocate public roles for women, Islamist women are not.

At a time when the major chorus of populist (mainly male) Islamist voices continues to call for women's retreat to the home, some Islamist women challenge this by insisting upon women's rights in the public sphere. Veteran Islamist Zainab al-Ghazali continues her earlier activism, after six years in prison under Nasser, inspiring and mobilizing young women who gather at her home and who read her writings including her weekly column for *al-Liwa al-Islami*. While she has always exalted women's roles as wives and mothers, she also demonstrates, by personal example and encouragement, the importance of *Dawa*, that is winning people to the true Islam to achieve an Islamic state and society. For professional women, which many of her followers are, this may be conducted within the context of their work.[34]

Safinaz Kazim, who started out as a Leftist in the 1960s, has remained on the scene as a writer and journalist since then (with spates in prison on three occasions). She prefers to view women and men simply as Muslims rather than gendered beings. She does not favor institutionalized gender separations. She decried, for example, the idea of starting an Islamic journal for women saying, "Dividing the forces of society into male and female is a Western practice." (It is interesting to note that she discredits this division by branding it Western).[35]

Kazim has promoted women's work and other societal roles in her column, "Personal Papers" in *al-Hilal al-Dawli*, a London-based Islamist journal. In an article entitled "Turuk al-Mar'a li al-'Amal Da'wa Shar'a Islamiyya" (Methods of the Woman in the Work of Propagating Islamic Doctrine, which appeared on October 16, 1987), she indicted as un-Islamic the call for women to quit their work. In "Quwwa al-Mujtam'a al-Islami" (The Power of Islamic Society, published in two parts: on September 16 and October 1, 1987), she reminded Muslims that women and men both constitute society and thus both sexes must build it together.[36] Kazim writes within the context of Islamist journalism abroad and for "secular" publications at home which have usually been reluctant to accept articles with an Islamic tone from her. However, in November 1990, the wide circulation women's magazine, *Nus al-Dunya* (Half the World), published her article entitled "Bi al-Tafkir al-Islami la Tujid Qadiyya li al-Mar'a" (In Islamic Thinking There is No Women's Question). Here she articulates both a gender-free and gendered approach to society stating that "there is no woman question," while acknowledging that "the woman has to regain her lawful rights guaranteed to her by Islam," including the right to work, to elect leaders, and "participation in building an advanced Islamic society." As a deputy editor of Dar al-Hilal Publishing House, a member of the editorial staff of *al-Musawwar* and through the very act of writing itself, Kazim engages in gender activism.

Some Islamists—many of whom are young women—have taken advantage of the new forum for airing their views provided by the first Islamist magazine for women which appeared in October 1990. A sister magazine to *al-Mukhtar al-Islami*, it is called *Hajir*. While women's magazines are typically under the editorship of women, *Hajir* has a male editor-in-chief called Jamal Sultan. He announced that the magazine intends to counter the negative influences of the women's and feminist magazines by providing an Islamic alternative. Female contributors to the new Islamic magazine include both conservatives and liberals. Among the issues discussed so far are public voices and roles for women. In "al- Adab al-Nisa'i wa al-Ham al-Qaumi" (Women's Literature and National Anxiety, in January 1991), Miral al-Tahawi stressed that women's writings are key in countering "the current of rigidity" and getting to "the root of problems." Hiba Su'ad al-Din in "al-Mar'a wa al-Siyasiya" (The Woman and Politics, in November 1990), argued that the Islamic path to women's freedom is through politics and that work is a woman's issue. If a woman or members of her family suffer because she works, al-Din claims it is not the woman but the state which is to blame for not providing proper support systems.

Meanwhile, Islamist progressive discourse on gender is being moved in a new direction by a young Islamist graduate student in political science at Cairo University, Hiba Rauf, who is attempting to develop a feminism within Islam. Rauf is examining the early sources of religion and Islamic history to evolve a theory of women's liberation. She rejects the term feminism because she sees it as anti-men and not because of its allegedly Western origins. Like the feminists, and like Kazim, she recognizes that women do not enjoy the rights accorded them by religion. For Rauf, as for Kazim, Muslim women's enjoyment in practice of their lawful rights is a step towards the realization of a true Islamic society.

Like all Islamists, Rauf is critical of the West, however, unlike most of them, she tends to critically examine phenomena attributed to the West rather than to reject them wholesale. Concerning feminism she says:

> Feminist questions can be very useful to us. When I read some feminist writings and saw what they were about, they helped me very much and gave me some ideas. But, I always go back to my Quranic dictionary, if I can use the term. The Quran is my dictionary and I can't move without it so for every term they use I go back and for every idea of theirs I go back and if I can find some legitimacy for them from the Quran I go on with them and see how they can help me with [new] ideas. ... It is the [universal] humanitarian things that concern me, but what is peculiar to them and is the result of Western ideas or experience and is not universal, I leave to them.[37]

She confesses, "As far as I know feminism negates religion." Although Rauf rejects the term feminism, she is looking for a way to express much of what feminism at base connotes. The challenge for her is to liberate women and to stay within the parameters of Islam as she understands it. While reading about women's experience in the West she discovered the American New Right. She feels that

The New Right can be of more use to Islamist scholars than radical feminism. The New Right doesn't reject Christian values and family life. Maybe we can find something in common and can raise some questions and have a debate but we have no starting point with radical and Leftist feminism.

Rauf is willing to admit that "Western" feminist movements have met with certain successes in Egypt and tries to analyze why rather than condemn them outright in the manner of mainstream Islamist discourse produced mainly by men but also by Islamist women such as Safinaz Kazim and Zainab al-Ghazali. The latter said in an interview, "The Egyptian Feminist Union [in the 1920s, 1930s, and 1940s] wanted to establish the civilization of the Western woman in Egypt and the rest of the Arab and Islamic worlds."[38] Rauf says:

They [conservative Islamists] say women's liberation movements were dominated by the West and were the tools of Westernization but they don't say why they succeeded to some extent. That [success] was simply because we as Muslims [kept] women in a very bad condition. They say that women have such and such in Islamic societies but they didn't [enjoy their rights]. When women's liberation movements started it was because Muslims had so much trouble in their family life and in society so that they [the feminist movements] had something to say and they were listened to. They don't analyze it that way. ... The problem is how can the Islamic movement initiate women's liberation from within? ... I would like very much to create such a movement. But this movement must liberate the entire society, women and men alike, and not be a separate movement for women. I would like this movement to be an item on the Islamic agenda.

Among the Islamists I interviewed, only one called herself a feminist. She admitted that she did not find any contradictions between feminism and Islam. Maha Sa'ud, a university graduate now engaged in development work, was a stewardess with Saudi Arabian Airlines for nine years before she took up the veil and accordingly was obliged to quit her job. Feminism for her is an everyday matter: an attitude and a way of conducting daily life. Women should have the freedom to choose how to live their lives and to freely express themselves in a way that is in general harmony with society. She believes this is possible.

Sa'ud does not see feminism as Western but rather as a universal that finds particular forms of expression in different societies. In this she stands out, not just among Islamist women but among many feminists and most pro-feminists as well.[39]

The pro-feminists mainly include women who typically are not concerned with ideology but are pragmatists who have carved out lives and careers for themselves and in the context of their professions tend to promote the general interests of women. However, pro-feminists also include women who are committed to socialist ideology and while attuned to matters relating to women have largely subsumed this concern under their socialism. The pro-feminists with whom I talked participate in public life through their work and their literary production. They are trying to confront what they see as a menacing regressive environment for women and to place their individual work in a larger perspective. Rather than debating feminism they address gender issues and explore new directions. Hanna Ayub, who is part of the development community, remarked,

Nowadays we are starting to get together as women interested in women's issues to discuss these things. We are a group of educated young women who happen to know each other. We are trying to network to make the group wider. We got together because we have one thing in common which is our interest in women's issues and because we realize what is happening to women ... such as asking women to go back to the home; it is threatening. ... The group is trying to counter-balance what is happening to other women. We see other educated women going back in big steps; our generation, women in their twenties and thirties.[40]

Development specialists Sumaiya Ibrahim Huber and Heba al-Khouly are members of the group. Both work with poor women in income generation projects; Huber works with Bedouin women in Sinai and al-Khouly works among poor Cairene women. Huber, al-Khouly, and Ayoub share a general perspective on the importance of women's roles in the workplace. Women in the group include pro-feminists and feminists (such as al-Khouly), but the emphasis is on practical issues rather than on ideological debate.

Experience has taught women like Ghada al-Howaidy that women can make practical gains in every day life which have incremental effects in opening out their lives on public and private fronts alike. Al-Howaidy who works in bi-national educational and cultural exchange does not call herself a feminist "because to me it's linked with [political] action."[41] She says that if a particular issue affecting women, such as the personal status case mentioned above, came to the fore, she would become an activist. Generally, however, she believes that women should not be singled out as a separate category. This is a common position among pro-feminists.

Gender activism at the university—where Islamism started to grow in the 1970s and is still strong—presents challenges. Huda Sadda is a professor of English literature at Cairo University where many of the students are conservative and the Islamist movement has many adherents. She and the many other women professors at Egyptian universities, a number of whom are department heads, serve as female role models by their very presence. The challenge is to open up new forms of awareness among students. Sadda says "If you shock students they don't listen to you and brand you Western, too affected by Western ideas, and they shut you out completely."[42] Her approach is to be sensitive to where they are coming from and proceed cautiously.

Among the ideological pro-feminists are writers Latifa Zayyat and Radwa Ashur, both Leftists. Zayyat was active in the student and the nationalist movements in the second half of the 1940s. In the early 1950s she joined the faculty at the Teacher Training School for Women at Ain Shams which later became the *Kulliyat al-Banat* (The Girls' College). In 1960 she published her much acclaimed novel, *al-Bab al-Maftuh* (The Open Door), about a young middle-class woman who found freedom from restrictions set by her family and society through participation in the nationalist movement. Although the author of a novel with a feminist theme, Zayyat has until recently shrunk from identifying with feminism which had no place in her socialist and nationalist ideology. However, in 1990 she confessed, "I have come more and more to realize that the status of women has been of great importance to me."[43] Her recent collection of short stories, *Shaikhukha* (Old Age), is "a celebration of self-reconciliation," which she asserts "no man could have written." She speaks of a woman's acceptance of old age and interrogates women's different kinds of relationships. In her writing she probes and expresses gender issues, and acknowledges her writing as a gendered enterprise.

Radwa Ashur, part of the 1960s student generation, a university professor in comparative literature, in addition to being a writer and critic. Like Zayyat, she finds feminism as a separate ideology problematic. She explains:

> I am very much preoccupied with women's liberation in the context of social liberation as part of national liberation. ... My feminist consciousness is one thread of a rich texture. I don't take this thread out of

the material and say this is the whole texture. That is why I don't conceive of myself as a feminist. ... I am aware of my problem as a woman. It is obvious in what I write because my personal experience makes me conscious of my womanhood and whatever hinders my womanhood but I am also aware that I am Egyptian, Arab, and Third World; being these three and a woman goes into the making of me.[44]

Like Zayyat, Ashur illuminates gender problematics in her books, and like Sadda and other women professors, her very presence as a university professor constitutes an important statement about gender.

Among the self-acknowledged feminists many operate in their everyday lives in ways not very different from pro-feminists. Meanwhile, others try to build and increase forms of collective activism. The Arab Women's Solidarity Association (AWSA) under Nawal al-Saadawi maintained the highest profile among feminists. AWSA feminism has been the most provocative and controversial in Egypt. AWSA's membership had grown in the mid-1980s at the time of the crisis over the personal status law, but subsequently decreased when rifts appeared. Nevertheless, the organization has evolved as a forum for feminist debate and outreach through its publications—including a quarterly magazine, *Nun*, launched in 1989—international conferences (in 1986, 1988, 1990), and monthly seminars. These events have attracted women of different ages, especially younger women, as well as men concerned with gender issues. Typically, the seminar speakers have been feminists or pro-feminists. However, early in 1990, an Islamist voice was heard when Safinz Kazim spoke on veiling and women's rights in Islam, drawing a particularly large audience. The talk provoked angry debate between AWSA feminists and Islamists revealing the depths of the ideological polarization between them concerning the role of Islam in everyday life and the nature of the ideal state and society. Interestingly, though, there was no disagreement about women's economic and political roles as such.

The government grew increasingly uneasy with AWSA and in the spring of 1990 prevented publication of the fourth issue of *Nun*. The following year it closed down the organization itself. AWSA, which is currently taking legal action, has received support from the Egyptian Organization for Human Rights.

Feminists who are members of the establishment and have made it to the top of their professions have confronted the call for women to retreat to the home. A group comprised of lawyers, journalists, professors, and Egypt's first woman ambassador collaborated in publishing a booklet entitled *The Legal Rights of the Egyptian Woman*, spelling out for women the rights guaranteed to them by laws and conventions so that they may practice them more effectively. The first chapter deals with laws concerning work. The third chapter, on personal status laws, makes the link between the "private" and the "public" and reminds women that they can stipulate in their marriage contract the right to work outside the home.

> The inclusion of a provision to that effect [the right to work outside the home] in the marriage contract in no way implies that a wife's right to work outside the home is contingent on her husband's approval. As explained above, this right is guaranteed by the Constitution and by law. However, it is advisable to include this provision to safeguard the wife's right to alimony in case of divorce as husbands have been known in some cases to use the wife's exercise of this right as an excuse to avoid making alimony payments, claiming that they were opposed to her working outside the home.[45]

The above feminists came of age in the 1950s and 1960s. Younger feminists, who were at university in the 1970s, are taking new initiatives to spearhead forms of collective activism. Members of the group that produce *The New Woman Magazine* circulated a letter in July 1990 clarifying their position and inviting collaboration:

> The New Woman Group is a progressive and democratic feminist group of women, who believe that while Egyptian and Arab women share with men the hardships brought about by backwardness, dependence and economic crisis, they have to carry a double burden and suffer from a variety of forms of subordination, oppression and suppression arising specifically from their position as women. Moreover, while we believe in the equal right of men and women to fight all forms of oppression and exploitation, we similarly believe that women's struggle will remain incomplete without their very own battles for freedom and equality and their rights to express themselves, to participate in public life and to take their own life decisions, their right to work and to equal pay, to mention just a few. We also stress women's right in determining what they want to do with their lives, whether in the public or personal sphere. We claim that this freedom will not be achieved unless women learn to organize themselves in a wide democratic movement, that has place for all Egyptian women in general and Egyptian women of the popular classes in particular. We are working with the objective that the New Woman Group which is one of several democratic women's groups in Egypt will be able to join together the widest possible number of those women

interested in the women's question and who work in fields related to women's concerns, interests, and rights and who fight to win those rights.[46]

Their strategy is to mobilize women to share their skills, expertise, and experience in a number of concrete fields including adult education, health, childcare, legal aid, income generation, and information for the benefit of the broad mass of under-privileged women.

Meanwhile, there are other feminists who are involved in individual forms of activism. These include the writer Salwa Bakr who attended university and participated in the democratic movement of the 1970s with many members of The New Women group. She says, "I object to the role of women being only in the home doing secondary work rather than doing effective work in society. She can't choose her life, her career, and her behavior." For these reasons, and others, Bakr calls herself a feminist. She is pessimistic, however, about the possibilities in the foreseeable future for an effective feminist movement. "Now there is no movement to develop society in general and so it is difficult for a women's rights movement to emerge." Bakr expresses her activism through her novels. "All the characters in my books are women. ... I know the world of women. ... I worry about the role of women which society forgets all the time so I speak about women going out on strikes, women in the hard times in our country. Everything in [recorded] history is related to men but this is not the way it was and so I write about women. ... I worry about the situation of women because I am suffering from it."[47]

While Bakr records women's recent history in fictional form, Huda Lutfy uses her historian's skills to look deeper into the past and write the history of Egyptian and Arab women. She does this as a self-conscious act of retrieval and validation of modes of indigenous feminist consciousness and behaviors:

I explore Middle Eastern history and try to find out how women felt, and perhaps sometimes try to identify with these women, psychologically, especially women who tried to assert themselves and to say, yes I am a woman but yes I can be influential, I can have my say, I can be a poet, a singer, I can be a musician, I can be a politician, a successful merchant and so on. By finding examples of these women even though they are rather exceptional, ... I don't have to deal with this guilt that it [female or feminist acts of assertion] is all Western, that women belonging to Middle Eastern society never questioned, never felt frustrated by the restrictions placed on them. ... It is not simply out of the historical experience of the West that women started to assert themselves and express themselves and to say that we want to do more than the role society imposes on us.[48]

Sensitive to this same issue Al-Khouly said, "I get very upset that the West should monopolize the concept of feminism. ... We had feminism in our history too."[49]

Feminists are active in the provinces as well as in the capital. In the Delta, in and around Mansura, the women of *The Daughter of the Earth* group are engaged in various forms of practical outreach such as training women in income-generating work. Jihan al-Sayyid, a member of the collective, articulates their approach and agenda: "Any movement like ours, in order to make contact with the masses, must work within their environment. We must work from below. It is long work and very difficult work. Writing is not enough; we must work with the people. *The Daughter of the Earth* must work with all classes: peasants, workers, and professionals."[50] Not only feminists belong to *The Daughter of the Earth* collective, some members are Islamists. In the Delta village of Kamshish, Shahinda Maqlad, a hero in the peasant uprising in the 1960s during Nasser's agrarian reform, is involved in similar forms of activism. In addition to her regular work, Maqlad organized a committee last year to plan a conference marking the twenty-fifth anniversary of the uprising. For Maqlad, women's liberation can only occur in the context of national liberation through socialism.[51]

Another gender activist who works among women in the rural areas of Egypt is Algerian-born Zohra Merabet. Permanently settled in Egypt, she heads her own development consulting firm. She says that her feminist consciousness first emerged during her childhood in the Aures Mountains of southeast Algeria and evolved more fully during her days in the student and women's movements in France in the late 1960s. Merabet's activism finds expression in the women's development projects she has worked on in different parts of the country. She has found a number of rural women affiliated with Islamic groups in both Upper and Lower Egypt and sees this at some level as a "feminist" function. She says:

It is hard for me to have a position on it. One has a functional reaction to it. ... The Islamization process is a process of awareness of the personality and one's position in society and it is very difficult for me to handle. In a way, I see it as a kind of progress. The women [who become Islamists] have discovered certain things and want to make a mark on society. I can understand it because I took a certain path [she had described earlier how important going to engineering school and becoming an engineer had been for her feminist actions] to make a mark on my society. These women took a different means, something that helped them to walk out of the family unit into a group to discuss and think. There's a certain group educational factor. Women who become leaders [as she observed in villages in the Nile Valley and oases] become *muhajjabat*. It enables them to take a stand, to do something. What goes on in the countryside is very different from what goes on in Cairo. ... Maybe the framework is too big in the urban setting. In smaller societies it is a very positive action because it gives women the chance to start articulating some ideas. They might not remain Islamists their whole lives. At the village level, Islamism empowers women. In Cairo the opposite may happen because one may be controlled by higher forces who are doing the articulating of ideology. In a complicated way village women [by becoming Islamists] are inventing themselves.[52]

Conclusions

This chapter has attempted to show that since the end of the 1980s, the positions of intellectual women as feminists, pro-feminists, and Islamists concerning women's roles in Egyptian society have been converging. Although women's rights to play roles in society, and the importance of these roles, have historically been central to feminist and pro-feminist thinking in Egypt, this has not been part of standard Islamist thought. Increasingly however, some women in the Islamist movement are advancing the cause of women's public roles through word and deed. I have used the term "gender activism" to describe this common approach towards women's public roles by feminists, pro-feminists, and Islamists. This has been an attempt to solve the problem of capturing the advocacy and practice by feminists and Islamists alike of women's roles in society as an inherent right—and one legitimized by Islam—by means of a new, and therefore unencumbered, analytical construct. Yet, I have cautioned that although women across the ideological spectrum engage in gender activism which is essentially a common pragmatic approach, women's moorings in divergent ideologies remain significant.

With the third feminist and Islamist phase from the late 1980s into the 1990s, the more stark adversarialism of the second phase from the 1960s well into the 1980s has been tempered. What accounts for this change? I would argue that this represents a pragmatic and political response on the part of feminist, pro-feminist, and Islamist women alike. At the end of the twentieth century, society in many ways is up for grabs; feminists and pro-feminists want to hold ground and Islamists want to gain (public) ground. Whereas committed feminists have evolved analyses of patriarchal supremacy, Islamist women have either internalized patriarchal thinking, even while at times acting on their own in contrary ways, or they have silently eschewed it. Both stances on the part of gender activists signal some awareness of patriarchal hegemony. While older Islamist women have not directly confronted this hegemonic framework, younger Islamist women are beginning to question male dominance and to see it as transgressing the bounds of correct Islamic parameters. Although this will probably not lead the new generation of intellectual women out of Islamism it will probably produce a gender reconfiguration from within.

Not only are there treacherous patriarchal shoals in Egyptian society, but the Egyptian state impedes the free flourishing of feminism and Islamism alike. Thus women like those mentioned here operate in a pragmatic mode: non-movement feminism holds out while liberal inroads are made within the Islamist movement. In Egypt, intellectual women will continue to articulate their positions, to stand their ground in society, and try to reach out across class, regional, and ideological divides. Their gender activism will remain grounded in divergent ideologies which in turn reflect their different configurations of identity and their overlapping yet distinct visions of the good society.

Egyptian women as feminists, pro-feminists, and Islamists all have a stake in retaining their presence in society and in promoting the public presence of other women. They have many common gender interests and common goals, despite the different primary contexts in which they place their projects. For feminists religion is primarily an individual and personal matter. They do not advocate an Islamic state and they have a pluralist attitude toward society. For the more ideologically concerned Islamists, the goal of an Islamic state and society is fundamental. They believe that when this is achieved women, and all other members of the *umma* (Islamic nation), will enjoy true liberation. These differences however have not precluded feminist, pro-feminist, and Islamist women from engaging in common forms of activism.

Notes

I would like to thank the Fulbright Islamic Civilization Program and the Ford Foundation for support during the period I collected material for this paper. I would also like to thank Dr. Ann Radwan, Executive Director of the Fulbright Commission in Cairo for her help in facilitating my research and Dr. Valentine Moghadam for organizing the richly stimulating conference where this paper was presented and for her careful editorial attention to the final version of my paper.

1. I made comparisons between the first two waves of feminism and Islamism in "Feminism and Fundamentalism: Emergence and Resurgence," paper delivered at Bard College, 1986 and in "Feminists and Islam in Egypt: An Historical Perspective," seminar paper for the Institute of Islamic Studies Research, McGill University, 1987. In "Competing Agendas: Feminists, Islam, and the State in the 19th and 20th Century Egypt" (in Deniz Kandiyoti, ed.), *Women, Islam, and the State*, London: Macmillan, 1991), I have examined feminist and Islamist experience under various state formations. In "Independent Women: More Than A Century of Feminism in Egypt" (in Judith Tucker, ed.), *Old Boundaries, New Frontiers: Women in the Arab World*, Bloomington: Indiana University Press, 1993) I discuss the feminist continuum in Egypt from the late 19th century to the present distinguishing various phases and their leaders. I dealt with the first feminist wave in *Huda Sha'rawi and the Liberation of the Egyptian Woman*, D. Phil. thesis, Oxford University, 1977.

2. See Margot Badran, "From Consciousness to Activism: Feminist Politics in Early Twentieth Century Egypt," in John Spagnolo (ed.), *Problems of the Middle East in Historical Perspective*, St Antony's College, Oxford monograph series (London: Ithaca Press 1991).

3. See, for example, Hamied N. Ansari, "The Islamic Militants in Egyptian Politics," *International Journal of Middle East Studies* 16 (1) (1984):123-144. See also the following by Saad Eddin Ibrahim: "Contemporary Islamic Militancy," *Ideen Unserer Zeit*, (Zurich: Rugger Verlag, 1987), pp. 109-27; "Anatomy of Egypt's Militant Islamic Groups," *International Journal of Middle East Studies* 12 (4) (1980):481-499, and "Islamic Militancy as a Social Movement: The Case of Two Groups in Egypt," pp. 117-37 in Ali Dessouki (ed.), *Islamic Resurgence in the Arab World* (New York: Praeger, 1982).

4. For a recent broad treatment of the Islamist movement see Saad Eddin Ibrahim, "Egypt's Islamic Activism in the 1980s," *Third World Quarterly* 10 (2) (April 1988):632-657. Books by Islamist men who take liberal views on women's roles in society include Muhammad al-Ghazali's *Istiqlal al-Mar'a fi al-Islam* (The Independence of the Woman in Islam) (Cairo: Dar al-Mustaqbal al-'Arabi, n.d.) and his *Qadaiya al-Mar'a bain al-Taqalid al-Rakida wa al-Wafida* (Issues of the Woman between Stagnant and Alien Traditions) (Cairo: Dar al-Shuruq, 1990). Jamal al-Din 'Atiya in a talk at a girls school in Constantine, Algeria on March 19, 1990 entitled "Muqarana bain al-Usra al-Mislima wa al-Namudhij al Mithali" (A Comparison between the Muslim Family and the Ideal Model), in addition to discussing women's family roles, spoke in favor of women's work and other public roles, and noted the need for an Islamist women's liberation movement. In an interview in Cairo in 1989, the Islamist intellectual and writer

Muhammad Yahia told me of the Islamist movement's need to draw women into active participation.

5. See Badran, "Competing Agandas."

6. Women who wear the niqab are particularly zealous. However, the issue of niqab is highly sensitive. Last year there was a series of articles in *al-Nur* under the heading "Tahrim al-Niqab," (The Face Veil is Forbidded) by Ismail Ben Mansur which elicited an impassioned outcry. The author published an article called, "Hiwar al-Ashab hawla Mand'a Niqab" (Conversation with Friends about Forbidding the Face Veil), *al-Nur*, August 19, 1990 discussing the 38 letters he had received from professionals and some students, including at least one woman student, which attacked him for his position on the niqab. There is controversy among religious thinkers concerning the niqab; many write in favor of it; however, Muhammad al-Ghazali attacks it in his book, *Istiqlal al-Mar'a fi al-Islam*, p. 7. It is important to mention here that I did not speak with any *munaqqibat*, women who wear the niqab, nor did I attempt to since I was led to believe they would not welcome this.

7. Kamila al-'Arabi, "Tuba li Man Ta'ti Ghadan bi al-Hijab" (Blessed is She Who Comes Tomorrow with the Hijab). Cairo, *Hajir*, October 1, 1990.

8. Interview with Sumaiya Ibrahim Huber, Cairo, July 16, 1990.

9. Interview with Eva Elias, Cairo, March 29, 1990.

10. Interview with Heba al-Khouly, Cairo, July 16, 1990.

11. Interview with Hala Halim, Cairo, August 12, 1990.

12. Interview with Huda Lutfy, Cairo, May 22, 1990.

13. Interview with Radwa Ashour, Cairo, May 24, 1990.

14. Interview with Latifa Zayyat, Cairo, May 3, 1990.

15. Interview with Hala Halim, Cairo, August 12, 1990.

16. Nassera Merah, "Women, Equality, and Fundamentalism in Algeria," paper prepared for the UNU/WIDER Roundtable on Identity Politics and Women. Not only feminists but secularists in general are often accused of leading society astray and promoting Western culture by not veiling. An example of a grassroots Islamist view is 'Abd al-Aziz al-Najjar, a science teacher from Kafr al-Shaikh in the Delta, who said in an article entitled "Iftira'at Ibrahim Madkur wa Amina Sa'id" (Fabrications of Ibrahim Madkur and Amina Sa'id) in *Al-Nur* (August 19, 1990) that the stand against veiling taken by Ibrahim Madkur, former President of the Arabic Academy, and Amina Sa'id would lead Egypt to become like Europe with all its immorality.

17. Huda Lutfy demonstrated this in "A Study of Muslim Popular Literature on the Role of Women in Contemporary Egyptian Society," a paper presented at the Conference of the Middle East Studies Group, London, 1988. Concerning a similar approach in publications in the 1970s see Yvonne Haddad, "The Case of the Feminist Movement," Chapter 5 in *Contemporary Islam and the Challenge of History* (Albany: State University of New York Press, 1982), and "Traditional

Affirmations Concerning the Role of Women as Found in Contemporary Arab Islamic Literature," pp. 61-86 in Jane Smith (ed.), *Women in Contemporary Muslim Societies* (Lewisburgh, PA.: Bucknell University Press, 1980); and Valerie J. Hoffman-Ladd, "Polemics on the Modesty and Segregation of Women in Contemporary Egypt," *International Journal of Middle East Studies* 19 (1) (February, 1987):23-50.

18. See Albert Hourani, *Arabic Thought in the Liberal Age, 1798-1939* (Cambridge: Cambridge University Press, 1983).

19. See Margot Badran, "The Origins of Feminism in Egypt," pp. 143-170 in Arina Angerman et al. (eds.), *Current Issues in Women's History*, (London: Routledge, 1989); and Badran, "From Consciousness to Activism."

20. See Margot Badran, "Independent Women: More Than A Century of Feminism in Egypt."

21. See Kathleen Howard-Merriam, "Women, Education and the Professions in Egypt," *Comparative Education Review* XXIII (1979):256-270; and Clement H. Moore, "Sexual Equality amid Professional Impoverishment," *Images of Development: Egyptian Engineers in the Search of Industry* (Cambridge, Mass.: MIT Press, 1980), pp. 131-43.

22. See for example, Muhammad 'Atiyya Khamis (ed.), *al-Harakat al-Nisa'iyyat wa Silatuha m'a al-Ist'mar* (Feminist Movements and their Relations with Colonialism) (Cairo: Dar al-Ansar, 1978); and Safinaz Kazim, "Mas'alat al-Sufur wa al-Hijab" (Questions of Unveiling and Veiling). I analyzed this in "Feminism as a Force in the Arab World," *Contemporary Arab Thought and the Woman* (Cairo: The Arab Women's Solidarity Association, 1990; and 1989 in Arabic).

23. This was observed and decried by many Egyptian women. See for example, 'Aziza Husain, Inji Rushdi, Saniyya Salih, Awatif Wali, Mervat Ittalawi, Muna Zulfiqar, and Magda al Mufti, *Al Huquq al-Qanuniyya li al-Mar'a al-Misriyya bain al-Nadhariyya wa al-Tatbiq* (The Legal Right of the Egyptian Women: Theory and Practice) (Cairo, 1988); and Nawal Al Sadaawi, "The Political Challenges Facing Arab Women at the end of the 20th Century," pp. 8-26 in *Women of the Arab World: The Coming Challange*, papers of the Arab Women's Solidarity Association Conference, edited by Nahid Toubia, trans. by Nahed El Gamal (London: Zed, 1988). Analyses of second wave Islamist discourse on women include those by Yvonne Haddad and Huda Lutfy (see Note 17).

24. Amina Sa'id was one of the first to attack the move to take up the veil which she saw as a large step backwards. Among her articles in *Hawa* in the 1970s are: "This Phenomenon, What Does It Mean?" (November 18, 1972); "Back to the Issue of the Dress, This Show of Fuss ... What does it Mean?" (November 25, 1972); and "Feast of Unveiling, Feast of Renaissance" (March 24, 1973). The latter commemorated the political unveiling by Huda Sha'rawi and Saiza

Nabarawi fifty years earlier at the beginning of the first organized feminist movement in Egypt. Analyses of the return to the veil in the earlier years of the second Islamist wave include Fadwa El Guindi, "Veiling Infitah with Muslim Ethic: Egypt's Contemporary Islamic Movement," *Social Problems* 28 (4) (April 1981):465-485; Zainab Radwan, *Bahth Zahirat al-Hijab bain al-Jam'iyyat* (A Study of the Phenomenon of the Veil among University Women) (Cairo: National Center for Sociological and Criminological Research, 1982); and John Alden Williams, "A Return to the Veil in Egypt," *Middle East Review* 11 (3) (1979):49-54. These studies accepted women's explanations that veiling helped smooth their movements in public stressing a positive functionalist approach. They did not elaborate the negative implications of the ideology accompanying the veil nor possible longer-term implications.

25. See Hoffman-Ladd, "Polemics" (see Note 17).

26. It is interesting to note that the opposite is true in Algeria, where Nassera Merah notes that many Islamist women are illiterate or semi-literate.

27. Interview with Zainab Al-Ghazali, Cairo, February 12, 1989.

28. Christian women in Egypt had started to unveil at the end of the 19th century. Among Muslims, Nabawiyya Musa who unveiled around 1909 was in the vanguard. It was not until after the unveiling of Huda Sha'rawi, and with her Saiza Nabarawi in 1923, as an overt political act that most Muslim women would finally end the practice.

29. Interview with Hala Shukrallah, a member of *Al-Mar'a al Jadida* Group, Sept. 1, 1990, during which she said how she and other students were influenced by the book. In an interview with the writer, Salwa Bakr, on May 18, 1990 she spoke of the importance of the book saying it was "very brave and useful."

30. At the 1988 AWSA Conference on Contemporary Arab Thought and the Woman, Syrian literary critic, Samar Attar, presented a paper on themes of sexuality in the *Thousand and One Nights*, which — although a literary analysis of fiction — gave rise to angry accusations of feminist promotion of immorality.

31. On the creation of AWSA see Toubia, *Women of the Arab World.*

32. Jihan Al-Sayyid, Suraya 'Abdul Rad'i, and Hala Isma'il, "Taqrir 'an al-Tajriba al-Majalla Bint al-'Ard" (Report on the Experience of the Daughter of the Earth Magazine), paper presented to the AWSA Conference on Arab Women in Publishing and Journalism; interview with Jihan Al-Sayyid, Cairo, September 6, 1990.

33. See Nadia Hijab, *Womenpower: The Arab Debate on Women and Work* (Cambridge: Cambridge University Press, 1988) and Sarah Graham-Brown, "After Jihan's Law: A New Battle Over Women's Rights," *The Middle East* (June 1985):17-20.

34. Interview with Zainab al-Ghazali, Cairo, February, 1989. During the interview several of her followers were present which gave me the opportunity

to talk with them as well. An indication of al-Ghazali's influence may be seen by the fact that her prison memoirs, *Ayyam fi al-Hayyati* (Days in My Life) are now in their tenth printing. On al-Ghazali's dual message to Muslim women see Badran, "Competing Agendas." Also see Valerie J. Hoffman, "An Islamic Activist: Zaynab al-Ghazali," pp. 233-54 in Elizabeth Fernea (ed.), *Women and the Family in the Middle East: New Voices of Change* (Austin: University of Texas Press, 1985).

35. Safinaz Kazim, "Quwwa al-Mujtam'a."

36. Badran, "From Consciousness to Activism."

37. This and subsequent quotes come from an interview with Hiba Rauf, Cairo, September 8, 1990.

38. Interview with Zainab al-Ghazali, February 12, 1989. For a similar view see Muhammad 'Atiya, *Harakat Nisa'iyya wa Silatuha ma' al-Isti'mar* (Feminist Movements and Their Connections with Colonialism) (Cairo, 1978).

39. Interview with Maha Sa'ud, Cairo, January, 1990.

40. Interview with Hana Ayoub, Cairo, March 29, 1990.

41. Interview with Ghada al-Ghowaidy, Cairo, August 20, 1990.

42. Interview with Huda Sadda, Cairo, May 5, 1990.

43. Interview with Latifa Zayyat, Cairo, May 3, 1990.

44. Interview with Radwa Ashour, Cairo, May 25, 1990.

45. Group of Egyptian Women ('Aziza Husain, Inji Rushdi, Saniyya Salih, Awatif Wali, Mervat Ittalawi, Mona Zulfigar and Magda al-Mufti, *al-Huquq al-Qanuniyyaa li al-Mar'a al-Misriyya bain al-Nadhariyya wa al-Tatbiq* (Cairo: 1989).

46. Letter from The New Woman Group, Cairo, July 1990.

47. Interview with Salwa Bakr, Cairo, May 18, 1990.

48. Interview with Huda Lutfy, Cairo, May 22, 1990.

49. Interview with Heba al-Khouly, Cairo, July 16, 1990.

50. Interview with Jihan al-Sayyid, Cairo, September 6, 1990.

51. Interview with Shahinda Maqlad, Cairo, May 1990.

52. Interview with Zohra Merabet, Cairo, Sept. 7, 1990.

11

Identity Politics and Women: "Fundamentalism" and Women in Pakistan

Khawar Mumtaz

Introduction

"The decade of the 1980s has truly been a decade of the women of Pakistan," wrote Hamza Alavi towards the end of an eventful decade for Pakistan.[1] Alavi's reference was to the women's resistance to General Zia-ul-Haq's military regime (1977-1988) and its proclaimed Islamic measures that in effect down-graded women. Undoubtedly the eighties were significant for the crystallization of an autonomous women's rights movement in urban Pakistan which strongly challenged, on both religious and political grounds, the government's so-called "Islamization" process.[2] However, the same period also saw the entry of heavily veiled women on the public scene who projected themselves as defenders of Islam and denounced the women questioning state-initiated measures.

Historically, the struggle for women's rights in Pakistan has been one of consistent opposition from the religious-orthodox quarters. Beginning in 1949 just after the country's creation, with the protest over the presence of two women parliamentarians in the Constituent Assembly of Pakistan, any move for even minimal rights for women has encountered opposition from these forces. Measures that had an appearance of crossing the boundaries of prevalent norms, that meant greater mobility, confidence, or independence, invited the wrath of the religious groups.[3] After 1977, the pressure from the religious elements

228

reached new heights and the accepted positions regarding women were challenged (the mode of dress, women's right to work, drive, to hold public office, vote, participate in sports, and so on). Following the election in 1988 of Benazir Bhutto as the first woman prime minister of Pakistan, a heated debate ensued over whether a woman can be head of government. A relentless and vitriolic campaign continued after Ms. Bhutto's premature removal from office.[4]

Gender and class politics frame the current debate on women's role and position in society. Located essentially in urban centers it has been a debate between obscurantist men from the lower middle class and the newly rich middle class with aspirations for political power, and women's rights activists belonging to the professional middle and upper middle class. Initiated by men, the debate reflects their perception of middle- and upper-class women as threats to the existing order. Built largely upon differentiation, it has led to the politicization of gender whereby those advocating women's emancipation are viewed as modern and as such opposed to Islam. The debate manifested through opposition of women on the basis of religion remained marginal up until 1977. Led by a small band of male *ulama* (religious leaders) and *maulvis* (clerics), dispersed over a number of religiously defined political parties it failed to make much of an impact on the evolutionary process of women's emancipation. But it intensified after 1977 with the military government's use of religion to legitimize its stay. With the weight of government behind them the position of the male antagonists of women's rights was bolstered as were their efforts for cultural hegemony. Women as the supposed carriers of cultural values became central to their political project. On the one hand was the relentless running down of women's rights activists, their "other-ness" being singled out for attack, and on the other active mobilization of women belonging to the emerging middle class was undertaken. It is in this context that the 1982-1983 entry onto the political arena of organized and vocal women articulating the ideology of the religious right should be viewed. An interesting if disconcerting new development, it highlights (a) the variance in perspectives of women belonging to different classes, and (b) the dynamics of the changing political framework.

For women's rights activists such women—referred to as "fundamentalists" for want of a more appropriate term—have been an enigma. They reject the concept of gender equality, accept women's primary role as that of reproducers and nurturers, see restrictions on women's mobility and curtailment of legal rights as protective measures prescribed by religion (and therefore unquestionable), and condemn women agitating for rights as westernized and un-Islamic. At the same time a number of these women are also professionals, working as teachers and doctors. They demand a ban on polygamy, reject divorce by repudiation, condemn exploitation of women by men—all concerns with which the women's rights activists are also occupied.

Who are these women? What are the compulsions that have brought them into the foreground? Which forces do they represent? What implications does their organized emergence have: (a) for themselves and (b) for the women's movement? Why do they see themselves different from the women activists? These and similar other concerns merit closer investigation. This chapter first examines the religious Right in Pakistan and its evolution in the political process, as it is in the backdrop of the rise of the obscurantist forces that the religious women's groups can be best understood. It then attempts to identify the "fundamentalist" women, their background, the needs and dynamics of their ideology, and finally the other less known mechanisms initiated to spread and consolidate the obscurantist right. The analysis is in a historical-sociological framework in the specific context of General Zia-ul-Haq's rule which catalyzed the rise of the phenomenon.

Political Background

The rise of the religious Right in Pakistan is closely linked with the peculiar nature of political development in the country. Soon after independence the ulama, who had opposed the creation of Pakistan as a state for the Muslims of India, appeared on the political scene. Isolated during the independence movement, they clamored for a share in state power and presented themselves as the sole authority for defining the nature of an "Islamic" state. Small in numbers and lacking popular support they were not taken too seriously by the governing elites.[5] However, their aggressive assertions of being protagonists of "purist" Islam and their indictment of those in power as "un-Islamic" put the latter on the defensive. The religious elements' capacity to create tensions and law and order problems on religious and sectarian grounds also gave them a certain amount of leverage upon the government of the day. The ruling elites used the religious groups (who were never a part of the power elites) to bolster their positions in their internal power struggles. In the process the use of Islam for political ends augmented as did the capacity of the religiously defined groups to gain a place for themselves in the system.

The tussle for power and the manipulations that ensued precluded the growth of democratic institutions and systems. Pakistan's political history is one of long spells of authoritarian military rules interspersed with short-lived civilian governments. With mass participation minimized in the political process the significance of well-organized pressure groups that were willing to be coopted by the various authoritarian regimes increased. Such situations benefited the religious obscurantist groups and their influence spread disproportionately to their numbers. The high point was reached after the military coup of 1977, when the interests and ideology of the state coincided with those of the religious obscurantists epitomized by the Jamaat-e-Islami, established in 1941 as the first party of Muslims in undivided India to voice obscurantist ideology. Jamaat-e-Islami is perhaps the most significant of all religiously defined political parties,[6] primarily because of (a) its highly organized and tightly knit structure; (b) the influence of the writings of its founder-ideologue, Maulana Abu A'la Maududi, within and beyond Pakistan; (c) its cooptation by Zia, who appears to have used the Jamaat-e-Islami's 1977 election manifesto as the blueprint for Islamization; and (d) the subsequent expansion in its influence because of the government support it received.

For women activists the fact that the most vocal and rabid opposition to women comes from the Jamaat-e-Islami, and that women who espouse religion-based positions are either supported by the Jamaat or belong to its student wing, renders it particularly important.

The social base of the Jamaat-e-Islami is the newly urbanized, upwardly mobile classes of Pakistan's expanding cities. These include the new entrepreneurs (traders and small business) who are socially and psychologically distinct from the older comprador bourgeoisie with whom they are now in competition. The party's influence is in urban locations where extensive industrialization has led to most rapid changes. On the one hand, these cities are experiencing the breakdown of existing social relations and economic structures and on the other attracting newcomers from small towns and rural areas. The newly urbanized youth, in particular, finds the religious idiom of Jamaat-e-Islami a source of self-identity. Arriving from areas where minimal or no remarkable change has occurred these young people are provided material as well as moral/psychological support to cope with the alien and rapidly-changing environment. Not surprisingly, the campuses serve as the training and recruiting grounds for Jamaat activists, a number of whom have entered national politics through this route.

Essentially an elitist party, the Jamaat-e-Islami is disdainful of the masses and ordinary people, who in Maudidi's words are, "foolish and thoughtless ... who cannot think and form independent opinions ... don't deserve attention and may, therefore, be ignored."[7]

A review of the Jamaat-e-Islami's political development reveals opportunism as a fundamental characteristic of the party. Desirous of gaining political power, the Jamaat has had no compunction in changing its stands for political exigency. Contradictions in what Jamaat-e-Islami states and what it practices abound. For example, Jamaat's declared position in 1951-1953 was that in an Islamic state there was no provision for a woman head of state, but in 1965 it supported Ms. Fatima Jinnah as the presidential candidate. In 1978, the Jamaat got into power through the backdoor, by joining Zia's cabinet but distanced itself when the General became politically isolated. It was at that juncture willing to make an alliance with the women-led Pakistan People's Party. In 1989 it entered into an alliance with the Awami National Party (ANP) which along with its leader had earlier been declared anti-Islamic, communist and traitorous. After the dissolution of the assemblies in August 1990 it sat with Syeda Abida Hussain, an independent woman politician and a federal minister, as part of the combined opposition. But the Jamaat-e-Islami chief walked out of a televized discussion because the program was being compered by a woman. In the October 1990 general elections it again tried to seek People's Party support on some seats.

The spectrum of other religion-based political parties ranges from the traditionalist Jamiat-Ulema-e-Pakistan (JUP) and Jamiat Ulema-e-Islam (JUI), and their various factions, to the fanatical Anjuman Sipah-e-Sahaba. Interestingly, none of these have a women's wing nor is there any evidence of their having women members in their ranks. Some, like the JUI, who took part in the struggle against military rule (Maulana Fazlur Rehman, head of JUI, stated when Benazir Bhutto was elected Prime Minister that whereas *Sharia* did not permit a woman to be head of government he accepts the verdict of the people) and have not succumbed to the attractions of state power through cooptation are viewed as having democratic tendencies. Yet a breakaway faction of JUI has supported authoritarianism. The authors of the controversial 1985 Enforcement of the Sharia Bill which was adopted by the Senate in May 1990 belong to this breakaway part of JUI. The Bill, incidentally, proposed to radically restructure the existing judiciary as well as the law-making procedures. The judiciary, manned by *muftis* (religious scholars) trained in the *deeni madrassahs* (seminaries/religious schools) and the International Islamic University (set up in early 1980s), would have the power to override any law enacted by the legislature. Thus, in effect, a nominated institution would take precedence over an elected representative one. A new version of the Sharia Bill was bulldozed through the National Assembly in May 1991. Ambiguous in wording, the Bill does not prescribe a formal role for the religions in judiciary—much to their displeasure. It nevertheless paves the way for greater control of the government over people's lives. The People's Progressive Party (PPP) and women's rights activists have strongly criticized the Bill.

Regardless of whether religiously defined parties profess to be democratic and notwithstanding the particular school of thought they belong to, they are all essentially conservative, particularly where women are concerned. Moreover, all of them have benefited directly or indirectly from the State's support for obscurantist forces during 1977-1988. For example, the Zakat and Ushr Ordinance of 1980 provides for employment of persons for Zakat Committees who have qualified from *deeni madrassahs* (religious schools, seminaries). The Ordinance opened job opportunities for the cadres of these institutions, run by various schools of Islamic thought. Similarly, employment by the State of *khatibs* and *imams* to manage mosques helps to strengthen the networks of the *maulvis* and increases their influence at the level of communities and neighborhoods. Thus in an environment that bolstered activities in the name of religion, the space of operation for all religious groups expanded.

An important point needing cognizance is that even those of the religious parties who had struggled for democracy did not question the so-called "Islamization" introduced through presidential ordinances. While several professed anti-authoritarianism, they did not reject a law, particularly an "Islamic" law, because of its undemocratic manner of promulgation. Obviously the parties realize that legislation of this nature would not be possible through representative assemblies. Not only were the 1979 Enforcement of Hudood Ordinances and the 1984 Law of Evidence not resisted by these forces but the Sharia Bill was passed for reasons other than ideological. The Bill, when first presented in the House in 1985, was strongly opposed by some of the religiously defined parties; the JUI opposed it on ideological grounds. But in 1990, JUI and other religious parties supported it largely because the Bhutto government was opposed to the Bill.[8] It appears that the religious parties recognizing their failure to win popular support see state enforced "Islamization" as the only means to find a decisive place in the political system.

Women of the Religious Right

Like men, women who believe in the ideology of the religious Right are first generation educated women who have for the first time entered universities and professional institutions and are working outside the home. And like men the ones appearing in the public area have largely been recruited from campuses. Some of the older women have come up from the "preaching" stream, often belonging to the families of ulama or *maulvis*. They give *dars* (preach) to women and have now been drawn onto the public platform.

The women of the religious Right are identified by the *burqa*, a "veil" that differs from the traditional one worn by other women. The burqa, which is a smartly tailored outfit in black or white silk/synthetic material, consists of a coat-like full-sleeved over-garment of knee to ankle length and a square piece of cloth that covers the head and face in a manner that only slits are left open for the eyes. In contrast, women of the urban poor wear a loose-fitting two-piece black garment; the top part covers the head with provision of two sheer pieces of cloth to cover the face if desired. The burqa of Pathan women of some of the tribal north-west small towns is made up of several meters of cloth gathered around a close-fitting cap with a laced bit for eyes; it is nowadays available in electric pinks, yellows and greens besides the traditional white. The "fundamentalist" women are in fact making a statement about their identity, for their burqa sets them apart from the underprivileged women on the one hand, and from the relatively privileged unveiled women of the middle and upper middle classes, on the other. That the burqa is used as a symbol of identity and a specific ideology is evident from the fact that it is not always worn by the women in activities related to their private lives. For instance Nisar Fatima, probably the most important "fundamentalist" spokeswoman wears the normal Pakistani dress (loose trousers, loose shirt and *dopatta*—a two-meter length of cotton or silk cloth used to cover head and body) when visiting relatives and friends. Her public appearances in the National Assembly, television, meetings and press conferences are however always in her favored white burqa.

The positions that the women of the religious Right take regarding women's role and status in society are often contradictory. On the one hand the leadership keeps reiterating its belief that men are the providers and women are depriving men of jobs by competing with them. On the other hand, they demand separate universities for women as well as arrangements for segregated work places which they argue will tap the productive potential of women. They strongly oppose women's participation in politics but have agreed to sit in the parliament themselves.

Over the years their positions have experienced shifts. In 1982-1983, for women to step out of the confines of their homes was considered an invitation to immorality. But over the years it has become acceptable for women to go out "if and when absolutely necessary." Where earlier paid employment was considered a male activity, women's right to work "in times of necessity" and not for "material needs" is now promoted. What distinguishes "necessity" from "material needs" is unclear. In any event, the focus of "fundamentalist" women is on complete gender segregation of society.

Mixing of sexes is considered the root of all ills in society. Corruption, polygamy, bribery are all laid at the door of desegregation which in turn is viewed as a manifestation of westernization. Segregation and other patriarchal structures which the women's rights activists view as responsible for keeping women subordinated are seen by "fundamentalist" women as being the "natural order."

Interestingly, unveiled privileged women are the targets of "fundamentalist" women's ire. The fact that over seventy percent of the country's women live in rural areas and participate in agricultural activities largely outside their homes and without the burqa is ignored by the religious Right, both men and women. Their concern is with the behavior of middle- and upper middle-class urban women. Nisar Fatima (and other women leaders of the conservative right) hysterically accuses the latter of leading the younger generation astray, of breaking the link with Islam, of not being aware of Islamic teachings but only of "decorum of clubs." The last of these allegations is particularly peculiar as desegregated clubs in Pakistan are exceptions rather than the norm. These are extremely exclusive and are open only to a minuscule section of upper-class men and women.

The Needs and Dynamics of "Fundamentalism"

In the earlier examination of the phenomenon of obscurantism/ "fundamentalism" and its impact on women,[9] one of the conclusions was that

> The "fundamentalist" discourse developed in response to changed material circumstances, offering guidelines to salvation in the midst of confusing times. One very important set of guidelines concerned the need to preserve the division of labour which nature herself has devised between the sexes that was being undermined by contemporary developments.[10]

In Pakistan, as in most other post-colonial states, the rapid transformation of the economic and social structures has resulted in a state of confusion and lack of control by men. In this shifting and bewildering reality the only area where control is possible is the domestic space, hence the compelling need to exercise it over women.

At the same time, however, women belonging to older professional classes of the dominant elite have over the years managed to expand the economic, social, and psychological space for themselves and present a dilemma to men. These women have entered spheres of activity considered to be solely male: they are in politics, in professions like engineering, town planning, banking and computer programing; they drive cars, can operate modern machines and are as competent as men in their work. They assert their right to be treated as equals, to be allowed to exercise choices and not be discriminated on the basis of gender. Despite being numerically small such women disturb men even when they are neither in competition with them for jobs nor are likely to enter their domestic space (through marriages). The men perhaps feel threatened because of "the indirect threat they present as role models (not least because of their class affiliations) or because they suggest a real possibility of change for women of their classes."[11]

Mernissi views the onslaught of the conservatives against women as "a defense mechanism against profound changes in both sex roles and the touchy subject of sexual identity."[12] This explains why the discourse in Pakistan over women's rights and their position in society has been between "fundamentalist" men and non-"fundamentalist" women.

This perceived threat has become an increasingly imminent reality with spiraling inflation and what Alavi calls the "crisis of the middle- and lower middle-class household economy."[13] Traditionally, the gender division of labor was neatly defined with men responsible for providing for the family and women bearing the burden of domestic labor. There was no confusion between the "external" (male) and the "internal" (female) spaces. However, this norm is no longer practical with the economic crunch necessitating women's cash contribution to the family economy.

While for the poorest sections of society the division between the male-female space of operation is blurred because of the exigencies of survival (in rural areas, in any case, the agricultural economy cannot be sustained without joint inputs of male and female members of the household), for the urban lower middle and middle classes it presents a major problem. Both men and women are placed under stress. Men have to cope with the sense of failure emanating from the inability to fulfil their primary responsibility, and the concomitant psychological loss of masculinity, in other words their identity. Women have to assume roles they are neither conditioned nor prepared for. Coming from highly segregated cloistered households, they have to deal with an unfamiliar and often mixed environment as the "outside" is both alien and insecure, they need a reassuring anchorage, and religion provides this. Thus, if women join obscurantist/"fundamentalist" movements it is because the latter respond to some of the women's needs and allay some insecurities.

These, however, are only partial explanations of "fundamentalist" women's visible emergence in Pakistan. An additional and important factor was the resistance to General Zia-ul-Haq's Islamization by women and women's organization from the platform of Women's Action Forum (WAF). It appears that WAF's questioning of the distorted interpretations of Islam to justify legal measures, rejection of the *maulvis* as self-styled guardians of Islam, and challenging of the patriarchal structures underlying women's subordination has had a greater impact than warranted by their numbers. The obscurantists have felt compelled to promote a vocal women's lobby of their own to counter WAF activities. The Jamaat-e-Islami had responded in a similar manner in 1974-1975 when a group of left-wing women students formed the Women's Front in Lahore's Punjab University. The Front was perhaps the first instance of feminist expression of women's rights that questioned patriarchal norms.[14] Within a short period the Jamaat had set up a women's section of its student wing. That was the first time that women students in the typical burqa associated with "fundamentalist" women made their appearance. The women students' section, Islami Jamiat Talebat, is now a permanent subsidiary institution of the Jamaat-e-Islami. Its activists use aggressive strong arm tactics typical of the male students' wing of the Jamaat (Islami Jamiat-e-Tuleba) against liberal women students. The Islami Jamiat-e-Tuleba has the dubious distinction of introducing fire arms in campuses and using violence in student politics.

It was, therefore, not a coincidence when Majlis-e-Khawateen, a women's organization unheard of before, came out with press statements against the progressive women's demonstration in Lahore protesting the Law of Evidence in 1983. That the Majlis had the support of Jamaat-e-Islami and the President himself became obvious over the years. Nisar Fatima, the president of Majlis, was elected member of the National Assembly of 1985 on the reserved women's seat with Jamaat-e-Islami support. She was also nominated by General Zia to the Council of Islamic Ideology (an advisory body responsible for examining existing laws for their Islamic content and proposing new laws) as well as the 1984 Commission on the Status of Women. The Commission was composed of 13 women and three men besides ex-officio members. Of the women at least 10 belonged to the professional elite class. Despite being hand-picked by a military government the Commission came out with an excellent report on women's oppression. It examined the prevalent social and cultural norms and critically reviewed the proposed and promulgated Islamic laws, concluding that the latter had been a setback to women. The report also made extensive recommendations. Nisar Fatima, the only "fundamentalist" representative on the Commission wrote a dissenting note. Her basic disagreement was with the Commission's perspective. For instance, she felt that the discussion on legal issues could only be undertaken by religious scholars; that instead of demanding equal opportunities the emphasis should have been on the importance of the family; responsibility of the male as earner, head of household and decision-maker; woman's place in the house as "obedient" wife and caring mother; strict segregation; and women's exclusion from professions that do not need them.[15] The unexpected candidness of the report and its obvious variance from official policies resulted in it being shelved; the only part that received publicity was Nisar Fatima's dissenting note.

Subsequently, Nisar Fatima appears to have had access to substantial funds to be able to organize international conferences almost every year since 1984, inviting women from the Muslim world under the aegis of the International Union of Muslim Women. Invariably, Shafiqa Zia, the President's wife, was the guest of honor in these conferences. More recently, in June 1990, Khawateen Nifaz-e-Shariah Mahaz (Women's Enforcement of Sharia Front) was formed with the blessings of the movers of the Sharia Bill following its adoption in the Senate in May 1990. A Nifaz-e-Shariat Conference was organized by the Front in the same month where "fundamentalist" women rejected democracy as an imported ideology and made the women's rights activists as well as the then prime minister, Ms. Bhutto, targets of its attack.

This, in fact, has been the pattern; any action or statement of WAF or a non-"fundamentalist" women's organization has invited an immediate and vitriolic response from women of the religious Right accusing the former of being westernized, alienated, and non-religious. Over the years these women have adopted the tactics and mechanisms used by women's rights activists to retaliate against them. Press statements, letter writing campaigns, seminars and conferences are used equally by both groups. In September 1986 the "fundamentalist" women for the first time brought out their own demonstration outside the National Assembly in response to the one organized earlier by WAF against the Sharia Bill at the same venue.

The action and reaction pattern has resulted in a strange and indirect dialogue between women of the two different classes. While there are common concerns shared by both—against violence and polygamy, over right of inheritance and owning property, over commercial exploitation of women—the antagonism between the two persists and suspicions are deep-seated.

The Future?

We have seen that at this juncture in Pakistan's political and economic development, the needs of some women push them towards obscurantist/"fundamentalist" ideology; conversely the needs of some religious political parties compel them to address and mobilize women. Thus the ideology appears to give succor, and provide the opportunity to these women to expand their operational space; and their emergence as a vocal lobby strengthens the right wing political parties, especially the Jamaat-e-Islami. So far most of the conservative right wing activists have come from colleges and universities. But now it appears that the religiously defined parties are taking a long-term view of instilling their ideology among a wider section of women. It is in this context that the mushrooming of *deeni madrassahs* for women in major cities and towns of Pakistan over the last decade assumes significance. Lahore alone has at least five registered *madrassahs* run by different Muslim schools of thought.[16] These institutions attempt to instil a particular version of Islam in women students and also prepare them for jobs in segregated settings as teachers of Arabic and religion in state-run primary and high schools for girls across the country.

The stated reason for establishing one such institution, *Madrassah Faisal-al-Banat* in Lahore, in 1979, was to rectify the neglect of women's spiritual education—considered essential to counter, in the words of the brochure of the *madrassah*, "Westernization that has affected women, who under the pretext of emancipation and liberation are in reality spreading obscenity and immorality."[17]

Madrassah Faisal-al-Banat houses 300 to 350 students at any given time. There are simultaneous programs lasting from two to four years. Once admitted, a student has to spend the entire period of her stay on the premises of the *Madrassah* with two-week breaks twice a year as home leave. A large number of girls seeking admission are from small towns and villages. The age group of students at the time of admission ranges from 11-15 years, depending on the course they opt for.[18] Educational requirements for entrance vary for different courses, but all students desiring admission are expected to have a certificate of good moral character from their guardians (usually parents), and, those above 15 years of age have to be in *purdah* (veiled) and are expected to be observing and practicing Muslims who pray and fast.

All students follow a rigorous, strictly disciplined and structured routine. A normal day begins with *tahajjud* prayers (one-hour before the pre-dawn *fajar* prayers) and ends at 10 pm. It includes at least six hours of academic work, prayers performed six times, and the reading of Quran. During study hours all students wear a uniform. Rules and regulations are very restrictive: only those persons whose names and photographs are registered with the *Madrassah* at the time of admission are permitted to visit the student; only *mehram* males (those ineligible for marriage like father, brothers, uncle, grandfathers) can meet the students—"cousins are not permitted under any condition" (because they stand as potential spouses); no student can write or receive letters without having them checked by the principal; radios, tape-recorders, cassettes are not allowed on the premises; students cannot keep any photographs with them, not even of their parents; they are not allowed to take interest in politics while in the *Madrassah*. No fees are taken from students except a nominal admission fee. Enclosed in high walls and a locked gate, the *Madrassah* is virtually a prison. All the staff except the guard, an old man, is female. "The *maulvi* who teaches Quran (by rote) is blind," the author was proudly told by a teacher, "and even then the girls sit behind a curtain."

Courses taught focus on the study of the Quran with translation and *tafsir* (explanations), *hadith* (transmitted tradition of the Prophet), Islamic history, spoken and written Arabic. The advanced course involves a more in-depth study of the religious texts, history of *hadith*, the *fiqh* (schools of thought), Islamic history and Islamic laws, among others.[19] There are special courses on women's place in Islam and more interestingly on "modern educated Pakistani's view of Islam and Islamic laws," and counter arguments to that view.

Of the students who graduate, some take up jobs as teachers, some give *dars* at home or open Quran classes for neighborhood children. The brighter ones go on to universities to specialize in Islamic History, Islamic Studies, and similar subjects. There appear to be links between *madrassahs* and conservative women activists. For instance, the founder of the Islami Jamiat Talibat in the Punjab University is currently the principal of one such institution (Ayesha Arabic Academy) in Faisalabad.[20]

Given the nature and content of the education imparted, combined with the formative ages of the students, the impact of the time spent in such seminaries can be well imagined. The hundreds of girls and young women, isolated in over-protected environment, following rigid routines, living away from reality, and only receiving a narrow and often bigoted view of the world through selected Islamic texts and discourses can only imbibe a particular kind of ideology.

The implications are indeed far-reaching and will certainly contribute towards generating retrogressive thinking and reinforcing patriarchal structures. Despite the tentatively emerging dialogue on one level, the divisions between right wing women and progressive women are likely to remain, if not sharpen.

The women's movement which creates new thresholds of women's acceptable activities has an indirect positive impact on all Pakistani women, as is reflected in the shifting positions of conservative women. For instance from prescribing only certain kinds of jobs for women (teaching and medicine) the field is now considered wide open. According to one Jamiat Talibat student activist, women can study journalism, be pilots, drive cars, do business, observance of *purdah* being the sole operational condition.[21]

Whether these women develop assertiveness vis-à-vis obscurantist men will be interesting to watch. It would be misplaced to believe that women who are vocal, articulate and strident will submit to controls that may limit their new found mobility. Will this lead to the closing of ranks between "fundamentalist" women and non-"fundamentalist" women on the basis of gender identity? This remains an important question for the future.

Notes

1. Hamza Alavi, "Pakistan: Women in a Changing Society," *Economic and Political Weekly*, Bombay, June 25, 1988.

2. The genesis of the women's movement in Pakistan and its resistance to "Islamization" has been documented in great detail in: Khawar Mumtaz and Farida Shaheed, *Women of Pakistan: Two Steps Forward One Step Back?* (London: Zed Books, and Lahore: Vanguard Books, 1987).

3. They objected to the formation of Pakistan Women's National Guards and Pakistan Women's Naval Reserve, both of which were para-military forces, on the pretext that women were appearing in public without their heads covered. The creation of the All Pakistan Women's Association (APWA), the first women's social welfare organization, was viewed as a step towards encouraging im-morality, and even the Family Laws Ordinance 1961, based on progressive interpretation of Islam was denounced as it included the provision for the delegated right of divorce for women and attempted to deter polygamy.

4. The assemblies were dissolved by the President on August 6, 1990, only 20 months into a five-year term.

5. The ruling group at the time of independence was a broad-based heterogenous group comprised of landlords, politicians, and professionals.

6. A number of parties cropped up during General Zia-ul-Haq's rule. These include the Tehrik-e-Nifaz-e-Fiqah Jaffaria (party of the Shias), Jamaat Ahle Hadith, Pakistan Awami Tehrik, Anjuman Sipah-e-Sahaba (anti-Shia party), Jamaat Mashaikh Pakistan, Hizb-e-Jehad; among others.

7. S. Abdul A'la Maududi, *Purdah and the Status of Women in Islam*, Islamic Publications Ltd., Lahore (9th ed.), 1987, in Farida Shaheed and Khawar Mumtaz, "Islamisation and Women: The Experience of Women," pp. 67-78 in *New Black Friars* 71 (835) (Feb., 1990) (Special Issue: *The World of Islam*), p. 72.

8. On the issue of the Sharia Bill the opposition to the Pakistan People's Party government was the driving force in bringing not only the various hues of religious political parties (who are otherwise at logger heads) but also the centrists (Pakistan Muslim League), the left-of-center social democrats (ANP) and the ethnicists (Mohajir Qaumi Movement, rivals of Jamaat-e-Islami). Majority of these had refused to support the Bill when originally presented in 1985. After the dissolution of the assemblies in August 1990 the issue of the enforcement of Sharia faded into the background. In early 1991 it had become a bone of contention between the sitting government and its electoral allies, the religious parties. The latter threatened street demonstrations if the government did not legislate the Sharia Bill. Its passage in May 1991, however, has left the religious parties disgruntled.

9. Shaheed and Mumtaz, "Islamisation and Women."

10. *Ibid.*, p. 74.

11. *Ibid.*, p. 76.

12. Fatima Mernissi, *Beyond the Veil: Male-Female Dynamics in Modern Muslim Society*. Revised Edition (Bloomington: Indiana University Press, 1987).

13. Hamza Alavi, "Pakistan: Women in a Changing Society."

14. Mumtaz and Shaheed, "Islamisation and Women," pp. 65-66.

15. Government of Pakistan, *Report of the Pakistan Commission on the Status of Women* (Islamabad, 1985), pp. 167-189.

16. *Darul-uloom, Al-nissa, Madrassah Taleem-al-Quran, Madrassah-Faisal-al-Banat* (two branches). The two well-known institutions of Faisalabad, the fastest growing industrial city in Pakistan, are: *Ayesha Arabi Academy* and *Madrassah Salfia-al-Banat*. There are reportedly others in Gujrat, Gujranwala and Karachi.

17. *Prospectus of Madrassah-Faisal-al-Banat* (Lahore, 1990), pp. 6-7.

18. Course for becoming a *hafiza*, that is, learning Quran by heart; the course for *qariya*, that is, special recitation of Quran; *Saanviyah Khasa*, intermediate level and *Shahadat-al-Aliya*, the course leading to B.A.

19. Details available in *Prospectus*.

20. *The Daily Jang, Lahore*, October 26, 1987.

21. *Ibid.*

12

Moving Away from a Secular Vision? Women, Nation, and the Cultural Construction of Hindu India

Sucheta Mazumdar

Introduction

An enormous change is in the making in India. On the political front this is marked by the unprecedented rise of Hindu fundamentalist groups at the level of national politics. Historically there was no such one religious affiliation; sects, regional interpretations of the sects, differences in practice and local culture were the distinctive feature of Hinduism in comparison to all other organized religions. Today terms such as "Un-Hindu" are increasingly in use, although the "Hindu" identity and religion are a creation of the political forces of the nineteenth and twentieth centuries, forces which could lead towards Fascism. How this religion was created, how its claim to "true" representation of national identity via the symbols of this religion came about, and what it means for women of all classes to have this religious construct as the accepted definition of nation and national culture are the subject of this chapter. I will also pose the question of whether it is possible to formulate an emancipatory and democratic discourse within the confines of what has come to be defined as Hinduism. Then I will show that the type of violence against women noted in contemporary India is clearly within this mode of Hindu cultural practice. In the conclusion I will return to some of the dilemmas confronting the women's movement. But let me first lay out the social and economic configuration which is contemporary India.

The Economics of Political Mobilization

During the 1980s the class polarization of the society sharpened considerably. Though 75 percent of the country continues to live in the countryside, there is now a middle class in the urban sector, comprised of perhaps 10-15 million people. These are people who benefited from an increase in jobs in the industrial sector, from the unprecedented explosion in the number of small-scale entrepreneurs, from the increase in the ranks of the professionals, and above all the dependents of some 5-7 million emigrants, many of them emigrants to the Gulf States and the Middle East who send remittances home. Then in the rural sector a stratum of rich farmers have emerged in the areas which have experienced the benefits of the Green Revolution, a stratum of 30-40 million people who have mobilized in the last decade demanding both remunerative prices and lower input costs. This group sees their interests often at odds with that of the urban minority. At the other end of the scale, depending on the region of the country 25-65 percent of the population remains below the poverty line. The landless agricultural workers in the rural sector and the urban poor are overwhelmingly from the Untouchable caste.

Those economists who believe an unfettered market economy will solve all problems see the potential buying power of this emerging middle class as the determining factor on the horizon of India's economic miracle. But in a population of 850 million, where 42 percent of the population is below the age of fourteen and another 120 million between the ages of fifteen and 24 years, it will take more than a miracle for the economy to produce enough jobs to provide for even one in every twenty in the 1990s.[1] The unemployment bureau has 30 million listed as looking for jobs, which does not count those who have stopped looking, or those who have found part-time employment. Over 2.8 million of those unemployed hold graduate or post-graduate degrees.[2] Inflation is an ever present spectre; prices for some commodities such as edible oil and tea have gone up 20 percent every three months.

Eleven percent of the population of India is Muslim and Muslims along with other religious minorities comprise over 115 million of the population. Another 15 percent (105 million) are Untouchables, who have little reason to consider themselves Hindus, and 52 million are tribals. The rest of the population is fragmented along lines of class, caste, religious sects, linguistic and other differences.

As in every other period of economic transformation and social mobility, there has been an increase in overt Hindu religious passions. The heartland of the Hindu revivalist movement is the North.

Beneficiaries of the Green Revolution, first-generation professionals and successful entrepreneurs, have sponsored temple-building, innumerable week-long or month-long recitations of the *Ramayana*, and other more elaborate rituals. The older, urbanized bourgeoisie, with educational patterns going back to the colonial period, with greater access to English-medium education, have become the representatives of the "polluted" West; their values and social attitudes based on reform Hinduism sufficiently distinct from conservative fundamentalist Hinduism to be labeled as "alien." The only vehicle that the nascent bourgeoisie have found which allows the alliances which camouflage the class and ideological differences between the urban and the rural is religious politics.

The Janata Party emerged in the 1977 elections as the representative of the aspirations of this class. The issues taken up included an attempt to block conversions to Christianity through national legislation and attempts were made to decertify textbooks that "failed to depict Hinduism in a sufficiently favorable light and glossed over the flaws of Muslims."[3] The conversion of a small number of Untouchables to Islam in Meenakshipuram was considered a portent by the upper-caste Hindu.

In 1982 the *Vishwa Hindu Parishad* (VHP, World Hindu Congress) came together with the leaders of the Bharatiya Janata Party (BJP) and the Rashtriya Swayamsevak Sangh (RSS). The latter, a party formed in 1925 to assert the right of Hindus to set policies, included many second-echelon Congress Party members who were simultaneously members of the RSS. The stated policies of the VHP are to prevent conversions to Islam or Christianity, to build temples, and prevent Hindu girls from marrying non-Hindus.[4] A measure of their success is that in Kerala, a state where Muslims and Christians form a substantial portion of the population, 962 temples have been built or renovated in the last decade.[5]

The RSS claims it has 25,000 *shakhas* or brotherhood units. The daily drills form the practice of the active members of the units; men in white shirts and shorts and saffron-colored caps go through a series of drills and exercises which begin with a Sanskrit prayer and conclude with a speech, generally warning of threats to Hinduism. Participation in the daily drills had increased from 1 million in 1979 to 1.8 million in 1989. In addition the RSS has thirty-eight front organizations with an additional membership of 5 million. It claims to have used its volunteers to distribute 20 million copies of an anti-Muslim anti-Christian leaflet entitled, "Warning: India in Danger." The Delhi branch alone has sold 5 million postcards and envelopes showing India,

Pakistan, Afghanistan, Nepal, Sri Lanka and Bangladesh under a saffron flag (saffron is the color of Hindu nationalism selected in the nineteenth century). The VHP has 3,500 branches and over a million members.[6] By contrast, the Communist Party of India (CPI) had 480,000 members in 1985 and the Communist Party of India-Marxist (CPM) 367,828.[7]

The main vehicle for political mobilization of the RSS/VHP/BJP has been marches from one end of India to another. Called *rath yatras* to evoke Hindu religious sentiment, these massive parades with thousands in tow have criss-crossed the country with their message of *Hindutva*. Each segment of the march concludes with rallies called *Ektamata Yajna* (or unity sacrifice rituals) honoring Mother India (*Bharat Mata*) deified as a goddess clad in a modest *sari* seated on the back of a lion. As the chief minister of the VHP declared, "You will soon see in this country a vertical divide within each political party – those who accept Hindu nationalism and those who don't."[8] The 1988-89 government of India was a coalition government with a majority formed with support from the BJP and the CPM; the Congress Party (I), defeated in the last elections has many members who are also RSS and VHP members and are switching political alliances.

Liberal and secular groups have attempted to voice concern and organize some forms of protest. There are also social movements of protest groups led by civil rights lawyers and others involved in trying to implement the existing laws to those organizing landless and the Untouchables (Dalits, the oppressed, the term Untouchable activists use), feminist and women's issues activists, eco-feminists, environmental activists, union organizers. But the agendas and the priorities of these various groups, not to mention class and caste interests have prevented the formation of any national coalitions. Their mobilization on the other hand has been a convenient issue for the guardians of "law and order" in society to further their own political interests, to raise slogans about "Hinduism in danger."

Escalating violence against women and minorities has become endemic in contemporary India. The confrontational techniques used by the Hindu Fundamentalist organizations at all political rallies, their overt support for killing minorities, had resulted in hundreds and thousands of deaths. Forcing Dalits to eat excrement was reported from Bihar, Karnataka, Trivandrum and Cochin in 1987 and 1988; in 1989 it was found that Dalit children in a village near Indore were not allowed to sit on the palm-leaf mats used by the other children in class-rooms for fear of pollution.[9] Rape, the age-old weapon of fear and coercion, has acquired a violent dimension, rape by the police. Gang rape of Untouchables activists and "uppity" tribals and Dalits has become so rampant by the police, that as one progressive journal described it, "The police in India consider the right of raping women as one of the perks of an underpaid job."[10] The signature of a police rape is usually to thrust the *lathi* (stick which the police carry) into the vagina when leaving the victim. But violence is seen, reported and mobilized against in a piecemeal fashion. Because these instances are seen in isolation from the fundamental logic of caste Hindu cultural practice, they are seen as amenable to legal or social reform.

India, from a constitutional viewpoint, is committed to being a secular state. Yet in the post-independence period (since 1947) and particularly since the 1970s, the overt use of caste-Hindu symbolism in public life has increased dramatically. National culture is defined and equated with Hindu culture; secularism itself has become a target of the fundamentalist Hindu religious movement.[11] What is the historical process through which this invention of national culture as Hindu upper-caste culture has taken place? Since many of the symbols of secular practice are considered to be of "Western" origin, they are rejected as inappropriate for an independent Third World country. Are progressive Indians, by selecting a Third Worldist and nationalist identity, lending support to the inegalitarian and sectarian world-views of caste-Hinduism? What is the genesis of the Hindu Indian nationalist identity and the intrinsic parameters of this identity?

Mass political mobilization presupposes a shared identity and shared concerns among the participants. At one level this identity is based on self-identification, a conscious selection of a given group of symbols (linguistic, religious, racial, and national). But in order to be viable as a political discourse, individualized identity is not enough; the symbols have to be shared by a group. The myths, the language, the religion, have to provide the glue as it were to hold and to construct this identity. The glue however, it seems, cannot be arbitrarily selected. It is the product of the specific social formation of the region, the social-property relations that have evolved in the region and the rules of production and reproduction by which that social entity has functioned since the beginning of its conscious history. Is it an accident that repeatedly over the last two hundred years, in periods of social mobility, in times of national identity formation, violence against women in socially sanctioned forms such as *sati* (immolation of a widow) have increased? Why is it that issues pertaining to women, such as the Abolition of Sati (1829), Widow Remarriage Act (1856), the Age of Consent Bill (1891), the Hindu Marriage Code (1954-1955), and most recently the sati of Roop Kanwar (1987) mark the periods when the cultural and political identity of particular groups was in the making and caste-class tensions were at the highest? Why is it that in contemporary India, the sharpest struggle for religious ideological domination has coalesced around the issue of building a temple to the mythical god-king Rama, who proved his own lofty virtue by rejecting his wife Sita who may have been tainted by a sexual assault while in captivity? Are these coincidental? Or have child marriage, the chastity and purity of women, the purported purity of the widow burnt on the funeral pyre of her husband and women's rights to property always been the terrain on which Hindu caste-class politics and identity politics been sorted out?

The Pre-Colonial Legacy

This section examines how religious identity came to be formulated. Many of my examples are drawn from the province of Bengal in particular, the area with the longest history of colonial rule. An historical perspective is necessary to clarify the process of selection of a cultural identity and to analyze how national culture came to be defined by the ideology of the minority upper-caste Hindus.

The British conquest of the Marathas (1818) for the first time in centuries brought Eastern and Western India under one imperial rule. There was no notion of a nation yet; the reality was a plethora of kingdoms with a multiplicity of languages and cultures, religions, castes, sub-castes and sects. The concept of community in the pre-colonial period was based on identities of locality, occupation, language, caste and sect. For the better part of the history of the subcontinent there had been no uniform religious identity readily identifiable as "Hindu." It was a term used first in pre-Islamic and then Islamic Arabic texts as a geographical nomenclature, *Al Hind*. Gradually it came to be used for people of the subcontinent, who were not believers in Islam or Christianity. In this usage it included all those considered the "other," making no distinction between the upper castes and the lower castes, the brahminical and non-brahminical. The usage of the term Hindu in non-Islamic sources in this sense of a religious grouping dates only to the fifteenth century.[12] In practice the particular sect of Hinduism such as Vaishnavite or Shaktya was more relevant, scriptural texts and their selections amenable to the *vyawastha* (arrangements and interpretations) of the local *purohit* or priest.

Given that the people of India did not have a unified conceptual framework for religion, Muslims too were not perceived as a unified body of people when they arrived. Indian Muslims did not discontinue their caste affiliations, which continued to form the basis of marriage relations and occupational categories well into the contemporary period.[13] The main distinction was among the higher caste Muslims claiming foreign decent such as the ashrafs and the indigenous converted. All foreigners in India, whether Muslim or Christian, Greek or Turkish, were called *mleccha* or unclean people, a term which had been used since the first millennium B.C. for non-Sanskrit speaking peoples, and this was the term most commonly used for Muslims. Persecutions at the level of national Muslim political authority were not necessarily translated into the village level. Conflicts which have been read as religious confrontations in the rewriting of history of this period in the twentieth century can also be read as examples of class conflict. For the vast majority of people, the village affiliation was the most important symbol of identity, and it was formulated in terms of caste.

The caste system fundamentally functions along two lines of distinction: the *varna*, which divided society into four orders, and the *jati*, birth distinctions based on local systems of ranked, hereditary and mainly endogamous groups. Although the division of society into the four orders (Brahmin or priestly category; Kshatriya or warrior, Vaishya or trader and agriculturist, and Shudra or menial) is considered to date back to the pre-Christian era, this ordering of society into separate orders is not unique.[14] It is caste understood as the jati system which made the South Asian social arrangement distinctive. The basis of the jati system is the opposition between "pure" and "impure," and "rules" based on the notions of pure versus impure governed inter-dining and sharing of ritual space.[15] It was the jati system according to which people lived their daily lives. The jati system evolved locally and the four orders were divided into numerous jatis, ten to thirty jatis depending on local practice. It is important to note that this caste system with its myriad categorizations and hierarchies of jatis was of necessity vague, its complexity and regional variations ensuring its malleability in the face of political convenience.

Social mobility, by which individuals of a lower caste gained higher caste status, was typically not an individual affair; more frequently the entire jati or even varna group collectively moved to a higher slot in the caste hierarchy though the impetus for such a move may have come from an individual. The seizure of political power and the acquisition of wealth were most the common routes for such caste-class mobility. Lower castes after seizing political power could and did declare themselves upper castes; tribal chieftains could and did enter the caste system through their seizure of power.

The articulation of caste mobility involved an overt practice of the accepted codified norms of "upper-caste" practice usually denoted by the term Sanskritization.[16] These included supporting Brahmins and temples, bringing in Brahmins from elsewhere with land grants or even creating a Brahmin caste if they did not exist locally and could not be enticed from elsewhere. In most areas of India such a process of Sanskritization also involved forsaking meat and liquor, for these were practices associated with the lower castes, tribals and mlecchas. But above all such demarcators of mobility involved women. Marriage of daughters with upper-caste men (hypergamy) with added dowry as compensation, was a common strategy. But even more specifically brahminical upper-caste status was accomplished by distinguishing marriage customs and control of female sexuality compared to those of the lower castes. Lower castes widows were and are permitted to remarry; in the upper castes they were not; the culture of the *pativrata* or the one who remains faithful to the husband was propagated as the norm. Divorce initiated by the wife was possible in the lower castes, forbidden among the brahminical upper castes till the 1950s. Polyandry, levirate and widow-remating were common among many tribes and peasant groups,[17] therefore *ipso facto* unacceptable as upper-caste brahminical practice.

Lower caste and tribal women worked outside the home, so seclusion of upper-caste women was imperative. Even stepping outside the home for visiting other women was considered a transgression of propriety and was subject to fines according to the *Arthashastra*.[18] The *Manu Smrti*, or *Laws of Manu* which are considered to be the guidelines for brahminical legal and customary practice was explicit in its concerns regarding the need to control female sexuality. It declared, "The father who does not give away his daughter in marriage at the proper time is censurable." "Proper time" was understood as before she had reached puberty and felt the first stirring of sexuality. This became the explanation for child marriage. Controlling the woman's sexuality remained the responsibility of males, "for unguarded they bring grief to both the families."[19] Sati, that final negation of right to life itself for the woman after the death of the husband by brahminical practice, also was related to caste-status mobility. The available inscriptional and archeological evidence suggest that prior to the nineteenth century sati was used by families of Kshatriya status or more typically by families seeking such a status. And, as in nineteenth century Bengal, some of the most prominent cases of sati in the eleventh century involved women from an upwardly mobile Shudra caste.[20]

Historically, then, it was women, their role in the family and the normative gender constructions which formed the core of brahminical ideological practice. This was ritualized; several of the important brahminical rituals involving the husband require the participation of the wife and remain incomplete without the wife's participation. Hindu brahminical wedding ceremonies require the participation of women who have husbands living. Within this ideological framework clearly it is not possible to sort out questions of status or caste or national identity without defining and redefining the normative gender roles. The articulation of this ideology in terms of women pre-dates colonialism; and that is why the challenges to this ideology presented by colonialism and capitalism have inevitably focused on women.

Urbanization and the Creation of a Hindu Identity

British colonization of India began in Bengal in 1757 and it was here that the first formulations of national identity were to emerge. This was in many ways a response to the fundamental transformation of society which occurred in the first century of British rule in Bengal. In the immediate aftermath of the colonial settlement some members of the old Muslim aristocracy lost privileges and new social classes emerged both in the countryside as well as in the new urban center of Calcutta. It was Calcutta, both as the administrative capital and commercial and industrial center, which was to become the city where the "new Bengal" was to be forged where the transition from the village identity to a national identity had to be articulated.

In the early nineteenth century Calcutta seemed to be on the verge of an industrial revolution. Several cotton mills, sugar refineries, rum distilleries and foundries were set up, manned by artisans and displaced village poor. This was the class which was called *chotolok* (literally the mean people or small people) in conscious contra-distinction to which the Bengali middle-class was to call itself the *bhadralok* (respected or refined people). This bourgeoisie consisted of the nouveau riche (or the *navya sampradaya* as they were called) as well as members of the older land-holding class who had begun investing in shipping and the new industrial concerns. Those with means built enormous European-style mansions with Italian marble, crammed them with imported chandeliers and Venetian mirrors and imitated "English ways." Many were upper-caste Hindus who had landholdings but were associated with British urban enterprises in business, government administration and the teaching and legal professions. Others were not from the upper castes, but by virtue of their wealth, their political and social power, their conscious adoption of strict Hindu brahminical models, they were "reclassified" as "upper caste."[21] To establish status in Bengali society, they built temples and *ghats*, supported Brahmin priests, held elaborate *shraddha* (funeral) feasts. Caste classifications, establishing a rigid hierarchy and supposedly dating back to the twelfth century were introduced. If hypergamy, child marriage, dowries and the polygamy of those men with such attractive caste attributes that they were much in demand were one type of manifestation of social restructuring, the rapid increase in widow immolations (sati) was another. It was on the issue of sati that the lines of debate on the women's issues between reformers, conservatives and the state were first drawn.

Between 1815 and 1828 the number of women dying as satis was recorded at 8,134. The vast majority occurred in the vicinity of Calcutta; in 1823, the caste background of the cases were 234 Brahmin, 25 Kayasth, 14 Vaisya and 292 Shudra.[22] It needs to be noted that in eastern India and Bengal the Dayabhaga system of property division prevailed where the women were entitled to a share in the immovable property of the husband upon his death. Was sati just a convenient murder of an inconvenient claimant? Was the increase in Brahmin sati related to changing property relations of this caste while satis of the Shudra caste related to status mobility? More research and individual case histories are needed before we can answer this. But as numerous eye-witness reports of the immolation ceremonies suggest, they were public events for which the whole neighborhood turned out and obviously the family sponsoring the sati was making an ideological and political statement regarding their caste status.

The petitions and counter-petitions about abolition of sati in the 1810s and 1820s came together with two other initiatives of the colonial state. To begin with, after 1813 Christian missionaries began arriving in increased numbers. Their ridicule of Hindu religion along with their increased success with conversions gave many elites cause for concern. Then there were the challenges posed by Anglicans and Utilitarians such as Macaulay who declared that "a single shelf of a good European library was worth the whole native literature of India and Arabia."[23] The upper-caste Bengali elites who had thus far experienced advantages as a result of their association with the British now had to deal with a necessary realignment in the contested realms of religious and cultural hegemony. Instead of Orientalist sympathy and admiration for Hindu Vedic religion which had developed in the late eighteenth century during Europe's (particularly Germany's) love affair with Sanskrit and had shaped British policy in the initial decades, the upper castes were now confronted with the scorn of the Anglicists and Evangelists. In the debates that followed on these issues, through a process of selection of specific ideas and normative ideals, the identity of the upper-caste

Hindu as representative of an Indian identity was articulated. Before the ideology and identity of a nation and a culture could be defended it had to be defined.

The nineteenth century definition of the Hindu community became based on the whole-hearted adoption of the "Aryan Race" theories by the upper-caste Hindus. The work of German Romantics, Orientalists and Indologists which gave rise to the Aryan theory of Indian history in the first half of the nineteenth century was eagerly seized upon. While Indologists later retracted and declared Aryan to be only relevant to a language group and not applicable to a race of people, this notion of Aryan origin became central to the process of creating a community and a distinct religious identity.[24] Upper-caste Hindus could now claim ancestral origins similar to those of Europeans and at the same time justify their superior status vis-à-vis lower castes and Untouchables. The theory of the Aryan race argued that the upper-caste Hindus were descendants of superior European Aryans who came in via the north and conquered the indigenous non-Aryan people. Aryan origin became the definition of the upper-caste Hindu community; all others were considered to pollute the purity of the upper castes. Like the guardians of racial purity among the white races who feared that through miscegenation the worst aspects of the inferior races would overwhelm the noble race, the upper-caste Hindus excommunicated those who were even touched by the shadow of the Untouchable.

It was in the process of marshaling arguments for and against sati that the discourse on the Vedic period had become articulated. Vedic texts such as the *Vedas* and *Upanishads* (the revealed or *Shruti* texts) were used by those Hindus who sought to reform society and argued these were the texts closer to the Aryan peoples and their ideology; the nobler version of the past without the accretions of *agama* and *tantra*. Orthodox Hindus turned to the *Smritis* and *Dharmashastras* which represent codifications and interpretations of the Shruti texts for their enlightenment. This revival of interest in the Hindu past, a rediscovery for most elites, coming as it did in conjunction with theories positing an Aryan migration from somewhere in Caucasian mountains further cemented another myth, the notion of an idyllic past. Thus began the creation and writing of a history of the "golden age of Hinduism" when Indian (read upper-caste Hindu) culture had flourished, produced great achievements in philosophy, mathematics and the arts. Tribals and Untouchables became simply a "people without history" who had contributed nothing to the great and glorious Hindu civilization.

The Aryan myth provided an opportunity for rewriting history and creating the notion of a golden age of Hinduism and Hindu culture "destroyed" by the depredations of Muslim invasions. Proponents of Aryan race theories in Europe had been increasingly turning towards anti-Semitism in the second half of the nineteenth century. Turkish and Arab rule in Greece and Spain came to be depicted as a struggle between European vigor and creativity and Muslim "decadence" and "sterility."[25] This framework was imported. The emerging nationalist historians of India found ready allies among British historians who were increasingly engaged in "rediscovering" the "martial races" of India such as the Rajputs, Marathas and Sikhs who had all stood up to foreign (Muslim) invasion. Indian history came to be written as demarcated into three periods, Hindu, Muslim and British.[26] By the late nineteenth century, Hindu Indian history was being portrayed as a history of glorious struggle against Muslim invaders. Muslims had had power, therefore unlike the Untouchables and tribals they could not be written out of history; but they could be seen as destroyers of the "true" and "legitimate" history.

What impact did this new identity of the upper-caste Hindus as Aryans have on the women? If upper-caste Hindus were but sun-burnt Europeans could the upper-caste women now be allowed the same freedoms as European women?

Female Education to the Rescue of Civilization?

The impetus to the education of women in India came most vigorously from the Utilitarians and their explicit equation of "civilization" with "the position of women." As James Mill (father of John Stuart) wrote in his *History of British India* (1817):

> The condition of women is one of the most remarkable circumstances in the manners of nations. Among rude people, the women are generally degraded; among civilized people they are exalted ... a state of dependence more strict or humiliating than that which is ordained for the weaker sex among the Hindus cannot easily be conceived.[27]

Indian social reformers like Rammohan Roy and others of the Brahmo Samaj, deeply influenced by the Unitarians, had taken up the issue of women's education along with issues of widow remarriage and abolition of sati. There were a handful of educated women, particularly from families where the fathers ran traditional schools (*tol*), where the women were part of the Vaishnavite tradition of women poets and composers or where the women were wives of reform-minded feudal princes.[28] But the issue at hand was not education for women for the sake of women, but for the sake of the nation and for the sake of men.

And what was this education to be like? As a Bengali newspaper of 1889 declared in the midst of a raging debate over women's education,

> The best system of education for Hindu females will be that which will take note of their character, capabilities and lifework, and implant in their minds those priceless domestic virtues which it is necessary for Hindu wives to possess. Considered from this point of view, it is not desirable that the Hindu girl should be given the *denationalizing* education which is given to the Hindu boy [emphasis added].[29]

So after thousands of impassioned debates since the 1830s, with the influence of the Brahmo Samaj on the wane by the 1880s, the curriculum of nationalist education for women had been firmly established with Sanskrit, Bengali, arithmetic, moral textbooks, culinary skills, and the learning of various *puja* (worship) rituals. The best puja performer received a prize.[30] And it was this curriculum and its acceptance by the Hindu bourgeoisie at Mahakali Patsala which signified the general acceptance of education for women in Bengal and with minor variations in the rest of India. The vast majority of those arguing for women's education invoked Gargi, Kshana, Matreyi and Lilavati, women from the Vedic and Upanishadic periods who were known for their knowledge and intellect, and suggested them as role models. The stories and sayings of Kshana are still popular and are still sold in little booklets at village fairs and city-sidewalks in Bengal and every Bengali girl reads some biography or other of these figures. And what is the moral of the story? Kshana defeated her father-in-law Varahamir in a learned debate, and then cut off her tongue to prove her obedience and filial piety. Gargi, when found to be getting the better of her competitor the sage Yajnavalkya was dismissed with, "Silence woman! Or your head will drop down dead on the floor." Education for women was to become a new class-caste demarcator in "new India," on condition that the woman was not "denationalized" by this education.

Of course, women's education and its accessibility to increasing numbers of middle-class women has had unanticipated outcomes, such as the growth of the women's movement in the twentieth century and challenges to the male-oriented gender ideology. But the dominance of the upper castes, their reincarnation as the upper class in contemporary India is underlined by examples such as even twenty years after independence in the elite professions such as the Indian Administrative Service, 65 percent were Brahmins, 30 percent Kshatriyas and 4 percent

Vaishyas with no Shudras among the Hindu members.[31] The nexus between class/caste/gender/national culture and politics makes the shaping of an emancipatory agenda and independent secular identity a particularly difficult challenge.

The Alliance Restructured

The Revolt of 1857 against the British shook not only British self-confidence; it also terminated their faith in following an active policy towards implementing social reform in India. The British concluded that it was a revolt of the old order against westernization and that it was in the best interests of the colonial state to be more conciliatory towards the upper classes and the "traditional" religious forces. The alliance between fiery radicals of Young Bengal and the Utilitarians eager to change society was replaced by the cautious Victorian imperialists who saw the collection of revenue and the keeping of the Indian subjects of Queen Victoria in line, with the races properly separated, as their main tasks. Between 1829 when the abolition of sati was legislated and 1885, the formal beginning of the Indian National Congress and the organized opposition to British rule, there was one item of legislation which had revolutionary potential for the condition of Hindu women. This was the passage of the Widow Remarriage Bill passed in 1856.

Opposition to this bill had been vociferous in some circles; it was even argued that it had contributed to the Revolt in its assault on upper-caste sensibilities.[32] The bill had very little actual impact on society at large, and received only tepid support from some elite Hindus. Orthodox Hindus organized against it. Those who had arranged for widow remarriage, such as G. Subramania Iyer who arranged for the marriage of his widowed twelve-year-old daughter, were boycotted by priests, cooks, and neighbors.[33] Campaigns for the promotion of intercaste-marriage and widow remarriage were perceived as "too radical" even by their financial supporters.[34]

But the Revolt of 1857 marked a deeper change, for a "national" identity had now been created. It was the first time Hindus and Muslims had united in political and military action against the British. Even more importantly a range of romanticized figures had been thrown up, the heroic Marathas and heroines like Rani of Jhansi. Canonized during the freedom struggle, she became the heroic woman, goddess and national spirit all at once; the woman as defender of the "Motherland" was born.

Defining the Spirit:
Stand Up and Be Proud if You Are a Hindu

[I]n the Arya system there is a preponderance of spiritualism, in the European system a preponderance of material pleasure. In the Arya system, the wife is a goddess. In the European system she is a partner and companion.[35]

By the time Bhudev Mukhopadhyay wrote his *Essay on the Family* in 1882, the creation of an Indian cultural identity as part of the nationalist discourse had already acquired certain specific traits. But there was a problem. The greatness of the Hindus clearly lay behind them; a posited racial equality with their British rulers via the Aryan race theories scarcely compensated for the daily indignities suffered by the colonized people. Earlier, during the first phase of its conscious formation in the mid-nineteenth century, emerging nationalist sentiments had posited a dichotomy between the "material" West and the "spiritual" East, and focused on the contributions of the East to the realm of moral values. The "spiritual superiority of the East" was to become increasingly a means of salvaging the national ego: "When the Occident wants to learn about the spirit, about God, about the soul, about the meaning and mystery of this universe, he must sit at the feet of the Orient to learn."[36] And over the course of the nineteenth and early twentieth century, the upper-caste Hindu Indian woman became the repository of this national spiritual essence; a "goddess" who must remain untainted by "westernization" and its implied pollution.[37]

It was also in 1882 that Bankimchandra Chattopadhyay's *Anandamath* was published. The theme is based on the Sannyasi Revolt of 1770, Hindu against Muslim. The theme poem, later set to music, was to be adopted by the Indian Congress Party as the national anthem. The second stanza is revealing:

> Every image made divine
> In our temples is but thine.
> Thou art Durga, Lady and Queen
> With her hands that strike and her swords of sheen,
> Thou art Lakshmi lotus throned,
> And the Muse a hundred-toned.
> Pure and Perfect without peer,
> ... Mother sweet, I bow to thee
> Mother great and free!
> — from *Bande Matram* [38]

Mere mortal women could only try to live up to this ideal. The Hindu Indian woman—her morality and behavior, her role in history—was no longer just to elevate class-caste status; equated with motherhood and goddesses, she was now the human face of the nation itself.

Seventy-three men, as representatives of "New India" and ten "sympathetic observers" came together in 1885 to form the Indian National Congress and take it upon themselves to "represent" some 250 million illiterate and impoverished peasants, women, and workers. Several of the men came from reform Hindu backgrounds, some were anglicized in their lifestyles. But most were comfortable with upper-caste Hindu identities, and "each took pride in his Hindu culture as faith."[39] At the second annual meeting—after the Parsi reformer B. M. Malabari's *Notes on Infant Marriage and Enforced Widowhood* had raised the question of social reform, and resulted in heated opposition from the Hindu conservatives—it was decided that Congress was a political body, "to represent to our rulers our political aspirations, not to discuss social reforms."[40] Most of the Congress leadership were pro-landlord interests in terms of peasant and tenant rights and not particularly interested in recruiting peasants or Muslims; none had any mass base.

The introduction of the Age of Consent Bill in the legislature in 1891 with a proposal to raise the legal age of marriage from ten to twelve ensured the identification and denunciation of all "enemies of Hindu civilization." The immediate cause for raising the matter in the Legislative Council was the death of eleven-year-old Phulmani from being raped by her husband. Scriptures were quoted to show it was contrary to religious precepts for husbands not to have intercourse with their wives on their first menstruation, forgoing the ritual of *garbhadhan* (inauguration of the womb). It was argued that the postponement of marriage until after menstruation would inevitably lead to unchastity; such a wife would remain evermore in a state of ritual impurity and would have to be barred from access to the kitchen.[41] Various other discussions on the subject in contemporary newspapers made it clear that the issue was fear of the woman's sexuality without appropriate male control. Reformers who sought to argue for support of the bill were physically attacked, and meeting halls rented to them were wrecked. As one commentator concludes, "The battle over the age of consent roused orthodox leaders throughout British India to a consciousness of the actual weakness and potential power of their position ... the cry of religion in danger had awakened a responsive chord in millions who otherwise took no note of public affairs."[42] Though the bill was made into law, the 1929 furor over the Sharda Act on the same issue showed that other than in Brahmo circles where the average age of marriage was higher anyway, the bill had little impact.

The brilliant social and cultural critic Ramabai was among the few women's voices raised in protest and comment. The case of her friend Rukmabai, however, made it abundantly clear to the educated women that the courts were not about to contravene the practice of Hindu law. Married as a minor to an illiterate and consumptive man, Rukmabai had refused to go and live with him, upon which the "conservative party all over India rose as one man and girded their loins to denounce the helpless woman." Large sums of money were raised to fight the case on behalf of the husband; the courts ordered Rukmabai to join her husband and ordered her arrest when she refused to do so. As Ramabai concluded, "There is no hope for women in India whether they be under Hindu rule or British rule."[43]

For the radical romantics, nationalism became a religious crusade. "What is nationalism? Nationalism is not a mere political program; Nationalism is a religion that has come from God," declared Aurobindo Ghosh. The Hindu religion was a sacred charge given to the "Aryan race to preserve through the ages."[44] Among these radical romantics and among the old guard Hindu conservatives, there was a rediscovery of the *Gita*, and it was reinterpreted as a call to action. New readings of the *Gita* were developed in Bengal, which made the "duty" of killing in the cause of the nation acceptable; goddesses such as Durga Shakti and Kali became symbols of the nation. Women from prominent Bengali families like Sarala Debi clearly found an acceptable niche in the early nationalist movement through this route. Emulating Kali in personal attire and hair-style, she started a gymnasium to train heroes in martial arts in 1902 and started a festival on the second day of the Durga Puja festival where Sanskrit verses were recited in honor of Hindu heroes like Krishna, Rama, Ranapratap, Shivaji and Pratapaditya, the Bengali "Hindu patriot who fought Imperial Muslim power."[45] This tradition was also to inspire the younger generation of romantic revolutionaries who undertook political assassinations. This ideology also created a romanticized martial culture for the upper-caste Hindus, invoking Shakti, Kali and Durga much in the same way as Kshana, Gargi and Matreyi had been in the cause of education. There was no emancipatory egalitarian concept of society or womanhood embedded in this vision. The woman became the last unpolluted sanctuary, the innate spirit of the Aryan nation:

If our womanhood is made to lose direction, then the nation's defeat would be complete. If, like the so-called enlightened westernized Indian man, the Indian woman also takes its western education and changes her own nature and religion then our subjection would be extended from outside to our innermost core.[46]

So the woman had to be kept pure, guarding the essence of national culture.

The reformist tendencies of moderates were to give rise to another version of Indian womanhood. As the nationalist movement turned into a struggle for independence and Gandhi became the undisputed leader of the Indian National Congress in the 1920s, he was astute enough as a politician and committed enough as a social reformer to believe all segments of society had to participate in the struggle. Upper-caste women set aside physical seclusion in the urban centers and began participating in Congress meetings. The Women's India Association was started in 1917 by Margaret Cousins, Anne Besant and Dorothy Jinarjadasa; the All India Women's Conference was formed in 1927 and was again initiated by Margaret Cousins. Of the 80,000 people arrested during the Salt March in 1930, 17,000 were women; at the next annual meeting of Congress in 1931, women were congratulated. In adopting the principles of the new Constitution at this meeting, the demand for women's suffrage and adult franchise was met with support from the Congress Party. As some of the leaders of the Congress pointed out, this also helped them say to the British that they were socially advanced and the issue of women's suffrage in India was dealt with in a far more civilized manner than in Britain.[47] Nehru was more outspoken as a social critic on women's issues, and was at least intellectually more aware of the connection between women's struggle against imperialism and against patriarchy at home. In the best tradition of Liberal Fabian Socialism he invoked Ibsen's *Doll's House*, and emoted, "The future of India cannot consist of dolls and playthings and if you make half the population of a country the mere plaything of the other half, an encumbrance on others, how will you ever make progress?"[48] Of course Nehru himself was yet to discover rural India and the conditions of life of working class women where they were anything but an "encumbrance on others."

Education for women in many of these upper-class/caste families was simply a statement of class access; they could educate even daughters abroad. But if the speeches of one of the most prominent women activists Sarojini Naidu (1870-1949) are any indication, care was taken that this participation in national politics and marches did not affect gender hierarchies. Educated in England, a noted poet, in close contact with English women's rights activists, she was a founding member of both the Indian women's organizations. Yet, she repeatedly referred to herself as a "mere woman" in her speeches, liberally sprinkling them with homilies like "I will confine myself as a woman should to domestic issues." The "domestic issue" in this case was the partition of India. Was she being sardonic? It is doubtful, for her vision of women's participation was, "Remember that in all great national crises it is the man who goes out, but it is the woman's hope and woman's prayer that nerves his arm to become a successful soldier."[49] "The essence of womanhood" remained Sita, the long-suffering wife of Rama who was a particular favorite model of Gandhi's. Of the numerous variations of the epic *Ramayana* that exist, the "official" version became the one where the chastity of the wife, her patience and her fortitude are key themes.

When the Child Marriage Restraint Act of 1929 was passed raising the minimum age of marriage to 14 for women and had a six-month waiting period before it came into force, millions of girls were married off at nine and ten years of age.[50] The Hindu Code Bill suggesting legislation banning polygamy, legalizing divorce and giving a widow the same share in her husband's property as the son, initiated in 1934 by the All India Women's conference was drowned out in opposition. In 1943, when the Bill was reintroduced, its opponents mobilized demonstrations against it in five cities and derailed it.

Inclusion/Exclusion: Legitimizing Hegemony

After 1917, when eventual self-government became a topic of discussion with the British government, Congress set about trying to bring all other social and political movements under its banner. The Untouchables, or Depressed Classes, had begun to organize themselves independently and since they represented one-seventh of the Indian population, note had to be taken of their political potential. Gandhi was probably among a handful of individuals who believed in a broader emancipatory movement as part of the nationalist struggle. But the reality was that this was not on the agenda as far as the vast majority of the leadership in Congress was concerned. My hypothesis that education for upper-caste men and women was indeed considered a part of sanskritization is borne out by the fact that despite all the paternalist rhetoric of untouchability being a "reproach to Hinduism," a 1924 resolution *requiring* all the national schools to accept Untouchables was shelved because it was not acceptable.[51] B. R. Ambedkar's Independent Labour Party Movement drawing support from the politicized Untouchables was to become second only to the Muslim

League in opposition to the Congress Party in numbers. Somewhat similar to the process of women being brought into the congress movement by Gandhi, Ambedkar also mobilized Untouchable women to participate in the 1927 movement to claim the right of Untouchables to take water from public tanks.[52] The parting of the ways between Untouchable national leadership and Congress came in 1956 when along with Ambedkar hundreds of thousands of Untouchables converted to Buddhism as a final gesture of separation from caste Hindu society and its cultural hegemony. In recent years various types of Dalit organizations have come to the fore. Although most Dalit activists continue to be from the Untouchable castes, the term is also being used by some to describe and assert their solidarity with all people who suffer social and economic exploitation and cultural oppression. A recent convention of Dalit writers in Maharashtra ended with homage to "the great African Dalit leader Nelson Mandela."[53]

Though Article 17 of the Indian constitution in 1950 declared, "'Untouchability' is abolished and its practice in any form is forbidden," the extent to which violence against Dalits (or the oppressed, as Untouchable women and men prefer to be called) has increased in the 1980s points to the vacuity of the statement. Even renaming an university in Ambedkar's name in Marathwada was enough to start off an upper-caste riot against Dalits followed by rape and burning of their villages. Rape of Dalit and tribal women has historically been one way upper-caste/class domination was reiterated. The access to state power by caste Hindus has increased rather than decreased the potential of abuse. While both Dalit women and upper-caste women are victimized by patriarchy, variant caste and class manifestations of patriarchy have by and large kept women from developing common political agendas. Though on the one hand information on police brutality and complicity of local officials with landlords and upper-caste Hindus have often been documented and reported systematically only in the urban educated feminist press, the investigations have also revealed instances of the complicity of upper-caste women in these atrocities.[54] And in April 1991, as a 16-year-old caste Hindu girl and her 18-year-old Untouchable lover were lynched by 500 people not even 100 miles from Delhi in a prosperous village, the mother of the girl defended the decision of the village to kill her daughter.[55]

The other major challenge to Congress hegemony had emerged in the 1920s and 1930s from the Kisan Sabha movement, where peasants of both Hindus and Muslim castes had organized to call into question the entire structure of landlord politics. The Communist Party had been formed in India in 1926 but due to British vigilance had effectively functioned only as an underground and illegal organization until 1942. The Congress Socialist Party had more of a presence, but successfully stifled by the Congress Party on the grounds that the only "responsible" (hence allowable) form of politics at the time was the anti-imperialist struggle. Any alternative vision of culture and nation that the upper-caste members of the Communist Party or Socialist Party may have had remained to be articulated. The Congress leadership was however not at a loss for words; Sardar Patel declared in 1938, "Comrade Lenin was not born in this country and we do not want a Lenin here. We want Gandhi and Ramchandra. Those who preach class hatred are enemies of the country."[56] In one fell swoop class enemies had been raised to the equivalent of enemies of the nation!

Though the communist movement of the 1930s and 1940s brought together many remarkable women who were intimately connected to the nationalist struggle, a coherent cultural critique did not emerge. Though many in their private lives adopted emancipatory practices such as abolishing Hindu marriage ceremonies, most retreated to a reformist stance on women's issues in the post-independence period. Class privileges also protected many of these women from having to deal with the stigma associated with divorce and widowhood in upper-caste society so that they were not impelled to take up these issues in public fora.

The Communist Party of India had always had a "right" wing which advocated a united front with the national bourgeoisie and a "left" wing which at least sloganeered about "people's democracy." There were also differences between the wings regarding the role of the proletariat versus the peasantry in the revolutionary struggle, the former position with leanings towards the Soviet Union, the latter towards China. The CPM was formed as a bifurcation of these ideological differences in 1962 and it has since formed majority governments in three states, West Bengal, Kerala and Tripura. In West Bengal (the eastern part became East Pakistan and then Bangladesh) where the CPM has been in power since 1977, and has achieved considerable success in land reform including land to tribals and lower castes, there has yet to be any overall agenda of a cultural critique of either Hinduism or of the status of women within the dominant ideology. As in the wider Indian society, women are conspicuously absent from any systematic public participation. In 1985 women constituted less than 5 percent of party membership in West Bengal and Kerala and 7 percent in Tripura.[57] Demographically, Bengal before independence had been a state with a Muslim majority 55 percent and Hindus 43 percent in 1931;[58] the axis of conflict and cultural consciousness since the nineteenth century had therefore been religion and upper-caste culture has not been challenged. Since independence, and the departure of many Muslims, Bengali Hindu nationalism has been at the core of the regional cultural identity. The CPM and its leadership has been comfortable in being able to draw on these earlier nineteenth and twentieth century symbols. Upper-caste Bengali culture with its romantic-reform tradition of Tagore and the Bengal Renaissance has sufficed as a form of alternative culture to that of Northern India. This "kinder, gentler" version of upper-caste culture retains intact the dominant norms of Hindu patriarchy.

In contemporary CPM-governed Bengal, as in other parts of India, caste Hindu culture is nurtured by the keepers of tradition of yore as hundreds and thousands of women perform numerous *vrata* (special ritual fasts and worship). One common vrata is *Lakshmi puja* performed by most middle-class women for the prosperity and well-being of the family. As part of the ritual, young girls sit around a married woman and hear her recite tales told in rhymed couplets. Normative gender expectations are manifest; the story-line is a denunciation of the improper conduct of women, such as loud laughter, rude talk, lack of respect towards parents-in-law, eating before the husband and not obeying him, dressing immodestly, and so on, all of which is said to have brought death, pestilence, starvation and unhappiness to all on earth. "Abandoning all modesty, grace and mercy, she goes hither and thither with careless freedom" scolds the goddess Lakshmi. Shades of the *Arthashastra*? These texts are still very popular and are sold all over the cities and even small market towns.

An analysis of the short stories in the new journal for upper-middle-class women started in Bengal by a well-known film director and actress Aparna Sen, shows that the value-system has changed only marginally. One of the special issues was devoted to the rituals and history of Santoshi Ma. A "new" goddess, popularized via a Bombay film in the late seventies, Santoshi Ma (the name of the goddess denotes fulfillment of desire) has suddenly become *the* goddess of choice for women's vratas. The cult seems to cross class boundaries.[59] My attempts to discern who is involved in carrying out this worship suggest a very broad segment, from those who are educated and "westernized" to those who are only nominally literate; most women I asked said, "of course everybody worships Santoshi Ma." The moral tales appended to the text for worship are filled with stories of long-suffering wives with unemployed husbands, whose prayers are answered when the husbands find jobs, usually in a distant land, upon which the husbands promptly forget their wives. Only the steadfast worship of the wife finally moves the deity so that she appears in a dream to the errant husband who then returns to the wife and shares his wealth with her. Gender socialization for the life of a woman in contemporary India?

Conclusions: Women, Hindu Practice, and Contemporary India

Three primary issues have drawn together women's activists from middle classes in India: dowry, "bride burning" and female feticide. In keeping with the pattern of Hindu caste-class mobility, hypergamy has become the norm and with it an enormous increase in dowry demands. A reflection of "status asymmetry" as the anesthetized terminology of anthropology calls it, dowry demands are a form of accumulation, where cash and commodities worth several hundred thousand rupees are extracted from the bride's family not only at the time of the wedding but on an on-going basis. This recurrent dowry-demand is a reflection of the traditional custom when with pre-puberty marriage, Hindu practice sanctioned the demand of "gift" when the marriage was consummated and with each ritual of *simanta* performed for the pregnant woman.[60] The Dowry Prohibition Act of 1961 is a law limited to the books; social practice of dowry has never been challenged because in the final analysis it would have to challenge Hinduism itself, a step even the most liberal politician is unwilling to take.

The associated institution of "bride burning" as the staged "kitchen accidents" and suicide by fire of women who fail to bring enough dowry are called, in 1989 claimed 4,006 women's lives, counting only those cases where police and hospital reports were made.[61] Then there was the case of Roop Kanwar, an educated woman who was burned as sati in September 1987 in Rajasthan so that her husband's family could keep her trousseau. It turns out there have been "a small number of sati (28)" in this area since Independence in 1947. The hundreds and thousands who were mobilized as a *celebration* of this ritual murder, were also treated to a special pamphlet, "An Appeal to Hindus" which points out sati is the "heritage" of many castes. Unfortunately crude as this attempt was to build cross-caste solidarity on the backs of patriarchy, it does refer to the historical role of sati in Hinduism as a route to sanskritic Hindu caste mobility.[62]

Of the 12 million girls born in India each year, 1.5 million do not survive their first year, another 850,000 die before they are five years old.[63] As one researcher has stated, "One can hypothesize that whenever daughters are much more expensive to raise than sons (for instance because of dowry required or lower returns from a daughter's labor than from a son's labor) female infanticide may be resorted to either consciously or unconsciously."[64] The value of daughters in Hindu religion has always been far lower than that of boys. Daughters cannot perform the funeral ceremonies for the parents, nor light the funeral pyre. The British had noticed some villages in the Indian northwestern plains had never raised even one daughter; since marriages are village exogamous, the women in these villages were daughters from other villages brought in as daughter-in-law. Based on very detailed demographic research, Miller had concluded that data for nineteenth and mid-twentieth century India indicate one-fourth of the population in the Northwestern region preserved only half the daughters born to them.[65] Though banned by the British in 1879, female infanticide obviously continued. The Kallar community in Tamil Nadu was reported to have 6,000 cases of female infanticide in the 1980s.[66] And for those who can afford the expenses of amniocentesis there is the option of feticide. The sex ratio in India by 1981, even before the widespread use of amniocentesis and female feticide, was 933 women per 1000 males. The average disguises sharper regional differences, with the North showing an even lower ratio of females to males.

This is then the cultural map which now defines the boundaries of India. Women's equality or caste equality are not on this cognitive map; they cannot be and have not been so historically even when there were not organized forces of fundamentalism arrayed against these aspirations. The anti-imperialist movement, which had necessitated a compromise on the part of the fundamentalist Hindus, is long past. The reformists are no longer needed. By choosing this terrain on which to introduce concepts of women's equality, as the Indian women's organizations who use terms such as "Sakti" or "Kali" as part of their nomenclature seem to have done, the women's movement seems to have entered the arena with one hand tied behind their backs. For example, the leading women's press in India calls itself "Kali for Women." One of the major journals in women's studies published in Delhi is called *Samya Shakti*. An active women's collective in Hyderabad, noted for its radical research work in women's history, nevertheless saw fit to take on the Sanskritized name "Stree Shakti Sangatana." By embracing the concept of nation that is not of their own making in culture or identity, their agenda at best can be a return to a reformist upper-caste Hinduism. At present, as class interests become more explicit, the local caste-class organizations are increasingly transformed into broader coalitions of "Hindus" versus the "others." The cultural hegemony of Hinduism which has always built its alliances through the propagation of certain institutions of patriarchal domination will continue to do so. There is no space here for a secular,

emancipatory, egalitarian vision; these concepts are as unnecessary as women who want to change "Hindu tradition."

The recent speech of the Chief Justice of the Supreme Court of India on 18 November 1990, on the Indian Constitution and its guarantee of equal rights to women underlines the very real danger ahead. Positing a mythical past when women were "superior" to men and given the status of "goddesses" he concluded:

(1) Let us not think of the articles in the Constitution and let us not try to implement those parts which give equality to women. (2) In accordance with the religious scriptures and the tradition of this country ... women 'certainly' have to be given an acknowledged role of superiority 'in playing their role as ladies, as mothers, sisters.' (3) What is necessary is that there must be a switchover (of women) from the office to the house. (4) If it is necessary for economic reasons to work outside the home, the women should put in 'extra labour' for it.[67]

A progressive Indian publication concluded the discussion of this speech of the chief justice with a commentary which chided the "privileged class centered myopic view."[68] But it is much, much more. It is the leitmotif of fascism, the demand for women to return to the home and hearth.

Finally, to summarize:

1. *Political Hinduism:* What is taking shape in India today is a **militant version** of Hinduism, not some vague resurgence of spiritualism. It is wrong to see it, as Ashis Nandy does, as the chiliasm of despair from among those battered by an alien urban economy.[69] In fact, the nerve-centers of the new Hindu-chauvinist mobilization are in the urban areas that have undergone a fairly rapid development of the commodity economy; and in the Green Revolution belt of North India. Clearly, the forces that are now redrawing the map of South Asia as a Hindu-Greater Indian *imperium* are not innocent lambs; saffron is the color of war.

2. *Political Calisthenics:* A further association with fascism comes from the mass mobilization of youth into brotherhoods performing calisthenics every morning in hundreds of towns and villages. These are not just good Hindu boys getting their bodies in shape; these are political exercises of a nation girding for war on internal enemies, among them Muslims, Dalits, and other national minorities; and presumably for later battles against external foes.

One thing we have learnt is that the price of "great nation" status in the modern world has always been accompanied by imperialism.

3. *Violence Against Women:* In the Indian context, these manifestations of political Hinduism are accompanied by a ferocious attack on women. Can anyone doubt that there is increased public and personal violence against women? From all that I have argued so far, the Hindu religion provides ample scriptural guides and practical precedents for all manner of oppression of women, including what is really the virtual rape of minor girls within the institution of child marriage. It is not enough to protest the abuses against women, while leaving the general ideological formation (Hinduism) and political formation untouched.

4. *Communalism as Fascism:* Gandhi and Nehru did not hesitate to call Hindu communalists *fascists*; in a context of communalized politics, and politicized religion, the advocacy of religion is itself tinged with fascism; whatever the justification for using religious symbolism for political organization in a prior time, now is not the time for innocence. We have to recognize there are only two political options: fundamentalist, fascist mobilization behind the symbols, practices and slogans of religion, or a resolute commitment to a fully secular politics behind an internationalist socialist ideology. There is no place for the third path, such as national socialism. Once the BJP-VHP-RSS-Shiv Sena and their front organizations come to power, and we are reduced to mothers in the fatherland, it will be too late to regret lost time.

5. *East Versus West:* There has been a great deal of rhetoric about East versus West, as if there is some essential cultural East which is being destroyed by the West. There is religious fundamentalism and oppression of women in the West, in the U.S. reaching as high as the Presidency and the Supreme Court; there are secular democratic movements in India, responding to purely local problems and circumstances. We have to get rid of the notion of rooted, essentialist differences. This after all is one legacy of colonialism and imperialism around which everybody seems to be rallying, not least the Third World elites and populists who have the most to gain from a diversion of energy from class politics.[70]

6. *A New Era of Internationalism for Women's Movement and Democratic Visions of Social Change:* The UN Decade for Women was problematic for international women's solidarity. Many U.S. and European feminists with a poor understanding of class, ethnicity and international political realities simply replayed colonial stereotypes of Third World nations, were extremely patronizing of

women from these nations, and often made no effort to separate the foreign policy objectives of their national governments from those of an internationalist women's movement. Third World women, for their part, rightly found this objectionable, and withdrew into a Third Worldist stance, replete with the rejection of feminism as a Western construct, omitting the fact that there is no such thing as "the Western woman," class, racial and other distinctions being obliterated in this simplistic view. This fed popular male perceptions, both the liberal and the left in Third World nations, that the women's movement was some concoction of female alienation in a commodity economy, and that it had no relevance in the collectivist ethos of Third World nations. This kind of discourse is common to Latin America, Africa and Asia.

Elite women from Third World nations themselves contributed to this mystification. Benefiting from state-provided resources to build up Women's Study Centers, with educational advantages which allowed them to take over the leadership of NGOs, these women reproduced the interests, in India for example, of class-caste politics, and became heirs to a Hindu-elite nationalist reconstruction of India.

What I am saying is that this is a dead-end. There is no political space in this emerging landscape for two visions of Hinduism, one, apparently spiritual and the other political. Religion is now ineluctably the property of right-wing forces. Women have to realize for their survival that they have to go beyond religion, indeed beyond nationalism. These are, after all, the pillars of the dominant political order.

Notes

I wish to extend many thanks to Vasant Kaiwar for contributing insights, time and energy to this paper.

1. Data from *India Today*, Sept. 30, 1990, p. 77; Arthur Bonner, *Averting the Apocalypse* (Durham, NC: Duke, 1990), p. 308.

2. *India Today* (September 15, 1990), p. 37.

3. Lloyd Rudolph and Susanne Rudolph, *In Pursuit of Lakshmi* (Chicago: University of Chicago Press, 1987), p. 43.

4. Their arm is long enough to reach the U.S.; Muslim members of the Committee of South Asian Women (an affiliate of the Association of Asian Studies), have been harassed by the organization for marrying Hindus.

5. Bonner, *Averting the Apocalypse*, p. 362.

6. Data from Bonner, pp. 352-353, 362-363.

7. T. J. Nossiter, *Marxist State Governments in India* (New York, 1988), p. 32.

8. Bonner, *Averting the Apocalypse*, pp. 362-363.

9. See numerous instances documented in Bonner.

10. Bonner, citing *Economic and Political Weekly*, p. 184.

11. This charge against secularism was voiced when in 1987 a young Rajput woman committed sati, immolation on the funeral pyre of her husband; when some segments of the urban elite succeeded in bringing government pressure to bear on the murder, the Hindu fundamentalist newspapers shot back with charges against the "irreligious minority overruling the rights of the religious majority." The Vishwa Hindu Parishad, the most organized of the fundamentalist groups, in a recent appeal to U.S.-based Indians to donate generously to the cause of building a Rama temple took out a full-page ad in the community newspaper *India West* (Aug. 31, 1990), p. 47. It is an appeal to all "Hindus-at heart" who are mislead by the "so-called champions of secularism."

12. Romila Thapar, "Imagined Religious Communities? Ancient History and the Modern Search for a Hindu Identity,"*Modern Asian Studies* XXIII (2):222-224.

13. The census of India in 1931 for example in Uttra Pradesh lists 14 castes with the most Muslims; Kingsley Davis, *The Population of India and Pakistan* (Princeton: Princeton University Press, 1951), p. 165.

14. The categorizations are remarkably similar to that of many pre-industrial societies: the Three Estates of clergy, aristocracy and commoner in pre-Revolution France or the samurai, agriculturists, artisan and merchant in Tokugawa Japan. Since many of the scholars working on Indian caste such as Louis Dumont have uncritically accepted the racialist theories of caste, i.e. that the upper castes are of Aryan origin, they have seen the caste system (*varna*) as somehow unique to India.

15. I am drawing on M. N. Srinivas, "The Nature of Caste Hierarchies" in *The Cohesive Role of Sanskritization* (Delhi: Oxford University Press, 1989) for this analysis.

16. First coined by M. N. Srinivas, the concept of Sanskritization includes that range of cultural and social practice usually associated with the two upper castes of Brahmin and Kshatriya. In his earlier writings Srinivas had totally neglected a discussion of how the regulation of women's conduct and sexuality was intrinsic to this process. Though in his most recent essays in *The Cohesive Role* he has sought to remedy this, it is still not a central theme in his analysis.

17. A very interesting article on *karawa* (widow remarriage) among Haryana jats, see Prem Chowdhry, "Customs in a Peasant Economy: Women in Colonial Haryana," pp. 302-336 in Kumkum Sangari and Sudesh Vaid (eds.), *Recasting Women* (New Brunswick, NJ: Rutgers University Press, 1990); Pauline Kolenda, "Living the Levirate: The Mating of an Untouchable Chura Widow" in Paul Hockings (ed.), *Dimensions of Social Life* (Berlin: de Gruyter, 1987).

18. *Kautilya Arthshastra,* translated by K. Shamasastry (Mysore, 1960), p. 177.

19. *Manu Smrti,* 3.55-57; translated and excerpted in Wm. Theodore de Bary (ed.), *Sources of Indian Tradition* (New York, 1958), Vol. I, p. 228.

20. Romila Thapar, "In History" in symposium volume on *Sati, Seminar* (Feb. 1988), p. 16.

21. See John McGuire, "Social Relationship Among Hindus" in Kenneth Ballhatchet and John Harrison (eds.), *The City in South Asia* (London: SOAS, 1980), for a discussion of caste mobility in early nineteenth-century Bengal.

22. *Parliamentary Papers on Hindoo Widows* cited in Lata Mani, "Contentious Traditions," in Sangari and Vaid, *Recasting Women,* p. 121, Fn 1.

23. de Bary (ed.), *Sources of Indian Tradition,* Vol. II, p. 45.

24. Thapar, "In History," p. 228.

25. Martin Bernal, *Black Athena: The Afroasiatic Roots of Classical Civilization* (New Brunswick, NJ: Rutgers University Press, 1987), refers to the Hellenomania and the depiction of Semites as both "female and sterile." See especially pp. 344-346.

26. As Romila Thapar, *Ancient Indian Social History* (Orient Longman, 1979), p. 4, points out, this was first done by James Mill in 1817 with the publication of *History of British India.* But she does not explain why this proved to be such a favorite framework for Indian historians ever after. Uma Chakravarti's article, "Whatever Happened to the Vedic Dasi?" in Sangari and Vaid, *Recasting Women,* is a path-breaking article analyzing nationalism and the writing of history from a feminist perspective.

27. James Mill, *The History of British India* (London, 1840, 4th edition) Vol. I, pp. 445-447.

28. See Brojendranath Bandhopadhya (ed.), *Sangbadpatre sekaler katha* (Calcutta, 1970 edition) Vol. I, p. 12.

29. Meredith Borthwick, *The Changing Role of Women in Bengal 1849-1905* (Princeton, 1984), pp. 92-93.

30. *Ibid.,* p. 100.

31. Joanna Liddle and Rama Joshi, *Daughters of Independence* (London: Zed Books, 1986), p. 72.

32. *Ibid.,* p. 30.

33. John McLane, "The Early Congress, Hindu Populism, and the Wider Society" in Richard Sisson and Stanley Wolpert (eds.), *Congress and Indian Nationalism* (Berkeley: University of California Press, 1988), p. 54.

34. Borthwick, *The Changing Role of Women,* pp. 142-144; Ranade in de Bary (ed.), *Sources of Indian Tradition,* pp. 135-136.

35. Bhudev Mukhopadhyay, *Paribarik Prabanda* (Essays on the Family) first published 1882, cited in Partha Chatterjee, "The Nationalist Resolution of the Women's Question" in Sangari and Vaid, *Recasting Women,* p. 243.

36. Vivekananda, 1894 in a speech given in New York, excerpted from the *The Complete Works of Swami Vivekananda*, edited by de Bary, p. 99.

37. Tanika Sarkar, "Nationalist Iconography: Image of Women in 19th Century Bengali Literature," *EPW* 21 (1987) has been an invaluable source for this discussion and I am indebted to her many insights.

38. de Bary, *Sources of Indian Tradition*, Vol II., pp. 159-160.

39. McLane, "The Early Congress," p. 54.

40. Eleanor Zelliot, "Congress and the Untouchables, 1917-1950", citing Dadabhai Naoroji, in Wolpert and Sisson (eds.), p. 182.

41. Borthwick, *The Changing Role of Women in Bengal*, pp. 127-128.

42. Stanley Wolpert, *Tilak and Gokhale* (Berkeley: University of California Press, 1962), p. 62.

43. Uma Chakravarti, in Sangari and Vaid, *Recasting Women*, pp. 73-74.

44. Ghosh speeches, reprinted in de Bary, Vol. II, pp. 176, 179.

45. Uma Chakravarti, "Whatever Happened to the Vedic Dasi?," p. 64.

46. Tanika Sarkar, "Nationalist Iconography," p. 2014, citing Motilal Ray, *Bharatlakshmi* which was published in 1931.

47. Liddle and Joshi, *Daughters of Independence*, p. 36.

48. Allahabad Speech, 31 March 1928, cited in Kumari Jayawardena, *Feminism and Nationalism in the Third World* (London: Zed Books, 1986), p. 98.

49. Sarojini Naidu, excerpts in P. Sengupta, *Sarojini Naidu, A Biography* (Bombay, 1966), pp. 73, 148.

50. Liddle and Joshi, *Daughters of Independence*, pp. 87-88.

51. Zelliot, "Congress and the Untouchables," pp. 185-187.

52. Meenakshi Moon and Urmilla Pawar, "We Made History Too," *South Asia Bulletin* IX (2) (1989), edited by Barbara Joshi.

53. Barbara Joshi, "Perspectives on the Dalit Cultural Movement," *South Asia Bulletin* VII (1 & 2) (1987), p. 68.

54. See Bonner, *Averting Apocalypse*, p. 323, when upper-caste women objected to Dalits carrying a bridegroom in a palanquin and started off the attack. See also Madhu Kishwar and Ruth Vanita (eds.), *In Search of Answers* (London: Zed Books, 1984), p. 184, where women were hired by a landlord to beat up a woman from a potter caste who had dared to bring rape charges against a landlord. Other incidents include the massacre of 21 men and women at Arwal in April 1986.

55. "Mehrana, Medieval Murders," *India Today*, April 30, 1991, p. 72.

56. Gyanendra Pandey, "Congress and the Nation, 1917-1947" in Sisson and Wolpert (eds.), *Congress and Indian Nationalism*, p. 129.

57. T. J. Nossiter, *Marxist State Governments in India*, p. 35.

58. *Ibid.*, pp. 119-121.

59. *Sananda* (Calcutta 1393/August 28, 1986).

60. Srinivas, "The Nature of Caste Hierarchies," p. 101.

61. Home Minister, Mufti Mohammed Sayeed, Report to Parliament, August 3, 1990, excerpted in *India West*, August 31, 1990, p. 11.

62. Kumkum Sangari, "Perpetuating the Myth," *Seminar* (Feb. 1988), p. 26.

63. "The Status of Female Children in Asia," *Women's International Network News* 15 (2) (1989), p. 49.

64. Barbara Miller, "Female Infanticide," *Seminar* (March 1987), p. 20.

65. *Ibid.*, pp. 20-21.

66. *India Today*, June 15, 1986.

67. Cited in Kameshwar Choudhary, "Debunking the Call for Women's Slavery," *EPW* (December 22, 1990), p. 2770.

68. *Ibid.*

69. Ashis Nandy, "The Sociology of Sati," *Indian Express* (October, 8, 1987).

70. In an 8-hour debate in Delhi on "What is Secularism?" the well-known journalist M. J. Akbar finds it appropriate to comment, "I think one of the greatest problems with this word secularism is that we never managed to get an adequate Indian word for what we wanted to say. We are still using an English word which is, I would suggest, even irrelevant to the Indian context." *India Today* (May 15, 1991), p. 65.

13

Identity Politics and the Contemporary Indian Feminist Movement

Radha Kumar

Introduction

In 1990, India was in the grip of a new series of agitations, stimulated by the National Front government's decision to implement the recommendations of the Mandal Commission Report of 1978. The Report advocated the broadening of caste-based job reservation in the administration, the public sector, and other state-controlled areas, such as education. It also suggested that the state classification of "backward castes" be altered, so as to include a large number of "other backward castes," and provided a long list of castes to be placed in this category. The agitation around this decision lasted several weeks, and led to considerable violence in different parts of the country. In its course a series of issues arose, concerning tradition and modernity, representation and the democratic state, caste, class, and the formation of bloc identities.

This is not the first time these issues have arisen in India. Interestingly, they were brought up in two agitations preceding this one: the Muslim Women's Bill campaign of 1985-86, and the campaign against *sati-daha* (widow immolation) in 1987-88. Both campaigns were engendered by attacks on women's rights made in the process of communal and/or caste assertions; in both, definitions of community identity appeared to center on religio-cultural definitions of women. Over the last ten years, India has witnessed increasingly strong communal and fundamentalist movements, many of which have sought to attack feminism. The Muslim Women's Bill agitation and the

274

campaign against sati-daha both launched attacks on feminism as being modernist, hegemonic and based on capitalist notions of equality within the market. In the course of both campaigns a series of questions came up concerning religious, ethnic and community identities, nationalism and nationalities, the nature of representative democracy, and the state. For feminists the attacks were not only a major setback, but especially sad because many of the issues raised were issues which feminists themselves had raised much earlier: for example, in the ongoing debate around personal law versus a uniform civil code. At the same time, while we are witnessing a series of identity movements which seek to dominate Indian society and its administration, the enormous range and variation of identities and identity politics in India is itself such that the universalist tendency of most fundamentalist movements is constantly undermined. One of the anticipated fall-outs of the Mandal Commission Report, for example, is that it will undercut the primarily upper-caste dominated chauvinist movement for a *Hindu Rashtra* (Hindu country). Whether this will happen, and to what extent it will constitute a real advantage for feminists is, however, unclear, as the inter-relationships between community, caste, and religio-political movements are ambiguous. This chapter seeks to explore some of these questions through analysing two campaigns: around the Muslim Women's Bill, and against sati-daha.

The Muslim Women's (Divorce and Rights to Maintenance) Bill

The issue of Muslim women's rights to maintenance on divorce became especially controversial for feminists in 1985, with what is now referred to as "the Shah Bano case." On April 23, 1985, a five-member Constitution Bench of the Supreme Court ruled that a seventy-five-year old woman, Shah Bano, was entitled to maintenance by her husband under Section 125 of the Criminal Procedure Code. Shah Bano's husband, Mohammad Ahmed Khan, had divorced her after roughly a half century of marriage. Ten years earlier, under pressure from her husband, Shah Bano and her children had moved out of the main house, into a sort of annexe. For two years her husband gave her Rs. 200 per month, and then abruptly ceased to do so. In 1978 she filed an application in the Indore magistrate's court, asking that her husband be ordered to pay her maintenance under Section 125 of the Criminal Procedure Code. Intended to prevent vagrancy due to destitution, this section entitles destitute, deserted or divorced women to support from their husbands, provided that latter are not destitute themselves.

Destitution, thus, defines the provisions of this section. The maximum amount allowed by it as "maintenance" is Rs. 500 per month, certainly inadequate for both shelter and subsistence. Shah Bano asked for the maximum, on the grounds that she was old and could not work to support herself. In other words, under Section 125 she had to show that she was unable to support herself before she could claim support from her husband.

While Shah Bano's application was still pending, her husband decided to divorce her, using the triple *talaq*[1] which the Quran names the most lowly form of divorce. Meanwhile, the magistrate ruled that Shah Bano was entitled to maintenance under Section 125, but fixed the amount at a ludicrous Rs. 25 per month. She went on appeal to the Madhya Pradesh High Court, which raised the amount to Rs. 179.20 (!). Now Mohammad Ahmed Khan went on appeal, to the Supreme Court, arguing that the High Court judgement exceeded its jurisdiction and violated Muslim personal law as stated by the *Sharia* (the text of Islamic law). In effect, several statements made up this contention: first, that as a Muslim he was bound primarily by Islamic law; second, that as maintenance from a husband related to the laws of marriage and divorce, which in his case fell under Muslim personal law, Shah Bano's application should be judged by this law and no other; and third, that if marriage, divorce and maintenance regulations fell under personal law, then criminal law should not enter the picture at all. In support of these arguments, he produced written statements acquired from the Muslim Personal Law Board, which said that under the Sharia the husband was not obliged to pay maintenance for more than three months after the divorce. Moreover, said the Board, the Sharia did not deal with the question of how the woman was to support herself after the three months were ended, and therefore the question was outside the purview of the Court.[2]

By the time the case was before the Supreme Court, thus, the distinction between maintenance on destitution (Section 125), and maintenance on divorce (which falls under personal law), was largely blurred. By virtue of this, the distinction between criminal and civil law was also blurred: at the same time, criminal law was banished from the territory of maintenance. Finally, the entire problem of female destitution was itself placed outside the purview of the Court, on the grounds that the text of personal law did not deal with it. And perhaps if the judgement of the Supreme Court on Mohammad Ahmed Khan's petition had ignored these points, it might not have been so controversial. It would, however, have been hard for them to do so, because these points were being argued before them, and countered by

Shah Bano's counsel, who cited two verses from the Quran to show that the provision of maintenance was regarded as a duty for the "righteous."[3]

The judgement can be summarized as follows: first, it upheld Shah Bano's right to maintenance from her husband, both under Section 125, and under Muslim personal law. Second, it asserted that Section 125 "Cut across the barriers of religion," that is, it transcended the personal laws of the religious communities which a given married pair might belong to. Third, it was critical of the way women "have been traditionally subjected to unjust treatment," and urged the government to frame a common civil code, saying:

> A belief seems to have gained ground that it is for the Muslim community to take a lead in the matter of their personal law. *A Common Civil Code will help the cause of national integration by removing disparate loyalties to laws which have conflicting ideologies.* No community is likely to bell the cat by making gratuitous concessions on this issue. We understand the difficulties involved in bringing persons of different faiths and persuasions on a common platform. But a beginning has to be made if the Constitution is to have a meaning. (Emphasis added.)[4]

When stated in such terms, it would have been difficult not to conclude that the judges were recommending a common civil code for the purpose of "national integration," rather than for reasons of justice alone. Following from this was the further conclusion that national integration entailed the abandoning of "loyalty" by Muslims to Islam and Islamic personal law.

Though feminists, liberals and secularists were all critical of the judgement for having entangled religious issues with matters of criminal law, the agitation which arose around it was almost immediately polarized along communal lines. Muslim religious leaders took it as representing an attack on the community and the *ulama* (scholar priests) issued a proclamation that it was against the teachings of Islam. Wide publicity was given to the proclamation. Claiming that Islam was in danger, Muslim communalists demanded that the Supreme Court judgement be repealed, and Muslim women excluded from section 125; jumping into the fray, Hindu communalists upheld the judgement, gleefully arguing that it supported what they had said all along, that Muslims were barbaric and anti-national.

In August 1985, a Bill seeking to exclude Muslim women from the purview of Section 125 was introduced in Parliament by a Muslim League M.P., G. M. Banatwala. The Bill was clearly in response to the

Shah Bano petition, and the feminist espousal of her cause, for it was introduced as the campaign against the judgement was mounting. The government decided to oppose the Bill, and deputed a Muslim minister, Arif Mohammad Khan, to argue against it in Parliament. Though he was asked to argue that Section 125 was intended to prevent vagrancy, and as such did not interfere with the personal laws of any community, Arif Mohammad diverged from his brief, delivering an impassioned plea for a humane reading of the Sharia. The ulama were outraged, and Arif Mohammad was denounced for his temerity in interpreting the Sharia as a lay person.

A massively orchestrated campaign against the judgement and in support of Banatwala's Bill now began. Over one hundred thousand demonstrated in Bombay, and at least as many in Bhopal. There were a spate of smaller demonstrations all over the country; in Hyderabad there was a *bandh* (a stoppage of all normal functioning for a day). In Lucknow the Muslim Personal Law Board called on all Muslims to boycott the Courts. As against this, the campaigns of Muslim liberals, feminists, and social reformers garnered small support: only a few hundred demonstrated in favor of the judgement. This may partly have been because those who did were threatened, and even attacked. The Talaq Mukti Morcha, for example, which was formed in November 1985, in a small town in Maharashtra, was forced to call off a march through Maharashtra to publicize Shah Bano's struggle before the march could be completed. The marchers were greeted with black flags at Miraj, threatened by a mob of four hundred in Parbhani, and stoned in Jalgaon. When they were surrounded by a mob of ten thousand in Ahmednagar, brandishing black flags, who stoned them, the marchers finally called off the march.

To understand why the issue became so heated one has to look at the context in which it arose. The 1980s witnessed a steep rise in communal violence all over India, both Hindu-Muslim and Hindu-Sikh. The November 1984 riots were particularly alarming: not only was Mrs. Gandhi's assassination treated as a communal issue by the Congress I, but no attempt was made either to punish the guilty, or even to investigate the charges of political and police involvement in the riots. The sense that Hindu communalism was acquiring increasing legitimacy in the eyes of the state was further strengthened by the Ram Janmabhoomi agitation which was launched in Uttar Pradesh.

In October 1985, the Vishwa Hindu Parishad, a relatively new Hindu communal organization, launched a full-fledged agitation demanding that a shrine in the precincts of the Babari Masjid in Ayodhya be declared the birthplace of Ram, and a temple be built on that spot. The question of worship at the shrine had become a source of conflict in the late nineteenth century, fomented partly by the British, and, pending a Court decision on the matter, the whole place was locked up. In the 1980s the case was revived by a "Hindu" advocate, and in the meantime the Vishwa Hindu Parishad led a two hundred thousand strong march to Ayodhya to "liberate" the shrine, and performed hundreds of fire-rituals all over the Hindi-speaking belt in 1985, to mobilize around their demand for a Ram Janmabhoomi temple to be built on the site where the mosque stands. Alarmed by the growing strength of the agitation, and the threat it posed, several Muslim religious leaders, politicians and others formed a Babri Masjid Action Committee, to defend the mosque.

The Babri Masjid issue and the Shah Bano case began to be linked as representing a Hindu communal onslaught on Indian Muslims.[5] Syed Shahabuddin, one of the leaders of the Babri Masjid Action Committee, and a member of the Janata Party, shot to prominence as a leader of the agitation against the Shah Bano judgement, organizing a petition against it which was signed by over three hundred thousand Muslims. In State elections in December 1985, Shahabuddin trounced his Congress I opponent from the Kishengaj constituency, despite an all out Congress I effort to win Muslim votes by putting up the secretary of the Jamat-Ul-Ulema-E-Hind, and bringing two hundred ulamas to canvass for their candidate.

On February 1, 1986, the district magistrate hearing the Ram Janmabhoomi-Babari Masjid case decreed that the shrine be opened to Hindus for worship. The Vishwa Hindu Parishad celebrated the decree with "victory processions." Muslims took out "mourning processions" in retaliation, and soon clashes between the two groups began, which escalated into riots in Delhi, Srinagar and parts of Madhya Pradesh. Alarmed by their loss in Kishenganj, and seeing a further loss of credibility in Muslim eyes, the Congress I began to backtrack on their assurance of Muslim women's rights under Section 125, announcing that they were considering a review of the judgement, and would introduce a bill along the lines of Banatwala's Bill. To many, this announcement displayed an utterly cynical willingness to sacrifice the rights of women for political expediency. Feminists and Muslim social reformers immediately lobbied the government against such a decision, but were unsuccessful. On the 25th of February 1986 the government introduced the Muslim Women's (Protection of Rights on Divorce) Bill, which excluded divorced Muslim women from the purview of Section 125, stating that the obligation of their husbands to maintain them ended with the three month period, after which their natal families would have to support them, or failing this, their local Waqf Board (these administer lands donated for the upkeep of Islamic religious establishments).

Opposition to the Bill took the form of public meetings, demonstrations, a concerted press campaign, and lobbying. The campaign, however, was not carried out under a single joint-action umbrella, even temporarily, as earlier feminist campaigns had been. Instead, a series of different identities and blocs appeared. The lack of any noticeable opposition to the Ram Janmabhoomi agitation from non-Muslims, especially Hindus, had left large sections of Muslims feeling more vulnerable than ever. Many Muslims who had earlier campaigned for a change in their personal laws, now became ardent supporters of it. Among them was Dr. Tahir Mahmood, an expert on Muslim personal law, who had earlier pleaded for reform of Muslim marital and divorce laws. In his book on the subject, he had, in fact, argued in favor of a uniform or common civil code. Now, in a revised edition, he withdrew the chapter on the need for a uniform civil code, and hailed the Bill as welcome. It is not surprising, then, that those Muslims who opposed the Bill felt impelled to form ranks within their own community. The Committee for the Protection of the Rights of Muslim Women, for example, which was formed by members of the two communist parties in India, together with "progressives" of various hues, solely in order to combat the Bill, decided to limit its membership to Muslims, allowing Muslim men to join, but not non-Muslim women.

For most of the autonomous women's groups this was a hard decision to accept, because it appeared to lend legitimacy to the idea that the rights of women could be defined by the religious community they belonged to, instead of arguing that religion and rights were separate and distinct. By implication, it also lent some support to two other arguments that feminists had had to contend with: one, that there is no such thing as a common category of women, because they are differentiated by caste, class and community, and therefore any definitions of rights have also to be based on these differences; and the other, that as different groups of women have different "interests," there is no real basis on which they can work together.

Interestingly, the Muslim Women's Bill of 1986, which took away Muslim women's right to maintenance from their husbands, also conferred a new right upon them which non-Muslim women do not have any equivalent of: the right to maintenance by the Waqf Board. One of the ironic outcomes of the agitation against the judgement has been that after the Bill was enacted there have been a spate of lower and higher court judgements granting divorced Muslim women much larger sums of maintenance than have been granted before. This should not, however, justify the Bill turned Act. By removing even the minor obligation which Section 125 imposed on husbands who had abandoned or divorced their wives, the Act made it legitimate for Muslim husbands to simply leave their wives stranded. The curtailment of the jurisdiction of Section 125, moreover, not only set a precedent for doing away with any checks on mistreatment of women under personal law, it also laid the foundation for excluding specific groups or communities from culpability for acts which abet crimes against women. It is especially significant that it was in the course of this agitation that the demand for legalizing sati-daha was first made.

Despite strong opposition to the Bill, it was forced through Parliament on the 6th of May, 1986, after an all night debate. A Party Whip was issued to all Congress I members of parliament, instructing them to vote for the Bill, no matter what their opinions on the matter might be. This was the first time that a Whip had been issued on a Bill concerning the rights of women.

For feminists, the campaign entailed a series of bitter lessons. Discovering the ease with which a "community in danger" resorts to fundamentalist assertions of self—amongst which, invariably, the subjection of women, justified as tradition, is of major importance— feminists were confronted with the associated discovery of the ease with which the Indian state chose to accommodate communalism (by taking no action against the Ram Janmabhoomi agitation), and balance this by a concession to fundamentalism (allowing personal law to cut into the application of uniform laws such as Section 125). For some years prior to this agitation, feminists had revived demands for a uniform civil code to replace religion-based and differentiated family laws ("personal law"), on the grounds that such laws sanctioned the oppression of women. Two initiatives against existing personal laws had received wide-spread support and publicity from feminists all over the country: Mary Roy's petition against Christian personal law, and Shahnaz Sheikh's petition against Muslim personal law. Filed sometime in the early 1980s, Shahnaz Sheikh's petition argued that Muslim personal law should be declared violative of Articles 13, 14, and 15 of the Indian Constitution, which guarantee equality before the law and prohibit discrimination on the basis of sex, religion or race. A great deal of pressure was put on her by conservative as well as fundamentalist sections of Muslim society, to withdraw this petition but she did not do so. The petition attracted so much press attention that some feminists feared that it would be adversely affected in Court. After the Shah Bano judgement and ensuing events, the issues raised by the petition lapsed into obscurity. In effect, the agitation interrupted developing critiques of personal law and moves towards some form of uniform civil code.

At the same time, the agitation posed certain issues which were to become increasingly important for feminists in the years to follow. First of all, there was the question of secularism, its definition and practice, in particular by the state, and its relation to religious freedom. By and large, opponents to the Muslim women's Bill espoused a classic liberal-democratic view of secularism as a system which separated religion from politics, which disallowed religious restrictions of the rights of the individual, and which allowed freedom of religious practice only insofar as it did not cut into the rights of the individual. Zoya Hassan, of the Committee for the Protection of the Rights for Muslim Women, for example, criticized the Bill on the grounds that it could hardly be called secular to pass a law which severely restricted the rights of the irreligious, while the memorandum drafted by the Committee argued that "by offering concessions to communal/sectarian groups with a view to short-term political or electoral goals," the "secular fabric of our society" was being frayed.[6] The signature petition which was jointly organized by feminists, social reform and far left groups argued further that all personal laws "have meant inequality and subordinate status for women in relation to men," and therefore religion "should only govern the relationship between a human being and god, and should not govern the relationship between man and man or man and woman."[7]

As against this, the government definition of secularism appeared to be radically different. According to the then Prime Minister, Rajiv Gandhi, "secularism is the right of every religion to co-exist with another religion. We acknowledge this by allowing every religion to have its own secular laws."[8] If this statement is not to be dismissed as sheer nonsense, then the only meaning to be extracted from it is that he defined personal laws as being secular—presumably on the grounds that as religion here defined the relationships between human beings (rather than between humans and gods), it was on secular terrain. Religion then, could formulate secularism. Implied, too, was the statement that all "religions" had the right to representation within the law—indeed, to make their own laws. While to a certain extent these rights have been present all through, the supremacy accorded to personal law re-affirmed the colonial codification of religion-based family laws, and ran counter to Constitutional promises of options from personal laws, and attempts to move towards uniform rights.

The second major issue which feminists were confronted with was the question of representation, or representativeness. Though the Committee for the Protection of the Rights of Muslim Women was formed partly to by-pass this issue (by offering solely Muslim support for Shah Bano and Section 125), and both Shahnaz Sheikh and Mary Roy were demanding reform of personal laws which affected them deeply, it was argued that none of them represented the "real" desires of "real" Muslim women. So much pressure was put on Shah Bano that she gave up the right she had fought for for so many years, asking the Supreme Court to record that she now repudiated the petition they had upheld, and renouncing the maintenance the Court had ordered. Upon this, she was welcomed back to the fold by Muslim fundamentalists, and hailed for having become a *true* Muslim woman.

This positing of the "real" or "true" woman, in opposition to the feminist, began to be widely made for the first time in the history of the contemporary feminist movement in the mid-1980s, and it is revealing that it arose in the course of communal and fundamentalist self-assertion. In the agitation around sati-daha which was to follow, the issues of secularism, religious representation, the Indian nation-state, and the symbol of the "real woman," as defined here, were expanded on even further, and used as sticks to beat the feminists with.

The Agitation Around Sati-daha in 1987-1988

In September 1987, an incident of sati-daha in Rajasthan sparked off a campaign which rapidly grew into a furious debate not only over the rights and wrongs of Hindu women, but over religious identity, communal autonomy, and the role of the law and the state in a society as diverse as India's. The debate raged for six to nine months, and in its course large sections of political opinion were polarized into twin camps of tradition and modernity. How and why this happened became matters of serious concern for Indian feminists, who found themselves facing intense hostility such as they had never faced before.

September 1987 was not the first time that Indian feminists encountered the problem of sati-daha. In Delhi the first encounter was in 1983, when a campaign to further popularize the ideology of sati-daha was launched by an organization known as the Rani Sati Sarva Sangh. The Sangh, which already ran several sati temples all over the country, got the government to grant them a plot of land in Delhi to build yet another sati temple, and decided to celebrate by leading a procession to the land. Delhi feminists heard of this plan and decided to hold a counter-demonstration along the route of the march, which they did with signal failure, partly because they had no time to mobilize and were thus outnumbered, and partly because this was the first time that they had had to confront a group of women in a hostile situation. This was in itself so distressing that it took the heart out of them. Most distressing of all, however, was the way in which the processionists appropriated the language of rights, asserting that they should have the right, as Hindus and as women, to commit, worship and propagate sati-daha. At the same time, they also appropriated feminist slogans, chanting, for example, "hum Bharat ki nari hain, Phool nahin, chingari hain" (we, the women of India, are not flowers but sparks). The feminists who attended the demonstration experienced, therefore, the humiliating sense of loss which accompanies the discovery that your own words can so readily be snatched and turned against you to serve an antithetical cause.[9]

The debate which arose in the 1987-88 agitation drew together some of the views expressed in 1983, and some of those expressed in the 1985-86 Muslim Women's Bill agitation. It was again couched in the language of rights, and the terms of definition which were predominant both marginalized and attacked feminist definitions of rights. It focussed, too, on issues concerning representation, the state, and identity politics, as the agitation around the Muslim Women's Bill had done, but this time the identity was not communal but caste based. In its course, the advocates of sati-daha were described as representing rural, traditional communities which were struggling to preserve themselves from the homogenizing tendencies of the Indian nation-state, while its opponents were described as representing elite, urban, modern sections of society, who were pressing the state to intervene in communities they bore no relation to, and were thus encouraging the Indian state to extend its sphere of control over civil society. At the same time, a furious polemic was directed against the Indian feminist movement, accusing Indian feminists of being agents of modernity who were attempting to impose crass market-dominated views of equality and liberty on a society which once gave the noble, the self-sacrificing, and the spiritual the respect they deserve, but which is now being rapidly destroyed by the essentially selfish forces of the market. Moreover, these views were defined as being drawn from the West, so Indian feminists stood accused of being Westernists, cultural imperialists, colonists, and—indirectly—supporters of capitalist ideology.[10]

The timing of this polemic was such as to lend legitimacy both to an ideology which claimed that the finest act a woman could do was to "die" with her husband, and to the specific event of Roop Kanwar's sati-daha. Yet the authors of the polemic did not address themselves to the question of what was happening in the village where it took place (Deorala), or asked under what conditions Roop Kanwar lived and died.

Roop Kanwar was eighteen years old and had only been married a short while when her husband died. She herself was a graduate, while her father-in-law was the headmaster of the school district. Her husband suffered from "mental disorders," and they had spent only about six months together. Her dowry included some thirty grams of gold. When, after her husband's death, it was announced that she would become *sati*, the impending event was announced in advance, because sati-daha is always a spectacle. Yet her family was not informed. Reports indicated that the local authorities knew of the planned sati-daha, but their only action was to dispatch a police jeep which had (supposedly) overturned on the way to the site.[11] Even more shocking was their general attitude, consisting as it were not of the usual tactic of slothful procrastination which our government uses when it wishes to avoid an issue, but of a kind of sullen paralysis in which over two weeks elapsed before any statement was made by government spokesmen, either at the state or at the center. No attempts were made to arrest anybody, despite mounting evidence of coercion— perhaps murder. When questioned by the press, some of her neighbors said that she had run away and tried to hide in a barn before the ceremony, but was dragged out, pumped full of drugs, dressed in her bridal finery, and put on the pyre, with logs and coconuts heaped on her. The pyre itself was lit by her brother-in-law, a minor.[12]

Immediately after the immolation, the site became a popular pilgrimage spot, and a number of stalls sprang up selling auspicious offerings, souvenirs (such as a trick photograph of Roop Kanwar sitting on the pyre with her husband's head on her lap and a blissful smile on her face, while the flames spurted about her), and audio-cassettes of devotional songs. Her father-in-law, prominent men from the village, and members of a newly formed organization, the Sati Dharm Raksha Samiti (organization for the defence of the religio-ethical ideal of sati), together formed a Trust to run the site and collect donations. What passes for modern technology in our country was used by the Trust to organize worship at the site: parking lots were arranged and traffic controllers appointed; a control tower was set up near the site and a fairly elaborate system of loudspeakers was strung around the area, through which instructions were transmitted to pilgrims and trust functionaries. Stalls selling food were set up by the Mahajans (members of the trading and moneylending community). Though no mention was made of how much money was collected by them, it was reported that within some three weeks the Trust itself had collected around Rs. 50 lakhs.[13] Sati-daha is big business. Despite demands from feminists and social reformers, the money was not impounded.

While aspects of this business side of sati-daha are neither new nor particularly modern, such as the site becoming a pilgrimage spot and stalls springing up, the scale and arrangement of the pilgrimage-event is obviously modern. Kumkum Sangari, in fact, has shown how the new and palatial sati temples replay the act of sati-daha through models of the woman, the dead man, and the pyre burning: she argues, further, that the worship of sati-daha or sati *dharm* is produced through commodification, for next to the new temples there are sati memorial stones which lie neglected.[14]

In other words, far from the feminists imposing crass market-dominated notions of equality on an anti-materialist society which celebrated self-sacrifice, the event revealed the gruesome materialism of a society which permits the production of "sacrifice" for profit. Historical research done by Sudesh Vaid, moreover, shows that sati-daha in post-independence India is not so much the continuation of a tradition, as the creation of a "tradition." Of the forty-odd recorded *satis* since independence, some three quarters have been in one district alone, known as Shekhavati. So, far from being an essential part of Hindu practice, sati-daha had practically ceased to exist in the country, apart from this one small part of it.

Even more interesting, sati-daha was not a traditional practice in Shekhavati before independence. Originally a small princely state, the area retained a semi-autonomous status under the British. When their prince ceded this status after independence, Shekhavati became just one province in the state of Rajasthan. Together with the introduction of land reforms in the 1950s (including a ceiling on land holdings), this led to a loss of some of the power held by Rajputs and Mahajans. First large and then small land holders protested against the reforms, and an agitation developed, in the course of which sati-daha began to be projected as exemplifying the true Rajput identity. The first post-independence sati-daha was in this area, in 1954, and at the same time, an old sati memorial in Jhunjunu was rebuilt. Annual sati *melas* (festivals) now began to be held at Jhunjunu.[15]

The general theory about why there have been so many sati-dahas in Shekhavati is that it began to be used by the inhabitants as a means of asserting their identity as a caste community, and through this they began to be seen as a political bloc to be courted. At one level, therefore, sati-daha became a way of regaining lost political and economic space.

One of the most dismaying discoveries for feminists was of the complex relations through which issues concerning women could be used to stake claims to power. Hard on the heels of Roop Kanwar's death, the Sati Dharm Raksha Samiti was formed in Jaipur city, whose leaders were all men, and most of whom were urban professionals or business men from land-owning families. Their sphere of control, thus, extended over both rural and urban areas. Together with the Deorala Trust, this Samiti announced that a *chunari mahotsav* (veil festival) would be held ten days after her death. While a ritual cremation of the veil is traditional in sati-daha, never before had it been called a festival.

Though feminists in Jaipur had petitioned the High Court to ban the ceremony, and the High Court had instructed the State government to prevent it from taking place, the *mahotsav* was performed. From an act of mourning it was transformed into a show of strength, a victory celebration, with the male marchers, traditionally dressed in Rajput garb, waving their fists aloft in triumph and shouting slogans. The site itself was transformed into a political rallying ground: a highly-charged state of siege atmosphere was created by sword-wielding youth, who surrounded the *sati-sthal* (the spot on which she died), and instead of singing devotional songs, they shouted slogans which were clearly modelled on mainstream political slogans. Madhu Kishwar and Ruth Vanita showed how these slogans fell into three major groups: (a) Slogans based on leader glorification, such as *sati ho to kaisi ho? Roop Kanwar jaisi ho.* (What should a true sati be like? Like Roop Kanwar.) This is clearly based on *Desh ka neta kaisa ho? Rajiv Gandhi*—or X—*jaisa ho.* (What should the leader of the country be like? Like Rajiv Gandhi.); (b) Victory chants, such as *Ek, do, teen, char, sati mata ki jai jai kar* (One, two, three, four, hail the sati mother). This is clearly based on *Ek, do, teen, char, Indira Gandhi*—or X—*ki jai jai kar.* (c) Slogans drawn from Hindu communalist movements, such as *Desh Dharam ka nata hai, sati hamari mata hai* (Ethics and nation are inseparable, sati is our mother). This is clearly based on *Desh dharam ka nata hai, gai hamari mata hai,* i.e., in place of the cow (*gai*), we have sati.[16]

Immediately after the event, several state level politicians rushed down to pay their respects at the site, among who were the state Janata Party chief, Kayan Singh Kalvi, the state Yuva Janata chief, a Bharatiya Janata Party member of the Rajasthan Legislative Assembly and a Lok Dal member, the acting member of the Rajput Sabha, and an ex-member of the Legislative Assembly from the Congress I.[17] So almost all the major center to right wing political parties sent representatives to the site, not to enquire into what had happened, but to stake their own claim to "tradition," and via this to the Rajput vote.

The process through which the "Rajput vote" became central here is a revealing one. At the policy maker and intelligentsia level the major argument of the pro-*sata-dana* camp was that if the state represented the people, then the Rajputs were a people among whom sati-daha was an ideal and a tradition, and as such it should be recognized and legitimated. On the ground, however, it was argued that a refusal to recognize sati-daha was a deliberate attempt to marginalize Rajputs. The widespread appeal of this argument became clear to feminists who were active in the campaign, for a majority of the Rajputs whom we met focussed on this point rather than a defence of sati-daha itself. Almost without exception, they asked why such an issue was being made of sati-daha, and—almost without exception—they said that sati-daha was just a cover to attack Rajputs.

The similarity between this and some of the arguments around the Muslim Women's Bill is striking. The question of maintenance for destitute Muslim women was seen as masking an onslaught against the Muslim community per se. And, as in the Muslim Women's Bill agitation, these arguments were taken a step further in the campaign around sati-daha by priests and fundamentalists. Two of the most influential temple priests, heading the Hindu religious establishments at Benares and Puri, issued statements that sati-daha represented the finest aspects not only of Rajput culture, but of Hindu tradition. As the ulama had argued before them, they also said that the interpretation of personal laws was their business, not that of either the law or the government. At the same time, they also raised the cry of "Hinduism in danger."

Just as the cry of "Islam in danger" was taken up by Muslim fundamentalists, the cry of "Hinduism in danger" was taken up by a section of extreme-right Hindu chauvinists, spearheaded by the Shiv Sena, a neo-fascist organization which has been active since the early part of this century. The Shiv Sena preach a martial crusading Hinduism: while they posit the Muslims as a major enemy of the Hindus, they also oppose the syncretic traditions of Hinduism. They assert that India is for the Hindus, but exclude the lower castes— especially the Untouchables or Dalits—from the fold. The Shiv Sena was especially active in the campaign for legalizing sati-daha along the "Hinduism in danger" line, arguing that the Indian state was perfectly willing to accommodate demands of minority communities (the Muslim Women's Bill), but was unwilling to do the same for the majority community.

Yet the Rajputs are not a majority community. And neither the practice nor the ideology of sati can be claimed to have been followed by the majority of Hindus. In effect, then, the statements of both the priests and the communalists revealed an inversion of minority into majority, a tactic which is frequently used here, perhaps because the upper-castes are numerically minorities, who—in order to maintain a dominance—constantly constitute themselves as the voice of a majority.

Fundamentalism, as we find all over the world, not only rationalizes the sexual oppression of women, but mobilizes them in support of their own oppression. Both the Muslim Women's Bill and pro sati-daha agitationists mobilized considerable sections of women in their support, the former on communal-fundamentalist grounds, and the latter on caste-fundamentalist (and partly communal) grounds. That is to say, they mobilized women who would appear to be directly affected by their demands. This allowed them to claim that they represented the "true" desires of "their" women, and to accuse feminists of being both unrepresentative and dictatorial.

The entry of their tradition versus modernity argument in this context delivered a fairly telling weapon into the hands of the fundamentalists. The bogey of modernism was so successfully erected that the fact that sati-daha was being used to create a "tradition" was successfully obscured. Tradition was defined so ahistorically that it obscured the fact that the issue of sati-daha was being used to create caste and communal identities along "modernist" lines, with modern methods of campaigning and organizing, modern arguments, and modern ends in view, such as the re-formation of electoral bases, and fundamentalist representation within the state. Worst of all, by polarizing women along the rural-urban, traditional-modern axis, it disallowed a whole series of questions and insights. Take, for example, the question of representation. Looking more closely at the nature of support for the pro sati-daha campaign, it immediately became obvious that this was nebulous, because at no point did the women themselves speak about the issue. Though their presence was ostentatiously underlined by the male leaders of the campaign, this presence seemed to consist of no more than traditionally dressed and heavily veiled bodies.

Secondly, an examination of the women who were mobilized for the pro sati-daha demonstrations made it clear that they were not in fact the women most directly affected by the issue. The figure of the widow was conspicuously absent. This absence of the widow was no mere accident. If one tragic consequence of the polarization of tradition and modernity was to obscure the process of casteism and communalism, then another was to obscure the way in which the pro sati-daha campaign actually legitimized the misery in which many caste Hindu widows live. Traditionally, widows of the three upper castes are forced into seclusion on widowhood. Their heads are shaved, they must wear only white, if they are lucky enough to be allowed to live with their marital or natal families then their position is a kind of cross between that of a poor relation and an unpaid servant; if the families are unwilling to keep them, then they are dedicated to temples instead, where they become the unpaid servants of the temple. The elevation of sati-daha into a tradition of idealized man-woman relations, in this context, indirectly rationalized the conditions of such widows: for if the widowed woman is not capable of living up to the sati ideal by immolating herself, then what better fate for her than to be condemned to servitude?

Conclusions

For the feminists, the realization of how the polarization between tradition and modernity successfully sidelined all questions of compassion or affection for women was a bitter one. Though they had long known, and said, that communalism, and the associated problems of fundamentalism and upper caste identity politics, center on women as both their victims and their constituency, the strength and speed with which this has been manifested at different times has left feminists relatively defenceless. Today, the real question is of how such a polarization can be anticipated and challenged, or transcended—which means finding ways to disrupt the formation of communal and upper-caste identities. Given the centuries for which such identities have existed and been grappled with in India, to even think in such terms seems laughable, and indeed we laugh ourselves when stating such intentions. Yet they are not as foolish as they sound. For the tradition versus modernity argument has one more crime to its name: that it successfully obscured not only the nature of opposition to sati-daha, but also the rising anti-caste and potentially anti-communal movements in this country.

Opposition to sati-daha came from both the right-wing Hindu reformist tradition and from maverick left-wing Hindu reformers such as Swami Agnivesh of the Arya Samaj, who challenged the pro sati-daha temple priests to a debate which they chickened out of. It also came from large sections of Gandhians, who held a rally of over ten thousand women in Puri to call the head priest of the Puri temple to account. And it also came from the anti-caste movement in Maharashtra, which had grown into a major and powerful movement of Untouchables or Dalits, who have had to fight the Shiv Sena in Maharashtra.

Looked at in this context, the National Front government's decision to implement the Mandal Commission Report, however opportunist or cynical, introduced an interesting new twist in Indian politics. Not only did it offer some degree of institutionalized support to lower-caste movements, including the anti-caste movement, it also changed the course of the "representation" argument, taking it away from communalists and fundamentalists. Occurring at a time when the Hindu communalist Ram Janmabhoomi agitation was at its height, the Mandal decision was hailed by many as leading to the disruption of Hindu communal formations and upper-caste attempts to hegemonize a Hindu identity. Matters, however, are never as simple as this.

The experiences of the feminist movement during the 1980s have shown the evolution of identity politics in this country, moving from the first indication of upper-caste identity mobilization through an attack on women's rights, to a minority fundamentalist attack in the context of rising communalism, to a now fully fledged upper-caste attack. If we first saw upper-caste and minority fundamentalist mobilizations on the basis of communal identities, with the aim of gaining a share in state power, then Mandal can be seen as expressing the development of a lower-caste, primarily peasant, identity, also now claiming its share of state power. Currently its most vocal, or prominent, sections are those who are already dominant groups in the countryside. It has not yet sought to assert itself through attacks on women's rights, but it has not espoused feminism either. Women, in fact, are pretty well absent in its rhetoric, though the same cannot be said of the opposition to it, in which women have been active (both mothers/relatives of upper-caste children who stand to lose by the reservations, and girls who would be affected).

Following, and somewhat overlapping with, the communal-fundamentalist attacks upon women's rights which we have seen, the last few years have seen the rise and increasing prominence of spokeswomen for Hindu communalism, and an invigorated mobilization of women in communal and far right women's organizations. (We are yet to see a parallel development in Muslim communal or fundamentalist organizations.) By and large, it is towns and cities which provide the site for this mobilization. Meanwhile, as the all-India feminist conference at Calicut in February 1991 showed, the women's movement has been growing, expanding to villages all over the country. Over two-thirds of the conference participants were rural women. Can this mean that while urban feminist groups find their space increasingly curtailed by identity politics, a large rural women's movement is growing?

Notes

1. One of several methods of divorce permitted by Islam, the triple *talaq* is the easiest, requiring only that one party say "I divorce you" three times.

2. Most of the information in this section has been compiled from press clippings from various national dailies. References are only being given for quotations, and sources other than newspapers.

3. The same verses were also quoted in the Supreme Court judgement (Supreme Court 945), and cited by Arif Mohammad Khan. They are:

Ayat 241	English Version
Wa li'l motallaqatay	For divorced women
Mata un	Maintenance (should be provided)
Bil maroofay	On a reasonable (scale)
Haqqan	This is a duty
Alal muttaqeena	On the righteous.
Ayat 242	
Kazaleka yuba iyyanullaho	Thus doth god
Lakum ayatehee la Allakum	Make clear his signs
Taqeloon.	To you: in order that you may understand.

4. Supreme Court 945, para. 32.

5. *India Today* (Jan. 31, 1986), "The Muslims: A Community in Turmoil."

6. Memorandum of the Committee for the Protection of the Rights of Muslim Women, *Mainstream* XXIV (27) (March 8, 1986).

7. Extract from the opening statement of the petition.

8. Quoted in brochure for the film "In Secular India," made by *Mediastorm*.

9. Recounted to me by Sheba Chhachhi and Nandita Haksar.

10. See, for example, "Bunwari" in *Jan Satta* (September 29, 1987), Ashis Nandy in the *Indian Express* (October 5, 1987), and Patrick D. Harrigan in the *Statesman* (November 5, 1987).

11. *The Times of India* (September 17, 1987).

12. The *Statesman* (September 18-20, 1987).

13. *The Times of India* (September 17, 1987).

14. Kumkum Sangari, "Perpetuating the Myth," *Seminar* 342 (Feb. 1988).

15. Sudesh Vaid, "The Politics of Widow Immolation," *Seminar* 342 (Feb. 1988).

16. Madu Kishwar and Ruth Vanita, "The Burning of Roop Kanwar," *Manushi* 42-3 (1987).

17. *Times of India* (September 17, 1987).

14

Women and Fundamentalism: The Case of Turkey

Binnaz Toprak

Introduction

This chapter will argue that Islamic fundamentalism in Turkey is primarily concerned with the status of women and defines the parameters of Islamic community in terms of a sexual differentiation of social and familial roles. The movement sees the defining characteristic of a Muslim society in its conception of women that in turn shapes the social organization without which Islam would have become a purely individualistic faith since it does not recognize a priesthood.[1] Fundamentalist politics reflect a struggle to redefine women's status in Turkish society.

Identity politics in the 1990s—whether in the form of religious, ethnic, linguistic, cultural, regional or local movements—shows signs of occupying a central position in the political agendas of both Western and non-Western societies alike. The nineteenth century ideology of the nation-state, which determined political borders and provided the conceptual basis of national identities, seems to be on the wane. The global economy has merged industrial, commercial and financial centers of individual nation-states and has produced a uniform market for consumption; the revolution in communications and technology is increasingly minimizing the centrality of indigenous cultural forms; English has become a true Esperanto; and political arrangements, such as the European community, seem to be in the direction of, if not global, at least regional cooperation and unity.

This move away from the parochial conception of the nation-state as a viable unit in itself has led to two responses. The first is a universalist response. It sees the future of human civilization in a collective effort to secure global peace and disarmament; in the universal acceptance of democratic principles and human rights; in a mutual protection of the environment; and in the obliteration of the gap between developed and underdeveloped nations. Possibly, it also sees the nation-state itself as an oppressive political unit which stands in the way of a global cooperation. There are already signs to support this view. For example, in a recent survey of attitudes towards the nation-state among West Europeans, the percentage of respondents who said that they would be willing to fight for their country in case of war was only 43 percent, a figure which would have been appallingly low for the generations that were of fighting age during the First and Second World Wars.[2]

The second is a particularistic response. It is a response to the technocratic structure of post-industrial society. It sees the emergence of a new universalization of values and patterns of behavior as a threat to both individual and cultural identity, hence attempts to formulate a new concept of community. This response takes on different forms such as regional separatist movements, religious fundamentalism or ethnic communalism. In each case, what is central to the movement's vision is the notion of a separate identity.

These two different responses to the universalization of economies and cultures form the basis of the major division and conflict in contemporary Turkey. The cultural aspect of this conflict has remained a permanent feature of political discourse in most non-Western societies as they have come under the influence and/or domination of the West in the last two centuries. The Islamic movement and its secular opponents in Turkey have inherited a debate which began in mid-nineteenth century with the Westernizing reforms in the Ottoman Empire. The impetus behind this debate has basically remained the same: to cope with Western industrial and technological advance. Whereas the Islamists of earlier generations thought that Western technology could be adopted without a wholesale acceptance of Western civilization,[3] contemporary thinkers within the Islamic movement have caught the very essence of modern technology as a synthesizer of cultural forms.[4] Hence, the cultural dimension of the Islamist alternative encompasses the rejection of identities shaped by the modern techno-structures.

There is also a structural dimension. Identity politics is not only a response to what the movement considers to be alien intrusions into its own culture, it is also a response to structural changes in the economy. Especially important in this context is the background characteristics of individuals within the Islamic movement, most of whom occupy marginal positions in a rapidly expanding economy. Therefore, the support for identity politics is both a means of registering economic discontent and a possible avenue for upward social mobility through the use of Islamic networks.[5]

The general characteristics of the Islamic movement in Turkey which have been transmitted into identity politics in recent years are especially visible in relation to the gender question. The Islamic fundamentalist movement is a reaction to industrial growth but at the same time provides the organizational mechanism to carve out a space for its members within the status hierarchy of Turkish society. What differentiates its goals from secular political alternatives, such as neo-fascist or socialist movements, is its demand to shape social organization and economic structuration on Islamic principles. Central to its vision is its view of the family and of women which is intimately connected with Islamic definitions of morality and community life. It is this conservative bias on the gender question which is the distinguishing mark of the fundamentalist movement and the major bases of the opposition to it. If this gender differentiation, which in turn fundamentally determines how social life is to be organized, was absent from the contents of Islam and of the movement, little would have remained to separate it from other contestants for power.

Hence, the gender question occupies a central position in the conflict between the secular and the Islamic groups in Turkey. Although this conflict originated in the nineteenth century over the question of Westernization, it would be anachronistic to analyze its contemporary phase in terms of Islam and the West. For reasons discussed above, the present dichotomy can no longer be posed in terms of Western versus indigenous cultures. This debate, which Islamic fundamentalism wants to revive, has been historically superseded with the structure of modern industry and technology which produces its own cultural forms. Therefore, the current conflict is not over the ultimate preference for, or rejection of, a "Western way of life." It is a controversy about the meaning and consequences of integration with the modern techno-structures. Such integration, by necessity, opens up the public space for women. Hence, a strict division of labor between the sexes which fundamentalism advocates, with women largely confined to the seclusion of their homes, is a political project which is not compatible with the demands of the new industrial order. It is precisely for this reason that the Islamist intellectuals are calling for the wholesale rejection of modern industry and technology.[6]

However, the fundamentalist movement itself is a product of this new technocratic environment as much as a reaction to it. The means by which it disseminates its ideology (for example, the use of video tapes, cassettes, and widely distributed publications), its organizational networks (such as Islamic banks and commercial firms), the importance it places on education (including the education of women), and its attempts to place its members within the state bureaucracies, attest to its articulation with modern structures. The implications of this for women within the movement is an issue which deserves attention, as will be discussed below.

Islam and Women's Status: The Structural Factors

An analysis of how Islam theologically looks at women's role in society is beyond the concerns of this chapter. As Deniz Kandiyoti argues, the position of women under Islam does not tell us much unless we understand the specific historical contexts of state formation which determined women's status in various Muslim societies.[7] The over-simplified view that Muslim states in history, because of their dependence on religious law (the *Sharia*), were theocracies does not hold true. In the case of the Ottoman Empire, for example, historians have argued that the often-used concept of *din-u-devlet* (merging of religion and the state) fails to take into account the much more complex nature of Ottoman administration which clearly demarcated the lines of authority between the sultan and the *ulama* (men of religion).[8] Moreover, there have been major differences in the relationship of the state and the religious hierarchy in Sunni versus Shia traditions. As Clifford Geertz has so cogently demonstrated in discussing Islam in Indonesia, how Islam is observed also changes in different cultural settings.[9]

Depending on the paradigmatic approach adopted, it could also be argued, for example, that patriarchy as the dominant form of gender relations in the Middle East is not necessarily attributable to the impact of Islam, and that male domination in most of the Middle East and North Africa is a characteristic shared by cultures in the Mediterranean basin. Indeed, anthropological literature has demonstrated that concepts of shame and honor in family and gender relations show similar patterns in Greece, southern Italy, Spain, and Portugal.[10] Hence, a Braudelian perspective of "la Méditerranée" would equally provide a framework for analysis as the Islamic paradigm.

The similarity of agendas of feminist movements in widely different cultural settings and socio-economic structures indicates the complexity of the factors that contribute to male dominance and sexual discrimination. Hence, one-factor analysis of the issue would fall far short of capturing its multi-dimensional nature. Nonetheless, Islam's unquestionable role in assigning a superior position to men is a major factor that has to be accounted for in any analysis.

The subjugation of women to the authority of men in Islamic law and the Islamic precepts about the enclosure of women, such as veiling, have undoubtedly resulted in their seclusion from public life in traditional Muslim societies. But, here again, structural factors have played a significant role in determining women's status. For example, although Ottoman society had characteristically excluded women from public life and imposed strict regulations on their public appearance (even the styles and colors of women's veils were at times dictated by imperial decrees), peasant women were never subject to such limitations because they comprised at least half of the labor force in agriculture.[11] Similarly, during the Balkan Wars and World War I, women began to be employed in hospitals, laboratories, post offices, and other service sectors due to the shortage of manpower, although theoretically Ottoman society did not allow the employment of Muslim women in workplaces open to the public.[12]

Republican Reforms on Women

Family law and the status of women was one area in the long list of legal reforms in the Ottoman Empire which remained under the jurisdiction of the Sharia courts until the republican period.[13] The resistance of the ulama to the secularization of laws on personal status demonstrates the crucial position of women and the family for the Muslim political project. As long as the Muslim family, and hence the Muslim community, remained intact, Muslim society could absorb the changes in economic and political arrangements. It is for this reason that the major reaction to Islamic fundamentalism in contemporary Turkey comes from women's organizations which correctly situate the enclosure of women at the center of the movement's political platform.

The radical break with Islam, following the collapse of the Ottoman Empire at the end of World War I and the subsequent establishment of the Republic of Turkey in 1923, has had no parallel in the Muslim world. The initial reforms undertaken by the Republic included the total secularization of the legal and the educational systems, the disestablishment of the ulama's official role in the affairs of the state, and the weakening of the symbolic structures of the Islamic community.[14] This militant secularism also involved a number of legal measures designed to ensure state control of religion as its organization was tied to the state bureaucracy and as Sufi religious brotherhoods (*tarikat*) were outlawed.[15]

In terms of the status of women, these reforms were truly revolutionary for a Muslim country. They included the introduction of co-education, with compulsory primary-school training and equality of educational opportunities for both sexes; the acceptance of a new Civil Code which outlawed polygamy and granted equal rights to men and women in marriage, divorce, child custody, inheritance, and property ownership; the promulgation of a new dress code which legally allowed women to unveil and outlawed the veil for civil servants; the granting of political rights, and finally, the opening of career and employment opportunities for women.[16]

Indeed, the Republic's success in emancipating women, although limited in terms of the percentage of women who benefited from it, was exemplary not only vis-à-vis Muslim countries but even in comparison to the condition of women in the West until recently. For example, in a comparative study based on data collected in the 1960s, the number of women in male-dominant professions, such as engineering, law, medicine and architecture, was strikingly high in Turkey. Whereas the composite index developed by the researcher, indicating the percentage of women in these professions was, for example, 2.3 for the U.S., 2.6 for Canada, 4.3 for Britain, 6.3 for France and 13.3 for Sweden, it was 25.0 for Turkey.[17] It was only after the impact of the feminist movement that the employment of women in high-level jobs increased in the West. The high percentage of women in law and medicine in Turkey, for example, with one in every five practicing lawyers and one in every six practicing doctors as women, still contrasts with many Western societies where these prestigious occupations are largely male dominant.[18]

The Fundamentalist Movement and Women

The history of the feminist movement in Turkey—however embryonic both in terms of aims and organization—goes back to the Second Constitutional Period (1908-1918) in the Ottoman Empire.[19] Although the emancipation of women was achieved only after the establishment of the Republic, the struggle nevertheless has seventy-five years behind it. It has especially gained momentum in the 1980s with feminist groups whose concerns reflect the perspectives of feminist organizations in the West. However, since the 1970s the movement has been beset with problems of focus. As in many underdeveloped countries, there are wide differences between urban versus rural, educated versus uneducated, professional and white-collar versus working class, city versus small-town women. Although the Turkish economy is rapidly integrating with world markets, and although both the development in communication networks and the increase in travel and tourism has opened up Turkish society to international influences, the fact remains that underdeveloped economies cannot produce uniform life patterns. Hence, the feminist movement in Turkey has had to struggle with the question of which strata of women it should focus on.

In the 1970s, the strongest groups within the movement were socialist-oriented, attempting to reach women of working-class and peasant backgrounds in the squatter cites of big industrial cities. After the socialist movement was suppressed following a military coup in 1980, the feminist political platform adopted more individualistic themes of sexual freedom, women as sex objects, sexual harassment, physical violence against women, prostitution, gender relations within the bourgeois family, and the like. Nevertheless, the consciousness that the nature of oppression changes for different categories of women has remained, a problem which the feminist project has to eventually tackle. To this long list of categorizations, yet one more category was added after 1980, namely, women within the Islamist movement.

As mentioned above, the major concern of the Islamists in contemporary Turkey revolves around the question of community morality which is intimately linked with the status of women. The Islamists are especially critical of Western influences on gender relations, the family, and social customs. In their view, republican education and legal reforms have destroyed the balance that Islamic society had achieved in the division of labor between the sexes. In contrast to the important role that Islam assigns to women within the family, republican secularism has led women to neglect their primary duties as mothers and wives and has encouraged them to seek public employment. The result has been the disastrous confusion of roles in the modern family.[20]

Hence the family, which is the foundation of any moral community, faces the threat of disintegration. Once the women no longer perform the essential duties of taking care of the children and the household, the whole structure of the family, with defined roles for its members, is thrust into a hopeless disarray. In the Islamist analysis, therefore, the changes in women's position in society from the private realm of the family to the public sphere has had important consequences for social morality. Women who choose their own destinies and are free from the control of the traditional Muslim community lose their direction in life. The society looks at them as sex objects, a perception which becomes internalized by women themselves as they come to define their existence in terms of a narcissistic quest to be fashionable, look young and sexy. This lack of perspective about their role and responsibility in life affects the whole structure of social morality as promiscuity in sexual relations, adultery, and even prostitution become acceptable norms of interpersonal behavior.[21]

Once women define their goals in terms of an individualistic ethic of self-satisfaction, little remains to hold the family structure. In the Islamist view, the tragic effect of women's liberation on the family and the community can be observed in patterns of modern living: women's bodies have become public show-cases of their sexuality; the consumption society has included pornography among the necessary lists of consumer goods; abortions have increased as women have come to shy away from the duty that God has given them to reproduce the human race; the traditional values of respect for the authority of elders, obedience of the wife and the children to the men in the family, mutual help and cooperation between the members of the Muslim society, as well as the ideas that the family and the neighborhood are sanctuaries of community morality have disappeared. In return, modern life has produced individuals who have no inner peace, are restlessly seeking satisfaction in pursuits which are external to their self, and are condemned to a lonely life designed by machines and bureaucracies.[22]

The alternative vision for the Muslim women places them in the context of Islamic precepts as determinant of their life patterns. Within this context, women, as true believers, should respect the authority of men who are endowed with the duty to provide for the necessities of the household. As long as the demands of their husbands are within the bounds that Islam legitimates, women should comply with their directives. Both the wish to divorce her husband or to punish him through refusal of sexual intercourse condemns a woman to hell. A true Muslim woman takes care of the children and the men in the household and guards the honor of her husband as the head of the family. To ensure this, she should neither go out of the house, nor accept visitors or speak to strangers without the permission of her husband. She should moreover protect herself from other men by covering her body and hair as Islam demands. Islam, in short, has given a major responsibility to women in terms of her contribution to the social order. This responsibility is primarily geared to her role within the family. A true Muslim woman accepts this responsibility which is in accordance with the design of the universe that God has created. It is because God intended different functions for men and women that he has created physical differences between them.[23]

Although the Islamic movement in Turkey defends these avowedly conservative views on the primary role of women as mothers and housewives, it has nevertheless come to accept a more active public role for Muslim women. For long years, the Islamic groups could not decide on the issue of mobilizing women for their political cause. The neo-Islamic National Salvation Party of the 1970s, for example, had a strong youth organization but was hesitant to establish affiliated women's associations. With the impact of the Islamic revolution in Iran and the role that militant Muslim women played in it, the Islamic groups in Turkey also began to profess active participation of women within the movement.

The most visible example of this new role assigned to Muslim women was their confrontation with state authorities over the question of covering their heads while attending the university. Islamic religion demands that women do not appear in public unless their hair and bodies are totally covered. This precept in Islam is the reason behind the veiling of women in Islamic countries. Although republican laws in Turkey never outlawed the veil, it was discouraged, and a separate dress code for civil service women banned it, which was *de facto* accepted by professionals as well. Until the 1980s, there were no veiled women among university students. However, they began to appear in relatively large numbers on university campuses during the 1980s, when radical fundamentalism emerged within the Islamic movement, which prompted the Council of Higher Education to ban what it called the "turban," which is a scarf securely tied around the head. The so-called "Turban Movement" started as a protest against the legal prohibition of the turban for women students but gradually became an issue of militant Muslim politics. The students wearing the turban claimed to do so because their faith demanded it and argued that their freedom of conscience was under a constitutional guarantee. But, what originally started as sporadic and unorganized demands for freedom of entry into universities soon turned into organized sit-ins and demonstrations.[24] Interestingly, therefore, it was the "Turban Movement" and the role of the women in it that became instrumental in radicalizing the Islamic cause. Here, again, is an example of the importance that the Islamic political project attributes to the segregation of the sexes. No other than the major symbol of this segregation, the covering of women's bodies and heads in public, became the cause of the confrontation with secular laws.

The education of Muslim women is a second example of the new understanding concerning women's role within the movement. Primarily, the Islamists view the education of women as important in terms of their crucial role in raising and socializing children. It is argued that educated women are better equipped to raise healthy children and to ensure a good education for them. Indeed, a major Islamic magazine for women regularly publishes articles on modern methods of child-care, suggestions for healthy living, advice on medical problems and the like, which are obviously addressed to women with some degree of education.[25] But more importantly, the Islamic movement has come to realize that it needs its own educated women in certain professions, such as gynecology.

As the above discussion demonstrates, the Islamic paradigm assigns a constricted role to women in social life. From a feminist perspective, the perception of women's status in the Islamic political project includes a retrogressive definition of sex roles. From the perspective of liberal democracy and universal human rights, it is a discriminatory project which refuses equal treatment before the law on the basis of gender differences. From the perspective of the modern industrial society, it is an ahistorical project which either fails to see the impact of the new techno-structures and the universilization of cultures on the status of women, or carries the anachronistic hope of returning to simpler structural arrangements that existed at a distant period in Islamic history.[26]

However, the evident gap between what Islam demands of women and what the new technocratic environment and the liberal society reveals to them is likely to have contradictory implications for women within the Islamic movement. For example, in a study of a major Islamic journal for women, Yesim Arat has argued that for the women who comprise the overwhelming majority of editors and correspondents contributing to its pages, the experience provides the opportunity to choose alternative life-styles. Instead of being confined to the limitations of the conservative backgrounds from which they come, work with the journal opens up new avenues for a search—however unexpectedly—of a more authentic, less community-defined, and perhaps eventually liberationist, life patterns.[27] Similarly, in a study of women wearing the turban based on extensive interviews, Nilufer Göle has argued that the sociological significance of the movement rests not on an understanding of the ideological orientation and religious belief of these women but on an analysis of their social practice. She points out that on the one hand, women with the turban refer to the basic foundation of Muslim society through the symbol of the veil, a symbol which is a reminder of the role assigned to women in the private sphere and the segregation of the sexes. On the other hand, however, through their claim to university education, they are already leaving this private sphere and developing individual strategies. Göle notes the paradox of ambiguous categories of traditional and modern identities.[28] Indeed, this ambiguity is becoming evident to some within the movement. For example, a leading weekly journal published a cover story under the title "Feminists with Turbans" in which a number of interviews with women within the fundamentalist movement showed that they were equally rebellious of the role patriarchal society assigns to them as their secular feminist counterparts. According to the journal, the discussion of patriarchy, feminism, and women's status in Islam was one of the most heatedly debated issues among Islamic groups.[29]

Conclusions

The fundamentalist movement in Turkey, as discussed in the first section of this chapter, is in essence a response of the marginalized sectors of society to rapid industrial growth and the concomitant structural and cultural transformation it brings. This marginality, in the Turkish context, is not always economic. It also includes marginality in social status as high status groups of republican society have consistently excluded Islamic traditionalists from their ranks. Since the mid-1970s, but especially in the 1980s, these groups have been bidding for social status, intellectual respectability, and political power. They have largely succeeded in entrenching themselves within the state and party bureaucracies, in commercial and industrial firms, and in intellectual circles. In short, they have become a counter-elite.

As such, the women within the ranks of the fundamentalist movement are part of this larger search of the marginals for respectability of status, and indeed, for a redefinition of status hierarchy. The turban and the long coat as "uniforms" serve the function of the bluejeans which women of these traditional backgrounds are most likely not allowed to wear. Both forms of dress are oblivious to status and class distinctions. This search ultimately includes the possibilities for upward social mobility, a prospect which some within the movement have materialized. Hence, identity politics is at the same time network politics.[30] It builds a web of within-group relations that become instrumental in terms of acquiring political power, economic wealth, intellectual prominence, or social respectability. To what extent women within the fundamentalist movement will be content with the newly-achieved status of the men in their family, or use these channels of upward mobility for determining their own life chances, ultimately depends on the Turkish social and economic transformation. Identity politics is a phase in this transformation when regional, ethnic, or religious differences overlap with lower levels of status hierarchy.

Notes

1. Unlike most other major religions, Islam has a political project of establishing a theocratic state which, through religious law, organizes the social order. For a discussion of this point, see Binnaz Toprak, *Islam and Political Development in Turkey* (Leiden: E.J. Brill, 1981), esp. Chapter II.

2. See Jean Stoetzel, "Defeatism in Western Europe: Reluctance to Fight for Country," pp. 168-180 in Mattei Dogan (ed.), *Comparing Pluralist Democracies: Strains on Legitimacy* (London: Westview Press, 1988).

3. For the views of these early Islamists, see Tarik Zafer Tunaya, *Islamcilik Cereyani* (Istanbul: Baha Matbaasi, 1962).

4. On contemporary Islamist intellectuals, see Binnaz Toprak, "Islamist Intellecuals of the 1980s in Turkey," *Current Turkish Thought* 62 (1987):1-19.

5. For an analysis of these structural factors which influence identity politics in Turkey, see Faruk Birtek and Binnaz Toprak, "Limits of Neo-Liberal Authoritarianism: Islam and the Secular State" (Unpublished).

6. See, for example, Ismet Özel, *Üc Mesele: Teknik, Medeniyet, Yabancilasma* (Istanbul: Dergah Yayinlari, 1984), and Ersin Gürdogan, *Teknolojinin Ötesi: Kaybolan Ölcü ve Bozulan Denge* (Istanbul: Nehir Yayinevi, 1985).

7. Deniz Kandiyoti, "Women and Islam: Is There A Missing Term?," paper presented at the workshop on "Women, Islam and the State" (London, May 15-16, 1987).

8. See, for example, H. A. R. Gibb and Harold Bowen, *Islamic Society and the West* (London: Oxford University Press, Vol. I, Part II, 1957), pp. 79-80. For a discussion of religious vs. secular laws in the Ottoman Empire, see Ömer Lutfi Barkan, "Türkiye' de Din de Devlet Iliskilerinin Tarihsel Gelisimi," pp. 49-76 in Türk Tarih Kurumu, *Cumhuriyetin 50, Yildönümü Semineri* (Ankara: Türk Tarih Kurumuru Basimevi, 1975).

9. Clifford Geertz, *Islam Observed* (New Haven: Yale University Press, 1968).

10. See, for example, the various articles in the collected volume by J. G. Peristiany (ed.), *Honour and Shame: The Values of Mediterranean Society* (London: Weidenfeld and Nicolson, 1965).

11. See Muhaddere Tascioglu, *Türk Osmanli Cemiyetinde Kadinin Sosyal Durumu ve Kadin Kiyafetleri* (Ankara: Akin Matbaasi, 1958).

12. See Tezer Taskiran, *Cumhuriyetin 50. Yilinda Türk Kadin Haklari* (Ankara: Basbakanlik Basimevi, 1973), pp. 27-63. Also see Zafer Toprak, *Türkiye'de "Milli Iktisat": 1908-1918* (Ankara: Yurt Yayinlari, 1982), pp. 314-318.

13. See H. A. R. Gibb, "The Heritage of Islam in the Modern World: Part II," *International Journal of Middle East Studies* 1 (3) (1970):221-237, especially pp. 233-34.

14. For a discussion of these changes, see Binnaz Toprak, *Islam and Political Development in Turkey*, Chapter III.

15. On the formal organization of religion in the Republic of Turkey, see Binnaz Toprak, "Die Institutionalisierung des Laizismus in der Türkischen Republic," pp. 95-108 in Jochen Blaschke and Martin van Bruinessen (eds.), *Jarbuch zur Geschichte und Gesellschaft des Vorderen und Mittleren Orients; Thema: Islam und Politik in der Türkei* (Berlin: Express Edition, 1985).

16. For a discussion of these reforms on women, see Binnaz Toprak, "Religion and Turkish Women," in Nermin Abadan-Unat (ed.), *Women in Turkish Society* (Leiden: E. J. Brill, 1981b), p. 288.

17. R. C. Blitz, "An International Comparison of Women's Participation in the Professions," *The Journal of Developing Areas* 9 (1975):499-510.

18. See Ayse Öncü, "Turkish Women in the Professions: Why So Many?," pp. 181-193 in Nermin Abadan-Unat (ed.), *Women in Turkish Society.*

19. See, for example, Zafer Toprak, "Osmanli Kadinlari Calistirma Cemiyeti, Kadin Askerler, ve Milli Aile," *Tarih ve Toplum* 51 (1988):34-38.

20. See, for example, the interview with a famous actor Ulvi Alacakaptan, who joined the ranks of the Islamists in *Kadin ve Aile* 14 (May 1986):20-22.

21. See the various issues of *Kadin ve Aile*, the leading Islamist publication for women, on the social problems stemming from the status of women and the family in modern Turkish society. See especially the following issues: No. 2, June 1985; No. 8, November 1985; No. 10, January 1986; No. 11, February 1986; No. 12, March 1986; No. 13, April 1986; No. 16, July 1986; No. 51, 15 June-15 July, 1989.

22. *Ibid.*

23. See, for example, Hüseyin Erdogan, *Islam' da Kadin, Tesettür, Izdivac* (Istanbul: Cile Yayinevi, 1979); Bekir Topaloglu, *Islamda Kadin* (Istanbul: Yagmur Yayinevi, 1980); Mehmet Hulusi Isler, *Islamda Izdivac ve Aile* (Istanbul: Türdav Basim, 1979); and Haci Sakir Efendi, *Mursid-i Muteehhilin: Kadinlara Dini Bilgiler* (Istanbul: Saglam Kitabevi, 1981).

24. On the "turban" controversy, see the weekly *Nokta*, January 18, 1987; the daily *Cumhurivet* and *Hürrivet*, March 1989; *Kadin ve Aile*, No. 9, December, 1985, No. 18, September 1986, No. 23, February 1987, No. 27, June 1987.

25. See the issues of *Kadin ve Aile.*

26. On this latter point, see the views of contemporary Islamist intellectuals in Toprak , "Islamist Intellectuals of the 1980s in Turkey."

27. Yesim Arat, "Feminizm ve Islam: *Kadin ve Aile* Dergisinin Düsündürdükleri," in Sirin Tekeli (ed.), *Kadin Bakis Acisindan 1980' ler Türkiye' sinde Kadinlar* (Istanbul: Iletisim Yayinlari, 1990).

28. Nilüfer Göle, "Ingénieurs musulmans et étudiantes voilées en Turquie," in Gilles Kepel and Yann Richard (eds.), *Intellectuels et militants dans les pays musulmans* (Paris: Le Seuil, forthcoming).

29. See the cover story in the weekly *Nokta*, "Feminists with Turbans," December 20, 1987. For a general discussion of the women within the Islamic movement, see Nermin Abadan-Unat, "Islam ve Kadin," *Cumhuriyet* 23 (September 1990).

30. On this point, see Birtek and Toprak, "Limits of Neo-Liberal Authoritarianism."

15

Halakha, Zionism, and Gender: The Case of Gush Emunim

Madeleine Tress

When the women come with their pots and their pans, their kids and their suitcases, then the government knows it's a settlement.

—Woman settler from Ofra[1]

Introduction

Despite more than 100 years of Zionist-related settlement and 45 years of statehood, the national question remains primary in Israel, superseding questions of class and gender. Unlike many Western or Third World societies Israel lacks a developed feminist movement—the contrast with India, for example, is quite sharp. The process of self-examination and study by Israeli women is less advanced than it is in other parts of the Middle East (for example, Egypt's Nawal El Sadaawi or Morocco's Fatima Mernissi). For many Israeli men and women, gender remains a non-issue. And yet gender is very much part of the Israeli social reality. Gender constructs and gender roles, I argue, have been largely shaped by both the *Halakha* (Jewish canon law) and Zionism. This will be illustrated by examining a specific case of the gender dynamics of religious law and national identity.

Years of Israeli military occupation of the West Bank and Gaza have polarized the Israeli public on whether Israel should trade land for peace. A public opinion survey published on 11 March 1991 in *Yediot Aharanot*, Israel's largest daily newspaper, indicated that 49 percent favor the idea and 49 percent oppose it.[2] The Palestinian rebellion or *Intifada*, the Persian Gulf War, and efforts on the part of the United

States to impose a peace settlement, have contributed to this polarization, and many questions raised in Israeli civil society about the occupation are still not fully answered. A major one has been how a seemingly marginal movement, Gush Emunim, has been able to effectively assert that part of its platform that refuses to cede any territory for peace. This chapter will focus on the specific role of women in the organization and how their identity as Jewish women empowered the movement and enabled it to operate with a certain amount of legitimacy in the arenas of both civil society and the state. I shall examine the role of women in Jewish law (Halakha) and tradition (*Aggadah*) as the guide for this exploration. This normative role will be juxtaposed against the actual role of Jewish women, both in the Diaspora and the Zionist enterprise. By focusing on the role of classical Judaism in Zionism we can see how the "new Jewish woman" operated in a sphere in which religion was hegemonic. Hence, the women active in Gush Emunim have to some extent been created by and have served the Israeli state.

To ground these assertions, I turn to the origins and evolution of Gush Emunim, the religiously-based settlers' movement that was born in the Gush Etzion region of the West Bank in 1974.[3] In Israel there were attempts at West Bank settlement before the official establishment of Gush Emunim, and all of these earlier pioneers would eventually play leading roles in the organization. Gush Emunim represents a sustained effort to form a synthesis among the three wings of the Zionist movement. It has combined the pioneering ideology (*Halutziot*) of the Labor movement, the maximalist territorial demands of the Revisionists, and the religious worldview of the Mizrachi movement. It is for this reason alone that the movement has been so successful and has been able to polarize Israel into two equal camps.

The discussion of Gush Emunim will focus on how women acting on behalf of an ascriptive collectivity ("the Jewish people") helped consolidate the military occupation of the West Bank and Gaza. Description of actions will be confined to the West Bank, particularly the Hebron area, for it is there that the first confrontation between what would become Gush Emunim and the Israeli state occurred. On April 4, 1968, the eve of the Jewish festival of Passover, which commemorates the exodus of the ancient Hebrew slaves from Egypt, a group of sixty Israelis, posing as Swiss tourists, arrived at the Park Hotel in Hebron, in the Israeli-occupied West Bank. The women in the group immediately set about cleaning the hotel's kitchen so it could be utilized for preparation of food according to Jewish dietary laws (*Kashrut*). At the end of the seven-day festival,[4] the group announced that its true intention was to reclaim the Jewish quarter of Hebron.[5] Eleven years later, in 1979, women veterans of the Park Hotel would occupy Beit Hadassah, also in Hebron, again to reaffirm Jewish right to live in the city.

The actions of these self-defined religious women illustrate how arbitrary Jewish law, henceforth referred to by its Hebrew name, Halakha, is in distinguishing between the private and public spheres, particularly in gender-related matters. Moreover, these women, who would later form the core of Gush Emunim, are not very different from the secular women pioneers who helped build the Israeli state. Finally, Gush Emunim women, as militant Zionists, have acted on behalf of that fraction of the state that has supported a policy of Greater Israel (that is, no retreat to the green line or pre-1967 borders and no compromise with the Palestinians).

Women in Jewish Law and Tradition

Of the 613 commandments or *mitzvot* in Judaism, only two apply to all women: the injunction to ensure that Kashrut, the dietary laws, are strictly adhered to in the household, and the keeping of the Sabbath. A third group of laws pertaining to menstruation (*niddah*) applies only to married women. None of these mitzvot have communal requirements at specific times. Furthermore, Halakha generally excludes women from religious activities, including study. They are not required to pray, except for their own satisfaction.

This exemption from public sphere religious activities extends into all of the public sphere. Religion is the privilege and responsibility of men. A woman is to facilitate this process by confining her activities to the private realm of home and family. The injunction in Genesis 1:28 to "be fruitful and multiply" becomes, in practice, a pro-natalist policy. Hence, a woman will receive great esteem if she fulfils her supportive role of bearing and raising children as well as providing a harmonious home so that men could study. In contrast, man's function is in the public sphere of business and politics. This lends credence to Rosaldo's point that it was the gender relations of traditional societies that resulted in a "differentiation of domestic and public spheres of activity."[6] Indeed, it is because of woman's "natural" function that the rabbinic literature credits her with more compassion and concern for the unfortunate than men.[7]

Women in the Hebrew Bible are predominantly adjuncts of men, and are legally and substantively dependent on them as well. Yet there is no one image of Woman in the text. Women can influence and maneuver others (Miriam and her brothers Moses and Aaron; Bathsheba and David; Devorah as judge). They are victims of rape, incest, and sexual harassment (Dinah, Tamar, and Susannah). They engage in female solidarity (Ruth and Naomi) as well. There are, however, no examples of women with political, social, or economic power. Indeed, the text addresses the community through its male members, and the key verbal form in the apodictic sentence, that is the style used primarily for the statement of religious obligations, is the second person masculine singular or plural.[8]

The family was the basic unit of society in ancient Israel. Women were to build up their husbands' homes. But in a world where society was an aggregate of households, women could collectively build society. Yet, even when women were historical individuals, they were primarily wives and mothers.[9] After the second Temple of Jerusalem was destroyed in 66 A.D. and the Jews were dispersed from the Land of Israel, the expectations of women began to change. Jewish leaders began to emphasize male and female involvement in charitable behavior and good deeds (*tzedakah*). Women were required to be pragmatists.

As print capitalism developed, a distinctive literature for women emerged,[10] creating—to borrow a phrase from Benedict Anderson—an "imagined community,"[11] consisting of Jewish women united by language and common cause of caretakers. All of these "women's" books emphasized their gender-related charitable obligations. Schultz reports that the most famous of these was *Ze'enah Ure'enah*, a Yiddish language companion book first published in Lublin, Poland in 1590 and written by Rabbi Jacob ben Isaac Ashkenazi. It was a best-seller for 300 years and went through 210 editions including translations into Latin, Italian, French, Hungarian, German, English and Hebrew.[12] It is significant that in the *Ze'enah Ure'enah*, communal interests are foremost when the rules of social behavior are emphasized. For instance, not only is the reader told that giving charity extends one's life expectancy, but in the earliest extant edition of 1622, the *Eshet Chayil* or worthy woman "is prepared to work day and night or to trade day and night to maintain her home, and to give charity to the poor from what she has produced or earned" [*was sie desarbet oder gewint*].[13]

Indeed, the early economic roles of Jewish women transcended their "natural" function as caretakers, such as trading. Finkelstein reports that the sixteenth-century Jewish legal movement toward women's rights "had its origins and compelling force largely in the fact that women began to occupy a prominent position in the economic world."[14] In the *shtetls* of Eastern Europe, it was the woman who dealt with government officials and peasants while her pious male relatives studied. While she had more movement than non-Jewish women, she was still limited as a European Jew in the period preceding the French Revolution. During the nineteenth century, there was a regression in Jewish gender roles. For example, the post-1850 *Eshet Chayil* only "works day and night to maintain her home and gives charity to the poor ... ."[15] Yet women were entering the labor force during that period in both the "feminine occupations" such as teaching or nursing, as well as office work and consumer goods production. Woman's work in the private sphere had become socialized so that she became engaged in many of the same things she had done in the household, albeit in a new locale and under new conditions.[16]

In contrast to labor outside of the home, the place of women as defined by the rabbinical tradition is much more circumscribed in the area of power and politics. Part of this is due to the tradition's roots in Islamic society, which produced most of the medieval Jewish authorities, such as Maimonides. Maimonides, also known as the Rambam, gave a ruling that "all appointments to positions of authority in Israel" were restricted to men.[17] Contemporary modern Orthodox thinkers have expanded this a little to suggest that it is acceptable in Halakha for women to have an influence on decision making, that is they can be voters or even advisory members of decision making groups, but not leaders per se. As recently as 1987, Dr. Sir Immanuel Jakobovits, the British Chief Rabbi, had declared that in the Orthodox communities under his jurisdiction "if what the women want is full participation, they can and will have everything. If what they speak is equal rights in a spurious quest for 'women's liberation,' they will have nothing."[18]

Indeed, both the socialization of private sphere work characterized by women's entry into the labor force and the Halakhic views on women's involvement in the political process would be reflected in the Zionist enterprise as well.

Women and the Zionist Enterprise

Since the beginning of Jewish settlement in Palestine in the late nineteenth century, women have been confined either to the private sphere or a socialized version of it. In Natalie Rein's study of women in Israel, she writes that starting in Degania, the first collective farm or kibbutz in the Land of Israel, there were political struggles over what role women would play in settling the land.[19] Women in the pre-state Zionist community in Palestine, known as the Yishuv, had to struggle for their place and right to participate in agricultural work, defense activities and political institutions. A combination of male resistance and harsh day-to-day conditions prevented women from fully entering the public sphere, however. As Rein writes: "Malaria and typhus were endemic, much of the country was either swamp or desert and [the early Zionist settlers] had come without agricultural or horticultural skills."[20]

There was another factor that helped prevent women from making any concrete gains, and that was the relationship between classical Judaism and the Zionist project. The Zionist elite was always opposed by a majority of the population in its midst. As Zionism developed in nineteenth-century Europe, it attracted only a minority of Jews. Secular Jews were bent on assimilation and most Orthodox Jews vehemently opposed the idea of Jewish sovereignty in the Land of Israel before the Messiah came. When the early Zionists came to Palestine, they were vastly outnumbered by the indigenous Arab population.[21] Moreover, those ultra-Orthodox or *haredi* Jews who had immigrated to the Holy City of Jerusalem in the early nineteenth century from the shtetls of Eastern Europe, in an attempt to escape the encroaching reformism of the Enlightenment political project, frequently denounced Zionist newcomers to the Ottoman authorities. Given its minority status, the Zionist enterprise needed a legitimating factor to unite the entire Jewish population against the indigenous population and to legitimate itself among the majority of Orthodox Jews in the Diaspora who were opposed to Zionism, so it would, at least, tacitly consent to the project. The religious discourse and symbols of the Hebrew Bible proved to be the unifying factor. Secular Zionists took an essentially religious document and put forward the claim that it provided a chronicle of Jewish history in antiquity. They used the Hebrew Bible to claim historic right to Palestine, using the borders described in the text itself as their geographic mandate. The Chosen People would reclaim the Promised Land.

This hegemonic role of classical Judaism conflated identity, ethnicity, and culture with the Zionist enterprise. Class and gender questions, while still there beneath the surface, seemed to have withered away. Hence, the woman who was engaged in halutziot still saw her role within the context of the Woman of Valor (*Eshet Chayil*). However, instead of one woman at home raising her own children, several women would raise the children of the kibbutz in its nursery. They became women of valor, the mainstay of the collective enterprise.

The Palestinian resistance to early Zionist settlement only served to reinforce this traditional role, for the civil societies of the Yishuv and Israel became increasingly militarized. The social culture became male-oriented, with woman as wife and mother assuming great importance. No women's movement ever emerged that challenged the ways in which women were confined and protected in the private sphere. If Halakhic injunctions prevented women from becoming transformed into consumer objects, it still made them status symbols so that woman's Halakhic role became intertwined with her national one; her primary purpose was to produce babies who would become soldiers in future wars.[22] Israeli-Jewish women are placed in a "demographic competition" with Palestinian women (both Israeli citizens and residents of the West Bank and Gaza) living under Israeli rule. Although abortion is legal, official government policy is pro-natalist.[23] Hence, Jewish women are generally denied access to contraceptives, even though they are legal. The haredi Agudat Israel party wants to introduce a bill in the Israeli parliament that would place strict limits on legal abortion.[24]

Zionist ideology considered women to be the embodiment of the home front. If the goal of the movement was to create the new Jewish man, the new Jewish woman was still a traditional one, albeit with a communal purpose.[25] Woman's ascriptive role was underscored. Ironically, this was further stressed when Golda Meir was prime minister (1969-73). By focusing on Jewish emigration from the Soviet Union and consolidating the occupation, Meir did little in terms of women's advocacy. While the United States and Western Europe were witnessing a burgeoning women's movement, what became magnified in Israel was the image of the earth mother producing children for the state. [26] Part of this was due to the persona of Meir herself, best described by Simha Dinitz, the current head of the Jewish Agency: "Since she is a Jewish mother and Jewish grandmother, she superimposes family feeling on national destiny."[27]

Paradoxically, Israeli women have more legal protection than many of their Western counterparts: The Equality of Sexes Act was passed in 1951 and there has been equal pay for equal work since the mid-1950s. Fully-paid maternity leave has been in effect since 1956, an Equal Opportunity in Employment Bill was passed in 1982 and there has been parity in retirement age since 1987. Much of this is due to the fact that the state itself, and not any social movement, has been the agent of change for women. Hence, women can become members of parliament and judges in the High Court, but only 5.8 percent of parliament members in 1991 were women (down from eight percent in 1984-88), the lowest proportion since the state was founded in 1948. There is not a single woman mayor in Israel[28] and Halakha, which adjudicates all personal matters for Israeli Jews, forbids women from either sitting on a bench in a family court or being a witness in one, since it does not acknowledge her right to sign a document.[29]

Women are poorly represented in Israeli public life. Despite universal conscription, they are not found in the upper echelons of the military. Within the military itself, there is sex segregation: Women are not assigned to combat and are frequently involved in "helping" roles—as office and kitchen workers. Indeed, there is a relationship between woman's role in the military and her lack of visibility in the parliament, for success in Israeli politics is often dependent on a strong military background.[30] Neither have women fared well professionally. Less than ten percent of Israeli academicians are women, although they comprise the vast majority of primary and secondary school teachers. While they seem to have made some inroads as physicians in the state-run medical system (*Kupat Holim*), much of this is due to the fixed hours they have working in a clinic, thereby making it easier to carry out their duties as wives and mothers in nuclear families. There are very few female physicians in private practice, however.[31]

Perhaps as a consequence, some of the most visible women in Israeli public life have been affiliated with Gush Emunim. As squatters in illegal settlements they were the embodiment of the home front, emulating both their Halakhic roles and those ascribed to them by the Zionist enterprise itself. As we shall see in the next section, rather than function as religious fundamentalists or radical dissenters, they were in fact created by and have served the state, albeit at arm's distance from it.

The Origins of Gush Emunim

Gush Emunim was founded in the Winter of 1974 by Rabbi Haim Druckmann at Gush Etzion, an area of the West Bank about fifteen miles due south of Jerusalem. Although it was preceded in the period after 1967 by the Movement for the Whole Land of Israel, some scholars trace Gush Emunim's origins to the early 1950s, in a group called Gahelet, translated as Embers, but also an acronym for Nucleus of Torah-Leaning Pioneers.[32] Gahelet considered the formation of the Israeli state to be the advent of a messianic era, an idea that became widespread in Israeli-Jewish civil society only after the June 1967 Arab-Israeli war, when the entire Land of Israel came under Israeli control. Gahelet activists unsuccessfully attempted to take over the National Religious Party (Mafdal) in 1963-64 and then began to recruit new members from various *yeshivot* associated with the Mafdal, its B'nai Akiva youth movement and the religious kibbutzim. The young rabbis active in the group and their wives would play prominent roles in both the Park Hotel and Beit Hadassah incidents in Hebron.

The Movement for a Whole Land of Israel, in contrast to Gahelet, consisted of both secular and religious Zionists. Its purpose was to make sure that all occupied territory remained under Israeli control. Some Movement adherents attached religious significance to the land; others used the argument of historic right. Its secular supporters included both right- and left-wing Zionists, including many prominent members of the Labor party. The religious supporters were affiliated with Gahelet as well as other civil society institutions associated with religious Zionism—B'nai Akiva, Mafdal, religious kibbutzim, Bar-Ilan University and *yeshiva* students. Nevertheless, by 1977, the religious forces had totally surrounded the Movement and both it and its newspaper, *This Land (Zot Ha'aretz)* were defunct, having been replaced by Gush Emunim, which justified settlement in the occupied territories on the basis of one thing only, Halakha.

Gush Emunim's roots in civil society institutions affiliated with the Mafdal, some of which existed in the Yishuv and helped to form the state, and were then later funded by the state, indicates that the movement is not peripheral to Zionism. As Beit-Hallahmi[33] points out, Lustick's use of the term fundamentalist to describe Gush Emunim is unfortunate.[34] Fundamentalism is a term that grew out of a uniquely North American phenomenon, referring to the five fundamentals of the Protestant Christians. Generally, fundamentalism has come to mean religious orthodoxy in confrontation with modernity.[35] In the specific case of Israel it usually refers to both the non-Zionist religious political parties and Gush Emunim. In terms of religious orthodoxy, however, Gush Emunim is not particularly fundamentalist. Moreover, since the Jewish tradition is based upon the authority of various commentaries on the text itself,[36] such as Talmud and Midrash, classical Judaism cannot be truly fundamentalist. If anything, secular Zionism, through its rejection of the Talmudic tradition and reliance solely on the Hebrew Bible, is more fundamentalist than the very forces it accuses of being so.

In terms of the Israeli continuum, Gush Emunim settlers are the dividing line between observant and non-observant Jews, and as Beit-Hallahmi notes, "just because of that they can be such militant Zionists."[37] This militancy was obvious by the movement's mode of operation throughout the mid-1970s: it would start an illegal settlement, be evicted by the Israeli Defense Forces (IDF), reappear, be repelled again, and so on, until the government would finally consent to the construction of a settlement on that site.

The Struggle to Settle Hebron

Since the Israeli occupation of the West Bank and Gaza began in 1967, Hebron has been a sensitive issue. Along with Jerusalem, Safad and Tiberias, it is one of the four holy cities of Judaism. Besides being the site of the Cave of Machpelah or Tomb of the Patriarchs, the alleged burial place of Abraham and Sarah, it also contains the tomb of Abner and was King David's first capital. Indeed, Hebron was a logical place to begin West Bank settlement, for it was the only holy city that had no Jewish presence in it after the June 1967 war. Furthermore, there had been a continuous Jewish presence there—some claim since at least the Roman Empire—for several hundred years. In 1929, as part of an aborted uprising against both the British administration and the burgeoning Zionist enterprise, sixty Hebron Jews were killed by local Palestinian-Arabs. Most of these victims were not Zionist settlers but members of an indigenous religiously-observant community. In 1936, during the beginning of the Palestine revolt, the Jewish population that remained abandoned the city. Together, these religious and historical factors provided the synthesis for a volatile emotional force that would produce in Hebron an enterprise reasserting and relegitimating a Jewish presence in all of Palestine.

Indeed, this is how the participants in the Park Hotel episode in 1968 saw their mission. The then-Labor government was divided on support for the Park Hotel group. Miriam Levinger, a group leader, recalled in a personal interview:

> Moshe Dayan was for us leaving [the Park Hotel] and Yigal Allon was for us staying. There were many elements in the government who were in favor of Jews settling in Hebron then. Those who were in favor visited us—Yigal Allon [and] Menahem Begin. Many people came to visit us and wish us luck.
>
> In the end [in late July], as a compromise, we were offered the choice of settling in the military compound as a government move. ... They made us homes from Hussein's old stables and feed rooms for the horses—a dining room, a living room, a school and a garden.[38]

Hebron is the third largest city in the West Bank and the major administrative, commercial and industrial center of the southern region. Moreover, the Arab population of Hebron has always been and is still considered to be the most traditional and least urbanized of West Bank residents.[39] Settlement in Hebron contradicted Labor party schemes, such as the Allon Plan, which called for inhabiting hilly regions in between Palestinian villages for security purposes. Yet in August 1968, the Park Hotel group was given space to worship in the Tomb of the Patriarchs. However, the group wanted more concessions from the government:

> We argued with them [the government]. After all, when we originally came, we had intentions of buying or renting homes in Hebron so we could free the Jewish property there. We thought we would rent homes which were former Jewish property and live in Hebron proper. But there were elements among us who said that if the government was letting us live in the governor's compound, then it was an indirect recognition of a new Jewish community in Hebron, so let's do what the government says. We went to the military compound.[40]

Within a year, the squatters were disobeying military orders by conducting aggressive prayer sessions at the Tomb of the Patriarchs, which is also a Muslim holy site. Five Jewish settlers were ordered out. But in the ensuing debate, the government backed down and the eviction order was countermanded. The historic right argument had won.[41]

By September 1968, plans were being readied for building a settlement at Kiryat Arba outside of Hebron. The first settlers took up residence in these eastern outskirts in 1971. Between 1969-73, the Israeli government spent over $10 million making Kiryat Arba viable, providing sewage facilities, electricity and other town services.[42] By 1975, there would be over 1,200 settlers living there, and in 1987, it topped 2,000, making it the largest Jewish settlement in the West Bank. The prize of Hebron, however, was not realized. Gush Emunim supporters associated with Rabbi Moshe Levinger and his wife Miriam continued to press for settlement in the heart of Palestinian areas, ostensibly for religious reasons. Despite the gains the movement had made in the 1970s, particularly after Menahem Begin became prime minister in 1977, by early 1979 it was once again resorting to renegade settlements. The most famous incident was one involving Beit Hadassah, a communal medical center in Hebron until the 1929 massacre. In early spring 1979, Miriam Levinger and a dozen women occupied the building. Gush Emunim had always considered settlement of Kiryat Arba, outside Hebron itself, to be a compromise. Moreover, a general state of economic recession and hyperinflation was to have its impact on the occupied territories. Settlement was not proceeding rapidly enough for Gush Emunim and Kiryat Arba was, in the words of Miriam Levinger, "gradually withering away."[43]

For individuals such as Levinger, who view the world in very mystical, anti-modern/Western terms, the failure to settle Hebron and the area adjacent to it had nothing to do with Israeli economic problems or international pressure on Israel vis-à-vis the Palestinians. Instead, she attributes the decision to take over Beit Hadassah to a conversation she had with a member of the Chabad-Lubavitch *hasidim*:

[He] said that the reason why this came upon us was because we compromised and we should never have compromised. We came to Hebron to live in Hebron and we agreed to the idea of settlement in Kiryat Arba. So because we compromised on Hebron we were getting neither Kiryat Arba nor Hebron. When he said that something clicked in my mind. I spoke with a few women friends and we came to the conclusion that he was right. And then we decided to move down to Hebron. [44]

It remains unclear if the women actually took the initiative or if they were acting on behalf of Rabbi Moshe Levinger: "I went to my husband and I said that the women wanted to live in Hebron. He consulted with others who came to the conclusion that we had a good idea. They worked out the plan."[45]

Since Israeli government policy was that Jewish settlement would not involve the direct dispossession of Arabs, the settlers' strategy rested on a demand to regain possession of Jewish property abandoned in 1929. The owners had given Gush Emunim the original deed to the property as well as the right to deed. The plan included moving a group of twelve women and thirty children into the building in the middle of the night. Beit Hadassah was occupied by an UNRWA-run elementary school at the time of the takeover. In addition, a few Israeli reservists were located on the top floor. Once the squatters appeared, the IDF proclaimed that whoever left the building could not return. The group lived with no running water and used kerosene lamps for six months. Supporters brought them food and clean clothing, and seed money came from the Israeli-born Nakash brothers, then living in the United States and owners of Jordache jeans.[46] On 23 March 1980, the government gave Gush Emunim permission to settle and establish a religious and field school in the heart of the city. It renovated the synagogue in Hebron's old Jewish quarter and completed two apartments. Jewish women had been given direct access to the rear of the Hall of Isaac in the Tomb of the Patriarchs so they would not have to mingle with men during hours of prayer. This, however, involved the clearing of a narrow passage in the "women's mosque."[47] Since Gush

Emunim considers equal rights to places of worship to be a concession (it regards Jewish historic rights as superior), major confrontations between Jews and Muslims began at the Tomb of the Patriarchs. In April 1988, a visiting yeshiva student was murdered in the center of Hebron's Arab market. The IDF placed the town under curfew and settlers from nearby Kiryat Arba ranged through the city. In the days that followed, five more Jews were killed and sixteen wounded. The IDF demolished the buildings that had shielded the Palestinian ambushers and expelled the mayor, Fawd Qawasmeh, to Lebanon. (No Jewish settlers were punished.) As tense as things were, and remained in 1991, Jews had won the right to live in Hebron.

The Identity of Gush Emunim Women

Jewish settlement would not have proceeded in Hebron without the squatting actions of women in Beit Hadassah. Although they had staged what appeared to be an autonomous women's action, they were acting totally within the framework of Halakha, which automatically separates women from men. They took their roles as wives and mothers in the private sphere and socialized them. All they did in Beit Hadassah was try to make the building habitable. They cleaned, cooked, did laundry, and raised children, in other words, maintained and reproduced their Jewish households.

Few women affiliated with the settlers' movement openly object to their ascribed status. Levinger, for example, denies that she ever acted in any leadership capacity: "I'm not a feminist at all, not a career woman. I'm devoted to my children, to my husband, and to Judaism. I went after my husband to Hebron, to Kiryat Arba, and then back to Hebron. I'm really just following his lead and his encouragement."[48]

This view was also echoed by Shoshana Mageni, another of the original Hebron settlers, who told Beata Lipman: "I don't mind that it should be all men deciding ... and the rabbis aren't all unsympathetic to us, either."[49] One of the things that men had decided to do, and which the women did willingly, was to be in the frontlines. Rather than view themselves as docile, they imagined themselves as Jewish fighters, "on the roof with a gun in their hand, fighting in the hills and on the mountains, one hand with their husband, one with their children."[50] Yet women have been deliberately excluded from all settlement councils. Indeed, Yuval-Davis reports that in some extreme religious settlements, women have not been allowed to vote in local elections.[51] Hence, it was Halakhically correct for Shifra Blass to serve as the spokesperson for the *Yesha* Council, that is the Council of Settlements in the West Bank and

Gaza.[52] She would, however, have very little say in formulating the policies she was defending.

Both Blass and Levinger are American-born and from religious families. Both were engaged in helping professions before becoming politically involved. Levinger came to Israel in 1956 when she was 18 and attended nursing school at Shaarei Zadek Hospital in Jerusalem. She married Moshe Levinger three years later and lived with him on various religious *kibbutzim* and *moshavim* until the June 1967 war, at which time Rabbi Levinger became active in the Movement for the Whole Land of Israel. Blass came to Israel on a one-year student program in 1970, returned to the U.S., and immigrated in 1972, working in hospitals and day-care centers. Unlike Levinger, Blass never viewed West Bank settlement in religious or mystical terms. Indeed, her view was practical, albeit somewhat naive:

> Settlement began as a personal issue for myself and my husband. We thought we could live someplace in Judea or Samaria on our own. We didn't understand that there was an organization. We were fairly new immigrants and didn't connect with networks that already existed. We saw the area, didn't understand any political problems connected with it. We saw that no one lived here, and said, "Why not we?" Then, as we went about our bumbling way trying to find a place, people started telling us, "This is the West Bank. These are all of the problems connected with the West Bank." After a year of banging our head against the wall, we joined a group, which we didn't even exactly understand was Gush Emunim. It was group for settlement in Shiloh. I did not think of myself as part of a larger network—I just saw people who wanted to live in Samaria.[53]

Blass's involvement in the *Yesha* Council came by default. Before its establishment in 1978, she had been speaking on behalf of West Bank settlement to foreign journalists. (Indeed, she continues to work for the Council when it needs its point of view represented in English.) When the Council was established, she was drafted. Levinger couches the return to Hebron in messianic terms, believing that the presence of Jews there will pave the way for the Messiah.[54] Blass, in contrast, views settlement in the occupied territories in classical Zionist terms. There is an

> [I]ntrinsic tie between the Jewish people and the Land of Israel, which is not negotiable. This means we can't accept the Diaspora as an alternative for Jewish life. It means that we should help Jews in other countries who have difficulties. It means accepting a position that a Jew who lives in

Israel should stay here and not leave. Another lifestyle elsewhere or one's personal development should not come before basic belonging to Israel.[55]

Blass's comments are illuminating for they bring into question just how religious Gush Emunim really is. Like all religious Zionists, the movement considers the injunction to settle the land to be the most important of the 613 mitzvot. It shares political Zionism's emphasis on the Hebrew Bible as the interpreter of Jewish history, beginning with Abraham and the divine promise in Genesis 15:18. Yet despite Gush Emunim's literal interpretation of the Bible, it has been quite liberal on other matters related to Halakha. It accepted the Israeli state; indeed, its roots indicate that it was to some extent created by it, and it was willing to work with secular nationalists in settling Greater Israel. It is not guided by a Council of Torah Sages, the paradigmatic governing body in rigorously Orthodox organizations, but a secretariat in which women serve.[56]

Gush Emunim's confrontational stance was essentially political, despite the religious justification for its actions. From the state, it appropriated the rhetoric of "security" and challenged the state on maintaining control of the Palestinians, while being entirely dependent on the tanks, helicopters and airplanes of the IDF for its survival. When dealing with the Palestinians, women were frequently in the frontlines, either as provocateurs or as victims. Gush Emunim actions against the Palestinians are informed by the movement's desire to protect its privileged position as Israeli "pied noirs" in the West Bank and Gaza but justified on Halakhic grounds. Hence, Palestinians are frequently depicted as the biblical enemies of the Israelite nation, Amalek. Officially, Gush Emunim claims to honor every person, since all people were made in the image of God, but ultimately believes that Palestinians are entitled only to individual rights, not political ones.

Attacks on Palestinians, while largely the purview of men, have also been carried out by women. A 1983 study conducted by David Weisburd found that out of a sample of 500 Jewish settlers, twenty-eight percent of males and five percent of females admitted to having participated in some sort of vigilante activity.[57] One of the most prominent examples of female participation in vigilante activity followed the death of Ofra Moses. Moses was a resident of the West Bank settlement of Alfei Menashe, located just over the green-line northeast of Tel Aviv. On April 11, 1987, a molotov cocktail was thrown at the family car as they passed a small Palestinian village on their way back to the settlement. The wife, five months pregnant, burned to death. Although her husband and four children escaped with burns, one of the children eventually died of his injuries. In response, Gush Emunim general secretary Danielle Weiss led a rampage of about 300 settlers through the town of Qalqilya, destroying shops and cars, burning fields and uprooting orange groves (on the grounds that the attacker used them as camouflage).

Gush Emunim publicly accused the government of apathy and claimed it was ineffective in dealing with security issues. When Ofra Moses was killed, it was more than another Israeli attacked by Palestinians, for a family had been attacked, and the primary care-giver was killed. In the Gush Emunim worldview, with its politicization of family life, the public-private distinction is less relevant and an assault on a mother required a strong vigilante response. Woman's domestic role became a ritualized public one for she was the mistress of the home, and those institutions most closely associated with the home such as education. By keeping Kashrut and the Sabbath she was the carrier of the morality that makes public communal life possible. The Weiss-led rampage through Qalqilya was an attempt to protect the family, and by extension, the nation. It had nothing to do with asserting women's rights or even protecting women. Indeed, Weiss explicitly rejects that any women's actions in Gush Emunim, including her own, are gender-related:

> When you have to fight for your rights, you're already inferior. ... A woman who does not recognize and take pride in the fact of having been born a woman is a miserable creature and cannot be an attractive person. ... Please understand, my role in the movement has little to do with feminist sympathies. It is based on the needs of the nation. The only sovereignty over these territories is Israeli, and the number one battle call is the settlement of these areas with Jews.[58]

In the parliamentary arena, this view is articulated by Tehiya MP Geula Cohen. Cohen has been involved in Zionist politics since the 1940s, when she was a member of the Irgun underground associated with Menahem Begin, and later joined the more radical Lehi or Stern Gang, responsible for a rash of terrorist activities, including the assassination of Count Folke Bernadotte, the UN Special Mediator for Palestine. Cohen entered parliament on Begin's Herut list, which she quit in early 1979 when the Egyptian-Israeli peace treaty (the Camp David accords) was ratified. Along with Yuval Ne'eman, a former Labor party activist who quit after the Sinai Disengagement treaty was signed in 1975, Cohen founded Tehiya, the political party most closely affiliated with Gush Emunim. Unlike other women associated with the settlers' movement, Cohen is not religious, preferring the label "traditional." She grew up in a religious household, but does not adhere to Kashrut either in or outside the home, and does not keep the Sabbath. Furthermore, she is divorced. Despite her background, Cohen has little regard for specific women's issues. Indeed, when Israel's abortion bill came up for parliamentary vote in February 1976, Cohen voted against it.[59] She has been an outspoken proponent of continued settlement, which like Blass she views in very practical terms. In her lexicon, real Jews are fighters. Gush Emunim is their army, while the Tehiya party is the political wing.[60]

Conclusions

The Halakhic injunctions against female participation in the public sphere and the belief that woman be keeper of the home and the family were also reflected in Zionist ideology and reinforced by the militarization of Israeli civil society. Gush Emunim women, on the line of demarcation between observant and non-observant Israeli-Jews, carry out the demands of Halakha and the Israeli state by protecting the private realm. Unlike the Israeli feminists, who link the militarization of Israeli civil society with the absence of a strong women's movement,[61] Gush Emunim women demand that the Israeli-Palestinian conflict go on indefinitely so they can fulfil their Halakhic roles. Indeed, the feminist calls for a completely different system that is egalitarian and democratic will undermine the role of Gush Emunim in general, and its women in particular. To some extent, Gush Emunim women have served the state as gate keepers in an attempt to turn the frontiers of the West Bank and Gaza into borders of a larger State of Israel. Moreover, as members of the hegemonic ethnic group,[62] Gush Emunim women, despite their actions, are not perceived as marginal. Like the ruling Israeli elite, they are petit bourgeois in class origin, fitting the general demographic profile of the Israeli pioneers (*halutzim*). By making Halakha primary, they have blurred all class and ethnic distinctions (such as Ashkenazi and Mizrachi) among Israeli Jews.

What impact the massive immigration of Soviet Jews, which began in 1990, and the May 1991 airlift of approximately 14,000 Ethiopian Jews will have on class, gender, and ethnic relations in the occupied territories remains unclear. Although few Soviet Jews have moved to the West Bank or Gaza, their arrival in Israel—approximately 500 per day in May 1991—has meant a concomitant displacement of working-class mizrachi Jews within the green line, who may be lured to the occupied territories with promises of cheaper and more spacious government-subsidized housing.

Moreover, although never stated explicitly, it is clear that a dialectic exists between the earth mother image of the Israeli woman and the Israeli-Palestinian conflict. Indeed, the national security situation has consistently been used against any kind of women's movement. As Aloni asserts: "It is an infallible excuse because *every* family in Israel has someone in the armed forces, and no Jewish mother or wife would do anything that might remotely harm her man."[63] Demilitarization of Israeli civil society, which as of this writing seems to be a remote prospect, will enable women to act on their own behalf. Although it is highly unlikely that the women of Gush Emunim will ever question their ascribed roles, the emergence of a strong women's movement will remove these women from center-stage and put them on the sidelines. At this writing (1992), given the continuation of the Palestinian Intifada, the influx of Soviet and Ethiopian Jews, ambivalence about the peace process, and a persistence of the arms race in the region, the future does not look bright either for peace or for feminism in Israel.

Notes

1. In David J. Schnall, *Beyond the Green Line: Israeli Settlements West of Jordan* (New York: Praeger, 1984), p. 55.

2. Joel Brinkley, "Israelis Kill 6 Armed Arabs Entering from Jordan," *New York Times,* March 12, 1991.

3. The research for this project grew out of a dissertation "Religion and the Secular State: Israel Since 1973," New York University 1990. This analysis is constructed from interviews with seventeen members of Gush Emunim, internal documents of the organization, and secondary materials. All interviews were taped and it is from these that the quotations have been taken. All were conducted in 1987 and transcribed by the author.

4. Jewish festivals are celebrated for one day longer in the Diaspora than they are in the Land of Israel. Hence, Passover lasts for seven days in Israel and eight outside of it.

5. Personal interview with Miriam Levinger, May 11, 1987, Hebron.

6. Michelle Zimbalist Rosaldo, "Women, Culture, and Society: A Theoretical Overview," pp. 1-30 in Rosaldo and Louise Lamphere (eds.), *Women, Cutlure, and Society* (Stanford: Stanford University Press, 1974), p. 22.

7. Judith Baskin, "The Separation of Women in Rabbinic Judaism" in Yvonne Yazbeck Haddad and Ellison Banks Findly (eds.), *Women, Religion, and Social Change* (Albany: State University of New York Press, 1985), p. 6.

8. Phyllis A. Bird, "Images of Women in the Old Testament," in Norman A. Gottwald (ed.), *The Bible and Liberation: Political and Social Hermeneutics* (Maryknoll, NY: Orbis Books, 1983), p. 259.

9. *Ibid.,* p. 268.

10. For example, *Mitzvat Nashim* was published in Venice in 1552, *Seder Nashim* in Prague in 1629, and *Mitzvat Ha'Nashim* in Hanau in 1677.

11. Benedict Anderson, *Imagined Communities: Reflections on the Origin and Spread of Nationalism* (London and New York: Verso, 1983).

12. J. P. Schultz, "The *Ze'nah Ur'enah*: Torah for the Folk," *Judaism,* 141 (1987).

13. The *Eshet Chayil,* recited at the Sabbath ...eal, consists of the concluding twenty-two verses of the Book of Proverbs (31:10-31). On the surface, it is a hymn to the perfect wife, who is the mainstay of her home. However, the chapter is supposed to be allegorical, with the Jewish woman chosen as the vehicle through which to describe such lofty spiritual manifestations such as the *Shechinah,* or female divine presence, the Sabbath, Torah, Wisdom, and the soul. See Rabbi Nosson Scherman (ed. and trans.), *The Complete ArtScroll Siddur* (Brooklyn, NY: Mesorah Publications Ltd., 1984), pp. 358-60, for a commentary on the text.

14. Louis Finkelstein, *Jewish Self-Government in the Middle Ages* (Westport, CT: Greenwood Press, 1924/1972), p. 379; see also Ze'ev Wilhelm Falk, *Jewish Matrimonial Law in the Middle Ages* (New York: Oxford University Press, 1966).

15. In Julius Carlebach, "The Story of A Book for Jewish Women," *L'Eylah,* 23, 1986, p. 43.

16. Suzanne MacKenzie, "Women's Responses to Economic Restructuring: Changing Gender, Changing Space," in Roberta Hamilton and Michele Barrett (eds.), *The Politics of Diversity: Feminism, Marxism and Nationalism* (London: Verso, 1986), p. 6.

17. Maimonides, *Hilkhot Melakhim* 1:5. For a comprehensive treatment of this theme see Rachel Biale, *Women and Jewish Law* (New York: Schocken Books, 1984).

18. Dr. Sir Immanuel Jakobovits, "Women in Community Service," *L'Eylah,* 23, 1987, p. 5. Ironically—and perhaps intentionally—this is a paraphrase of Stanislas de Clermont-Tonnerre's famous statement to the French National Assembly in 1789, in which he proclaimed: "One must refuse everything to the Jews as a nation but one must grant them everything as individuals; they must become citizens" (in Arthur Hertzberg, *The French Enlightenment and the Jews* [New York: Schocken, 1968], p. 360). Jewish women, then, like the Jews of the post-revolutionary France, could be free as individuals but not as a corporate community.

19. Natalie Rein, *Daughters of Rachel: Women in Israel* (Harmondsworth, Middlesex: Penguin, 1979).

20. *Ibid.,* p. 39.

21. After the establishment of the Israeli state in 1948, the Ashkenazi Jews of European descent who founded it were quickly outnumbered by Jewish immigrants from North Africa and the Middle East (the *mizrachim*), who were totally peripheral to the Zionist project, so that in 1991 about 35 percent of the Israeli-Jewish population is of Ashkenazi descent, while the other 65 percent is of mizrachi descent. Moreover, the addition of a million and a half Palestinians in the West Bank and Gaza after 1967 only served to marginalize the Zionist elite even more.

22. For further elaborations on this theme, see Shulamit Aloni, "Israel: Up the Down Escalator," pp. 360-364 in Robin Morgan (ed.), *Sisterhood is Global: The International Women's Movement Anthology* (Garden City, NY: Anchor Press/Doubleday, 1984); Beata Lipman, *Israel: The Embattled Land. Jewish and Palestinian Women Talk About Their Lives* (London: Pandora, 1988); and Nira Yuval-Davis, "National Reproduction and 'the Demographic Race' in Israel," pp. 92-109 in Yuval-Davis and Floya Anthias (eds.), *Women-Nation-State* (New York: St. Martin's Press, 1989).

23. Abortion has been legal since 1976. It can be performed if the woman's life or her physical or mental health is endangered, if the pregnancy resulted from incest, or if she is under the age of 17 or over 40.

24. Joel Brinkley, "Religious Party Joins Shamir Alliance," *The New York Times*, November 17, 1990.

25. Naomi Chazan, "Gender Equality? Not in A War Zone!," *Israeli Democracy*, (Summer) 1989.

26. See *ibid.*, and Rein, *Daughters of Rachel.*

27. Rein, *ibid.*, p. 81.

28. Alice Shalvi, "Israeli Women: Are the Gains Secure?," presented at the General Assembly of the Council of Jewish Federations, Miami, 1987.

29. Aloni, "Israel: Up the Down Escalator," p. 361.

30. See Chazan, "Gender Equality?"

31. These comments are based on personal observations of the *Kupat Holim* system while I was living in Israel as well as conversations with female physicians and Israeli academicians studying health-care policy. It should be noted that no one ever mentioned how difficult it would be for an Israeli woman to set up a private practice, thereby giving her no other choice but to work within the *Kupat Holim* system. Instead, all emphasized the advantages of working in a state-run enterprise.

32. For a comprehensive discussion of Gahelet, see Gideon Aran, "From Religious Zionism to Zionist Religion: The Roots of Gush Emunim," in Peter Y. Medding (ed.), *Studies in Contemporary Jewry*, Vol. II (Bloomington, IN: Indiana University Press, 1986).

33. Benjamin Beit-Hallahmi, "Review of *For the Land and the Lord: Jewish Fundamentalism in Israel* by Ian S. Lustick," *Journal for the Scientific Study of Religion* (28) (1989), p. 382.

34. Ian S. Lustick, "Israel's Dangerous Fundamentalists," *Foreign Policy*, 68, 1987, and *For the Land and the Lord: Jewish Fundamentalism in Israel* (New York: Council on Foreign Relations, 1988).

35. See James Davison Hunter, "Fundamentalism in Its Global Contours," in Norman J. Cohen (ed.), *The Fundamentalist Phenomenon. A View From Within; A Response From Without* (Grand Rapids, MI: William B. Eeerdmans, 1990).

36. See Leon Wieseltier, "The Jewish Face of Fundamentalism," in Cohen, *The Fundamentalist Phenomenon*.

37. Beit-Hallahmi, "Review of *For the Land and the Lord*," p. 382.

38. Personal interview with Miriam Levinger, May 11, 1987, Hebron.

39. Michael Romann, *Jewish Kiryat Arba Versus Arab Hebron* (Jerusalem: The Jerusalem Post, West Bank Data Project, 1985), p. 11.

40. Personal interview with Miriam Levinger, May 11, 1987, Hebron.

41. Howard M. Sachar, *A History of Israel. Vol. II. From the Aftermath of the Yom Kippur War* (New York: Oxford University Press, 1987), p. 16.

42. *Ibid.*, p. 16.

43. Personal interview with Miriam Levinger, May 11, 1987, Hebron.

44. Personal interview with Miriam Levinger, May 11, 1987, Hebron. In Sachar (*A History of Israel. Vol. II*, p. 161) Levinger claims that she had a dream in which King David appeared and ordered her to restore a Jewish presence in the heart of town. This dream was not mentioned at all when I interviewed her, leaving me to wonder if she had invented it in 1979 and had then forgotten about it eight years later.

45. Personal interview with Miriam Levinger, May 11, 1987, Hebron.

46. Geoffrey Aronson, *Creating Facts: Israel, Palestinians and the West Bank* (Washington, D.C.: Institute for Palestine Studies, 1987), p. 154.

47. Romann, *Jewish Kiryat Arba Versus Arab Hebron*, p. 57.

48. In Schnall, *Beyond the Green Line*, p. 51.

49. In Lipman, *Israel: The Embattled Land*, p. 19.

50. Geula Cohen in Lipman, *ibid.*, p. 16.

51. Yuval-Davis, "National Reproduction and 'the Demographic Race' in Israel," p. 105.

52. *Yesha*, which means salvation in Hebrew, is also an acronym for Judea (Yudea), Samaria (Shomron) and Gaza (Azza), the names used by Israeli annexationists and their international supporters for the occupied territories.

53. Personal interview with Shifra Blass, June 30, 1987, Halemish/Neve Tsouf.

54. Personal interview with Miriam Levinger, May 11, 1987, Hebron.

55. Personal interview with Shifra Blass, June 30, 1987, Halemish/Neve Tsouf.

56. It should be noted that religious Zionism was always more liberal on women's matters than the more rigorously Orthodox parties. For example, Tova Sanhedrin of the Religious Workers Party was elected to the parliament in 1959. She served as a member for fourteen years and was deputy speaker for ten.

57. See Ehud Sprinzak, "From Messianic Pioneering to Vigilante Terrorism: The Case of the Gush Emunim Underground," *The Journal of Strategic Studies,* 10, 1987, p. 212.

58. In Schnall, *Beyond the Green Line,* p. 55. It should be noted that this rationale for women's social action as part of a larger identity movement is hardly unique to Israel. See, for example, Sondra Hale in this volume.

59. See Rein, *Daughters of Rachel,* p. 152. It should be noted, however, that Cohen has publicly admitted to having an abortion when she was younger.

60. Personal interview with Geula Cohen, June 9, 1987, Jerusalem.

61. This is recognized by a small group of Israeli feminists, Women in Black, who hold vigil in front of Israeli-government offices throughout the country every Friday afternoon. They demand an end to the occupation and the creation of an independent Palestinian state. See also Chazan, "Gender Equality?," Judith Karp, "The Legal Status of Women in Israel Today," *Israeli Democracy* (Summer 1989), and Yuval-Davis, "National Reproduction and 'the Demographic Race' in Israel."

62. As stated earlier, the Ashkenazi Jews who settled Palestine comprise only about 35 percent of Israel's total Jewish population. However, over 80 percent of the settlers in the West Bank and Gaza are Ashkenazim.

63. Aloni, "Israel: Up the Down Escalator," p. 363.

16

The Role, Place, and Power of Middle-Class Women in the Islamic Republic

Shahin Gerami

Introduction

The focus of this chapter is urban middle-class women's assessment of their role and place in the Islamic Republic of Iran. The rise of Islamic fundamentalism provides a unique opportunity to explore women's attitudes toward their proper role and place. In addition to redefining women's status, Islamic fundamentalism has also affected their power in the family and society; directly, by redefining women's role and place, and indirectly, through their participation in the movement. Increased politicization due to participation in a movement contributes to empowerment. As a result, one can predict that women will express more willingness to hold and exercise power in the family and society. Closely tied to the above factors is an increased sense of group identity and solidarity among women.

This chapter provides a survey analysis of middle-class Iranian women which measures their attitudes toward spatial versus functional distinctions of sex roles, their relation to power at home and in society, and their extent of feminist consciousness against the background of the fundamentalist movement. The survey was carried out in Tehran during the summer of 1989.

Functional and Spatial Social Divisions

Division of labor, which is the essence of many social organizations, has invariably incorporated a sexually segregated pattern of social

329

responsibilities and rights. Culturally defined sexual distinctions determine men's and women's political, economic, and geographical positions within the social organization. Religious ideologies that solidify these functions also promote identity politics that further reevaluate and redefine previously established sex roles. Current fundamentalist movements within Islam and Western Christianity promote reconstruction of rigid sex roles. In the Christian system "the association of women with nature and therefore, by anatomical analogy, with childcare has long provided an excuse for excluding them from the political realm."[1] In the West the fundamentalist movement has created a vocal conservative group of women who champion the merits of the patriarchal family, a moral society, and a conservative political agenda.[2]

Unlike Islam, Christianity prescribes sex only for reproduction and does not attribute strong sexual power to woman and insatiable sexual drive to man. Therefore the urgency to seclude woman and make her asexual does not permeate Christian dogma. Rather this system is more concerned with delineating woman's role within the family and to safeguard man's authority against intrusion by the other sex.[3] The functional system places feminine roles in the family and society against masculine roles in each of these domains. In this system the emphasis is more on the functions of each sex than on their proper places. This system allows women limited participation in public life as long as they respect the demarcation between the masculine and feminine functions. As it is improper for a woman to assume a masculine function, it is also undesirable for men to intrude into the feminine realm.[4] This functional duality restricts and rejects women's equal access to power and economic resources, and limits their spatial mobility. However, compared with the spatial system, this provides women more independence by allowing them to participate in the public domain, and thus in the formal sector of economy.

Like the functional order, the spatial dichotomy is also part of a social system of roles, responsibilities, and distributive rewards. In Islamic societies cultural interpretation of women's biological distinctions are cast in terms of the place of women in society which in turn affects their social functions. By starting from woman's "natural" abilities the Islamic doctrine sequesters her in the private sphere, which in turn restricts her functions. The result is a multi-dimensional exclusionary practice that by all accounts is currently more restrictive than other patriarchies.[5] In Islamic societies women's identity reflects varied adaptations of these principles:

1. *Biological determinism of woman's place.* Woman's reproductive power has been used to justify her confinement to the private domain. Islamic jurists—sometimes influenced by Greek philosophers—have claimed that women are physically weaker, emotionally unstable, and intellectually inferior to men. Thus, they belong in the domestic sphere engaged in home-making and childrearing.[6]

2. *Woman's sexual power.* Islamic texts abound with the declaration that woman's sexual power, left unchecked, is destructive to the Islamic social order. Man with his primordial lust for woman is no match for her alluring schemes. To safeguard the sanctity of the family and *umma* (community), men must be saved from their insatiable search for sexual gratification. To this end, Islamic patriarchy confines women to the private domain and restricts their movement in public. Should women appear in public, they are required to observe dress and behavioral standards (*hijab*) that obscure their sexual identity. The extent of seclusion and the forms of hijab are subject to the culture, history, economy, and climate of a society or even a group.

3. *Geographical segregation.* Numerous examples in the language and folklore of Muslim societies confirm the idea of sex segregation. In Iran, in the traditional family, women are referred to as *manzel* (home), and *andaruni* (inner section). Many middle- and upper-class homes used to contain a *beruni* (outer house) where men resided, entertained, and conducted business, and an andaruni which was the women's section.[7]

4. *Woman's function.* As a raison d'être and as a result of this segregated policy, woman's functions are limited to motherhood and housekeeping. While this may sound tautological, considering the philosophical exchange between Roman/Greek and Islamic patriarchies,[8] this is both the cause and effect of the seclusion. According to *Sharia* (Islamic canon law) jurists, Allah created men and women differently and assigned each distinct responsibilities to be performed in their proper domain.[9] Therefore, spatial separation that identifies each sex's functions leads to duplication of some functions.

Like the functional order, the spatial system limits and rejects women's equal right to political and economic resources. Furthermore, since the formal job sector is all in the public domain, particularly in cities, spatial segregation restricts women's economic opportunities more than the functional order. Youssef proposes that seclusion of

Muslim women has affected their participation in the nonagricultural sector.[10] A cross-cultural study I undertook shows that, after controlling for the effects of economic growth and modernization, Muslim women have lower labor force participation and higher fertility than Catholic women in Latin American countries.[11]

Nevertheless, it must be pointed out that these dichotomies are not mutually exclusive. Some students of sex roles have applied the spatial distinction to the study of women's roles in America,[12] while others have expanded it to include Christian dogma in general. Thus, these categories serve as typology, not concrete boundaries. Indeed, the overlaps between the categories generate elastic boundaries that fluctuate with the cultural, economic, and socio-political conditions of societies. For instance, in Saudi Arabia a bank run by women ensures seclusion of women clientele, while Kuwaiti women enjoy greater freedom in public environment.[13] In a cross-cultural study, Kagitcibasi found that "the similarities between Turkish and Greek family cultures and sex roles were much greater than those between Turkish and Indonesian family cultures and roles."[14] While post-War modernization has relaxed sexual segregation in some Muslim countries, the rise of Islamic fundamentalism has revived spatial separation as the core of its ideal society. As in the West, there is strong support for this movement among women.

Women in the Midst of Islamic Fundamentalism

After World War II, a period of Westernization in many Middle Eastern countries reduced the intensity of spatial segregation, particularly in urban areas. Increased participation of women in educational and occupational activities, delayed marriage, legal changes in Sharia, and decreased use of veil implied some modification of exclusionary practices in these societies. Industrialization increased the female labor force who shared the public domain, though unequally, with men. These trends signaled the declining significance of spatial separation.

The return to the Islamic symbols and principles first became visible when female college students started wearing Islamic hijab.[15] Islamic hijab is often translated as "veil" which can be misleading since hijab constitutes different meanings and behavioral standards, and has distinct social implications.[16] Veil implies a sense of spatial and functional seclusion, which the Islamic hijab does not necessarily. In this chapter, I will use the term Islamic hijab which is *Hijab-e-Islami* in Iran, *al-Ziyy al-Islami* (the Islamic dress) in Egypt, and *chador* in Pakistan.

This trend goes far beyond symbolism and has far-reaching consequences. The new traditional woman whether in Egypt, Iran or Pakistan, has been losing ground in terms of legal family protection, political rights, and perhaps even employment and educational opportunities. A return to Sharia in many countries has eroded restrictions on men's unilateral right to divorce, polygamy, and child custody. Although women are not banned from higher education, there is a move in some countries to exclude them from "masculine" fields, such as engineering, and to encourage them to major in "feminine" disciplines.[17] The oil glut and general depression in the region has eliminated many jobs of guest workers in Arab countries and has reduced the local job market as well. In this context, repatriated and local workers facing unemployment are calling for women to return to home and open jobs for men. Protective laws in Egypt, Iran, and Pakistan call for early retirement, or mandatory part-time jobs for employed women, or penalize men with working wives in promotion, insurance, bonuses, and so on. Although the percentage of women in the nonagricultural sector has shown a modest increase,[18] there are conflicting reports about their share in the informal and agricultural sectors. It is too early to determine the consequences of fundamentalism for women in the region.

Putting Women in Their Place: The Islamic Republic Style

Nowhere has this movement been stronger than in Iran. It was in Tehran where the early signs of Islamic fundamentalism among women became observable. College and high school students started wearing the Islamic hijab as a sign of resistance against the Pahlavi regime in the early 1970s. Despite the regime's policy of banning hijab in schools and workplaces, hijab spread rapidly. During the revolution, hijab and chador (full-length veil) became women's symbol of resistance. Many of those who donned the hijab voluntarily as a sign of solidarity with the movement did not intend and could not foresee its becoming a mandatory dress and behavior code. The Ayatollah's decree in early March of 1979 that all working women should wear the hijab created strong resistance among middle- and upper-class women of the major urban centers.[19] This opposition movement, like many others, was eventually suppressed and the grip of hijab became harsher and stronger.

With the move to cover women came a concerted effort to return working women, particularly those in civil services, to their homes. A campaign of harassment, purges, mandatory retirement, or monetary incentives for husbands of housewives, made it extremely difficult, particularly in the early years of the revolution, for women to continue to work. Since then the woman question has been a major issue, and often a headache, for the new Republic.

Women's status has been a subject of debate not only among scholars, but leaders of the Republic as well. While the leaders share some general ideas about the place of women in the Islamic society, they are far from united. In more recent years a divergence of views is more apparent. It is imperative to point out that while government policies concern all women, the regime has paid particular attention to urban middle-class women. This is the group who was better positioned to take advantage of the Shah's reforms.[20] Therefore, the current regime has targeted it more specifically as deviating from Islamic principles.

What are these principles? How have middle-class Iranian women deviated from them? Here again, close observation can reveal that beneath an apparent unity there are conflicting approaches. The united front is primarily concerned with the place of women in society which subsequently defines their role. The zealots, who at the early stages defined a program of action, prefer a completely sex-segregated society in which women are relegated to the private sphere and men reign in the public, with one exception: women are needed in the streets to defend the revolution, denounce imperialism, and rally against any opposition. In an ideal situation, middle-class women would have abandoned their positions in the formal labor market when called upon by the leaders. Zealots have sought to establish a new vice squad to fight symbols of Westernization and *bad-hijabi*, or mal-veiling. The latter refers to any deviation from strict Islamic standards, from bright colors to boutique windows displaying women's clothing.

The regime has recognized that a completely sex segregated society, though desired by some elements, is not practical. Policies have varied due to political and economic exigencies over time. The main reasons are the following:

1. Economic necessities have made women an important part of the labor force. While women were included in the purges of the civil service, it proved impossible to remove them altogether from government jobs. Later, some of those who had been removed from the judiciary, higher education, and media were invited to return.
2. Young pro-regime women with a high school education replaced the purged professionals. This action itself created two unforeseen consequences. Many of these women, though loyal, were blatantly

unqualified for their positions. Secondly, those who managed to maintain their positions while supporting the regime's basic premises about women's role became weary of the zealots' effort to exclude and degrade women and expressed dismay at some of the government's actions, such as the crackdown on bad-hijabi. One such woman is Zahra Rahnavard, wife of a former prime minister and a well-known figure in her own right.

3. Despite pressures, economic incentives, and harsh treatment, many women refused to leave their work and return home.[21] Harassments were not limited to mixed environments; even in all women environments, like schools, working women faced abuse by pro-regime elements. Nevertheless, many stayed. During the summer of 1989, I interviewed 35 professional women about their family and occupational status in Tehran. Their reasons for working varied from economic need to professional fulfilment and even resistance against the regime.

Women have found various ways of resisting the regime, and the government's continuous obsession with women's behavior in public suggests that they have met with less than absolute compliance. Many middle-class women have refused to return to the private domain.

Research Questions and Survey Participants

Discussion and description of private versus public has been conducted primarily by Western anthropologists and the data have been overwhelmingly ethnographic. Two views predominate among the Western observers. One view is that the private is subservient to the public and that women's status is absolutely subservient to that of men.[22] Simpson-Hebert in her article about hospitality among Iranians claims that while women are responsible for preparation of feasts, men are organizers of the events that serve their public and familial interests.[23] Others maintain that this spatial distinction is a result of Western observers imposing their cultural constructs on the mystical world of the Middle Eastern women.[24]

Thus far the bulk of evidence for the existence of a spatial separation of sexes has come from participant observation studies. It is imperative to provide a definition of spatial versus functional distinctions by women themselves. Such research can also lay the foundation for a synthesis of the dichotomies based on any overlap that might be observed. In particular, a survey of Iranian women's attitudes toward the changes in their proper role and place, as the call for a return to the "true" Islamic principles continues, will add a new dimension.

Due to the politicization of gender, it is essential to explore women's attitudes toward power and their relation to it at home and in the public domain. Islamic scripture is very specific about the "inherent" inability of women to handle power or to make rational decisions. Causal links are drawn between woman's weaker physique and her intellectual inferiority. It is further proposed, and taken as a proven fact, that woman's delicate physique and weak mind make her unsuitable for politics and the judiciary.[25] Given women's support for the fundamentalist movement either through direct political participation or indirectly by increased adherence to the Islamic principles in their daily lives, it is important to understand their vision of power, in general, and in particular their own empowerment, as a result of participation in the movement.

An expected consequence of political participation is an increased degree of group solidarity and cohesiveness. Although the majority of women during the Iranian Revolution did not mobilize for furthering women's causes per se, given their participation in the revolution and the controversy surrounding their status in the new system, one can expect an increased degree of feminist consciousness.

Feminism as an ideology of sex role description and political action is arguably a recent Western phenomenon.[26] As such, aspects of it are exported to Third World countries in bits and pieces. There is little systematic evidence as to the nature and extent of this diffusion. But some principles such as equality of the sexes (particularly intellectual equality), women's right to self-determination, and desegregation of the sexes are transferred.

On the other hand, women's pioneering role in the fundamentalist movement and their rejection of Western values have given rise to the proposition that there is another brand of feminism in Muslim countries that is conceptually different from Western feminism. While the exact components of this ideology remain unclear, at least two ideas stand out. In the political scene, women have the right to express their opinions within the framework of the Islamic principles. In family and in the society, sex roles are complementary rather than conflicting and competing. An increased number of women in higher education and in the labor market suggests their support for equality of employment and educational opportunities for women. Therefore, it seems that there are elements of Western feminism combined with the Islamic sex role ascription as part of this Islamic feminism. As far as feminism is concerned, three areas are explored in this study: equality of the sexes, group consciousness, and group solidarity.

Questionnaire items are divided into four scales. A series of descriptive statistics are followed by a graph of the composite of each index.

Answers to four questions are explored:

1. Do Iranian women see a spatial segregation of sexes?
   a. The extent of their support for sex segregation.
2. Do Iranian women perceive a functional duality of sex roles?
   a. The extent of overlaps between these demarcations.
3. Are women intellectually incapable of handling power and making rational decisions?
   a. The extent of women's power at home and in society.
4. Are Iranian women feminist?
   a. The extent of group consciousness among women.

Research Design: A questionnaire with four scales was developed in Persian and English. Two scales deal specifically with woman's place versus her role. Another scale measures women's perception of power and power management. The last scale measures group consciousness and the extent of support for feminist issues.

Previous studies have clearly indicated that Islamic fundamentalism is a middle-class phenomenon. In the intial stages of the revolution all strata of middle-class urban women participated in the movement. Supporters of Islamic fundamentalism came mostly from the middle or lower middle class.[27] Additionally, during the Pahlavi regime educational and occupational opportunities were concentrated in the large urban centers where middle-class women were better situated to take advantage of them. They were also better informed to benefit from legal reforms. At the time of the revolution working women were present in government and business offices of large cities. To the leaders of the revolution, this group symbolized decadence and the usurpation of Islamic principles of the patriarchal family and seclusion. They became the target of a widespread campaign of coercion and intimidation to enforce the new order. Thus, it is plausible to concentrate on the middle-class women of urban areas.

During the summer of 1989, the questionnaire was administered to a sample of women students in two universities in Tehran. Additionally, a leading women magazine, *Zan-e-Rouz*, agreed to publish the questionnaire for their readers to complete and return.[28] The result was a national sample of 1098 responses of which 103 were completed by men. Due to the small number of this group, their responses are not included here. The total number of completed questionnaires by women are 854, of which 54 percent are from Tehran, 20 percent from other major cities, 12 percent from small towns, and the rest unspecified. This is not a random sample, but when compared to characteristics of middle-class women in urban areas as reported in the 1986 national census, this group comes very close as representative of middle-class women.[29]

The majority of respondents were students, followed by housewives, which leaves about 40 percent of the sample as either full-time or part-time employed. In terms of education, 80 percent of respondents had high school or less than high school education. Some 13 percent reported college and higher education. Generally, this sample was young, single or married with small families, and high-school educated. Among those who were employed, the largest numbers were teachers, civil service employees, and secretaries.

Feminine/Masculine Functions: A scale with 7 items measured attitudes toward woman's proper role (see Table 16.1). Calculation of means and standard deviations showed some consistency among respondents with regard to woman's proper place. Two questions in particular dealing with the primacy of man's occupation and the wife's responsibility to support his job (#1 and #2) showed that women agree on the greater importance of a man's job compared to a woman's job. They also agreed that their primary function is motherhood. This does not, however, suggest that they should remain out of the formal job market. An overwhelming majority of 93 percent believed that a woman should emphasize her work as much as her husband's job (#3). The next three questions showed clear support for the functional duality of feminine versus masculine occupations. Therefore masculine occupations such as mechanics are not suitable for women (#5), while teaching is more compatible with her "nature" (#6). These results would support some of the Islamic Republic's policies of sex role allocation, which recognizes and elevates motherhood and housekeeping as woman's primary responsibilities.

The next question was: Are women happy with their current status? This, of course, cannot be specifically and openly addressed in a general questionnaire. Item 7 was designed to provide some indication of women's satisfaction with their status, and the result was that women do not consider their lives easier than men's. Indeed over 81 percent reject this notion. If ambiguities of modern values during the previous regime created discontent,[30] promoting a traditional role for women has not removed the discontent.

Further statistical calculations of this scale showed that the idea of woman as mother is closely linked with the notion of man as breadwinner.

TABLE 16.1   Women's Function: Percentage Distribution

	SA	AS	DS	SD*
1 Women give up their job interfere family	63.6	20.5	7.7	8.2
2 Men's job to bring money, women's family	31.3	31.2	18.3	19.2
3 Woman should emphasize her job as much as his	80.1	12.7	4.7	2.5
4 Woman's job should suit her femininity	63.0	25.4	6.1	5.5
5 Carpentry, mechanics not women's job	69.4	13.6	7.5	9.4
6 Best occupation for women teaching	30.3	33.0	15.3	21.4
7 Women have easier life	5.2	13.4	19.2	62.3

*SA = Strongly Agree, AS = Agree Somewhat, DS = Disagree Somewhat, SD = Strongly Disagree.

Private/Public Spheres: Another scale with 6 questions was designed to measure women's attitudes toward spatial segregation of the sexes (see Table 16.2). Item 8 indicates that 86 percent believe woman's happiness is inside the home regardless of her achievements in the outside world. This reaffirms the findings of the previous scale that housekeeping and motherhood are perceived as women's primary functions and home as their primary domain. But while agreeing on their primary functions, women reject restriction on their options in terms of role and place. They overwhelmingly reject the idea that working women are unfeminine (#9). The majority do not believe that women should stay out of the job market to open up jobs for men (#10), or that girls' education should be limited to training for mothering (#11), or that happiness for girls is in marriage and for boys in education. In other words, women do not see any contradiction in combining their traditional roles with other opportunities. Mothering should not limit their other options. Taken together, results of items 9-11 display women's rejection of spatial seclusion.

According to both custom and Islamic scripture, men are guardians of women, both spiritually and physically. A man's honor is closely linked to the behavior of his womenfolk. To safeguard their honor men prefer to seclude women.[31] Question 13 directly asked women if proud husbands dislike their wives to work. A mean of 2.67 showed that a slight majority of 54 percent report moderate disagreement with this idea. But a standard deviation of 1.12 also suggested that women are not clear about men's preference. The small number of men who responded to this questionnaire were also divided. The result indicates moderate disapproval of this proposal. Altogether respondents clearly reject seclusion for women. Women support sex role specialization but they do not support spatial segregation. This scale supports the results of the previous index that women put emphasis on their nurturing roles as mothers and housewives; it also indicates that they reject seclusion because of these roles. It seems that women support functional duality more than spatial duality.

TABLE 16.2 Women's Place Index: Percentage Distribution

		SA	AS	DS	SD
8	Women's happiness, homemaking, regardless her achievement outside	56.9	29.4	7.2	6.6
9	Woman wants outside job unfeminine	4.8	20.1	13.5	61.6
10	High unemployment, women stay home	19.9	23.9	19.3	36.9
11	Girl's educ. should be suit. for her future roles as mother and housewife	71.1	23.0	15.5	44.4
12	Boys' happiness is in education and girls' in marriage	7.5	14.5	15.7	62.3
13	Proud husband dislikes wife working	17.5	28.6	23.6	30.4

Women and Power: Another scale with 6 items measured women's relation to power (see Table 16.3). This index treats three related issues with regard to women's power. Questions 14 and 15 seek information about women's general idea regarding their ability to make decisions and handle power. Questions 16 and 17 measure practical applications of men's and women's power in the family. Items 18 and 19 measure women's support for Islamic principles of female subordination.

Responses to items 14 and 15 seemed to record contradictory messages. Participants reject the idea that women are incapable of making important decisions (# 14), but 60 percent of them believe that men are more capable of handling power than women. Other statistical measures of these two items (not shown here) indicated that women do not see these points as contradictory. Indeed women reject the notion of being innately deficient but perceive inadequacy in power management. Questions 16 and 17 provide an interesting picture of women's relation to power in the family by overwhelmingly rejecting men's unilateral power in deciding family matters. Shortly after the revolution, the new regime abrogated the Family Protection Law, enacted by the previous regime, and restored men's unilateral right to divorce and their custody of children. Question 17 specifically asks women's opinion about this policy. The results showed women's unanimous disapproval of this policy.

TABLE 16.3   Relation to Power Index: Percentage Distribution

	SA	AS	DS	SD
14 Women incapable making important decisions	5.6	30.1	21.6	42.6
15 Men are more capable in handling power	20.0	39.4	15.8	24.9
16 Father important decision for future children	7.2	26.8	23.8	42.2
17 Father should be guardian in divorce	5.3	7.4	19.3	68.0
18 Women have weaker mental & psychol. capacities due to their weaker physical structures	3.4	6.1	8.2	82.3
19 Women do not have mental strength necessary for politics & judiciary	11.5	19.7	23.9	44.9

Taken together, these four items suggest that at an abstract level women do not see themselves as power-holders and decision-makers. At the family level they strongly reject their subservient position with regard to men's power.

Islamic literature contains references to woman's physical and mental weakness and her emotional instability. For these reasons women are barred from the judiciary and some political positions like presidency. Questions 18 and 19 specifically address these issues and are rejected. Some 92 percent of the respondents with a mean of 3.69 and a standard deviation of .74 refute women's inherent intellectual inferiority. About 70 percent dispute women's intellectual inadequacy for politics and the judiciary. The statistical analysis found a difference between means of 3.69 for #18 and 3.02 for #19; this could be due to the fact that since women are barred from these occupations in Iran, some respondents, addressing #19, were stating the fact rather than their opinion. However, their responses leave no doubt that they strongly disagree with this Islamic principle.

The results for this index imply three points: (1) Women do not concede that they are innately inadequate to handle power and make rational decisions; (2) They agree in general that they are not competent power-holders and decision-makers; thus, in practical matters they relegate decision-making to men; (3) With regard to family matters, however, men's unilateral decision-making does not receive women's support. The apparent inconsistency between the first point and the last two is due to the difference between theory and practice. Women reject the notion that they are ill-equipped to hold power, but they realize that men are power-holders and make important decisions. This also could be due to socialization. Men are socialized to hold power and have historically been the decision-makers. Women may recognize this and prefer to allow them to continue.

This reluctant abdication of their right does not, however, extend into family matters. Here, in practical matters such as the future of children, women want their right to participate in decision-making. One explanation is that respondents interpret power in political and administrative terms.

Feminism: A scale with 7 items designed to gauge women's attitudes on feminist issues ranging from financial and educational opportunities for women to solidarity and group consciousness provides surprising results (see Table 16.4).

In the statistical analysis, three items measuring equalitarian relationships between the sexes in the family and society received positive responses from the participants. The first item asks a general question about equality between the sexes. The results show an affirmative response by the majority of the sample. Equality of education for boys and girls measured by item 21 is supported by 72 percent of the respondents. Equalitarian relations in household responsibilities, measured by item 22, also received strong support from the respondents. Similarly, early marriage of girls measured by item 24 is strongly rejected. Taken together these items show that women support some aspects of gender equality at the family level.

Anthropological studies have recorded group support and cohesiveness among women in the extended family or community in the Middle Eastern societies.[32] At the same time, traditional hostility among the in-laws and fear of polygamous marriage can lead to lack of trust and adversary relations among women. The present study attempted to measure the degree of conscious support, reliance, and trust among women, and the extent to which practical behavior translates into a collective consciousness of solidarity with other women. The three items that are designed to measure group consciousness, trust, and solidarity suggest a moderate level of cognitive feminism. The majority of the sample (60 percent) reject adversary relationships among women, measured by item 24 (with a mean of 2.85). They also dispute the statement in question 25 that women are not trustworthy (with a mean of 2.9). The last item, 26 (with a mean of 2.82) relates a moderate degree of solidarity among the sample. Since all of these means are within a 95 percent range of the population mean, one can detect some level of cognitive solidarity among the middle-class urban women of Iran. Further statistical tests supported the descriptive statistics that urban middle-class Iranian women express some degree of feminism as measured by familial equality between the sexes and group solidarity.

TABLE 16.4   Feminism Index: Percentage Distribution

		SA	*AS*	*DS*	*SD*
20	Women can perform any job men do	19.2	41.5	27.4	11.9
21	Educational materials girls = boys	62.4	16.0	9.0	12.6
22	Fair to expect husband help with chores	54.8	30.9	9.9	4.4
23	Best for girls to marry early	5.5	10.6	14.1	69.8
24	Worst enemies of women are other women	16.6	23.0	19.6	40.8
25	Cannot trust a woman with a secret	12.7	26.4	18.9	42.0
26	Generally no solidarity among women	11.6	31.4	19.9	37.1

Re-testing Some Old Hypotheses: It has been suggested that women's socio-economic status affects their degree of feminism, acceptance of gender equality, and in general their perception of sex roles. A series of analyses of variance were conducted to measure the degree of association between respondents' education, occupation, marital status, age, and place of residence, and the four indexes tested here. The results are presented in Table 16.5.

TABLE 16.5 Analysis of Variance (ANOVA)

	Function	Place	Power	Feminism
Education	38.39	72.85	16.5	12.58
	p = .03	p = .01	p = .2	p = .3
Employment	89.40	500.0	126.8	.008
	p = .00	p = .00	p = .00	p = .9
Marital status	41.92	298.0	92.58	6.77
	p = .02	p = .00	p = .00	p = .4
Age	4.46	34.03	34.57	28.9
	p = .3	p = .9	p = .1	p = .1
Residence	9.95	.95	110.0	24.0
	p = .5	p = .9	p = .01	p = .36

This procedure treats each status variable, such as education, as an independent variable and tests its effect on each dependent variable, that is, respondents' attitude toward their role. Statistically significant relationship allows generalization from the sample to the population, suggesting that the same relationship exists in the population. As Table 16.5 shows, education influences women's participation of their proper role and place. It fails, however, to show a significant relationship with women's relation to power and their feminist consciousness. Considering the youth and moderate education of this sample, a lack of relationship between education and feminist consciousness challenges others' findings. Women's employment status influences their perception of feminine and masculine functions and their attitudes toward spatial restriction. It also positively contributes to a sense of empowerment (ANOVA = 200). But as far as feminism is concerned, employment shows no relationship with feminist consciousness.

A surprising result is the significant contribution of marital status to women's perception of sex roles. Analysis of variance between marital status and attitudes toward functional duality reports a positive and strong relationship. A stronger ANOVA of 500 is observed between this status indicator and the place index. Marital status affects rejection of sex segregation. This variable also affects women's relation to power and their own empowerment. As in previous indicators, however, marital status shows no significant relationship with feminism.

Respondents' age also does not contribute to our understanding of variations in their attitudes. Given the general youth of this sample, this result is not surprising. Neither does place of residence further our understanding of their attitudes. The only significant relationship observed here is between place of residence and relation to power. Neither age nor residence relay significant relationship with feminist attitudes. Indeed, none of the status variables seems to affect women's degree of support for feminist issues. Feminism as measured here receives positive support from the sample. Nevertheless, neither education nor employment nor any other indicators of respondents' characteristics show any relationship with feminism.

Conclusions

The main object of this research was to explore women's perception of spatial versus functional duality of sex roles within the context of Islamic fundamentalism in Iran. Are these theoretical constructs supported by women's cognitive recognition? The result shows that women identify functional duality to be more salient than spatial segregation. They clearly identify separate functions for men and women and recognize feminine functions as women's primary responsibilities. Recognizing that, they then reject restriction on their opportunities in the job market. Spatial segregation as measured here is clearly rejected by the respondents.

With regard to the dichotomies, the findings identify four areas: (1) Woman's nurturing capacity dictates her familial obligation as her primary responsibility; (2) This responsibility is not ground for her spatial seclusion; (3) Feminine occupations are recommended as women's outlet in the labor market; (4) Consequently, functional duality is recognized and approved more readily than spatial duality.

The result for women's relation to power and their capacity for rational judgement indicates two points: (a) rejection of women's intellectual inferiority; and (b) their belief in men's superior capacity to make important decisions and hold power. While there is some support for their reluctance to assume power there is strong evidence that they believe men are better decision-makers. One can conclude that Iranian women have not internalized the ideology rationalizing patriarchy, but have been socialized to accept it as practical.

As far as their power in the family is concerned, we have clear indication as to where women stand. The Islamic patriarchy that defines man as the ultimate decision-maker in the family is challenged and rejected. It is important to point out that this study did not address the legitimacy of man as the head of household. Numerous interviews and contacts have convinced this observer that Iranian women do not question the authority of man as the head of household. Rather these findings suggest that man's unilateral power is questioned and woman's right in decision-making at the family level is recognized.

With regard to feminism, three specific areas were measured: gender equality at the family level, group consciousness, and group solidarity. As measured here, middle-class Iranian women display a substantial degree of feminism by supporting familial gender equality, group consciousness, and group solidarity.

To explain this unanimous display of feminism the effect of status predictors on feminism were explored. The result did not show variations in terms of education or employment of the respondents. This can be due to the fact that feminism as measured here is so universally of concern to women and so elementary that women in Iran, regardless of their education and employment, support these basic rights. The experience of participating in the revolution can also foster a sense of solidarity and support for basic equal rights of the sexes. Finally, overshadowed by attention to anti-women rhetorics of the regime, the efforts of enlightened clergy and women activists inside the regime are obscured. The latter promote women's rights within the framework of Islamic doctrine presenting women as competent and dignified members of the umma. Woman's role delineated by her reproductive capacity is focused around the family and supportive services to men's activities. This type of feminism focuses on a functional sex role model which to some extent also delineates each sex's place in the society.[33] All of these contribute to support for women's equal rights in the family and a sense of common bonds and shared interest.

In sum, the middle-class Iranian women who participated in the Islamic revolution have not internalized the gender identity that the Republic has decreed for them. Notwithstanding years of mass propaganda and restrictive policies they reaffirm their right to occupy the public space as they choose. This clearly shows that a sex segregated ideal society envisioned by the revolutionary leaders has failed to enlist the middle-class women's support. While Islamic identity politics has reaffirmed their belief in complementary sex roles in society and family, it has failed to justify men's right to dictate women's public behavior. This study investigated women's response to an ideal Islamic society, promised by the revolution, in which women know their proper place. Women have clearly declared that their place is where they choose it to be—not where it is decreed to be. They know their places.

Notes

I wish to express my gratitude to the editorial board of *Zan-e-Rouz* for their sincere cooperation with the survey.

1. Cynthia Epstein, *Deceptive Distinctions* (New Haven: Yale University Press, 1988), p. 14.

2. See Rebecca Klatch, "Coalition and Conflict Among Women of the New Right," *Signs* 4 (1988):671-694, and in this volume.

3. C. Henning, "Canon Law and the Battle of the Sexes," in Rosemary Ruether (ed.), *Religion and Sexism* (New York: Simon and Schuster, 1974).

4. Ruether (ed.), *Religion and Sexism*.

5. Susan Marshall and R. Stokes, "Tradition and the Veil: Female Status in Tunisia and Algeria," *The Journal of Modern African Studies* 4 (1981):625-646; E. White, "Legal Reforms as an Indicator of Women's Status in Muslim Nations," in Lois Beck and Nikki Keddie (eds.), *Women in the Muslim World* (Cambridge: Harvard University Press, 1978).

6. For an elaboration, see Shahin Gerami, "Privatization of Women's Role in the Islamic Republic of Iran," in M. Benavides and R. Daley (eds.), *Religion and Political Power* (Albany: State University of New York Press, 1989).

7. Hossain refers to *mardana* (men's sections) and *zanana* (women's section) in Bengali culture. These words are Farsi and used in the same manner in Iran, too. See Rokeya Shakhawat Hossain, *Sultana's Dream* (New York: The Feminist Press, 1988).

8. Rifat Hassan, "Equal Before Allah?: Woman-Man Equality in the Islamic Tradition," *Harvard Divinity Bulletin* 2 (1987):2-7.

9. Murtiza Muttahari, *Nizam-i Huguqi zan dar Islam* (Women's Right in Islam) (Tehran: Islamic Press, 1359 [1980]).

10. Nadia H. Youssef, *Women and Work in Developing Societies* (Berkeley: Institute of International Studies, University of California, 1974).

11. Shahin Gerami, "Women's Public Power in Muslim and Catholic Countries," unpublished, presented at the meeting of Society for Study of Social Problems, 1988.

12. B. Hargrove, et al., "Religion and Changing Role of Women," *Annals, AAPSS* (480) (1985):117-131.

13. N. Ramazani, "Arab Women in the Gulf," *The Middle East Journal* 2 (1985):258-276; L. Bahry, "The New Saudi Woman: Modernizing in an Islamic Framework," *The Middle East Journal* 4 (1982):502-515.

14. C. Kagitcibasi, "Status of Women in Turkey: Cross-Cultural Perspective," *International Journal of Middle East Studies* 18 (1986), p. 487.

15. Y. Ibrahim, "Inside Iran's Cultural Revolution," *New York Times*, 23 July 1982, p. 4, and 18 April 1983, p. 2.

16. El Guindi and Williams make the same point, but use the word "veil" nonetheless. F. El Guindi, "Veiling Infitah with Muslim Ethic: Egypt's Contemporary Islamic Movement," *Social Problems* 4 (1981):465-485; J. Williams, "A Return to the Veil in Egypt," *Middle East Review* 3 (1979):49-54.

17. This was the explicit policy of the University of Tehran in 1985.

18. World Bank, *World Tables 1987* (Washington, D.C.: Oxford University Press, 1988).

19. Azar Tabari and Nahid Yeganeh (eds.), *In the Shadow of Islam: The Women's Movement in Iran* (London: Zed Press, 1982).

20. Val Moghadam, "Women, Work, and Ideology in the Islamic Republic," *International Journal of Middle East Studies* 2 (1988):221-243.

21. *Ibid.*

22. Mary Douglas, *Natural Symbols: Explorations in Cosmology* (New York: Random House, 1970).

23. M. Simpson-Hebert, "Women, Food and Hospitality in Iranian Society" in Angeloni (ed.), *Anthropology* (Guildford: Dushkin Publishing Group, 1990).

24. Cynthia Nelson, "Public and Private Politics: Women in the Middle Eastern World," *American Ethnologist* 3 (1974):551-565.

25. Muttahari, *Nizam-i Huguqi zan dar Islam.*

26. Karen Offen, "Defining Feminism: A Comparative Historical Approach," *Sign* 1 (1988):119-157.

27. Azar Tabari, "Islam and the Struggle for Emancipation for Iranian Women," in Azar Tabari and Nahid Yeganeh (eds.), *In the Shadow of Islam: The Women's Movement in Iran;* Anne Betteridge, "To Veil or Not to Veil: A Matter of Protest or Policy," in Guity Nashat (ed.), *Women and Revolution in Iran* (Boulder, CO: Westview Press, 1983).

28. Gerami, "Privatization of Women's Role."

29. *Census of Iranian Population* (Tehran: Statistical Center, 1987). Furthermore, means and standard errors calculated for all variables indicate a probability of .05 that this sample may not be within 95 percent range of the population mean.

30. Michael M. J. Fischer, "On the Changing Concept and Position of Persian Women," in Lois Beck and Nikki Keddie (eds.), *Women in the Muslim World* (Cambridge: Harvard University Press, 1978).

31. Lila Abu-Lughod, *Veiled Sentiments* (Berkeley: University of California Press, 1986).

32. Erika Friedl, *Women of Deh Koh* (Washington, DC: Smithsonian Institution Press, 1989).

33. International Institute for Adult Literacy, n.d, "Woman's Place" (Tehran, mimeograph).

17

Paradoxical Politics: Gender Politics Among Newly Orthodox Jewish Women in the United States

Debra Renee Kaufman

Introduction

One issue emerging in this book on identity politics and women is how to analyze and evaluate the relationship between the worldwide rise of fundamentalist identities (Christian, Jewish, Islamist) and the gender politics of a feminist identity. At first, there appears to be little to discuss, as such identities are politically and theoretically incompatible. Yet recent theoretical trends suggest that this might too easily overlook the complexities of identity formation in general, and the potential for ambiguities, if not contradictions, in the specification of either a fundamentalist or a feminist identity over the life course.

The formation of a religious or a gender identity involves power-laden negotiations between the "self" and the "other." Both are developed within the constraints of culturally available meanings and specific power constraints and conditions. As Dorinne Kondo asserts, the identities that make up our concepts of self may be more like "strategic assertions" rather than "fixed essences."[1] Neither a fundamentalist nor a feminist identity is "fixed," as both are constructed and emergent. Moreover, neither a fundamentalist nor a feminist discourse is limited to just one invariant socio-historical tradition or one set of political possibilities. In this chapter, I shall explore more fully some of the counter-intuitive aspects of the gender identity politics of a non-Christian subset of fundamentalist women in the United States (newly Orthodox Jewish women) and compare and contrast their politics to those of contemporary radical, cultural feminists.[2]

In each chapter in this book we see how women are central to the construction of religious and ethnic identities. Jewish Orthodoxy is no exception. As women do in other fundamentalist traditions, orthodox Jewish women mark religious/ethnic boundaries (only children born of a Jewish mother are considered Jewish) and by their behavior and dress signify who belongs to the collectivity and who does not. They are seen as the cultural carriers of orthodoxy and are expected to transmit that heritage to future generations.[3] As with other fundamentalist groups,[4] gender politics, and consequently gender identity, are at the heart of Jewish orthodoxy.

Historical Backdrop to the Orthodox Jewish Revival: Youth and Its Discontents

The return to fundamentalist Biblical religion among the New Christian right in America has been accompanied, with less media attention, by a renewed interest in Jewish orthodoxy.[5] And, while this phenomenon of "return," as it is translated from the Hebrew, is of interest in general, the turn to orthodoxy, or for that matter any patriarchal religious tradition among women, in the closing decades of the twentieth century, is particularly intriguing.

The 1960s marked a period of social turbulence in the United States— rapid technological advances, the full emergence of the civil rights movement, urban riots, the assassinations of the Kennedy brothers, Malcolm X, Martin Luther King, anti-war protests, the beginnings of the women's movement, racial pride among Blacks, flower-children, drug culture, and strong anti-establishment feelings, particularly among young people. The countercultural upheavals of the 1960s gave birth to an upsurge of cults, quasi-religious therapeutic movements as well as an evangelical and neo-pentecostal revival. Jewish Orthodoxy, unfashionable and outmoded throughout the 1950s and into the 1960s participated in this neo-orthodox revival and "new" religious ferment.

The links between this heightened spirituality and the counterculture are many. The "hippie" movement, as the counterculture has often been referred to, was characterized both by its anti-rational thrust and its rejection of conventional values, particularly those that represented a technocratic, bureaucratic society dependent on science as the primary source of truth.[6] The countercultural rejection took many forms: expressed at times through drugs, or politics, or music. At times the values were contradictory—"tuning in, turning on, and dropping out" versus political struggle against racism, sexism, poverty and war. At times God was declared dead, at other times only moribund, and sometimes rediscovered. Among the newly orthodox women in my study, more than two-thirds (104) were involved in one form or another of the countercultural turbulence of the sixties and seventies.

Although there had been neo-orthodox revivals before the counterculture, the "hippies" attraction to such movements recast and popularized them. The *ba'al teshuvah* (contemporary orthodox revival) movement in America originated in this period of "hippie" religious sentiment.[7]

The Study

The data reported in this chapter reflect in-depth interviews conducted with 150 newly orthodox Jewish women (called *ba'alot teshuvah* in Hebrew) in the mid-1980s, in five major urban areas across the United States.[8] Interviews with leading rabbis, lay community leaders, and known ba'alot teshuvah in each of five major urban cities across the United States helped locate newly orthodox women within three identifiable frameworks in contemporary orthodoxy—modern orthodox (25), strictly orthodox (40), and ultra-orthodox (85).[9] While all orthodox Jews acknowledge that *Halakha* (Jewish law) is basic and essential to Judaism, they vary in their style of dress, their relationship to the secular world, and their interpretation of some laws, with modern orthodox being the most "liberal," and ultra-orthodox the most "stringent."

Although it seems obvious why men might be drawn to religious communities steeped in patriarchal tradition and staunchly opposed to any changes in the clear sex-segregation of religious roles, it is much more difficult to explain women's attraction. But what is most puzzling is that although many ba'alot teshuvah openly reject feminism or what they perceive feminism to represent and advocate, they simultaneously maintain a gender consciousness that resonates with some aspects of contemporary and past feminist ideology. Like some feminists, these newly orthodox Jewish women celebrate the female, her life-cycle experiences and feminine attributes, however, they eschew feminist politics by choosing to enhance the status of women and to protect them as a group within the boundaries of patriarchal religion and social structure.[10]

Sixty-six percent of the women I interviewed (99) were in their late teens and early to middle twenties in the decade between 1966 and 1976. Therefore, most of the women in this study began their journeys toward orthodoxy in their youth during the counterculture, or in its wake. Of these women, almost seventy-one percent (70) identified with the "hippie" counterculture of the sixties and early seventies. That is, they either had ties to the seemingly apolitical lifestyles associated with the counterculture (such as drugs, music, dress) or to radical political organizations and protests. Few characterized themselves as leaders in any of the groups of which they were a part. Although some began their protest as teenagers in high school, most were involved during their college years. The most common radical politics among this group included civil rights demonstrations, university protests, marches, and/or anti-Vietnam protests, and, for a few, farm protests.

Twenty-five women claimed to have identified with and/or participated in the women's movement. Ten had been actively involved in feminist consciousness raising groups. Although twelve women were active in the pro-choice campaigns of the early seventies, most of the women under study described themselves during their searching years as pro-choice and claimed that certainly in appearance they were "liberated" women. Their embracing of orthodoxy, long before most even believed in it, demanded that they give up the freedom many of them had come to associate with jeans/pants and little underwear. Although the drastic change in their lifestyles at first seems contradictory, on closer observation, their change from radical left to radical right appears congruent with the most important issues these women faced at that stage of their lives.

Those women who had identified with the women's movement, for instance, eventually were disappointed by what they perceived to be the concerns of the early women's movement. For many, the focus on individual rights and personal independence left the larger issues of "how to live one's life" in a meaningful manner unformulated. One woman elaborates on this theme:

> I was in a feminist consciousness raising group. We talked a good deal about our problems ... about being women, students, lovers, and working women. ... We talked about whatever it was that was going on in our lives at that time, but we never really were able to formulate anything beyond or larger than ourselves. ... We were good at defining the negatives. ...

Those attracted to other politically liberal causes found that, both as women and as whites, they felt marginalized. For instance, women who had been involved in "left politics," felt, in their words, that "men ran the show ... we ran off the leaflets and made the coffee." Others, by the end of the sixties, no longer felt "comfortable" as whites and as Jews, in the Civil Rights movement.[11] Other studies of that same period corroborate some of these sentiments. For instance, in their study of the Jesus Movement, Richardson, Stewart, and Simmonds note that former political activists felt that the Civil Rights movement had excluded whites by the end of the sixties.[12]

Many of these ba'alot teshuvah describe the late sixties and early to mid-seventies as a time of growing disillusionment and frustration for them. They describe themselves as concerned about the Draft, the War in Vietnam and later, for some, the Watergate scandal and the Kent State University killings. As one woman put it: "You know, all the 'macho' issues." Disillusioned, feeling marginal, and perhaps as Richardson, Stewart and Simmonds note, shocked at a state that was willing to kill its children, either abroad or at home, forty-nine of these self-identified countercultural women moved from secular, political, activist identities to Jewish orthodoxy. Twenty-one detoured on their way to Jewish orthodoxy by joining either one of the "new" religious or one of the personal growth movements of the late sixties and early seventies.

Overall, over one-third of all the ba'alot teshuvah joined or participated in the "new" religious or quasi-religious therapy movements of the sixties and seventies, ranging from the oriental/mystical traditions (such as Zen, transcendental meditation, Buddhism, Hinduism, Taoism, sufism, and yoga) to the personal growth movements (such as est or scientology). Yet despite the attraction, all fifty-four of those who had joined or participated in "new" religious, or quasi-religious therapy or personal growth movements, found them disappointing.

Reflecting back on those years, the majority of those involved in Eastern mystical groups (30) felt that such groups were too focused on the self through "inner spiritual awakening" and "intrapsychic" consciousness, and too unfocused on fixed moral codes as a guide for their everyday behavior. One woman referred to her early seventies experiences with transcendental meditation as if it were "a great big organized be-in." She remembers that "Something was missing, I didn't want to be, I wanted to do. I wanted to feel I could make decisions that would lead to 'right' actions." The focus on self and "inner consciousness" troubled many who had become involved in quasi-religious therapy, therapeutic, and human potential movements as well. The relativistic and subjective moral systems of monistic movements, and the predominant focus on inner consciousness in the quasi-religious therapy groups,[13] forced many of these women to continue searching for a coherent system of beliefs and a stable moral community meaningful to them.

For the remainder of the ba'alot teshuvah, that is, even for those who were not politically aware during the sixties, or who had come into their young adult years in the late seventies, and/or who were not from upwardly mobile, middle-class families, similar themes emerged: their search for a moral community of both public and private virtue, and, above all, their need for a moral framework in which to make decisions. The need, as one woman put it, for "official values." Jewish orthodoxy provided these women with clear ethical guidelines and both historic and transcendental ties. Moreover, it was a tradition with which many of them were, if not knowledgeable, familiar.

Findings

Most ba'alot teshuvah describe themselves as trying to make moral sense of their lives. As they told their stories of return, women reported a common experience: that their lives had been spiritually empty and without purpose before their return. Regardless of age, virtually all women suggest that they were "searching." Some labeled that quest a "journey homeward." I was to find some irony in that designation, for although it initially implied that they were seeking their roots as Jews, it also served as a metaphor for what orthodoxy meant to them—home, family and a moral community with clear dictates about how to live both one's public and private life. Their "return" to orthodoxy, in some fundamental way, constitutes a protest against secular society which many characterized as masculine in orientation and organization.

In this context of a search for guidelines, the very admission that orthodoxy may not be the literally revealed word of God destroys orthodoxy's claims to truth, and therefore, to the certainty about guidelines it offers for moral, ethical, and meaningful decision making. Therefore accommodations to the law which are commonly found in the more "progressive" wings of Judaism (Reform, Reconstructionist, Conservative), while serving some contemporary needs, also serve to undermine any claim to absolute authority.

However, there is more to orthodoxy's appeal than moral certitude. What maintains these ba'alot teshuvah's commitment was couched in terms of women's personal needs. For many, one of the most troubling qualities of contemporary living (most realized perhaps in the fragmentation of a postmodern context) was expressed as the culture's confusion and ambivalence toward women, women's sexuality, family and gender roles. Even for those who had been part of the women's movement, many did not feel that there was a coherent set of social norms governing expectations about gender roles. On the contrary, they believed that the dismantling of many of the gender-related norms, spurred by the women's movement, often left women more vulnerable to men's manipulation than ever before. Most felt this was particularly true in the area of sexuality.[14] One young woman noted:

I needed something that spoke to me directly about being a woman ... decisions about my sexuality, for instance. I had had enough of one night stands ... orgasm alone was just that, an orgasm—masturbation could and did fulfill the same function. I didn't want moralizing, I wanted to know how sexuality would fit into my life, you know over the long haul. Orthodoxy had an answer to that ... when I learned about the family purity laws ... they immediately made sense to me. In fact, my boyfriend and I practiced *taharat hamishpacha* [family purity laws, regulating sexuality and requiring a two-week abstinence each month during the woman's menstrual cycle] while we were living together. Neither of us could take our sexuality or me for granted.

A recently engaged woman expressed her search for familial values in a community which supports those values in these terms:

Both my fiancé and I are on the job market together. Since we have become orthodox we have made some very important decisions. We are looking for jobs which give both of us real flexibility. I mean we want time for ourselves and time for family in our lives. An orthodox life-style promotes that—family comes first. It is clear to both of us right from the beginning that our family life will have priority over everything else we do. Menachem [fiance's fictitious name] will be a part of a community that enforces that commitment and I will be part of a community that makes that commitment real.

"You know," volunteered one older, divorced woman

Orthodoxy provides a game plan. At first you accept a whole system, letter perfect, that has survived thousands of years. Yet, even though it has such history it speaks directly to you on a day to day, week to week, season to season basis. It speaks to you about the most personal things in your life—the way to go about dealing with others, your friends, your husband, your children, even how to go about having sex.

Interestingly, these women claim that their "return" to the patriarchal setting of orthodoxy put them in touch with their own bodies, in control of their own sexuality, and in a position to value the so-called feminine virtues of nurturance, mutuality, family, and motherhood. Indeed, they describe orthodoxy as "feminine in principle," correlating that which is associated with the female in orthodoxy with the spiritual and sacred meaning of life. It is in orthodox Judaism, they assert, that they have found their identities as women. "You know," says one unmarried twenty-three year old, "I think this is the first time in my life I have felt really good about being a woman."

The specialness of woman and the importance of her sphere of activity were stressed throughout the interviews and often juxtaposed to a rather rigid conception of what they described as feminism. The majority of these women define feminism as a movement which dismisses differences between men and women and focuses on the world of work, where equal pay is the most important issue. Most felt that the priorities set by feminists neglected the family and what they believed to be important feminine values. In general, these women believed they had gained a new dignity through their orthodoxy and especially through their roles in the family, a pride they felt feminists either disregarded or devalued.

The ba'alot teshuvah share the "official" patriarchal belief system of orthodox Judaism and a belief system that emerges organically from their everyday lives as women in a highly sex-segregated community. They believe that community is critical if orthodox Jewish life is to be preserved.[15] For them, female activities and systems of meaning are as vital to orthodox Judaism as are men's. They do not see their sphere as inferior, but rather as a place where they are free to create their own forms of personal, social, intellectual, and, at times, political relationships. Whether intentional or not, sex-segregated living seems to provide these women with the resources on which they can build a community of meaning and action. By accepting and elaborating on the symbols and expectations associated with gender difference, these ba'alot teshuvah claim they have some control over their sexuality and marital lives. They seem to transcend the domestic limits set by patriarchal living, not by entering a man's world, but by creating a world of their own. Awareness of gender hierarchy and empowerment issues are less focused for these newly orthodox women in such a sex-segregated environment. The solidarity, self-esteem, and strength they receive from this world reinforces them in their celebration of difference and woman-centered values.

Comparisons Between Newly Orthodox Jewish Women and Radical Feminists

Both newly orthodox Jewish women and some contemporary feminists, despite radically different politics, argue for celebrating women's culture and women's "unique" biological, emotional, temperamental, psychological, and spiritual qualities. For both newly orthodox Jewish women and some contemporary radical feminists, the male-defined culture of secular society typically is seen as a source of social problems: war, violence, and aggression. The radical feminism referred to in this chapter is described by Allison Jaggar as sparked by the "special experiences of a relatively small group of predominantly white, middle-class, college-educated, American women in the late 1960s." However, writes Jaggar, since its inception radical feminism has undergone some critical changes. In general, younger radical feminists are no longer as active in left organizations nor are they influenced as much by Marxist categories. Indeed, argues Jaggar, they are not "identified by adherence to an explicit and systematic political theory."[16] She notes:

> Instead, they are part of a grass-roots movement, a flourishing women's culture concerned with providing feminist alternatives in literature, music, spirituality, health services, sexuality, even in employment and technology. ... Because of the nature of their political practice, some of those whom I identify as radical feminists might now prefer to call themselves cultural feminists or lesbian feminists.[17]

It is to the more contemporary radical feminist movement and to the cultural radical feminists that the ba'alot teshuvah are compared in this section. Drawing on the works of such writers as Mary Daly and Susan Griffin, Jaggar concludes:

> The contemporary radical feminist movement is characterized by a general celebration of womanhood, a striking contrast to the devaluation of women that pervades the larger society. This celebration takes many forms. Women's achievements are honored; women's culture is enjoyed; women's spirituality is developed; lesbianism is the preferred expression of sexuality. ... Women's special closeness with nature is believed to give women special ways of knowing and conceiving the world. Radical feminists reject what they see as the excessive masculine reliance on reason, and instead emphasize feeling, emotion and nonverbal communication.[18]

Ynestra King supports Jaggar's characterization of radical feminists by suggesting that there are essentially two schools: radical rationalist feminists who repudiate the woman/nature connection and radical cultural feminists who celebrate the woman/nature connection. She writes: "The major strength of cultural feminism is that it is a deeply woman-identified movement. It celebrates what is distinct about women, challenging male culture rather than strategizing to become part of it."[19]

The contemporary radical feminists, Jaggar considers, believe that women are closer to nature than men. Jane Alpert describes the qualities unique to women in the following: "Feminist culture is based on what is best and strongest in women ... the qualities coming to the fore are the same ones a mother projects in the best kind of nurturing relationship to a child: empathy, intuitiveness, adaptability, awareness of growth ... ."[20]

In sum then, the radical feminists to whom Jaggar and King refer emphasize and celebrate the biological and psychological differences between the sexes wishing to develop new values based on women's traditional culture. In general, however, radical cultural feminists tend to ignore the complex, multidimensional and historically divergent life situations of women. Radical cultural feminists frame their understanding of human nature, and, consequently their politics, in an ahistorical context.

Not unlike many of these contemporary radical cultural feminists, the ba'alot teshuvah frame their understanding of gender differences in an essentialist framework as well. They, like radical cultural feminists, appear to attack those aspects of liberal patriarchy which focus on acquisitive individualism, self-indulgence, and a lack of value consensus (other than individual rights).[21] For the radical cultural feminists described by Jaggar and King and the newly orthodox Jewish women in my study, self-identity is not independent of separatist and sex-segregated social structure. However, unlike the radical cultural feminists, while many newly orthodox Jewish women acknowledge that secular culture and masculinist culture are essentially the same, they do not associate a masculine ethos with orthodox Judaism. Rather, they insist that Jewish orthodoxy is "feminine in principle." They hold this belief despite the fact that Jewish orthodoxy has maintained a religious-legal system that supports only heterosexual marriage, recognizes only the husband's right to divorce and leaves public religious leadership and devotion only in the hands of men.

As noted earlier, Orthodox Judaism's very attraction to these ba'alot teshuvah is that its moral certitude is embodied in the inviolability of

Jewish law. Therefore, to use their newly found collective female identity to radically transform any of the ritual or law would undermine orthodoxy's authority, certainty and appeal. Therefore, these women do not challenge male hegemony in the public, legal community that is identified as Jewish orthodoxy (the world of synagogue and study). They accept the very premise of orthodoxy which places men at the center of the religious community as rabbis, leaders, and as those who study and interpret the heart of orthodoxy—religious law. They do not explicitly acknowledge that the "feminine" virtues they celebrate also help to maintain a gendered religious division of labor. In this sense, they do not use their gender identity for confrontational politics with patriarchy.

The newly orthodox Jewish women derive a great deal of strength from their highly sex-segregated living. Women-centered support groups define and reinforce their sense of identity and worth. Significantly, Jaggar notes that a distinctive feature of radical feminist strategy for social change is to extol separate and autonomous women's organizations as the best means to accomplish women's liberation. As such, claims Jaggar, radical feminists tend to focus their energies into developing alternative social arrangements, rather than organizing direct confrontations with patriarchy.[22]

Like women-centered feminists, many ba'alot teshuvah and, indeed, other women of the new religious Right in America, celebrate gender differences. For many radical cultural feminists and for these ba'alot teshuvah, women represent a source of special strength, knowledge and power. Jaggar contends that radical feminists give "special value to women's reproductive functions and to the psychological characteristics that have distinguished women and men."[23] So, too, many of the ultra-Orthodox ba'alot teshuvah claim that there are natural differences between the sexes, and that women's superior moral sensibilities arise from their greater intimacy with the everyday physical world.

There are, however, clear differences between newly orthodox Jewish women and the radical feminists to whom Jaggar refers. Significant differences exist in the ways those radical feminists and the ba'alot teshuvah develop their feminist and feminine identities. The radical feminists *choose* sex-segregation as a way of resisting male dominance and as a way of shaping society. Sex-segregation and separatist institutions are a result of their feminist demands to be autonomous. The ba'alot teshuvah accommodate themselves to sex-segregated living established by patriarchal tradition. Therefore, the latter develop a female consciousness limited by the parameters of patriarchy. The former develop a feminist consciousness shaped by their resistance to patriarchy. Both newly orthodox Jewish women and radical feminists emphasize the significance of sexuality, procreation, and mothering, but in significantly different ways. Where radical feminists often challenge the heterosexual and patriarchal definitions of sexuality and maternity, the ba'alot teshuvah do not. Radical feminists politicize the reproductive sphere, believing that it determines how economic production, as well as other forms of culture, are organized.[24] The ba'alot teshuvah have no analogous understanding of the politics of sexuality. They reclaim the value of sexuality and procreative practices, but within the limits of patriarchal definition.

Gender Identity Politics and Fundamentalism

Newly orthodox Jewish women emphasize their uniqueness and difference from men in their efforts to rectify what they see as injustices and failures within liberal patriarchy to provide a clear set of moral values (other than those related to individual rights) and to bring public remedy to private injustices, especially those that exist between men and women. It would be too facile to describe the "return" of these contemporary women to religious orthodoxy as simply reactionary, or merely as their search for order, stability, and security in a world bereft of overarching standards. Explanations must also include their perceptions of how familial and gender-role experiences have directed that search as well. Indeed, the burgeoning literature on wife abuse, child abuse and rape within marriage reveals many of the stresses in contemporary familial living.[25]

There is the growing recognition that liberal feminism (at least as a popular movement) may have failed a significant number of women because it has not been able to develop a "politics of the personal," particularly for heterosexual women amid the destabilized family and work conditions of the past few decades.[26] For instance, vigorous legislative reforms aimed at promoting gender equality often fail to bring about real changes in the private arena of life, most particularly, in the role behavior of men.[27]

Although these women selectively adopt and even incorporate "protofeminist" attitudes and values into their familial lives, their female-consciousness is limited, at best, to mild reformist tactics and most certainly to concerns of only orthodox, heterosexual, Jewish women. Since these women's most important roles involve their functions as wives and mothers, unmarried, divorced, widowed, separated, and childless women face clear problems within such communities. Like many of the radical cultural feminists described earlier, the ba'alot teshuvah approach their gender politics from an ahistorical and essentialist framework characterizing all women as similar in needs and motivations. Furthermore, while Jewish orthodoxy may provide them with a woman-centered identity and communal recognition of the importance of female-linked practices and symbols, newly orthodox women lack any power to change the social structural arrangements which reinforce essentialist formulations which become, by definition, unchangeable and therefore potentially repressive. These newly orthodox Jewish women differ markedly from feminists in that they argue their identity politics within the boundaries of patriarchal religious definition. They do not challenge patriarchal politics either sociologically or theologically.

Conclusions

Gender identity and consequently gender politics are at the center of the practice of Jewish orthodoxy. As with other fundamentalist movements, women mark the boundaries of the group and are considered the carriers and transmitters of the tradition. Women not only produce religious differences, but their behavior signifies who belongs to the collectivity and who does not. But identities are negotiated as well as constrained. As women live longer and spend more time without children and without husbands, as most demographic projections suggest,[28] will the issues concerning their spirituality in the public religious community, as opposed to the private sphere of home, become more important to these newly orthodox Jewish women? Will the virulent attacks against the women, including orthodox women, who attempted to pray at the Western Wall in Israel (without violating Jewish law),[29] for instance, become more troublesome for these ba'alot teshuvah when they find more time for public rituals and spirituality? Will the aggressive stance taken against the Palestinians and the vigorous defense of Israeli settlements in the West Bank lead these women to question their belief that a "feminine ethos," as collectively defined, is at the heart of orthodoxy?

As the dimensions of the private sphere of life change and as the female community continues to grow more knowledgeable in Jewish law, perhaps these women will be able to articulate more definitively and authoritatively the clear contradictions between what orthodoxy preaches and what it practices (for example, the potential for blackmail and coercion of husbands against wives in granting a divorce). Different historic times, like different lifecycle stages, demand different strategies. Because those strategies and the discourse presented in the support of those strategies change, no patriarchal setting is quite the same or continues to be the same over time. And while "orthodoxy" is presented as the inviolable, ahistoric and only authentic voice of Judaism, the focus and the language of these, and other "born again" women, set at least some of the terms for ongoing discussions within fundamentalist communities. That some challenge has emerged to patriarchal law in Jewish orthodoxy is clear from both the slow, incremental changes for women in public rites and private rituals, and from the way feminism has entered into the authoritative discourse, even if only to be railed against.

Like religious discourse, feminist discourse(s) and strategies have shifted over time as well. All identities, religious or gendered, are negotiated, multiple, and potentially shifting over the life course and over time. Moreover, despite the clear differences between the radical feminists discussed earlier and these ba'alot teshuvah, it is not unreasonable to argue that some of the latter's values, goals, and strategies represent a variation on both contemporary and past feminist discourse and strategy. One of the many issues raised in this chapter has to do with the way in which cultural constructions of the female, female-linked symbols and separatism may be used as a political strategy.[30]

Some feminist theorists claim to base their theories in observation and to "acknowledge their construction as rooted in the concerns of the present."[31] This turn in feminist scholarship—wariness toward absolutes, recognition of complexities in our analyses and the political ramifications of our particular "fix on feminism"—helps us to reassess gender identity politics. Women have used their gender identity to culturally resist or challenge aspects of patriarchy, capitalism, technology, and, even feminism, as each is commonly understood at a particular socio-political moment in history.

The newly orthodox Jewish women raise important questions about the meaning of family, fundamentalism, the politics of gender identity, and feminism. Their stories, and those of other born-again women, reveal more than the antipathy of an anti-feminist religious Right. Their voices are the voices of women trying to cope with the inequities and imbalances of liberal patriarchy in a postindustrial order.[32] Therefore, despite many "born again" women's distrust of feminism, their focus on raising women's status, promoting female interests, and altering the gender-role behavior of men as fathers and husbands, resonate with issues long of concern to feminists and feminist identity politics.

I have been cautious about generalizing beyond the boundaries of the white, female, primarily middle-class, urban-dwellers I studied. I have tried to base my theories "in observation" and to acknowledge that they are "rooted in the concerns of the present."[33] However, although I may locate a particular group of women in place and time, they are never stably fixed there; individuals negotiate their "locale" both in terms of their own histories and within the framework of the institutions that surround them. I am aware that the narratives these newly orthodox women recount resonate with other stories of women from the past and in the present, different from them in religion, class and ethnicity. However, comparisons to other groups of women, both past and present, are predicated on the assumption that similarities are artifacts of similar social constructions, not universal definitions.

I believe we are approaching a new stage in feminist intellectual history. A stage which maintains a tolerance for contradictions, ambiguities and fluid boundaries. By approaching, for instance, religious Right women from this perspective we can more readily see the contradictions and ambiguities and the challenges to fixity and unity their identity politics present. And while I may not be able to present "a truth" about newly orthodox Jewish women in the closing decades of the twentieth century, I hope I have added to a less false[34] set of narratives about gender, identity, feminism, and politics.

Notes

This chapter draws from material in Chapter 6 of my book, *Rachel's Daughters* (New Brunswick, NJ: Rutgers University Press, 1991).

1. D. Kondo, *Crafting Selves* (Chicago: The University of Chicago Press, 1990), p. 10.

2. See A. Jaggar, *Feminist Politics and Human Nature* (Totowa, N.J.: Rowman and Allanheld, 1983), and Y. King, "Healing the Wounds," pp. 115-141 in A. Jaggar and S. Bordo (eds.), *Gender/Body/Knowledge* (New Brunswick: Rutgers University Press, 1989).

3. See Yuval-Davis in this volume on ethnic identity and women for a more elaborate discussion.

4. See N. Ammerman, *Bible Believers* (New Brunswick, N.J.: Rutgers University Press, 1987); E. Brusco, "Columbian Evangelicalism as a Strategic Form of Women's Collective Action," *Feminist Issues* 6 (2) (Fall 1986):3-13; R. Klatch, *Women of the New Right* (Philadelphia: Temple University Press, 1987).

5. As with religious renewal in general, there is controversy about numbers and the meaning of Jewish orthodox revival. In particular, there is some controversy about whether the indicators of growth are signs of numerical growth or a by-product of increased organizational coherence and affluence

among Orthodox Jews (and therefore an increase in institutions serving that population).

6. See T. Roszak, *The Making of a Counter Culture* (New York: Doubleday, 1969); C. Glock and R. Bellah, *The New Religious Consciousness* (Berkeley: University of California Press, 1976); M. Yinger, *Countercultures: The Promised Peril of a World Turned Upside Down* (New York: The Free Press, 1982).

7. M. H. Danzger, *Returning to Tradition: The Contemporary Revival of Orthodox Judaism* (New Haven, Ct.: Yale University Press, 1989).

8. The five cities include: Boston, Cleveland, New York City (including Crown Heights), Los Angeles, and San Francisco.

9. Once within these settings, the referral method or snowball technique of sampling [J. Coleman, *The Adolescent Society* (Glencoe, Illinois: The Free Press, 1971)] was employed, thereby identifying smaller interactive groups of *ba'alot teshuvah* within each community. No claims are made that the women under study were randomly drawn as a sample of a defined universe nor can the interviewed be considered statistically representative of those who return to orthodoxy or of orthodoxy itself.

10. For a fuller discussion, see D. Kaufman "Women Who Return to Orthodox Judaism: A Feminist Analysis," *Journal of Marriage and the Family* 47 (3) (1985):543-555; "Feminism Reconstructed: Feminist Theories and Women Who Return to Orthodox Judaism," *Midwest Sociologists for Women in Society* 5 (March 1985):45-55; "Patriarchal Women: A Case Study of Newly Orthodox Jewish Women," *Symbolic Interaction* 12 (2) (1989):299-314; *Rachel's Daughters, Newly Orthodox Jewish Women* (New Brunswick, New Jersey: Rutgers University Press, 1991).

11. Some feminists have written about anti-semitism in the feminist movement as well. See Letty Cottin Pogrebin, "Anti-Semitism in the Women's Movement: A Jewish Feminist's Disturbing Account," *Ms* (June 1982), pp. 15-19.

12. James Richardson, Mary Stewart and Robert Simmonds, *Organized Miracles* (New Brunswick, N.J.: Transaction Books, 1979).

13. S. Tipton, *Getting Saved in the Sixties* (Berkeley: University of California Press, 1982).

14. Even some feminists have recanted on their earlier positions. Germaine Greer vehemently argues that the sexual revolution never happened: "Permissiveness happened, and that's not better than repressiveness, because women are still being manipulated by men" (Cited in *New York Times*, March 5, 1984, C 10).

15. For an historic example of Jewish women's claim to the preservation of human life, see Temma Kaplan, "Female Consciousness and Collective Action: The Case of Barcelona, 1910-1918," *Signs* 7 (13) (1982):545-566.

16. Alison Jaggar, *Feminist Politics and Human Nature*, pp. 83, 84. It is interesting to note that there are some strong demographic similarities between

radical feminists described here and the newly orthodox Jewish women in this study.

17. *Ibid.*, p. 8.

18. *Ibid.*, p. 95.

19. Ynestra King, "Healing the Wounds," p. 123.

20. Cited in Jaggar, *Feminist Politics and Human Nature*, p. 97.

21. In her comparisons between American and Japanese women, Kondo suggests that in "Western" culture, "the relationally defined self of American women still remains solidly within a linguistic and historical legacy of individualism" while in Japan, selves are inextricable from context. See Kondo, *Crafting Selves*, p. 33.

22. A. Jaggar, *Feminist Politics and Human Nature*, pp. 102, 104.

23. *Ibid.*, p. 97.

24. *Ibid.*, p. 105.

25. For the majority of American women, work and family demands are incompatible. Despite massive increases in the labor force and legislative reform, women still earn less than men in every occupation, irrespective of their training, skills, and qualifications. (See Kaufman, "Patriarchal Women.") Moreover, well-trained and educated women may find their career lines limited by informal barriers to success, barriers which are hard to legislatively reform or even publically address. And while the structural conditions in the labor force have been difficult to change, the normative expectations surrounding households have not changed significantly either. Irrespective of paid employment, women maintain the major responsibility for domestic and child-care activities. See J. Pleck, "The Work-Family Role System," *Social Problems* 24 (1977):417-424; M. Fox and S. Hesse-Biber, *Women at Work* (Palo Alto, CA.: Mayfield Publishing Company, 1984).

26. In fact, feminists have been most aware of this problem. Among the earliest to address this concern was Zillah Eisenstein, *The Radical Future of Liberal Feminism* (Boston: Northeastern University Press, 1981). For a good analysis of religion's appeal, see Judith Stacey and Susan Gerard, "We Are Not Doormats: Post-Feminist Evangelicalism in the U.S.," unpublished manuscript (Davis, California, University of California, 1988).

27. E. Brusco, "Columbian Evangelicalism," pp. 3-13.

28. See J. Giele, *Women and Future* (New York, N.Y.: The Free Press, 1982); Helena Lopata, *Women as Widows: Support Systems* (New York: Elsivere, 1979).

29. See, for instance, the article by Rabbi Susan Grossman and R. Susan Aranoff entitled: "Women Under Siege at the Western Wall," in *Women's League Outlook*, Spring 1990, pp. 7-10.

30. The strength of American feminism prior to 1920, argues Freedman, was the separate female community that helped to sustain women's participation in both social reform and political activities. She writes:

When women tried to assimilate into male-dominated institutions, without securing feminist social, economic, or political bases, they lost the momentum and the networks which had made the suffrage movement possible. Women gave up many of the strengths of the female sphere without gaining equally from the men's world they entered.

(E. Freedman, "Separation as Strategy: Female Institution Building and American Feminism, 1870-1930," *Feminist Studies*, Fall 1979, p. 524).

31. L. Nicholson (ed.), *Feminism/Postmodernism* (New York: Routledge, Chapman and Hall, Inc., 1990), p. 5.

32. See J. Stacey, "Sexism by a Subtler Name?," *Socialist Review* (Nov./Dec. 1987):8-28.

33. L. Nicholson (ed.), *Feminism/Postmodernism*, p. 5.

34. I am paraphrasing Sandra Harding's analysis of feminist epistemologies (S. Harding, "Feminism, Science, and the Anti-Enlightenment Critiques," in L. Nicholson. ed., *Feminism/Postmodernism*, pp. 83-106.)

18

Women of the New Right in the United States: Family, Feminism, and Politics

Rebecca E. Klatch

Introduction

Although the first wave of feminism in the United States granted women the vote, it was not until the second wave of feminism during the late 1960s and 1970s that women were integrated into the main-stream of political life. The past two decades in American politics have been marked by an extraordinary degree of activism by women. Yet, paradoxically the very success of the feminist movement's increase in female participation in politics has also meant the increased involvement by women opposed to the goals and values at the core of feminism.

In particular, the enormous social changes provoked by the civil rights, anti-war, and feminist movements of the 1960s fomented a counter-reaction, a resurgence of conservative activism commonly termed the "New Right." While no consensus exists on the exact boundaries of the New Right, generally the phrase is used to delineate a network of people and organizations that came into prominence in the mid-1970s including conservative politicians such as Jesse Helms, Orrin Hatch, and Jack Kemp; conservative think-tanks such as the Heritage Foundation; general purpose organizations such as the Conservative Caucus, the National Conservative Political Action Committee, and the Committee for the Survival of a Free Congress; as well as the religious sector, including prime-time preachers, the Moral Majority, and groups working against such issues as abortion, gay rights, and pornography. The New Right was associated with the election and re-election of

President Reagan in 1980 and 1984 and with shifting the political agenda from the progressive social change measures instituted during the 1960s and early 1970s to limited government, militant anti-Communism, and opposition to affirmative action, welfare, and other social issues promoted by liberals of the 1960s.

In fact, the New Right is not a cohesive movement whose members share a single set of beliefs and values. Rather, there is a fundamental division within the New Right based on different—and even opposing—views of human nature, men's and women's roles, the function of government, and the ideal society.

Although the "New Right" implies a movement distinct from the "Old Right" associated with McCarthyism and right-wing groups of the 1950s, in fact the schism within the New Right is historically based and continuous with the Old Right. Seymour Martin Lipset and Earl Raab's classic study of the American Right from 1790 to 1970 finds a constant marriage of interest between two groups: those based in the less educated, lower economic strata, who are highly religious and drawn to the non-economic issues of right-wing movements; and those rooted in the highly educated, higher income strata, who are less religious and committed above all to economic conservatism.[1]

While social conservatism is not a distinguishing mark of the New Right, what is unique about the New Right is the visible presence of women throughout the conservative movement.[2] While virtually all past research looked exclusively at male activists, recent research, particularly by feminist scholars, examines women's involvement in the Right. Although these studies are a welcome and necessary addition to the lack of knowledge about women, virtually all of the research concentrates exclusively on women's participation in anti-feminist activities.[3] Typically, conclusions are reached about "right-wing women" based on involvement in anti-ERA (Equal Rights Amendment) or anti-abortion organizations. This is a limited portrayal of women of the Right. By only focusing on women involved in the social issues, we get an incomplete picture of female activism. Just as the New Right is not one cohesive movement, neither are right-wing women a monolithic group. To discuss women's role in the religious Right, it is essential to also understand how this contrasts with women's involvement in the secular Right. There are significant differences, for instance, in each sector's view of gender and relationship to feminism.

My study, based on two years of field research in the 1980s, reveals a fundamental division in worldview among a diverse group of female activists on the Right. My research consisted of in-depth interviews with thirty women activists,[4] extensive field notes taken as a participant-observer at conservative conferences and organizational meetings,[5] and examination of the printed literature of organizations affiliated with those interviewed as well as literature obtained at conferences and meetings.[6] The fundamental division between right-wing women that emerged from these sources can be presented as two distinct ideologies or ideal types: the social conservative and laissez-faire conservative worldviews.[7]

Social Conservatism and Laissez-Faire Conservatism

Every ideology has a central lens through which the world is viewed. Vision is refracted through this lens, shaping all perception. Social conservatives view the world through the lens of religion, meaning specifically, Christianity or the Judeo-Christian ethic. In looking at America, social conservatives see a country founded on religious beliefs and deeply rooted in a religious tradition. The family stands at the center of this world, representing the building block of society. The family's role as moral authority is essential; the family instils children with moral values and restrains the pursuit of self-interest.

Implicit in this image of the family is the social conservative conception of human nature. Humans are creatures of unlimited appetites and instincts. Without restraint, the world would become a chaos of seething passions, overrun by narrow self-interest. Only the moral authority of the family or religion tames human passions, transforming self-interest into the larger good. The ideal society, then, is one in which individuals are integrated into a moral community, bound together by faith, by common moral values, and by obeying the dictates of the family and religion.

Next to this ideal, the social conservative sees contemporary America as a morally decaying country in which the basic unit of society is crumbling. The social conservative activist's special mission, then, is to restore America to health; to regenerate religious belief; to renew faith, morality, and decency; and to return America to the righteousness of the founding fathers.

Laissez-faire conservatives, in contrast, view the world through the lens of liberty, particularly the economic liberty of the free market and the political liberty based on the minimal state. Laissez-faire belief is rooted in the classical liberalism associated with Adam Smith, John Locke, and John Stuart Mill.[8] Hence, the concept of liberty is inextricably bound to the concept of the individual. As the primary element of society, the individual is seen as an autonomous, rational, self-interested actor. Laissez-faire conservatives view humans as beings endowed with free will, initiative, and self-reliance. The larger good is not ensured through the maintenance of moral authority and the restriction of self-interest. Rather, the laissez-faire ideal is a society in which natural harmony exists through the very pursuit of self-interest. The aim of the good society is to elevate the potential of individuals by bringing their creative and productive nature to fruition.

Proponents of this view award America a special role in history as the cradle of liberty. Yet, like social conservatives, laissez-faire conservatives deplore the current direction and spirit of America. The erosion of liberty, rather than moral decay, however, is their utmost concern. America's departure from the ideal of the limited state and the unfettered market threatens the individual's economic and political liberty. Thus, laissez-faire conservatives unanimously name economic problems and, secondarily, defense issues as the top priorities of the nation.

Perceptions of Gender Roles

The two constituencies also differ in their perception of the proper roles of men and women in society. Social conservative women believe in a strict division of gender roles as decreed by the Scriptures. Gender is envisioned as a hierarchical ordering with God and Christ at the top, followed by men, and then women.

While male and female roles are each respected as essential and complementary components of God's plan, men are the spiritual leaders and decision makers in the family. It is women's role to support men in their positions of higher authority through altruism and self-sacrifice. At the 1982 Moral Majority conference in Washington, D.C., pro-family leader Connie Marshner gave a speech entitled "The New Traditional Woman." She explained: "A woman's nature is simply, other-oriented. ... To the traditional woman self-centeredness remains as ugly and sinful as ever. The less time women spend thinking about themselves, the happier they are. ... Women are ordained by their nature to spend themselves in meeting the needs of others. And women, far more than men, will transmit culture and values to the next generation. There is nothing demeaning about this nature: it is ennobling."[9] This belief in women's natural orientation to others is also reflected in the words of a pro-family activist in Massachusetts who told me:

Being a mother has enhanced my life *so much*. [My children] really brought me out of myself. Before I had children I was always worried about how my hair looked or my clothes, but now I no longer worry about that as much. I'm no longer self-centered. It feels so good because now I put six people ahead of me. I don't think about myself all the time. ... I am giving something important to my children and to future generations. I am leaving behind a legacy to them. So I really see all this activism as a part of being a housewife. Cleaning house is part of the short-run goals of being a housewife; but my activism leaves something for the long run.

The social conservative world, then, is rooted in a firm conception of the proper and separate roles of men and women, which, divinely ordained, are essential to the survival of the family and to the maintenance of a moral, ordered, and stable society. Because gender roles are delineated in such unambiguous terms, any blurring of roles is viewed as a threat. A Family Forum member in Massachusetts expressed her fear of this threat in the following story:

You know, tonight we took the kids out to Papa Gino's for dinner. While we were sitting there, these three girls came in dressed up in baseball outfits. They looked just like boys. From the back you couldn't tell the difference. They had it all down—even drumming on the table [imitates a drum-player]. And the way they walked, everything! They were about fourteen. I mean, here's my twelve-year-old son sitting there and what is he to think? What effect does that have on my son to see this sameness? He won't be able to tell the difference between the sexes seeing things like that.

The ultimate fear underlying this concern over confused gender roles is the fear of homosexuality. One social conservative woman declared: "The increase in homosexuality is just one of the social disorders that is an outgrowth of gender-role blurring."[10] In order to reaffirm the essential line dividing the sexes, Jerry Falwell sermonizes about the super-masculinity of Jesus. Denouncing the portrayal of Christ as having long hair and wearing flowing robes, Falwell asserts: "Christ wasn't effeminate. The man who lived on this earth was a man with muscles. Christ was a he-man!"[11]

No such clear distinctions between gender roles are visible in the laissez-faire conservative's view. There is a notable absence of commentary on women's and men's roles. There is particularly no mention of the need for male authority and for female submission or of women's natural orientation toward others. In fact, these beliefs contradict the fundamental values of the laissez-faire conservative worldview. One woman active in public education says, for example: "I believe women used to be considered property; that was terrible. I do believe in differences between the sexes. We're not all the same. There are biological differences. For example, I can't do all the things men do in terms of strength; but difference does not mean inferiority. I think women are strong, competent, able. Women have to get over their roles as shy, pretty, helpless, and always nice. Men who are successful and competent get really scared and threatened when they discover a strong woman. I've had people treat me that way." Later, this activist commented, "The other day when I was collecting petitions it really made me mad—I could see why women want the ERA! All of these women would say, "Gee I can't sign—I'd have to talk it over with my husband." Or "No, my husband votes in our family." Aren't they thinking people?"

In short, the social conservative vision of a hierarchical ordering of authority of men over women is antithetical to the laissez-faire conservative ethos. Faith in individual self-reliance and free will, and belief in the liberty and autonomy of every individual, extends to women as well as to men. One woman interviewed, who heads an anti-tax organization, reacted to my description of this study by saying, "Why study *women* in politics? After all, women are no different than men." In contrast to the social conservative activist who praised the selflessness of the mother role, the tax reform activist responded to her days as a homemaker by saying: "Ontological guilt—do you know what that is? The feeling that you're not doing enough, that if only you could do more, get something more from your life—that is what I felt as a homemaker. I felt I was not working to my capacity. Now I have really found myself. I never feel as if I haven't done enough. Every moment is consumed in my work which is a fulfillment of my beliefs."

The gap between the two worlds' perceptions of gender roles is also apparent in a comment made by one Washington leader active in defense and Republican women's organizations. Reacting to the ideas of social conservative leader George Gilder, she said: "I've read part of Gilder's book. He makes some pretty strong arguments. It would be almost like saying I don't belong in the workplace to believe that stuff, wouldn't it? There's sort of an over-emphasis on family, that every woman's got to have children to be fulfilled kind of thing and you've got to give your twenty years in the kitchen or whatever. ... You can only vacuum a house so many times before you start sucking up the carpet!" In sum, laissez-faire conservatives view women's submission to men as abhorrent. They believe both men and women are self-interested actors, capable of and responsible for autonomous action.

Perceptions of Discrimination Against Women

Because social conservatives adhere to a hierarchical ordering, they believe positional differences between women and men do not imply inequality, and, therefore, they deny the existence of discrimination. For example, Connie Marshner argues:

> Feminists like to blame everything on men. ... Women are second-class citizens, they say, because men degrade women. But it is important to put things in correct perspective. Women earn fifty-nine cents for every dollar earned by men. But women themselves choose to work part-time, or only temporarily. When you factor in the part-time and temporary nature of the work, the fifty-nine cent statistic falls part. It becomes approximately eighty percent parity. Only eighty percent, feminists would still screech, why not 100%? They would say it is because women are discriminated against. They would not entertain the idea that women may not want to work as hard or that in school they may not want to take as challenging courses. Such ideas would be heresy to a feminist.[12]

Similarly, Phyllis Schlafly claims: "The fact that there may be only eighteen women out of 535 members of Congress does not prove discrimination at all. The small number of women in Congress proves only that most women do not want to do the things that must be done to win elections."[13]

Laissez-faire activists, on the other hand, in their adherence to individualism, are inclined to recognize and deplore discrimination against women. For example, Jeane Kirkpatrick argues that in order to overcome men's resistance to the inclusion of women in politics it will be necessary "to abandon the notion, still supported by some religious denominations, that men are the natural governors of society ... that femininity is inexorably associated with the submissiveness of female to male. ... What must also go is the expectation that the male will have prime responsibility for the financial support of the family and the female for its nurturance."[14]

Recognition of the discriminatory treatment of women in politics is also evident in another activist's story:

> Once I was on this panel debating the mayor and he argued against my comments about waste in government by saying, "When was the last time you cleaned out your refrigerator? Didn't you throw anything out of that?" And then, "Why aren't you home with your children?" I got the audience on my side because I said, "Gee, it's embarrassing. I can't remember when the last time was that I cleaned my refrigerator. Actually,

I think my husband did it." And then I went up to him afterwards and said, "Why did you have to say something like that? My husband is at home with my son and he's perfectly capable of taking care of him." I hate that kind of attitude.

Another laissez-faire activist complained about the tendency to pay men for their political efforts while expecting women to volunteer their time.

Laissez-faire conservative women are also more likely to acknowledge discrimination against women in the workplace. An engineer active in the Libertarian party reports:

I once worked for a corporation. I came up for promotion. It was between me and this man. They gave it to him. I asked my boss, "Was I qualified to get the promotion?" and he said, "We gave it to him because he has a family." I said, "I didn't ask you if he had a family, I said was I qualified." I quit two weeks later. I figure any place that doesn't value me and my work doesn't deserve me. Those places lose all their most productive people. If you don't reward them, they'll go somewhere else. Sure, there's discrimination. But I'm not going to get upset over a person's attitude about women or blacks. I can go somewhere else.

Although laissez-faire women share with feminists a recognition of discrimination, they react to such bias purely in voluntaristic terms. Women who are discriminated against should, on their own initiative, leave the job and enter the free market to choose another one. Individualistic solutions, rather than collective actions, are the way to fight unequal treatment.

Perceptions of Feminism

To social conservatives, feminism represents one of the primary forces of moral decay responsible for America's decline; by challenging the traditional roles of men and women, feminism threatens the family and religious dictates. Among laissez-faire conservatives, in contrast, there is a noticeable absence of commentary on feminism. In fact, laissez-faire women adhere to part of the feminist vision.

Social conservatives charge feminists with renouncing the family as a source of repression and enslavement, a tool used by men to entrap and oppress women.[15] As one local pro-family activist put it:

The libbers want to abolish the family. That's what Gloria Frie—I mean Steinem—says. "Women will not be liberated until marriage is eliminated." Have you seen the "Declaration on Feminism"? They state quite clearly there that they want to eliminate the family. That's why when I hear people say they support ERA, I say to them, "Do you know what that means? Do you know what they want to do?" The feminists want to abolish the family. But the family is the basis of everything. It is the foundation of our society; if that crumbles, everything else goes.

The International Women's Year Conference held in Houston in 1977 concretized the perception of feminism as an anti-family force. Sponsored by the United Nations, the conference brought together women from all over the country to consider "women's issues." Social conservatives were shocked by the delegates' overwhelming support for the ERA, gay rights, federal funding of abortion, government sponsored child care, and contraception for minors without parental consent, all seen as threats to the traditional family. In opposition to such measures, a network of activists and organizations came together and called themselves "the pro-family movement."

Inextricably bound to the view that feminism is anti-family is the perception of feminism as an extension of the new narcissism, a symbol of the "Me Decade." Pro-family leader Onalee McGraw explains:

The feminist movement issued an appeal that rapidly spread through our culture urging women to liberate themselves from the chains of family life and affirm their own self-fulfillment as the primary good. ... The humanist-feminist view of the family is that it is a biological, sociological unit in which the individual happens to reside; it has no meaning and purpose beyond that which each individual chooses to give it. Thus, the autonomous self, freely choosing and acting, must satisfy its needs. When, by its very nature, the family exercises moral authority over its members, it thereby restricts the self in its pursuit of self-fulfillment and becomes an instrument of oppression and denial of individual rights.[16]

Feminism threatens to replace the higher moral authority of the family with women's self-interest. When individuality and freedom of self are paramount, the ultimate result is what Connie Marshner labels "macho feminism:"

Feminism replaced the saccharine sentimentalizations of women and home life and projected instead a new image of women: a drab, macho feminism of hard-faced women who were bound and determined to serve their place in the world, no matter whose bodies they have to climb over to do it. Macho feminism despises anything which seeks to interfere with the desires of Number One. A relationship which proves burden-some? Drop it! A husband whose needs cannot be conveniently met? Forget him! Children who may wake up in the middle of the night? No way! To this breed of thought, family interferes with self-fulfilment, and given the choice between family and self, the self is going to come out on top in their world. Macho feminism has deceived women in that it convinced them that they would be happy only if they were treated like men, and that included treating themselves like men. Feminists praise self-centeredness and call it liberation.[17]

If everyone pursues his/her own interest, no one will be left to look out for the larger good, to be altruistic, to be the nurturer, the caretaker, the mother. The underlying fear of social conservative women is of a total masculinization of the world.

Further, social conservatives believe that feminism also denigrates the very status of the homemaker. One woman interviewed, a national organizer for the Eagle Forum, explains:

The women's liberation movement really resents homemakers. There's a great Chicago magazine out that gives great quotes about how they think it's an illegitimate profession being a homemaker. Now when they get a lot of media coverage saying things like that ... they really caused the split to occur. They caused a resentment to grow between homemakers and working women. ... The women who used to say "I'm a homemaker" with pride now say "I'm just a housewife." That's a terrible change in attitude. ... Why it's really unfortunate is because girls getting out of college don't get the choice. They think they have to make long-range career plans, they have to go to graduate school. They have to keep a job. They put their children in day-care centers.

Feminists' call for women to go beyond the housewife role, to step into the male world of paid labor, denies the importance and the satisfaction derived by those content with their homemaker status. As one pro-family activist explains: "The feminists want all women to work. But all women don't want to work. I talk to women all the time around here who really want to stay home with their children. It's not because they're misled or not liberated. They honestly want to stay home with their children." Or, in another local activist's words: "The women's liberation movement looks down on the housewife. She should be the most respected person as she is bringing up future generations. But women's liberation puts her down and says "All she does is stay home all day and wash dirty diapers." ERA won't do anything for these women."

The conflict between feminists and homemakers is a tug-of-war between two lifestyles. Rather than valuing the lifestyles of women who work outside and inside the home, social conservatives view feminism as promoting new roles for women at the expense of the old, thereby disregarding the worth of women's work in the home. Social conservatives are appalled, for example, by feminist assessments of the monetary value of housework, believing such efforts reduce a relationship based on love to purely quantitative value. Similarly, Phyllis Schlafly argues that feminists are contemptuous of volunteer services performed by women because "in their inverted scale of values, they judge every service by money, never by love."[18]

While feminists—not men—are blamed for attacking the status of homemakers and for degrading the traditional female role, beneath this blame is an underlying distrust of men, particularly evident in discussions of the ERA. In social conservative eyes, the ERA would have eliminated the homemaker's most valuable property right: the right to be provided for by her husband. The existing remedies a wife has if her husband neglects his responsibilities, such as purchasing goods on her husband's credit and letting the store handle collection of payment, would be destroyed. As one anti-ERA activist put it: "Marriage as a full equal partnership is discrimination against women because the man is no longer responsible for his wife. Under the Judeo-Christian tradition, men *are* responsible. I did not get married as an equal partner." Worst of all is the fear that a man who stops loving his wife, or who finds a new woman, will be freed of all responsibility to support his spouse. Phyllis Schlafly warns:

> Consider a wife in her 50's whose husband decides he wants to divorce her and trade her in on a younger model. This situation has become all too common, especially with no-fault divorce in many states. If ERA is ratified, and thereby wipes out the state laws that require a husband to support his wife, the cast-off wife will have to hunt for a job to support herself. The most tragic effect of ERA would thus fall on the woman who has been a good wife and homemaker for decades, and who can now be turned out to pasture with impunity because a new, militant breed of liberationist has come along.[19]

The underlying assumption is that men are creatures of uncontrollable passions and lust, who have little sense of loyalty or commitment. Only moral and legal authority can restrain the savagery of male nature. Opposition to the ERA, then, speaks to the fear that homemakers will be left most vulnerable if legal binds on men are lifted. Feminists are responsible for removing the safety valves which currently protect women. As Mrs. Billy Graham put it, the women's liberation movement is "turning into men's lib because we are freeing them from their responsibilities. I think we are being taken for a ride."[20]

Ironically, this same fear of women's precarious position is voiced by feminists in recognizing that all women are just one man removed from welfare. Yet while social conservative women try to ensure women's rights and entitlements within marriage, thereby binding men to a stable family unit, feminists seek security through ensuring women's economic independence from men. Where social conservatives reject feminism for blurring the sacred differences between women and men and for encouraging women to be self-interested, laissez-faire conservatives do not reject feminism. They see no threat because they do not uphold separate spheres. Rather than viewing women's self-fulfilment as narcissistic, laissez-faire conservatives applaud each individual's attempt to rise to their talents, believing it adds to the wealth of the nation. If anything, laissez-faire conservatives have created the ideology of the upwardly mobile "me generation" that social conservatives abhor.

Laissez-faire conservatives also opposed the ERA, but they did so because they viewed the ERA as a misguided way to eliminate gender discrimination that implied the growth of big government. The ERA symbolized the expansion of bureaucratic control, the federalization of one more area of life, resulting in encroachment on individual liberty. One female activist put it this way: "There are two parts to the ERA. The first part regarding equality I agree with, but I don't think we need that. That's already established by the Constitution. But the second part I don't agree with. The second part gives the government the right to enforce equality." Typically, laissez-faire conservative activists responded to the ERA by calling for individual efforts to fight discrimination or by proposing changes on a state or local level.

This fundamental opposition to big government is also evidenced in the stance laissez-faire conservatives take toward other "women's" or "family" issues. While opposition to day care, the right to have an abortion, and gay rights is at the very core of social conservatism, laissez-faire conservatives support these very issues. To them, abortion and homosexuality are private, individual matters; government legislation of such issues intrudes on individual liberty. As one activist states: "I believe life begins at conception, but I don't see how you can legislate that. I much prefer the way it is now ... women are not butchered. But do I want government to pay for abortions? Well, no, because that's not morally justifiable. But then I also don't want those teenage mothers to be a drag on the system, so it's a complex issue. ... Ideally, those people should have contraception, but realistically, will that happen? Hopefully, each generation will be more liberated." Typically, this laissez-faire activist is pro-choice but against government-sponsored abortion. The government has no right to deny a woman's choice but should not fund her abortion either. Many laissez-faire activists also support day care as long as it remains in private hands. In the words of one federal government administrator under Reagan: "I think we need to expand day care. ... If a woman has to work an eight-hour day to make money, she needs day care. I just don't believe the government should pay for it. I think it should be in private hands."

Although laissez-faire conservative women are closer to feminists in their view of gender roles and gender discrimination,[21] the means to achieve women's equality which they advocate separates laissez-faire conservatives from most feminists. Feminists call for federal support in addressing women's needs, but laissez-faire conservatives oppose any further reliance on big government. While feminists look toward collective solutions as a way to end discrimination, social conservatives believe that measures such as affirmative action threaten to encroach on individual freedom. In short, liberty must not be sacrificed in the quest for equality.

The Paradox of Right-Wing Women's Activism

Given their adherence to traditional roles in which men are breadwinners and protectors, and women are helpmates and caretakers, how do social conservative women understand their own position as political activists in the public arena? Does their activism contradict their beliefs? Social conservative women do not see a tension between their political activism and the traditional female role. In fact, these "new" political roles are defined within the bounds of traditional gender ideology. Female political activism is conceptualized as the power behind the throne, women altruistically working for the benefit of a larger cause. Phyllis Schlafly, for example, includes an assertive political role in her ideal of womanhood, what she terms "The Positive Woman." "The Positive Woman accepts her responsibility to spin the fabric of civilization, to mend its tears, and to reinforce its seams. ...

God has a mission for every Positive Woman. It is up to her to find out what it is and to meet the challenge."[22]

Pro-family leader Connie Marshner has another name for this expanded female role: "the traditional woman." In explaining the new traditional woman, Marshner distinguishes between conventions and traditional values. Conventions are mutable; thus, certain changes in gender roles must be seen as a mere shift in conventions. For example, the fact that more women today feel that boys should be as responsible as girls for doing the laundry does not challenge traditional values; this merely indicates a change in convention because doing laundry is a morally neutral act. On the other hand, traditional values are eternal; traditional values are moral norms that must be followed without exception. Fidelity is a moral norm; thus, adultery is always wrong. Similarly, a man being the head of the household is a traditional value. It is not immoral for a woman to earn as much or more money than her husband does, but it is immoral to reject his authority.[23]

Thus, both Marshner and Schlafly see no contradiction in the political activism of the social conservative woman. It is, in fact, woman's role as moral gatekeeper that allows her to adopt new positions, to be a voice of righteousness in the political world, bringing moral purity to a world filled with sin.

Because laissez-faire conservatives do not see women as bound to traditional roles, there is no seeming contradiction between their beliefs and their roles as public leaders. Jeane Kirkpatrick speaks of the need for more women to be in positions of power in order to break traditional stereotypes of women.[24] Laissez-faire conservative women in politics see themselves as no different from men, self-interested actors working for a political cause.

The paradox of right-wing women is not that social conservative women are vocal and active as they advocate women's submission to men. Despite the prevalent assumption that anti-feminist women are "a brainwashed flock,"[25] "lackeys" of men,[26] the paradox is that those women who are furthest from feminists in their beliefs actually do act in their own interests as women, while laissez-faire women, who partly share the feminist vision, do not act collectively in the interest of their gender. Far from suffering from false consciousness, in fact, social conservative women are well aware of their interests and act to defend their status as women.

To borrow a phrase from Marx, social conservative women act as women *for* themselves, while laissez-faire conservative women remain women *in* themselves.[27] Gender identity is central to the political involvement of social conservative women; recognizing their commonality with other traditional women, they seek to protect women's place as a group. Laissez-faire women's activism is not motivated out of concern regarding gender; they do not act in the collective interest of women and therefore remain women in themselves. For laissez-faire conservatives, it is individuals, and not men and women as men and women, who are threatened by the foes of freedom. Thus, laissez-faire women act as members of the marketplace not as members of their gender group in their effort to return America to strength and freedom.

Clearly there is a relationship between a woman's social location and her values and beliefs. It is not coincidental that a woman with a devout religious upbringing who is a full-time homemaker is more likely to see the family at the center of the world and to adhere to a traditional ideology regarding gender. Nor is it a coincidence that a single professional woman in her mid-thirties who is devoted to her career does not see the family as central and holds nontraditional attitudes about men and women's roles. Traditional gender roles "work" for social conservative women because they themselves are likely to be in life situations that correspond to traditional roles. Laissez-faire women, in contrast, who are more likely to be single, divorced, or living with men outside of marriage, and who have higher levels of education and hold more professional positions than do social conservative women, are in life situations and have social resources outside of the traditional female sphere.[28]

Interestingly, the differences in background and lifestyle of social conservative and laissez-faire women in this study parallel findings of other studies regarding the social bases of anti-feminist and feminist activists. Most anti-feminist women are white, middle-aged housewives, married or widowed, new to politics, and oriented toward single issues. Protestant fundamentalism and Catholicism play a primary role in motivating these women to political action. Feminists, on the other hand, are typically somewhat younger than anti-feminist women, employed outside the home, and often are single, divorced or separated. Feminists tend not to be new to politics, have more years of education, and have a more secular orientation than anti-feminist women. Finally, feminist women tend to be much more oriented toward careers than anti-feminist women, whose life goals involve taking care of others.[29]

The views of conservative women may also be shaped by ever-encroaching economic realities. Each year more and more women are forced by economic necessity to enter the labor force,[30] and employed women are more likely to believe in equality between the sexes than are full-time homemakers.[31] Thus, as women become paid laborers, a decline in women's social conservatism may follow.

In short, the inevitable results of social conservative women's activism may undermine their beliefs. However, given the deep-rooted nature of worldviews and the resilience of ideology, a mass exodus among social conservative women is unlikely. Even so, social conservative women certainly exist as crucial role models to a generation of daughters. Whether daughters of social conservative women will follow in traditional ways or whether their mothers' vocal and active roles in the political world will provoke their own departure from tradition remains to be seen.

Coalition and Conflict

Despite the mutual views of laissez-faire women and feminists concerning gender and discrimination, laissez-faire women are unlikely to change from women in themselves to women for themselves. Although an alliance between feminist and laissez-faire women may be possible on specific single issues, such as the need to protect a constitutional right to abortion, an enduring coalition is unlikely. The laissez-faire opposition to government involvement restricts the possibility of any broad agreement on the issues. Laissez-faire women, for example, might be persuaded to rally in support of abortion rights or to appeal to a company to set up day-care facilities, but they would not support government aid to poor women to ensure the right to abortion nor would they endorse public support for day care.

A second limitation to an alliance is that laissez-faire women's support for issues related to the economy and defense supersedes their concern about women's issues. In a May 1984 meeting of the Republican National Committee's National Women's Coalition, a group of seventy business and professional women conceded that while they disagreed with President Reagan on a number of women's issues, they agreed that the state of the economy overrode these concerns. In their view, only when inflation and interest rates were down, and employment was on the rise, would both men and women prosper.[32]

Finally, what is the likelihood of continued coalition between the two worlds of the New Right? Although social and laissez-faire conservatives united to "get government off our backs" in electing and re-electing Ronald Reagan, in fact the two worlds hold diametrically opposed positions regarding the role of the state. Both social and laissez-faire conservatives criticize the existing state. However, social conservatives wish to replace the values and interests now embodied in public institutions with their own set of beliefs and values, while laissez-faire conservatives wish to cut back or eliminate the public sector altogether.

Conclusions

While by some absolute scale the increased activism and leadership of women in the New Right indicates opened doors and new roles, certainly the content of women's grievances, particularly by social conservatives, does not indicate a feminist victory. Too often, however, feminists and those on the left dismiss the right as being fanatics or pathological. Yet if one listens closely to the underlying fears expressed by social conservative women, one hears concerns which speak to real social problems.

Social conservatism speaks to problems and fears created by the enormous social upheaval of the past few decades in the United States, which witnessed changes in blacks' relations to whites, women's relations to men, and children's relations to parents. The pro-family movement expresses fears resulting from teenagers' cultural independence from parents; it expresses parents' concerns about their children's getting pregnant, having abortions, abusing drugs, or being sexual without a context of responsibility. Added to this, the pro-family movement speaks to fears regarding women's precarious position in society. During a time of increased divorce and the feminization of poverty, women seek to assuage their anxiety, to secure their place in the social structure. Social conservatives also react against the vision of a society steeped in self-interest. They criticize the hedonism and obsession with self of a society that has taken individualism to an extreme, in which self-fulfilment takes priority over responsibility to others.

For these reasons, we must take seriously these movements in their own terms and confront the very real concerns being expressed—regarding family relations, women's economic security, and the need for responsibility and community.

Notes

An earlier version of this chapter was published in *Signs: Journal of Women in Culture and Society* 13 (4) (1988).

1. See Seymour Martin Lipset and Earl Raab, *The Politics of Unreason: Right-Wing Extremism in America, 1790-1970* (New York: Harper and Row, 1970).

2. Because so little data exists on female activists in the Old Right, there is no way of knowing how women of the Old or New Right compare in terms of number of participants, degree of involvement, or social background. The vast majority of research on the Old Right makes no mention of female activists, but it is not clear whether this lack of attention is due to the small number of female participants in the movement or to the male bias of the researchers.

3. See Theodore S. Arrington and Patricia A. Kyle, "Equal Rights Amendment Activists in North Carolina," *Signs: Journal of Women in Culture and Society* 3 (1978):666-80; David W. Brady and Kent L. Tedin, "Ladies in Pink: Religion and Political Ideology in the Anti-ERA Movement," *Social Science Quarterly* 56 (1976):564-575; Pamela Johnston Conover and Virginia Gray, *Feminism and the New Right: Conflict Over the American Family* (New York: Praeger, 1983); Andrea Dworkin, *Right-Wing Women* (New York: Perigee Books, 1983); Zillah Eisenstein, *Feminism and Sexual Equality: Crisis in Liberal America* (New York: Monthly Review Press, 1984); Kristin Luker, *Abortion and the Politics of Motherhood* (Berkeley: University of California Press, 1984); Andrew H. Merton, *Enemies of Choice: The Right-to-Life Movement and Its Threat to Abortion* (Boston: Beacon, 1981); Carol Mueller, "Rancorous Conflict and Opposition to the ERA," paper presented at the American Sociological Association Meetings (New York, 1976), and "Women's Issues and the Search for a New Religious Right: A Belief Systems Analysis, 1972-1980," paper presented at the American Political Science Association Meetings (New York, 1981); Rosalind Pollack Petchesky, *Abortion and Women's Choice: The State, Sexuality, and Reproductive Freedom* (Boston: Northeastern University Press, 1984).

4. All activists are self-identified and labeled by others as conservative. The women included in the sample were referred to me by others either because I explicitly stated that I wanted to talk to women of the New Right or because of their affiliation with organizations identified as part of the general movement called the "New Right." The entire sample supported the 1980 election of Ronald Reagan, with nearly all criticism falling to the right of Reagan's policies. Many of the women interviewed worked for or supported the 1964 presidential campaign of Barry Goldwater as well. Thus, the organizations and political beliefs represented in this study range from the conservative branch of the Republican party to the more "extreme" ideology of such groups as the Libertarian party and the Moral Majority. Approximately one-quarter of the total sample were national leaders interviewed in Washington, D.C. Due to limited funding, all interviews with local activists took place in Massachusetts. The final sample includes organizational affiliations with the following groups: American Legislative Exchange Council, College Republicans, Conservative Caucus, Eagle Forum, Family Forum, Free Congress Foundation, Libertarian Party, Moral Majority, Morality in the Media, Pro-Family Forum, Republican

National Committee, Women for Constitutional Government, Women's Republican Club, and local antibusing, antitax, and antigun-control organizations. Because confidentiality was assured, all excerpts from the interview data included in this paper remain anonymous. For futher discussion of the methodology and ethical issues involved in carrying out this study, see Rebecca Klatch, *Women of the New Right* (Philadelphia: Temple University Press, 1987), and "The Methodological Problems of Studying A Politically Sensitive Community," in Robert G. Burgess (ed.), *Studies in Qualitative Methodology Vol. 1* (Greenwich, Conn.: JAI Press, 1988).

5. Conferences attended include Phyllis Schlafly's Over the Rainbow Celebration of the Defeat of the ERA (July 1, 1982, Washington, D.C.); Family Forum II: Traditional Values Work, a national conference held in Washington, D.C., July 27-29, 1982, co-sponsored by the Moral Majority and the Free Congress Foundation; the Conservative Political Action Conference (February 17-20, 1983), co-sponsored by the American Conservative Union and Young Americans for Freedom; and local meetings in Massachusetts of the Libertarian party and the South Shore Pro-Family Forum.

6. The textual analysis of printed materials included regular and miscellaneous publications from the following groups: Alabama Christian Educational Association, American Conservative Union, Christian Voice, Center for Family Studies, Citizens for Educational Freedom, Coalition for Decency, College Republican National Committee, Conservative Caucus, Eagle Forum, Free Congress Research and Education Foundation, Free the Eagle, Freemen Institute, Home Education Resource Center, Intercessors for America, John Birch Society, Libertarian Party, Moral Majority, National Federation of Parents for Drug Free Youth, Pro-Family Forum, Republican National Committee, United Families of America, Utah Association of Women, and Young Americans for Freedom.

7. Comparing the background of the women in the sample reveals the varying social bases of each type. In particular, while all activists interviewed are white, there are notable differences between social and laissez-faire conservative women with regard to age, religion, education, marital status, and occupation. The overall sample includes women ranging in age from their late twenties to late fifties. Social conservative women tend to be somewhat older than laissez-faire conservative women, with the average ages being forty-five years and thirty-eight years, respectively. Although the sample as a whole is disproportionately Catholic, due to the location of the majority of the interviews in Massachusetts, the social conservative group is virtually all Catholic and Fundamentalist Christian, while the laissez-faire conservative camp is divided between Catholics and more ecumenical Protestants, with a minority of Jewish constituents. Further, while the sample overall is highly educated, with nearly all women having completed a college education, laissez-

faire conservative activists hold more postgraduate degrees than do social conservative activists. Overall, there are slightly more married than single women. Of those married, more fall into the social conservative group, and all but two of the married women have children. The laissez-faire group includes two divorced women who are living with men, as well as another woman living with her fiance, a lifestyle not found among any of the social conservative activists. While the clear majority (90 percent) of the sample are employed outside the home, all women who are full-time homemakers are located within the social conservative group. Half of the overall sample holds jobs directly tied to their political beliefs, e.g. employment in conservative organizations, federal government administrators, etc. The laissez-faire group, however, includes more women who have training and/or who hold professional positions distinct from their political work, e.g. engineer, college professor.

Obviously, one must be cautious in generalizing from the small sample in this study to the population as a whole. While the interviews with local activists took place in Massachusetts, a state that is disproportionately liberal and Irish Catholic, the field data from conferences and the textual analysis do draw on a national pool of activists. Moreover, because the basic division in political beliefs at the heart of this analysis is consistent with the findings regarding the dual social bases and ideological tensions historically present in the American Right, there is reason to believe that the findings here are true for the New Right as a whole. For parallel findings of the Old Right see Richard Hofstadter, *The Paranoid Style in American Politics* (Chicago: University of Chicago Press, 1952); Lipset and Raab, *The Politics of Unreason*; Grace A. Pheneger, "The Correlation Between Religious Fundamentalism and Political Ultra-Conservatism," M.A. Thesis, Bowling Green State University, 1966; Immanuel Wallerstein, "McCarthyism and the Conservative," M.S. Thesis, Columbia University, 1954; Raymond Wolfinger, *et al.*, "America's Radical Right: Politics and Ideology," in Robert A. Schoenberger (ed.), *The American Right Wing: Readings in Political Behavior* (New York: Holt, Rinehardt, and Winston, 1969).

8. Whether the founders of classical liberalism would associate themselves with laissez-faire conservatism is another question. In fact, while Adam Smith advocated free trade and extolled the self-regulating market, he also expressed much skepticism about the morals of businessmen. His view of the self-interested nature of individuals was also accompanied by belief in a natural sympathy toward others; see Adam Smith, *The Theory of Moral Sentiments* (New York: Kelley, 1966).

9. See Connie Marshner, "Who Is the New Traditional Woman?," paper presented at Family Forum II Conference, Washington, D.C., 1982.

10. See Jaynann M. Payne, "Teach a Child to Be a Winner!" in *The Child: Who Cares?* (Salt Lake City: Utah Association of Women, 1978), p. 33.

11. See Frances Fitzgerald, "A Reporter at Large — A Disciplined, Charging Army," *New Yorker*, 57 (May 18, 1981), p. 110.

12. See Marshner, "Who Is the New Traditional Woman?"

13. See Phyllis Schlafly, *The Power of the Positive Woman* (New York: Jove, 1977), pp. 45-56.

14. See Jeane J. Kirkpatrick, *Political Woman* (New York: Basic Books, 1974), p. 245.

15. See Onalee McGraw, *The Family, Feminism and the Therapeutic State* (Washington, D.C.: Heritage Foundation, 1980).

16. *Ibid*, pp. 1, 19.

17. See Marshner, "Who Is the New Traditional Woman?"

18. See Schlafly, *The Power of the Positive Woman*, p. 75.

19. *Ibid.*, p. 100.

20. *Ibid.*, pp. 72-73.

21. In particular, laissez-faire conservatives come close to the views of liberal feminists; see Zillah Eisenstein, *The Radical Future of Liberal Feminism* (New York: Longman, 1981).

22. Schlafly , *The Power of the Positive Woman*, p. 177.

23. Marshner, "Who Is the New Traditional Woman?"

24. See Kirkpatrick, *Political Woman*.

25. For discussion of the "false consciousness" of right-wing women see Shirley Rogers Radl, *The Invisible Woman: Target of the Religious New Right* (New York: Delacorte, 1983), p. 117. A notable exception to this assumption of the "false consciousness" of the anti-feminist woman is Luker, *Abortion and the Politics of Motherhood.* Luker carefully and sensitively portrays both sides of the abortion debate, revealing how the pro-life and pro-choice positions are rooted in different sets of interests and values.

26. See Dworkin, *Right-Wing Women*, p. 17.

27. I am indebted to Kristin Luker for making use of this distinction drawn from Marx. Marx discusses a class in itself and a class for itself in discussing how capital creates a mass of people in a common situation who share common interests. See, for example, Karl Marx, "The Poverty of Philosophy," in Robert C. Tucker (ed.), *The Marx-Engels Reader* (New York: Norton, 1978), p. 218. While I argue here that social conservative women are motivated out of gender interests and laissez-faire conservative women out of their self-interest as actors in the marketplace, I believe both act to protect both status and class interests. Contrary to much previous research on right-wing movements, I think it is a mistake to separate the motivation for political activism into two distinct types. The social conservative woman's defense of traditional gender roles protects a particular economic arrangement in which the male is the breadwinner of the family. So, too, while laissez-faire conservative belief is premised on support for small business, belief in individual liberty and anti-Communism are deeply

held values that translate into more "symbolic" behavior as well, e.g. petitions condemning Polish repression of Solidarity and participation in counter-demonstrations to the nuclear freeze movement.

28. See note 8 above.

29. See Catherine Arnott, "Feminists and Anti-Feminists as True Believers," *Sociology and Social Research* 57 (1973):300-306; Arrington and Kyle, "Equal Rights Amendment Activists;" Janet K. Boles, *The Politics of the Equal Rights Amendment: Conflict and the Decision Process* (New York: Longman, 1979); Brady and Tedin, "Ladies in Pink;" Carol Mueller, "Oppositional Consciousness and ERA Activists in Three States," paper presented at the American Sociological Association Meetings (San Francisco, 1980); Carol Mueller and Thomas Dimieri, "Feminism vs. Anti-Feminism: The Structure of Belief Systems Among Contending ERA Activists," Working Paper No. 47 (Wellesley, Mass.: Wellesley Center for Research on Women, 1980).

30. See U.S. Department of Labor, *Employment in Perspective: Working Women: Annual Summary* (Washington, D.C.: Government Printing Office, 1981).

31. See Virginia Sapiro, *The Political Integration of Women: Roles, Socialization, and Politics* (Urbana: University of Illinois Press, 1983), p. 182.

32. See Sandra Salmans, "Women's Panel Using Economy to Back Reagan," *New York Times* (May 22, 1984).

PART THREE

Dilemmas and Strategies

19

The Preferential Symbol for Islamic Identity: Women in Muslim Personal Laws

Marie-Aimée Hélie-Lucas

Introduction:
Fundamental Movements and Muslim Identity

Fundamentalist movements in the Muslim world emerged under diverse political and economic circumstances. Although they are present everywhere and display some similarities, it would be erroneous to analyze them as a single and homogeneous movement.[1] An ahistorical image of fundamentalism can only confound the opportunity to confront politically its various forms. There is not one uniform fundamentalist "monster," but rather several fundamentalisms. This being stated, one should add that what fundamentalisms do have in common pertains to identity politics and affects women directly.

Fundamentalists' discourse offers a consensus on two points which are intertwined: the quest for identity and the woman question. Their discourse presents striking similarities in political and historical contexts which are drastically different: whether Muslims are a majority or a minority, whether the state declares itself socialist or capitalist, whether it is a democracy or a kingdom, whether it has been Islamized long ago or recently, whether it has been under foreign rule for a long time or independent, fundamentalists declare Islam to be in danger.[2] Islam as both religion and cultural identity is always in danger, whether it is threatened by colonialism, imperialism, capitalism, socialism, foreign ideologies or other dominant religions. When a group identity is threatened, those who do not unconditionally devote their energy to its survival, defense and resistance, or who challenge any aspect of its culture, become traitors to the group. Consequently, although the threat is generally described as external (the West, imperialism, or another religious group) the worst enemy will always be the alienated national elites who have lost their identity and play the Trojan Horse vis-à-vis the group's identity.

Failing to describe identity in positive terms, as well as to promote any specificity in Islamic politics or Islamic economics,[3] fundamentalists have only succeeded in identifying one area as the essence of Islamic identity: the private sphere. They therefore concentrate their efforts on Personal Law and on the family, which become the epitome of Islamic politics, a condensation of all other identities, and a place of refuge. Whoever challenges this refuge threatens all the multiple identities at once, as well as the essence of identity.

The "external threat" to identity is perceived and described as monolithic, deprived of internal contradictions and therefore of potential allies.[4] To this monolith one opposes another monolith. Inner contradictions must be veiled and their solution postponed to a utopian moment in time when identity will no longer be under threat: after the liberation struggle, after rebuilding the nation, after the war, or after reconstruction of the economy.[5] Priority is thus given time and again to other problems and exclude both popular demands and women's claim for a better status in their society. Moreover, any attempt to raise questions other than defense of the threatened identity could divert attention from it, and are equated to betrayal of the nation, community, culture, or religion.

Identity is thus defensive and closed upon itself. The concepts used to describe this secluded identity[6] explicitly refer to a retro-movement: "going back to our sources," "going back to our roots," "going back to our authentic values," "going back to our Islamic values," "going back to our traditions." Both religion and traditions are seen as ahistorical, fixed and immobile in the past. This quest for a transcultural and transhistorical Muslim identity completely negates the diversity of traditions and cultures in which Islam has been propagated, as well as their living history. It denies re-interpretation of Islam and does not take into account the fact that Islam has expanded and is still expanding in all continents and in the "developed West" as well.[7]

A Question of Definition: Islam and Muslims

Fundamentalists speak in the name of Islam, and unfortunately there is a common tendency to conflate Islam and Muslims. We feel that the adjective Muslim should be used to describe the social reality of the Muslim world as it is—people, countries, states, laws and customs—without assuming that what Muslims do is Islamic. The term Islam should be used for religion as such, theological reflections and interpretations of the Quran. In other words, we do not believe that Islamic states exist, but that there are Muslim states.

Debates often take place among Muslims about what Islam is or should be. Rather than speculating about a true and authentic Islam, we would simply use the term Muslim to describe what those who claim to believe in Islam and those who claim to live according to rules edicted by their God and those who claim to build nations which abide by those, do in the real world. In other words, Islam as it should be, Muslims as they are.

Women as Pillars and Weak Points
in the Construction of Identity

In spite of their diversity, although Muslim fundamentalist groups represent a variety of interests and classes, and fulfill different psychological and political needs, their discourse centers around identity in three senses: identity as threatened; identity as a process of "going back"; and, identity confined to the private sphere. And although the threat is generally external, monolithic and all-evil, educated elites and women are the weak points in the defence system as well as the potential allies of the external enemy. This in turn justifies the closing of identity upon itself, like a fortress, and the closing of women within the fortress.

The practical consequences of this ideological stand shape women's lives as well as their responses to fundamentalists. At a political level, they fear being accused of betrayal, since challenging any aspect of identity is betraying the whole; at a cultural level, traditions are defined as immutable; at a religious level, the end of interpretation of the Quran confines women into a model of society, way of life, dress and behavior as close as possible to the historical model born in the Middle East 14 centuries ago; and finally, at a legal level, the emphasis is on Personal Laws as the means to defend identity.

Fundamentalists do not merely share a common discourse on identity and women; they also achieve common immediate goals: They have successfully put pressure on governments to adjust Personal Laws to their definition of Islamic identity. Personal Laws directly affect women: they pertain to questions of marriage, divorce, child custody, and inheritance. Therefore they also determine what a Muslim woman's behavior should be and link her to the defense of the threatened identity.

To be the guardians of identity and culture is an honor in the fundamentalist discourse. Women are honored for as long as they keep culture and religion in the way they are told to do; breeders and raisers of good Muslims, women should behave as a model for the sons, who are warriors of Islam. Recently published studies on women in Nazi Germany provide elements of comparison with women living under or participating in Muslim fundamentalism.[8] What is common to both is the ideal of Mothers and of Family keepers tied up with the notion of reproducing the best possible group (race or religion) in the context of an economic crisis and expansionist views over other nations. Being the guardian is so central to the threatened identity that it is also identified as the weakest point, the most vulnerable to be protected from alien influences. Being the guardian is being a potential traitor who should therefore be closely watched. Laws should be codified which clearly fix the private sphere as central to protection of the threatened identity, bind women to their role of guardians and prevent them from any possibility to fulfill the dark part of their natural mission, to show the other profile of their Janus face, prevent them from betrayal and the destruction of the community—national, religious, or communal.

Women Living Under Muslim Laws

About 450 million women live in Muslim countries and communities, throughout five continents. The majority of them live under "Muslim laws," that is, Muslim Personal Laws, also known as Family Codes. These laws are presented as "Islamic" and consequently as the unique and untouchable transcription of the word of God. They have many commonalities but also significant differences from one country to the other. This is due to two reasons: the incorporation of local traditions and the political use of religion.

Islam is a religion which constantly expands—probably the only one to do so nowadays. In the process it invariably incorporates ways of life and customs from different cultures. Muslim laws as they exist in the real world today result from the combination of interpretations of the Quran entwined with local traditions. It is important to fully realize that although they are not "Islamic," traditions are enforced upon women in the name of Islam. Belonging to a specific Muslim community is equated with accepting all the religio-cultural aspects which make for this society. The Semitic tradition of veiling and/or secluding women in the Middle East and North Africa; female genital mutilation in Egypt, Sudan and other countries of West Africa; or the Hindu tradition of caste and dowry in India and Sri Lanka are all specific to the regions where they prevail.[9] Nevertheless, Muslim peoples and certainly women are made to believe that their local traditions are part and parcel of being a Muslim and—in the final analysis—are Islamic.

Muslim states also interpret Islam in ways which suit their local policies, even on very crucial ideological issues. An example of the fact that Muslim states do not have a common policy inspired by Islam can be found in the diversity of stands taken on the question of contraception and abortion. Both are legal in Tunisia; both are enforced on women in Bangladesh together with sterilization for both sexes; contraception is allowed but abortion forbidden in Pakistan. Algeria has forbidden both for a long time (from 1962 till 1974) in spite of a *fatwa* issued a year after independence by the High Islamic council in Algiers; it finally allowed contraception when our annual population growth rate had reached 3.5, threatening the wealth and privileges of the ex-socialist bureaucrats who by then had turned into a classical bourgeoisie owning the means of production.[10] All these countries claim that they defined their population policy according to the spirit of Islam. In each country, people and certainly women are made to believe that the rules enforced locally or nationally reflect the spirit of Islam and are injunctions of God that Muslim states apply in their legislation. Moreover, the official discourse implies or eventually states that these laws are Islamic.

The mere confrontation of women from various Muslim backgrounds is in itself enlightening in so far as it permits challenging the notion of one homogeneous Muslim world and the existence of a Muslim law which would genuinely be Islamic.[11] On the contrary, it draws attention to the fact that Muslim Laws are grounded in history and culture, *hic et nunc*, as well as to the fact that they are used for political purposes.

Fundamentalists and the State

In July 1984 the first Action Committee of Women Living Under Muslim Laws defined themselves as "Women whose lives are shaped, conditioned and governed by laws, both written and unwritten, drawn from interpretations of the Quran tied up with local traditions." The Action Committee later stated that "generally speaking, men and the

State use these (laws) against women, and have done so under various political regimes."[12]

During the past two decades and more especially during the last one, Muslim Personal Laws have been at the center of Muslim identities; new Muslim Personal Laws have been passed, reinforced, or modified in ways which are highly unfavorable to women. This phenomenon could be interpreted as the expression of the power of fundamentalists, and as the collusion of states with fundamentalist movements.[13] No matter whether fundamentalists are in power or in the position of a powerful main opposition party, or whether they are just growing, in most cases, their claim to an "Islamic" private sphere through the adoption of personal laws is very generally heard by those in power.[14] This happens whatever their general political stands would otherwise be.[15] Is it that the woman question is so sensitive, as they pretend, that their authority and their position could be challenged on this issue? Or is it rather that women's subordination is thrown to the crowd to amuse itself with, like crumbs are thrown to the poor, while serious political matters remain in their hands? Are we the *monnaie d'échange* they use to remain in power? Could it also be that the control of women prepares for a brutalization of the society which suits the needs of the powers-that-be to control people? Although states may resist on other points the rise of fundamentalists, family affairs and women's subordination are generally, with rare exceptions, the reflection of the fundamentalist definition of identity, and laws are passed or modified in order to meet their demands. The past decade has seen increasingly the collusion of states with fundamentalists in these matters. It is interesting to note that this happens even in countries where fundamentalists are otherwise fought, banned, and imprisoned for their challenge to the state.

For example, in 1984 the first Family Code was passed in Algeria, 22 years after independence. It deprives Algerian women of the right to marry (they have to be given in marriage by a *wali*, a matrimonial tutor), to divorce (except for very specific cases, only husbands can initiate a divorce), to have permanent custody of their children (the children may stay with their mothers until the age of five for a boy and ten for a girl, after which they will be returned to their guardian).[16] Women are also granted an unequal share of inheritance. Men are allowed polygamy and the right to repudiate their wives. In the same year, 1984, Egyptian women lost the right to remain in the marital home with their children after a divorce, a right which they had won after a decade-long battle. In 1985, the Central Government of India passed "the Muslim Women Protection of the Right to Divorce Bill" by which Indian women from the Muslim community are now deprived of the right to maintenance after divorce. This "protection of the right" obviously refers to their right to be Muslims and therefore deprived of maintenance, rather than to their rights as women and Indian citizens, including the right to maintenance. In 1986 Sri Lanka appointed a Commission to reform Muslim Personal Law in a way which was most unfavorable to women. In 1987 and 1989 the ostensibly socialist and secular government of Mauritius accepted the project pushed forward by the Muslim main opposition party to reintroduce *Sharia* for the Muslim community. This will amount to depriving women born in the Muslim community of rights that all other Mauritian women will enjoy in the country: for instance, right to divorce and equal right to inheritance. In 1990 the Algerian government decreed that each man could vote by delegation for three women in his family. On the 15 of March 1990 the secular Iraqi Revolutionary Command Council decreed that each man could kill a well-defined list of kinswomen on the accusation of adultery. Similar attempts have taken place in several other countries in Africa. Sharia is being passed in several countries (including Sudan and Pakistan) which will supersede Muslim Personal Laws and restrict even further women's freedom, given the present interpretations of Sharia.

In countries of emigration, such as Britain and France, and in the Caribbean, Muslims have demanded that Personal Laws be introduced. Migrants from Muslim communities in France therefore demand a major constitutional change from secularism to a multi-religious state. It is interesting to note that the first right to be claimed as symbolic of Muslim-ness is polygamy, as one could observe in *Le Courrier des Lecteurs of Le Monde* during the 1988 controversy. Reports from feminist Muslim groups in Sri Lanka, Malaysia and India indicate the desire for polygamy as a major cause for conversions to Islam. We have no reports yet from African countries in which Islam has been expanding rapidly in the past 20 years, and where polygamous tradition preceded conversion to Islam. This does not seem to apply to converts in Western Europe and North America, where federal laws forbid polygamy.

Construction and Enforcement of
a Transnational Muslim Identity

One could examine these legal changes in the light of the internal politics of the concerned countries which lead to compromise with rising fundamentalist groups. This would fail to take into account the international dimension of this phenomenon. Not only is there concomitance between the various attempts to promote more "Islamic" versions of Muslim laws, but there are also obvious interconnections. For instance, after the Shah Bano case in India, the Sri Lankan government invited an Indian scholar as adviser for its Commission to reform Muslim Law. More recently, the main opposition party in Mauritius, the Muslim Party, is proposing the Indian Muslim Personal Law as a model for the Mauritius Muslim Personal Law, and it too has brought in an Indian adviser. In many other instances we found Saudi, Pakistani, or Iranian advisers. It is important to fully realize the extent of fundamentalists' attempts to enforce their views of Islamic society through the adoption of Muslim Personal Laws.

The same spirit of internationalism is to be found in military training of the Muslim youth and in setting up fundamentalist groups both for men and for women, with attached privileges. These efforts imply a wide circulation of funds. Research on the origins and circuits of the funds may allow identification of the connections between Muslim private capital, the involvement of states in promoting fundamentalist movements, and the fundamentalist groups operating locally, nationally and regionally.[17]

Women's Internalization of Identity Politics

Women's responses to this state of affairs show the impact that fundamentalist ideologies have, not only on governments and subsequent legal decisions affecting women, but also on the women's movement itself. Women's organizations range from participating in the fundamentalist movement, to working for reform within the framework of Islam, and to fighting for a secular state and secular laws. In spite of this wide range of tendencies and strategies, all of them have internalized some of the concepts developed and used by fundamentalists. In particular they have internalized the notion of an external monolithic enemy, and the fear of betraying their identity— defined as group identity, rather than their gender identity in the group. To a large extent, they also accept tradition, not as a living history which informs their present and future, but as a dead body to be revived and maintained in its former (imagined) shape. And finally, they acknowledge their central role in identity politics.

In the same way that those who lived for a long time in a state of lack of democracy have difficulties in reinventing democratic practices (even if they fought for reaching such a stage), it is not easy today to step out of ideological constructions of the fundamentalist women-centered discourse on identity. One should not underestimate the impact of this discourse on women's minds. Its consequences are clearly visible in the efforts that women have to make in order to question not only fundamentalist discriminatory practices against women but also the premises which inform these practices.

Internalization by women of fundamentalists' philosophy, concepts and biased hypotheses has many consequences at the level of their strategies. Internalizing the notion that Islam is in danger—therefore that the community is in danger—implies that in their practices, women must abide by an established set of priorities. Thus they become an easy prey for political manipulation: Since facing an external threat requires total unity of the group, then wars, communal tensions, any suitable political event will be used against women to compel them to join the nation's unity and postpone their demands. We could provide many examples.[18] The Algerian case is a landmark insofar as women not only postponed their demands but were later forced to renounce them until very recently. For decades, they were fully cheated.[19] Even in recent history, in Palestine for instance, where women are trying to build an autonomous movement, priority is still given to the liberation struggle, and women's struggles will still come as their second or third priority.

As the Left before them, women who try to defend their rights in Muslim contexts are generally accused of importing a foreign ideology whenever they ask for more social justice. But while the Left's response was to point at universal values of social justice, women accept the fundamentalist premises that in matters concerning the private sphere, universal is equated to being West-dominated. Consequently defending universal values of social justice becomes unacceptable when it comes to the woman question. This is why, instead of going straight to the point, women first try to demonstrate that they are truly and genuinely rooted in their own culture, that they are not alienated in non-indigenous ideologies, that they do not side with external enemies. Trying in vain to legitimize themselves and their struggle according to the criteria for legitimacy set by fundamentalists, they expend considerable time and energy trying to distinguish themselves from "Western feminists" as "Third World feminists"—as if these categories too were homogeneous aggregates of interchangeable individuals, without ideological differences, without classes and conflicting interests, a very mechanistic model indeed. To a certain extent, one could say that women thus also abide by the notion of the superiority of Muslims over other religious groups, a xenophobia which theologians denounce as contrary to the spirit of tolerance in Islam, but which is also present in the policies of some contemporary Muslim states.

It sometimes takes very long before individuals dare transgress the "betrayal complex," and try and identify their allies both inside and outside their community. It is only after experiencing again and again that the time for women's demands is never now, but always later (reasons given for it may unfortunately be very convincing, as for instance when Palestine is under brutal attack by Israel, or in Pakistan under Benazir Bhutto,[20] or during the Gulf war) that women dare make a breakthrough out of the fortress of communal, national and religious identity.

Women's Responses and Strategies

A sort of intermediate step is offered by the network Women Living Under Muslim Laws which allows women from Muslim contexts to speak out freely in the secure space of the Muslim *umma*, without interference from outsiders. It also provides for the first cross-cultural comparison between the various forms of Muslim ways of life and laws affecting women, and a first insight to their entwinement with indigenous cultures—therefore allowing women to make crucial distinctions between what is specifically religious, what pertains to traditions, and what is the political use of both religion and traditions in their own set up.[21]

Many women's groups in Muslim countries and communities devote time to research their feminist ancestors, not only in an effort to recover their own history as women, but also in the vain hope of stopping accusations of Westernization by rightists, and in quest for their legitimacy. They may also try and excavate traditions in an attempt to show that traditions were not necessarily unfavorable to women if placed in their historical context.[22] This again refers to a definition of traditions as a thing from the past, to be opposed to "modernity," while modernity should be understood as the present stage of traditions, the normal evolution of tradition and culture evolving from the past to adjust to the present context. However, it is very clear that many traditions which were indeed favorable to women are at present being eradicated,[23] while our rulers introduce new "traditions" directly inspired by Western colonization, without ever being accused of betrayal and collusion with the West, not even by women's groups themselves. In this general context, one can identify three main strategies in the women's movement in Muslim countries and communities:

1. Women joining fundamentalist groups—a strategy which I tend to see as a sort of entryism. On the one hand this strategy avoids challenging Muslim identity, and it frees from the fear of betrayal;

on the other hand, because fundamentalist groups have both the will and the funds to do so, they offer various gratifications and advantages to their members, such as grants to study, free medical care, and loans without interest. Women followers also benefit from social and parental recognition, the right and encouragement to study (although they may not freely choose their subject, as there are areas of knowledge which are forbidden to women), a chance to choose their husband within the group instead of going through an arranged marriage, and so on.[24] An increasing number of women join fundamentalist groups throughout the world. We cannot dismiss this important social and political phenomenon by stigmatizing these women and their ideological alienation. Neither can we simply say that there are material benefits which no other group ever offered them. We believe that a serious reason for their choice is that no alternative—at the religious and therefore at the identity level—ever existed until recently.[25] Fundamentalists are the first ones to consider and use women and their needs to try and reach out to them, and to acknowledge them as a political force which can be maneuvered and is worth trying to gain to the cause. The new strategy, described in the following paragraphs, will hopefully provide for the philosophical needs of those who at present see no way out of the religious frame hijacked by fundamentalists.

2. Women working from within the frame of Islam, both at the level of religion and at the level of culture. Although they are not yet very visible, there are feminist theologians and historians within the Muslim world. They represent a very important ideological current and offer a real alternative to the previous strategy. Women theologians in search of a "true" Islam are currently trying to promote a liberation theology in Islam by reviving the tradition of reinterpretation of the Quran. Several men in recent history have devoted their time and paid with their lives for their progressive interpretations of the Quran[26] and if there were women interpreters of the Quran in modern history, we have lost track of them. But there are now women who have attained a high level in theology and who feel that progressive male interpreters of the Quran have not fully explored it from the point of view of women. They go back to the original Arabic text and will propose, in the spirit of what they believe is true Islam, their own interpretation of the verses on which fundamentalists base their oppression of women.[27] They also point to the historical context of the text which may lead to more enlightened interpretations.

Similarly, women historians attempt to track and recapture women's history, to show the historical role of leading women in the transformation of customs and traditions. They stress that this role was seen neither as threatening to the group's identity nor as cutting them off from their cultural or religious roots. Both theologians and historians have worked in isolation for a long time. They now have opportunities to come together and reinforce each other as well as opportunities to reach out to their real audience, to women activists who are craving for such knowledge. Even though such approaches are indeed seen as betrayals by fundamentalists, women feel secure that these strategies do not cut them off from the masses, and challenge the accusation of betrayal by closing themselves within an Islamic frame of thought. We nevertheless believe that if such women theologians and historians would gain audience of women in masses, they will, as their male counterparts did, pay with their lives for the social change that their religious and philosophical work aims at.

3. Women fighting for secularism and for laws which would reflect the present understanding of what human rights are and should be in the world today. Those are under the fiercest attacks. These women are left unprotected because they step out of both religious and cultural frames. Although they state that they did not renounce their religious, cultural and national identities, they are perceived as having lost them all, and are regarded as outcasts. Not only are they accused and rejected but each of them as a single individual is treated as if their sole betrayal would endanger both their society and the whole of the Muslim world.[28] They advocate that religion is a private affair for individuals to choose and plead for the separation of religion from the state.[29] They believe in values which are neither the property of Muslims nor of the West and tend to turn to internationalism as the only way for them to build up their legitimacy, as well as a strategy for information, support and solidarity amongst themselves across national, religious and cultural boundaries.

But it is interesting to note that internationalism in their view does not transcend and erase their belonging to a cultural-religious compound in which they still want to grow their roots; nor does it come into conflict with forms of nationalism drawn from the full consciousness of imperialism and memories of the time of colonization. Although they are in a minority, they seem to me the only alternative to identity politics as defined and shaped by fundamentalists, the only hope for the recognition of concomitant non-antagonistic, multiple identities in each individual.

Notes

1. One witnesses various attempts to globally qualify fundamentalism in political, religious or cultural terms, for instance as totalitarianism, revivalism, traditionalism, etc. We believe these generalizations to be both inadequate and dangerous. See Olivier Roy, "Fundamentalism, Traditionalism and Islam," *Telos* 65 (1985):122-127; also see Hassan Hanafi, "The Origins of Violence in Contemporary Islam," *Development* 1 (1987), Special issue on Culture and Ethnicity, pp. 56-61; and also Tibi Bassam, "Neo-Islamic Fundamentalism," in *ibid.*, pp. 62-66.

2. This is true from socialist Algeria to rich capitalist Arabia, from the Middle East where Islam was born to the Pakistani state set up "for Muslims only" in 1947 or to recently converted sub-Saharan African countries, from Arab countries with nearly 100 percent Muslims to Indian or Sri Lankan minorities, etc.

3. See for example, Charles Issawi, cited by Anwar H. Syed in "Revitalising the Muslim Community," *Race and Class* XXVIII (3) (1987). According to Issawi: "Islam does not identify preferred modes for organizing production, but its injunctions regarding property have implications relevant to economic organization. First it secures the right to property for individuals, groups, and the community. The economies of many Muslim countries are actually mixed. Their governments have taken over banking, insurance, transport, communications, mining and some large scale manufacturing. This has happened partly from nationalizing enterprises once in foreign or domestic ownership. In addition, these governments regulate industry and commerce in the private sector. Considering Islam's disapproval of unearned income, exploitation and excess in all matters, ceilings on profits in both public and private sectors would also be appropriate." Syed concludes that "there is general agreement that since 661 no Muslim government has qualified as Islamic."

4. It is especially clear when it comes to "the West" and "Imperialism," but the same simplistic analysis applies to any other external enemy. Without denying imperialism as such, one should be aware of the fact that presenting Western societies as homogeneous, classless and casteless, without any progressive forces attempting to oppose their government policies, deprives us of making fruitful alliances and strengthening each others' knowledge, awareness and activities. This causes immense damage on both sides by narrowing our perspectives. In our countries, Marxists thirty years ago and feminists more recently have renounced positive alliances for fear of being accused of siding with the West and "importing foreign ideologies." Similarly,

the fact that Western media now present Islam as the threatening devil (in place of the Reds) will initiate the same defense mechanism.

5. Algeria is a very good example of how women's demands were declared a non-priority during the liberation struggle and after. In spite of their attempts to avoid such a trap, one is not sure that Palestinian women will be able to push forward their demands while their people live under such a pressure. Cf: Marie-Aimée Hélie-Lucas, "The Role of Women During the Algerian Liberation Struggle and After," in Eva Isakson (ed.), *Women and the Military System* (London: Harvester-Wheatsheaf, 1988), pp. 171-190.

6. Women's veil could be seen as a sign of the secluded identity and apartheid of the whole society.

7. In the past thirty years Islam has spread very rapidly throughout Africa. The "going back to our traditions" movement did not lead to a return to animism, but to the choice of Islam — the religion of slave traders — against Christianity — the religion of colonizers.

8. Claudia Koonz, *Mothers in the Fatherland, Women in the Family and Nazi Politics* (New York: St Martin's Press, 1986). Cf. *Cahiers du Feminisme*, November 1990, on Women and Nazism.

9. Cf. Dossiers *Women Living Under Muslim Laws*, nos. 1 to 6 (1986-1989), edited by M-A. Hélie-Lucas.

10. M-A. Hélie-Lucas, "La politique de formation en Algérie, comme indicateur d'une situation de classe," *Temps Moderne*, no. special "Du Maghreb," Paris 1974. See also M-A. Hélie-Lucas, "Women in the Algerian Liberation Struggle and After," presented at a conference at the Transnational Institute, Amsterdam, 1984.

11. See Documents *Women Living Under Muslim Laws Exchange Programme* (1988), and *Aramon Plan of Action* (1986).

12. In 1988 the Women Living Under Muslim Laws network organized an Exchange Programme by which women from 18 different Muslim countries were sent to each others' countries; they were hosted by women's groups and introduced to the diversity of cultures and practices all believed to be inspired by religion. This exercise enabled them to distinguish in their own set up what pertains to religion, what pertains to culture, and what is the political use of both, or, as Salma Sobhan once described it: "It helps us analyze how all these have been woven together to form a particular garment that women have to wear willingly or unwillingly."

13. The debate on the Woman Question and the nature of the State is very important among feminists from Muslim countries. See essays in Deniz Kandiyoti (ed.), *Women, the State and Islam* (London: Macmillan, 1991).

14. In France and in Britain, the debate on "respect of the other's culture" has been raging over the past few years. The traditional Left caught into its white colonial guilt is so afraid to be labeled racist that they have lost all shame and

are prepared to cover crimes against women in the name of respect of culture, while feminists try to link up with indigenous women's demands. The most fruitful alliance of this kind is the London-based group "Women Against Fundamentalism," which takes up issues against Christian fundamentalism in Ireland, Muslim fundamentalism in Britain, and racism in the U.K. Britain has accepted that separate schools for Muslim girls be set up, where the curriculum is drastically different from both the curriculum of British children in British schools and of Muslim boys in Muslim schools. Women in France (both French and migrants working together) who take to court parents who practice female genital mutilation on their baby daughters are fiercely attacked both by fundamentalists of all sorts and by the liberal Left who support "the right to be different."

15. On March 15, 1990, the Iraqi Revolutionary Command Council declared it legal for Iraqi men to kill their mothers, wives, daughters and their paternal nieces and cousins accused of *zina* (fornication and adultery); the decree specified that they could "not be brought to justice" for acting as prosecutors and executioners of the suspected women, who then had no chance to even try and prove their innocence. Until recently, the Iraqi Baath government was the main exemplar of a secular Arab state which did not draw on Quranic interpretations for its laws and policies. The fact that it did take inspiration from other Muslim states on the issue of zina in drafting this decree (and made it worse, to the horror of believers who protested) did not attract attention, except from women activists inside and outside the Muslim world.

16. That is, provided the ex-husband is satisfied with her way of bringing them up, otherwise he can take them back, being the official guardian. Mothers cannot remarry without losing their children; they also have to live close enough to where their ex-husbands live so that he can exercise his right to control the children's education as often as he likes. In other words, mothers are used as cheap labor to bear the burden of raising small children, while all rights remain with fathers.

17. There is a need to study the source of fundamentalist funding and how funds are spent. We believe that the obvious sources of funding (such as Saudi Arabia and Iran) are not the only ones and recently discovered that massive funding comes from the U.S. We are also aware of the fact that funds coming from one specific country go to a second one in order to provide military training for the youth of a third one. It is therefore very difficult to track down. As far as the arms trade goes, we would welcome research which would account for both arms traders and arms buyers.

18. On the Sheenaaz Sheikh case, see *Women Living Under Muslim Laws Dossier* 1 and 2 (1986).

19. Hélie-Lucas, "Bound and Gagged by the Family Code," reproduced in *Women Living Under Muslim Laws Dossier* 5/6 (1989).

20. Under Benazir Bhutto, Pakistani women reproduced the experience of Algerian women under "specific socialism": for fear of giving reasons for fundamentalists to attack the legal government, they did not make any demands which could have aggravated the situation, thus losing precious time.

21. See Documents *Women Living Under Muslim Laws Exchange Programme* (1988).

22. Most progressive theologians and interpreters of the Quran introduce a historical factor in their analysis of the improvement that Mohammad brought to women in his time; for instance, they would quote his opposition to female infanticide. Others would research on rights for women to end their marriage or own property, looking at it both from the point of view of religious rights and customary rights.

23. For example, in the Arab and Middle East tradition women would keep their father's name throughout their lives and would be known as X, daughter of Y (or would also be referred to as X, mother of Z). Now bureaucrats are imposing the Western tradition of the husband's name. Considering the number of divorces and repudiations, women will now have to be called by 4 or 5 different names in their life. Their sense of self-identity will certainly be shattered. Bureaucrats do not seem troubled with this introduction of such an alien tradition.

24. Though women who join fundamentalist groups claim that they get all these benefits, it clearly appears as self-justificatory. Nevertheless, one has to admit that neither the Left nor governments have even pretended to cater to the needs of people the way fundamentalists do. As an example, in Algeria in the late 1970s, when there were neither food on the market nor clothing in the shops to buy (regardless of prices), the Muslim Brothers were the ones who distributed semolina (the basis of couscous, a very popular basic dish), as well as "Islamic dress" at the mosques on Fridays. This is how the *hijab* Iranian style — definitely an untraditional women's dress in Algeria — was introduced in our country. The Muslim Brothers in Algeria and fundamentalist groups in many other countries are the only ones who have both the will and the money to afford to be populists. Their money obviously comes from various state sources, which allow them to generate income and finance their projects. The powerful Arkam, who was visited by a woman activist in Malaysia, has branches in many countries both in Asia and in Africa, as well as in non-Muslim countries (for instance in Australia); they own factories, produce for their own communities who live in autarchy, both in terms of self-subsistence, and for grants, teachings, and religious education.

25. In 1988 the network Women Living Under Muslim Laws planned to explore the possibilities of gathering and circulating information on progressive interpretations of Islam; this project later evolved into identifying feminist interpreters of the Quran, then gathering and circulating their work. In 1988 an

international working group on feminist interpretation of the Quran was launched which held its first meeting in July 1990 in Karachi; since then the group meets regularly; the research done is circulated within the network Women Living Under Muslim Laws.

26. Male progressive interpreters of the Quran have often paid with their lives for their decision to undertake *Ijtihad*. In recent years Tahar Haddad was persecuted in Tunisia, Asghar Ali Engineer escaped bombs in India, and the Sudanese Nour Mahmoud Mohamed Tahir was killed in 1984. The latter's books were publicly burnt, his body buried in a hidden place to prevent pilgrimage, and the possession of his books was punishable.

27. See various publications by Women Living Under Muslim Laws network: *Information Kit on Marriage Contracts and the Delegated Right of Divorce Talaq et tafwez* (1989); *Proceedings of the Meeting on Interpretations of the Koran by Women* (1991); *Les Femmes dans le Coran: Kit d'information préparé pour la réunion du Groupe International de Travail sur les Interprétations Coraniques par les Femmes,* (Juillet 1990, Karachi: Femmes Sous Lois Musulmanes); *Women in the Qur'an: Information Kit prepared for Women Living Under Muslim Laws,* (July 1990), International Working Meeting on Qur'anic Interpretation by Women (Karachi).

28. The claim by fundamentalists that any individual is a threat to the whole of Islam is well illustrated by the Rushdie affair.

29. On the forefront of secularism and the separation of religion from the state are the Algerian women, whose stands are published in *Dossier no. 7* and *8, Women Living Under Muslim Laws.*

20

Identity Politics and Women's Ethnicity

Nira Yuval-Davis

Introduction: Identity Formation

The notion of a generic "woman" functions in feminist thought much the way the notion of generic "man" has functioned in Western philosophy: it obscures the heterogeneity of women and cuts off examination of the significance of such heterogeneity for feminist theory and political activity.[1]

This problematization of the notion of sisterhood which we have started to witness in the last few years in feminist theory and politics, promoted to a large extent by the writings and activities of black feminists, is long overdue and is welcome. However, some of the ways this heterogeneity has been constructed in Left politics in general and feminist politics in particular are problematic. This chapter will examine some of the theoretical and political issues involved, concentrating on the notions of identity, ethnicity, and their specific implications for women. The main argument is that ethnicity cannot be collapsed into identity and/or culture. Ethnicity is also a political category; ethnic movements are political projects, and consequently women's ethnicity can and should be distinguished from men's. This is the context within which Stuart Hall's call for "the return of the subjective" to politics as the epitome of "identity politics" should be evaluated.[2]

The study of identity formation in general and of ethnic identity in particular has preoccupied many social scientists and philosophers. A central dilemma in the field of identity formation is the duality of the individual and society and the equation of "society" with the small group of "the family" or even more specifically with "the father" (as has been the case with Freudian theory regarding the super-ego). Ethnic identities have often been studied in terms of the person's identification with or distancing from fixed external reified ethnicities.[3] On the other hand, post-structural analyses which attempted to go beyond this duality of separate reified realities often lead to the denial of the individual's existence by speaking only of human agencies—subjective manifestation of the general symbolic order. A basic question has been the extent to which one can talk about an essential self, a unitary self or even a minimal self.[4] Whatever the answer to this question, identity constitutes the conscious "self"—the answer, or rather answers, to the question "who am I?" Whether or not the multiple and changing answers to this question constitute different identities (or the Parsonian "roles"), sub-identities or different facets of a unitary construct, they represent the ways individuals experience themselves at specific times. While some of the answers to the question "who am I?" may be transitory or situational (being of a certain age or occupation, or having certain relationships), others are perceived to be permanent and "natural" (sex and familial/ethnic/national origin). All identity dimensions can, in specific social contexts, have higher or lower salience, but often the primordial components of one's identity provoke the most powerful emotions for the individual, through processes of identification which in extreme cases can blur individual and collective boundaries.

However, even these primordial identities are often far from being fixed and unproblematic, because in spite of their "naturalist" character the collectivities with which they identify are far from being fixed and unproblematic themselves. Recently, with the rise of post-modernist theories, identities have become a focus of renewed interest. The exile, the person with fragmented identity, who belongs everywhere and nowhere, has become the symbol of the post-modern epoch. Within the discourses of post-modernism, or of the *New Times*, identities have a "formative, not merely an expressive place in the construction of social and political life."[5]

In order to be able to evaluate Hall's statement, we need to examine both the nature of the relationships between identities of individual subjects and more collective social constructs, as well as the nature of these collective constructs themselves. For the purpose of this chapter, I shall concentrate on ethnic collectivities, although they are by no means the only collectivities in relation to which individual subjects construct their identities.

Ethnic Collectivities

Floya Anthias and I have previously argued that "the only general basis on which we can theorize what can broadly be conceived of as 'ethnic phenomena' in all their diversity, are various forms of ideological constructs which divide people into different collectivities and communities."[6] Historically these collectivities and communities have been formed in many different ways—conquests, colonizations and immigrations have all played their part. Although each of them has to be analyzed in an historically specific manner, one cannot differentiate in an abstract way between ethnic, racial, national and religious collectivities—although one can and should differentiate between their different discourses and projects.[7] What is common to them all, in all their diversity, is that they divide people into collectivities or communities—"imagined ones," to use Anderson's terminology,[8] as they assume a sense of fellowship towards people they do not and can never know, unlike a real community. Moreover, in different social and historical contexts, the same collectivities would be labeled as one or the other. For instance, the same immigrant community in Bradford may be constructed in ethnic, racial and religious discourses as Pakistani, Black and Muslim; or in different times and countries, Jews have been hegemonically constructed as a religious, ethnic, national or racial collectivity.

The exclusionary/inclusionary boundaries which form the collectivities tend to focus around a myth (which may or may not be real) of a common origin or a common destiny, so that membership of the collectivity is normally, although not always, obtained by birth. The boundaries of such collectivities can shift—they can cross-cut, expand or shrink in specific historical or socio-psychological situations. Nor do they have to be symmetrically shared by insiders and outsiders, who might have different criteria or signifiers for membership of the collectivity. For instance, for the Nazis, whoever had a Jewish grandparent was Jewish; for Orthodox Jews only those who have Jewish mothers or who converted according to the *Halakha* are Jewish; and to many secular Jews, if one considers oneself Jewish, then that person is Jewish. Another example is South Africa, where people of mixed-race origin have legally constituted a separate racial category of Colored, while in Britain they are usually considered Black—unless they can "pass" as White.

As we have seen, although the boundaries are ideological, they involve material (biological, legal, social) practices and therefore have material origins and effects. They involve struggles, negotiations and the use of ethnic resources (such as language, culture, religion, material assets and state political powers) in their power relations with other collectivities. Ethnic practices can be used for countering disadvantages or for perpetuating advantages stemming out of the inclusionary/ exclusionary boundaries and the relations of power, of dominance/ subordination which are aspects of this. Within this general framework, national projects would specifically involve demands and/or practices for separate political representation and/or territory for the collectivity; racial projects would involve the use of ethnic categories as signifiers of a fixed immutable deterministic genealogical difference for the purpose of exclusion/inferiorization/exploitation of members of the collectivity thus labeled; and religious projects would involve the establishment of a moral/social order within which the collectivity would be constructed as a centerpoint.

Ethnic collectivities, even when not religious, can provide the members of the collectivity (and often others dominated by it), with a mode of interpreting the world, based both on shared cultural resources and shared collective positioning vis-à-vis other collectivities. Ethnicity, therefore, can provide its members not only with the Andersonian "imagined communities," but also with what Deutch and Schlesinger have called "communicative communities."[9] According to Deutch: "Membership in a people consists in wide complementarity of social communication. It consists in the ability to communicate more effectively, and over a wider range of subjects, with members of one large group than with outsiders."[10] This characterizes all collectivities and not just those minority ones known as ethnic. Hegemonic ethnicities, however, often have the power to "naturalize" their *weltanschauung*, usually using their privileged access to the state apparatus. Thus, they can construct any different ethnicity as deviant in some way or another.

Ethnicity, therefore, cannot be equated with culture, as it is a political phenomenon which uses cultural resources to promote its specific purposes. Moreover, because the struggle for hegemony takes place, at any specific moment, not only between collectivities but also within them, different and sometimes conflicting cultural resources can be used simultaneously by different members of the collectivity. Examples are the use of different *Suras* in the Quran for and against abortions in Egypt, and the promotion of Hebrew versus Yiddish by Zionists versus Bundists. Although at certain historical moments there might be a hegemonic construction of the collectivity's culture and history, the dynamic, evolving, and historical nature of the ethnic phenomenon continuously re-invents, reconstructs, reproduces and develops the cultural inventory of various collectivities. In extreme cases, these processes involve not only the redefinition of ethnic boundaries and their signifiers but also the complete dissolution and/or transformation of the collectivity and its positioning of difference from other collectivities. Examples are the absorption of German-origin Americans into the co-called WASP group, and the evolving category of the Black British.

The existence of a conscious ethnic identity is not even a necessary condition for the construction of ethnicity, although it can often promote it. Ethnicity may be constructed outside the group by the material conditions of the group and its special representation by other groups or by the state. This is often the case where migrant laborers of various ethnic origins are categorized as an ethnic collectivity by state legislation and are viewed and treated as ethnically distinct by the indigenous population. Conditions of reproduction of the ethnic collectivities, as well as their transformation, are related to other forms of social divisions, such as class and gender. For example, class homogeneity within the ethnic group will produce a greater cohesion of interests and goals. Access to state apparatus might support "naturalization" of ethnic culture into hegemonic ways of viewing the world, and special legal status would help to reproduce the boundaries of the ethnic group.

Ethnic identity and often solidarity may occur either as a prerequisite for the group or as an effect of its material, political or ideological positionings. As such, they can provoke the strong passions that Anderson and Kitching have discussed.[11] These passions are linked to the naturalizing elements which are so powerful in the construction of membership in collectivities. They provide "an entity transcendent of the individual both in space and (more importantly) in time, in the name of which sacrifices (including 'the ultimate sacrifice') can be made."[12] In certain historical conditions racial, religious, national and other forms of ethnic projects can aspire to such identifications and investments of the self.

To emphasize the inessentiality of ethnicity and its historical, dynamic and often contested cultural construction, therefore, is not to underestimate the important and powerful role it often plays in social relations in which it is often enmeshed but to which it cannot be reduced. What, then, is the relationship between ethnicity and ethnic identity, and what is the relationship between either of them and what has come to be popularly known as identity politics?

It is clear from the above that ethnicity is much more than a question of ethnic identity. It certainly cannot be summed up as a personal characteristic of the members of the collectivity, as argued in the writings of the British Ethnic School, for example. But it also cannot be summed up as simply "a collective sentiment"[13] even if we can accept, which is doubtful, that the notion of a collective identity does not necessarily involve a process of reification. Ethnicity involves both practice and political struggles.

Women and Ethnicity

Sexual difference and biological reproduction, which form the ontological basis of gender, are usually constructed in a way which assumes "natural" and necessary social effects in terms of the sexual division of labor and other aspects of gender relations. The ideological construction of these necessary social effects involves material practices which are enmeshed in class and ethnic relations and cultural discourses defining the boundaries of feminine and masculine social roles. There is no inherent "femininity" or "masculinity" transcending social relations which construct the biological differences between the sexes. Gender divisions often play a central organizing role in specific constructions of ethnicity, marking ethnic boundaries and reproducing ethnic difference.[14] The "proper" behavior of women is often used to signify the difference between those who belong to the collectivity and those who do not; women are also seen as the "cultural carriers" of the collectivity and transmit it to the future generation; and being properly controlled in terms of marriage and divorce ensures that children born to those women are not only biologically but also symbolically within the boundaries of the collectivity. At the same time, different categories of women within the collectivity may participate in ethnic processes in different ways, according to their class position, age, marital status and sexuality. They develop their own "patriarchal bargains,"[15] although the notion of "womanhood" tends to have a unified ideological connotation within ethnic, as well as within feminist discourses.

There is no space here to carry out an historical survey of the various positions found within the women's movement, in the West and worldwide, concerning the form and contents of feminist actions. A major debate has focused on the extent to which women should struggle alone, or should prioritize common struggles with the male members of their collectivities. A corresponding debate has been about the concrete foci of women's struggles and the extent to which such struggles can be universal beyond cultural and political differences. Examples are the anti-abortion versus reproductive rights campaigns, and the anti-family versus family reunification campaigns. Ultimately these debates have been concerned with the extent and the form with which sisterhood or women's solidarity can and should be achieved. Does the empowerment of women depend primarily on their positions within their collectivities or on the positions their collectivities occupy within the wider society and the state?[16]

There is a certain paradox with respect to women's empowerment, especially when women are members of minority or non-Western collectivities. Often, the particular culture they would like to assert vis-à-vis the hegemonic culture includes also elements which they feel subordinate them as women and which they would like to resist and transform within their own community.

Identity Politics

The above analysis should help us to clarify certain confusions which exist concerning identity politics in general and identity politics and women in particular. Some of these confusions have emanated from equating culture and ethnicity on the one hand, or identity and ethnicity on the other hand. The different discourses and practices of culture, ethnicity and identity have been collapsed together within the tradition of consciousness raising, and when practicing the political slogan of "the personal is the political."[17] Consciousness-raising is a powerful tool which has been used for a number of positive and important purposes within the feminist and other leftist as well as ethnic movements since the late 1960s. It can empower people, bond them together in a sense of solidarity which is emotional as well as intellectual or political, and can also problematize arenas of life and social norms which tend to be "naturalized" within hegemonic cultures and which were formerly considered to be outside the arena of "normal" politics.

On the other hand, consciousness-raising techniques assume as a basis for political action a reality that has to be discovered and then changed, rather than a reality which is being created and re-created when practiced and discussed. Moreover, this reality is assumed to be shared by all members of the social category within which the consciousness raising movement operates who are perceived to constitute a basically homogeneous social grouping sharing the same interests. Individual identity has become equated with collective identity, whereas internal differences, rather than being acknowledged, have been interpreted by those holding the hegemonic power within the movement as mainly reflections of different stages of raised consciousness. Although to a large extent this has been acknowledged by the women's movement in recent years, the solution has often been to develop essentialist notions of difference, such as, for example, between black and white women, or middle class and working class women. And within each of these prototypes, the previous assumptions about discovered homogeneous reality usually continue to operate.

As Rosalind Brunt rightly put it (but did not pursue) in her paper on the politics of identity,[18] the issue of representation is the starting point of any politics of identity. However, as Brunt also correctly pointed out, there are two separate questions which need to be asked in relation to the issue of representation. The first is how our identities are represented in and through the culture and assigned particular categories; the second is who or what politically represents us, speaks and acts on our behalf.[19]

In the next section of this chapter, I shall examine critically some of the political practices which have been adopted within the British Left, especially during the late 1980s, to respond to these questions. I shall first address the question of political representation of the "community."

Identity Politics and "Community Representation"

Within the New Left politics, "the community" has been presented as an alternative model to that of "class" or "party" politics,[20] although the definition of "the community" has always been vague, inconsistent and contradictory, with boundaries ranging from a specific housing estate in the Inner City to the whole of Western Europe. Within social policy, the term community assumed a homogeneous group of people who basically related to each other in a caring and non-alienated fashion, who comprised family, neighborhood and parish, and who conformed to a hegemonic culture, often English and usually working class. It was against this model that the "popular planning" approach of the Greater London Council (GLC) and other radical local authorities developed in the late 1970s and early 1980s. It attempted to correct this dubious model of the community by including in it all those previously excluded and which, at least in some areas of the "Inner City," constitute a major part of the local population. However, as Harriet Cain and I have argued elsewhere, in doing so, the hegemonic answer to the question of "who is the community" has made three conceptual jumps and the following conflations:

- From focusing the attention on disadvantaged sections of the population, motivated by populist and democratic aspirations, "the community" in actuality has become to a large extent reduced to the categories of "Equal Opportunities"—previously excluded to a large extent from definitions of the community.

- From focusing on the "Equal Opportunities" disadvantaged sections of the population, the politics of "the community" have become reduced to the voluntary sector and local government-sponsored organizations which aspire to represent and serve them.
- From focusing on the disadvantaged section of the population, "the community" has, to a large extent, become reduced to the professional "community activists."[21]

This construction of the community which conflated discrimination and disadvantage (against which equal opportunity policies are established), had an unfortunate and unintended consequence. By excluding the working class as a category, it opened the door for a backlash of all those who felt they were not represented in such a construction.

There were even more problems arising from this approach to issues of representation. In spite of genuine attempts by the GLC and other radical authorities to widen circles of consultation, especially in relation to the women's committee and the race and ethnic minorities' committee, the methods they used inevitably led them to those who work in various community projects. The latter tend to have been sitting as "community representatives" on various management committees in which a certain "closed shop" network of "community activists" has developed, in which the "representatives" have never been selected or elected to represent anyone in any democratic fashion. This is not necessarily a critique of the work and politics of these activists themselves, the majority of whom have been deeply committed and hard working. Moreover, any attempt to establish a democratic procedure of representation would inevitably run into highly practical difficulties. Nevertheless, they should be seen as advocates rather than as representatives, and no homogeneity of interests should necessarily be assumed between them and the sections of the population they supposedly represent.

The question arises, therefore, about the extent to which their representation of the community is more valid than that of other political activists. The argument that they are more valid relies on common ethnic origin (or color, or sexuality, or disability) and assumes a common personal experience between the representative and those whom s/he represents, in the spirit of "the personal is the political." Shared experience and social positioning is assumed to have created the basis for a common *weltanschauung*, that "communicative community" that Deutch has spoken about, giving the activists insights into the specific difficulties from which these people suffer, and also making it easier to find ways of convincing them to join the cause. While this may be so, there are certain assumptions in this construction of community representation which are important to point out:

1. It assumes a commonality of interests of all members of the specific collectivity represented. In reality the "community activists" of necessity often come from a different class background and/or live outside the neighborhoods where the people they "represent" live. In other words, this politics of identity assumes that primordial boundaries of ethnicity or gender are of greater importance than the actual life experiences of the people involved.
2. Often, as a result of scarce resources, one representative may represent people of different equal opportunities categories. In other words, this politics of community representation assumes that the interests of women, blacks, and disabled people, for instance, are inherently non-conflicting and intrinsically the same, because they are all categories of disadvantage. In other words, in actuality, the politics of identity often devalues the actual separate, and often conflicting experiences of the people it attempts to represent.
3. As can be seen from the equal opportunities categories mentioned above, they are constructed in such a way as to reify one component of a person's identity as opposed to the reality of people's experiences which are multi-faceted, and are attached to one category or another: that is, one has to be black, or a woman, or gay or disabled. As real material benefits have often been attached to such choices, struggles have broken out as to whether, for instance, monies given to a certain project for black women, should be channeled through the women's or the race unit. Representing an identity category can thus turn into a form of power brokery, struggles for control, which can become bitter and degrading, let alone divisive.

This is the situation not only in relation to different identity categories, but also within them, especially in regard to racial and ethnic categories. What should be, for instance, the boundaries of the category "black"—are only people of African descent included in them, or are also those from Asian origin? And if Asians are a separate category, what are the implications for someone of Hindu (or Sikh or Muslim) origin representing "the Asians," or a person born in India, rather than a person born in Britain, or a man rather than a woman, and so on? In other words, the form of political representation which has grown out of identity politics and which has attempted to represent social difference more genuinely, has created an impossible mission for itself. One unintended result of such politics has been to create a space in which new fundamentalist leaderships have arisen in minority communities.[22]

This issue links the issue of representation in community politics to the other level of representation mentioned by Rosalind Brunt—that of cultural representation.

Identity Politics and Multiculturalism

Multiculturalism has been the most common policy promoted during the last twenty years or so by liberals, as well as (with some reservation) by the Left, in order to establish a way for minority cultures to be represented in school curricula and other cultural institutions in pluralist societies. Multiculturalism was a reaction against earlier policies of the absorption of immigrants which assumed one-sided assimilation and suppressed minority cultures. The Inner London Education Authority document of 1977 promoted multiculturalism as a policy "which will ensure that, within a society which is cohesive though not uniform, cultures are respected, differences recognized and individual identities are ensured."[23]

Basically, multiculturalist policies graft customs, celebrations and other symbolic signifiers of the cultures of immigrant communities onto the hegemonic culture. In addition, in countries like Australia and Canada where multiculturalism has been adopted as a major social policy tool, and in Britain to a lesser extent, special services geared to fulfil the special needs (linguistic, religious, and so on) of these communities are also funded by central government. Those on the Left who criticized multiculturalism objected to it as an ineffective anti-racist policy.[24] They rightly pointed out that concentrating on cultural difference, rather than on issues of discrimination and disadvantage, would not enable any major shift in class and power relations between the black minority and the white majority. At the same time, the policies of the Equal Opportunities Community discussed above, also helped to break the monopoly of traditional leaderships and constructions of cultures in minority communities. Unlike the structure of earlier periods in the British Race Relations Industry, projects which catered to specific and often oppositional groups within these communities were funded, such as alternative youth centers and Black women's organizations.

However, anti-racist and community politics generally incorporated rather than replaced the old structures. The traditional organizations continued to be financed together with the new, and when the cuts started, again it was the religious and cultural organizations which proved to be the most resistant to cuts, together with the constructs of cultural difference they evoke. These assume cultures to be static, ahistoric and in their "essence" to be mutually exclusive from other cultures, especially that of the host society. Moreover, "culture" in the multiculturalist discourse often collapses into "religion," with religious holidays becoming the signifiers of cultural difference within school curricula.

Fundamentalist leaderships have benefited from the adoption of multiculturalist norms.[25] Within the multiculturalist logic, their presumptions about being the keepers of the "true" religious way of life are unanswerable. External dissent is labeled as racist and internal dissent as deviance (if not sheer pathology, as in the case of "self-hating Jews"). In the politics of identity and representation they are perceived as the most "authentic" "others." At the same time, they are also perceived as a threat, and their "difference" as a basis for racist discourse. Unlike older versions of multiculturalism, fundamentalist activists refuse to respect the limits of multiculturalism which would confine ethnic cultures to the private domain or some limited community cultural spheres. Fundamentalists aim to use modern state and media powers in order to impose their version of reality on all those whom they perceive as their constituency.[26] In societies where their constituency is only a minority, they might not get involved in the general politics of the state.[27] However, they also vehemently refute any notion of internal pluralism which has been the basis of leftist popular planning and of feminist-socialist identity politics in recent years. This has proved to be very confusing for the Left. On the one hand, the contents of the ideology promoted by religious fundamentalist activists are often anathema to all they believe in, especially in terms of women's equality and individual freedom. On the other hand, the ideology of autonomous self-determination and empowerment, which is at the base of identity politics and multiculturalism, forbids intervention in the internal affairs of the community as Eurocentric and racist, part of a tradition of cultural imperialism that has to be rejected.

As Val Moghadam has pointed out, the Left has been caught in what can be seen as an insoluble dilemma: "Does a critique of Orientalism and of Eurocentrism mean a hands-off attitude towards the cultural artifacts of non-Western and/or Islamic countries?"[28] Val Moghadam's argument, with which I agree, is that this dilemma, in its present dichotomous construction, is misleading, because, as Sami Zubaida has claimed, "The world of thought was and remains universal in the sense of generating forms of knowledge, thought and argumentation which were drawn upon by intellectuals from different cultures and religions to formulate problems and solutions relevant to their particular contexts."[29]

Constructing a discourse of cultural difference which is based on mutually exclusive categories denies the possibility of such a universality. However, such a discourse can serve other purposes. As Trin T. Minh-ha claims: "Differences that cause separation and suspicion therefore do not threaten, for they can always be dealt with as fragments."[30] Such differences become part of a hegemonic ideology of multiculturalism. They are also part of the hegemonic culture because, according to her, accepting this model of thinking about "differences made between entities comprehended as absolute presences—hence the notions of pure origin and true self—are an outgrowth of a dualistic system of thought peculiar to the Occident."[31]

Thus, establishing a system of identity politics as a form of resistance to Eurocentrism, Orientalism and racism, fails exactly because its basic assumptions have been formed within the discourse of difference that it most wants to attack.

Whence Politics? Towards a Conclusion

What are the implications of the above for forms of political action and organizing? Two recent major positions which relate directly to "identity politics"' but which differ thoroughly in their attitudes to it, are those of Jenny Bourne and Rosalind Brunt.[32] Jenny Bourne vehemently objects to identity politics. She claims that identity politics have come to replace political struggles which aimed at social change and the transformation of society which were articulated as the primary purpose of the first British Women's Liberation conference. For her, identity politics are "separatist, individualistic and inward looking. The organic relationship we tried to forge between the personal and the political has been so degraded that now the only area of politics deemed to be legitimate is the personal."[33] According to Bourne, a major pitfall in the politics of identity is that it tends to reify cultural resources as signifiers of identity and thus overlooks, or even reverses, the "difference between asserting who we are and trying to recreate who we no longer are."[34] "What we do," claims Bourne, "is who we are." Moreover, "we do not need to seek out our identity for its own sake, but only to discover in the process 'the universality inherent in the human condition'."[35]

Rosalind Brunt, on the other hand, sees identity politics as indispensable. Partly for reasons with which Bourne might agree, she argues that if political activists recognized their own identities as the base of their social positioning and of their difference from each other, rather than repressing all parts of their identities except for their identification as political activists, this could eliminate the polarization between the "vanguard" and the "masses," and the self-righteousness which lead to politics in which the end justifies the means. Brunt argues that "unless the question of identity is at the heart of any transformatory project, then not only will the political agenda be inadequately 'rethought', but more to the point, our politics aren't going to make much headway beyond the Left's own circles."[36]

Brunt, however, who situates herself within the tradition of Gramsci as well as Foucault, perceives the political arena in an overall more complex and contradictory manner. Reflecting upon one's separate identities, the return to the subjective does not imply for her (and for Stuart Hall) withdrawal from politics, but rather the opposite—locating grids of power and resistance which are horizontal and not just vertical, while keeping political frameworks of action heterogeneous and floating. She rejects the logic of "broad democratic alliances" and "rainbow coalitions" which emanates from Bourne's argument, because, she argues, political action should be based on "unity in diversity" which should be founded not on common denominators but on "a whole variety of heterogeneous, possibly antagonistic, maybe magni(fi)cently diverse, identities and circumstances ... the politics of identity recognizes that there will be many struggles, and perhaps a few celebrations, and writes into all of them a welcome to contradiction and complexity."[37]

As a positive example for this type of political struggle Brunt points to the support activities which surrounded the miners' strike in 1984-1985. This is, however, an unfortunate example, because this strike ended up in such a crushing defeat, not only of the miners and the trade-union movement, but of the anti-Thatcherite movement as whole.

Real politics aside, Brunt's model of politics seems very seductive—it incorporates theoretical insights of highly sophisticated social analysis, is flexible, dynamic and totally inclusive. However, it in this last point that the danger lies. What ultimately lies behind Brunt's approach is a naive populist assumption that in spite of contradictions and conflicts, in the last instance all popular struggles are inherently progressive. She shares with the logic of multiculturalism the belief about the boundaries of difference which has been precisely the source of the space that has encouraged the rise of fundamentalist leaderships.

It is beyond the scope of this chapter to recommend specific modes of political action. Moreover, this task is senseless outside specific and concrete historical situations. The general principle, however, should be not so much Brunt's unity in diversity but rather universality in diversity. Political struggles do not have to be uniform, nor do they have to be united. Differences of interest and of foci of struggles should be recognized, otherwise any notion of sisterhood or other forms of solidarity would be inherently racist, sexist and classist. However, the boundaries of solidarity and co-operation should also be very clear within specific historical contexts, and they should be based upon the shared universal dialogue discussed above.

Notes

1. E. V. Spelman, *Inessential Woman* (London: The Women's Press, 1988), p. ix.

2. *Ibid.*, p. 120.

3. K. Lewin, *Field Theory in Social Sciences* (London: Tavistock, 1952); A. L. Epstein, *Ethos and Identity* (London: Tavistock, 1978).

4. E. Hirsch, *The Concept of Identity* (Oxford: Oxford University Press, 1982); S. Shoemaker, and R. Swinburn, *Personal Identity* (Oxford: Blackwell, 1984).

5. See S. Hall, and M. Jacques (eds.), *New Times* (London: Lawrence & Wishart, 1989). See also S. Hall, "New Ethnicities," in ICA (Institute for Contemporary Arts) Documents: *Black Film in British Cinema* (London: ICA, 1990), p. 27.

6. F. Anthias and N. Yuval-Davis, "Contextualizing Feminism: Gender, Ethnic & Class Divisions," *Feminist Review* 15 (1983): 62-75.

7. *Ibid.*, and Anthias and Yuval-Davis, *Racialized Boundaries: Race, Nation, Gender, Colour, and Anti-Racist Struggle* (London: Routledge, 1992).

8. B. Anderson, *Imagined Communities* (London: Verso, 1983).

9. K. W. Deutch, *Nationalism and Social Communications: An Inquiry into the Foundations of Nationality* (Cambridge: MIT Press, 1966); P. Schlesinger, "On National Identity: Some Conceptions and Misconceptions," *Social Science Information* 26 (2) (1987): 76-98.

10. Deutch, *ibid.*, p. 97.

11. Anderson, *Imagined Communities*, and G. Kitching, "Nationalism: The Instrumental Passion," *Capital and Class* 25 (1985):98-116.

12. Kitching, *ibid.*, p. 109.

13. Schlesinger, "On National Identity," pp. 234, 269.

14. N. Yuval-Davis, "The Bearers of the Collective: Women and Religious Legislation in Israel," *Feminist Review* 4 (1980):15-27; Anthias and Yuval-Davis,

"Contextualizing Feminism;" Yuval-Davis and Anthias (eds.), *Woman-Nation-State* (London: Macmillan, 1989).

15. D. Kandiyoti, "Bargaining with Patriarchy," *Gender and Society* 2 (3) (1988):274-290.

16. For an elaboration of this debate see N. Yuval-Davis, "The Bearers of the Collective," and "Zionism, Anti-semitism and the Struggle against Racism," *Spare Rib,* September 1984, pp. 18-22; Anthias and Yuval-Davis, "Contextualizing Feminism;" and Spelman, *Inessential Women.*

17. Yuval-Davis, "Zionism, Anti-semitism and the Struggle against Racism."

18. R. Brunt, "The Politics of Identity," in S. . all and M. Jacques (eds.), *New Times.*

19. *Ibid.,* p. 152.

20. A. Gortz, *Farewell to the Working Class* (London: Pluto Press, 1982); H. Wainwright, *Labour: A Tale of Two Parties* (London: Hogarth Press, 1987).

21. H. Cain and N. Yuval-Davis, " 'The Equal Opportunities Community' and the Anti-Racist Struggle," *Critical Social Policy* 29 (Autumn 1990), p. 6.

22. G. Sahgal and N. Yuval-Davis, "Refusing Holy Orders," *Marxism Today* (March 1990):12-16; and Sahgal and Yuval-Davis (eds.), *Refusing Holy Orders: Women and Fundamentalism* (London: Virago, 1992).

23. Inner London Education Authority, *On Multiculturalism* (London: ILEA, 1977).

24. C. Mullard, *Racism in Society and Schools* (London: The Institute of Education, 1980).

25. Sahgal and Yuval-Davis, "Refusing Holy Orders," and Sahgal and Yuval-Davis (eds.), *Refusing Holy Orders: Women and Fundamentalism.*

26. N. Yuval-Davis, "Fundamentalism, Multiculturalism and Women in Britain," *Revue Internationale de Sociologie,* new series, 2 (1990).

27. Although in Britain recently a Muslim party has been established, and the representatives of the "Muslim community" continue to pressure the government for state-funded Muslim schools.

28. V. Moghadam, "Against Eurocentrism and Nativism: A Review Essay on Samir Amin's *Eurocentrism* and Other Texts," *Socialism and Democracy* 9 (Fall/Winter 1989), p. 96.

29. *Ibid.,* p. 97; S. Zubaida, "Islam, Cultural Nationalism and the Left," *Review of Middle East Studies* 4 (1988): 28-29.

30. T. T. Minh-ha, *Woman, Native, Other* (Bloomington, Indianapolis: Indiana University Press, 1989), p. 90.

31. *Ibid.,* p. 40.

32. J. Bourne, *Homeland of the Mind: Jewish Feminism and Identity Politics* (London: Race and Class pamphlet no. 11, 1987); Brunt, "The Politics of Identity."

33. Bourne, *ibid.,* p.2.

34. D. Attar, "Why I am not a Jewish Feminist," *Shifra* 2 (1985):16-21.
35. Bourne, *Homeland of the Mind*, p. 22.
36. Brunt, "The Politics of Identity," p. 150.
37. *Ibid.*, p. 158.

21

International Standards of Equality and Religious Freedom: Implications for the Status of Women

Division for the Advancement of Women,
United Nations

Introduction

The principle of the equal rights of men and women is well-established in international law. The Charter of the United Nations, formally binding its 159 Member States, reaffirms in its preamble "... faith in fundamental human rights, in the dignity and worth of the human person, in the equal rights of men and women and of nations large and small." Article 1, paragraph 3 of the Charter lists among main purposes of the United Nations the achievement of "... international co-operation in promoting and encouraging respect for human rights and for fundamental freedoms for all without distinction as to race, sex, language or religion."

The Universal Declaration on Human Rights (1948) states that "everyone is entitled to all the rights and freedoms set forth in this Declaration, without distinction of any kind, such as race, colour, sex, language, religion, political or other opinion, national or social origin, property, birth or other status." The Declaration provides for both equality between women and men and freedom of religion. Specifically, Article 7 states that "All are equal before the law and are entitled without any discrimination to equal protection of the law. All are entitled to equal protection against any discrimination in violation of this Declaration and against any incitement to such discrimination." It also provides for freedom of religion in article 18, which states that "Everyone has the right to freedom of thought, conscience and religion; this right includes freedom to change his religion or belief, and freedom, either alone or in community with others and in public or private, to manifest his religion or belief in teaching, practice, worship and observance."

In adopting the Charter, the Universal Declaration of Human Rights and subsequent international human rights instruments, no country has argued that freedom of religion and the principle of equality between women and men are inconsistent or in conflict.

The practical meaning of equality and means to achieve it has been reflected in the United Nations Convention on the Elimination of All Forms of Discrimination Against Women, adopted on 10 December 1979. Like all international conventions, this multilateral treaty is binding on States that have ratified or acceded to it. In addition, States that have signed the Convention have indicated an acceptance, in principle, of its provisions. The Convention entered into force on 3 September 1981 and as at 1 September 1990 had 104 States parties. In addition, another 13 States have signed the Convention, although they have not yet ratified it. It is, in terms of speed and number of ratifications and accessions, one of the most successful international treaties.

Similarly, the type of actions necessary to achieve equality by the year 2000 are set out in the Nairobi Forward-looking Strategies adopted by the General Assembly by consensus in 1985. While the Strategies are not legally binding, they reflect a moral consensus of the international community and provide an understanding of how equality should be interpreted in practice.

The Strategies strongly emphasize the necessity of full observance of the equal rights of women and the elimination of *de jure* and *de facto* discrimination. They address in particular the social, economic, political and cultural roots of *de facto* inequality. They assert that adequate legislation exists in the majority of countries and it is their ineffective implementation that is a major obstacle to the full participation of women in all spheres of life. Consequently, the Strategies provide a set of measures to improve the *de facto* situation of women with regard to social participation, political participation and decision-making, role in the family, employment, education and training, equality before the law, health and social security.

The Universal Declaration on Human Rights, the Convention and the Strategies are all intended to set out universally-agreed norms. They were framed by people from diverse cultures, religions and nationalities and therefore were intended to take into account such factors as religion and cultural traditions of countries. For that reason, perhaps, the Convention makes no provision whatsoever for differential interpretation based on "culture or tradition." Instead, it states clearly in Article 2 that "States Parties ... undertake ... to take all appropriate measures, including legislation, to modify or abolish existing laws, regulations, *customs and practices* [emphasis added] which constitute discrimination against women ... ."

The Strategies, even though based on a broader consensus, only admit the concept of national differences based on culture and religion in one of its 372 paragraphs. This is related to family law and even there the Strategies do not accept that differences based on culture and religion replace or modify the universal principle of equality. Thus, with regard to custody rights of children in a divorce (paragraph 74), the Strategies state: "Without prejudice to the religious and cultural traditions of countries, and taking into account the *de facto* situations, legal or other appropriate provisions should be made to eliminate discrimination against single mothers and their children." No similar qualification is made with regard to any of the major development issues (employment, education or health), political, economic or social participation.

It is from the basis that sexual equality and religious freedom are fully consistent in international law that religious practices covered under the generic term "fundamentalism" as well as cultural practices should be seen. The issue is whether, *de facto*, certain religious or cultural practices can lead to discrimination against women. The analysis that follows first explores the meaning of equality and religious freedom and some of the social and economic origins of religious and cultural fundamentalism as they impinge on equality. It then examines some of the effects of culture and religion on advancement of women, by comparing those states that have accepted the international norms embodied in the Convention with those that have not fully accepted them. This analysis is based on the situation in 1989, when there were 104 States Parties. By July 1992 the number of signatories had increased to 114.

Religious Freedom and the Practice of Equality

It might be asserted that religious fundamentalism is inherently contrary to equality. This would not be accurate. All religions are both simple and complex. They are simple in that they place, in one way or another, the individual human being into a relationship with the Divine.

In this all individuals are equal and all religions assert the essential equality of persons. Religions are also complex, with sacred writings, rules, customs and interpretations based on history and practice that are immensely varied and sometimes derive from millennia of experience. At different times and places, in all religions, there have been movements to focus on what are perceived to be the simplest and most essential in religious belief and practice. In this sense, fundamentalism has been an essential component of broad religious experience. However, fundamentalism can also go beyond the essential and timeless proposition of equality of the human being in relation to the Divine and include aspects of the more complex historical practice that also characterize most religious practice and which may accept or even justify inequality on earth.

Religious Freedom as an Exercise of Choice

Based on its expression in the Universal Declaration on Human Rights, religious freedom as a human right can be said to mean being able to choose, as an individual, one's religion and how to practice one's religious beliefs. It implies freedom from coercion either by the State or by other religious groups. It also implies that one cannot seek to impose one's own religious beliefs by coercion.

This choice can, and often does, imply deviation from prevailing societal norms. For example, many religions call for material poverty and an adherent can choose not to seek wealth. Some religions emphasize humility and subordination for all adherents or venerate life by refusing to participate in violence.

However, some religious practices encourage and strengthen de facto inequality of women in the family and in the society. This may be in terms of role definition and it can be reinforced within the religion itself by denying women the same access to priestly functions, decision-making or adjudication of religious law as men. That this is not inherent in religious belief itself is suggested by the fact that branches of the same religions accord priestly functions, decision-making or adjudication of religious law to women as well as men. However, in some interpretations of religious law in terms of the family women may be accorded fewer rights than men. The issue of choice here is whether women adhering to a given religion freely choose to accept a lesser position. If so, this would be an exercise of religious freedom that would not be inconsistent with the principle of equality. But whether a choice is freely made is itself a complicated issue.

Obviously, if a woman were compelled, by civil law or the State, to accept inferior conditions on the basis of dominant religious practice, or would not have the opportunity to choose an alternative, this would contradict both the principle of equality and the right of religious freedom as set out in international norms. The test, in this case, would be whether the legal system in place provided for full equality and whether its interpretation in practice also guaranteed equality. In some countries civil and family laws can be contradictory to constitutional guarantees of equality. In these cases, although the constitution may proclaim the equality of women and men, the civil and family codes can contradict those principles by enacting more detailed regulations that are discriminatory to women.

More complicated is the effect of long-term social pressure on women that constrains their ability to choose. If women are subjected to religious practices that give them lesser status throughout their lives, live in a rigid and often intolerant social and cultural environment without the economic means to survive, women will have practically little choice, if any. This lack of choice would not be limited to religious practice and belief, but also to other basic decisions concerning their lives such as life-style and dress to education, birth control and participation in public life. Freedom of choice in this context will be difficult to measure and non-confirmity becomes difficult. What can be said, however, is that if the legal system reflects equality, it becomes more difficult to enforce—over the medium- or long-term—the practice of inequality.

Socio-economic Factors in Fundamentalism

The practice of religion is anchored in the experience of individuals in their societies and therefore is closely related to processes of social and economic change. Religious beliefs allow an individual to place her or himself in context, to give purpose to life and to provide an explanation for events. The current rise of what have been called "fundamentalist" movements should be seen in this context.

It has been found historically that at times when social and economic change has been fastest or most abrupt, many people have adhered to religious interpretations that can be regarded as "fundamentalist" in the sense of emphasizing what are held to be basic religious values and practices, with their accompanying cultural practices anchored, often, on the past.[1] In the present period, while the phenomenon is probably universal, it has particularly emerged in certain regions, as a response to prolonged instability, decline in living standards and economic and social change. It has taken on different forms, depending on the underlying cultural traditions and specific conditions of individual countries, and can be found in all of the major religions of the world, but especially within Judaism, Christianity and Islam. In their interpretation, a common characteristic of all fundamentalistic movements is return to traditional values and structures of the past which are considered to be necessary to re-establish a perceived previous social order and stability.

In a search for a historical anchor for religious belief and preferred behaviors, this type of "fundamentalism" often focuses on values and practices of what is perceived to be a "better" or more "moral" past as an alternative to social/cultural changes, new values and ideas that are perceived to be threatening. This has often implied, as a matter of belief, a return to "traditional" social roles, including the place and role of women in the society and the family as an important aspect of ideology. The perception that women are the main transmitters of societal values has often meant that the changing role of women is associated with changes in values and behaviors that are perceived to be at odds with religious belief. As a result, in some societies, efforts are made to try to reimpose those perceived "traditional" behaviors for women as a remedy for crisis and destabilization. This may include refusal to accept any change in women's status as part of a rejection of other social changes, innovations and reforms.

It should be noted that maintaining women in an inferior position is a kind of "least common denominator" principle under which any man can feel superior to any woman, regardless of objective merit. This may be accompanied by a theoretical "respect" and "protection" for women in their traditional roles, as a form of compensation which does not change fundamental economic and political structures. In this sense, maintenance of "traditional" behavior intends, even if unconsciously, to maintain societal power relationships intact.

An Empirical Examination of Some Effects of Cultural and Religious Tradition on the Status of Women

There is no clear definition, at a national level, of where religious or cultural beliefs may be affecting the status of women since there is no accepted definition of what constitutes fundamentalism or similar practices in measurable terms. However, a proxy indicator can be found in cases where, on the basis of religious or cultural principle, the international norms of equality embodied in the Convention are not accepted. Non-acceptance can be measured either because a state has not signed or acceded to the Convention or where reservations based on religion or culture have been entered on ratification. The relationships between the status of the Convention for countries and indicators of equality in various spheres of life can be examined as a broad indicator or some of the main relationships between acceptance of international norms and the *de facto* status of women.

Who Adheres to the Convention and Who Does Not?

From the legal perspective it can be noted that countries that have ratified the Convention—who have become States Parties to it—have accepted its terms as having the force of law for national purposes. States who have signed the Convention have accepted its terms in principle, but have not yet accorded it with force of domestic law. In 1989, out of 164 member and observer states of the United Nations, 60 were not parties to the Convention. They had neither ratified nor acceded to it, although thirteen of them had signed the Convention without yet having ratified it.

The 104 countries that had ratified or acceded to the Convention were found in all regions of the world and included the most materially rich countries and the most materially poor. They ranged from the country with the largest population in the world to island states with among the smallest populations. They included countries that reflect all of the major religions of the world. They had in common their commitment to equality.

The analyses of countries which in 1989 had neither ratified the Convention nor acceded to it allow the following conclusions:

1. One group of countries (13) had signed the Convention, but had not ratified it. Some of them (the Netherlands, Switzerland and the United States) had not ratified it mainly because of a national requirement to first eliminate (or agree to eliminate) any incompatibility between the Convention and national or local laws. For example, Netherlands held that it must first pass a national equal opportunities law before it can ratify. Switzerland held that, under its federal system, cantonal law must be in conformity with the Convention before ratification (and one half-canton did not yet permit women to vote, for example). The United States has not ratified the Convention in part on the grounds that the necessary adjustment of state laws has not yet been made, as well as a general reluctance to ratify international conventions. It should be

noted that in these cases, the reasons for non-ratification are not formally of a religious or traditional/cultural nature.[2]

2. In the case of a few other countries that had signed the Convention the reason for not ratifying the Convention could include difficulty of reconciling religious law and practice with the Convention. This could include the cases of India, where family law may follow either civil or religious codes, and Afghanistan, Jordan and Israel.[3]

3. A large group of 47 countries had neither signed nor acceded to the Convention yet. In a few cases, non-ratification had to do with specific circumstances, as for example, in the case of Namibia which was only recently independent and had only recently begun to consider accession to international conventions, or in the case of Lichtenstein, which had only recently joined the United Nations. Almost half of these countries have large Muslim populations (Albania, Algeria, Bahrain, Brunei Darusalaam, Comoros, Chad, Djibouti, Islamic Republic of Iran, Kuwait, Lebanon, Malaysia, Mauritania, Morocco, Niger, Oman, Pakistan, Qatar, Saudi Arabia, Somalia, Sudan, Syria, and the United Arab Emirates). Many of them have incorporated Muslim law in their civil or family codes and this may be a factor in non-accession. Religion may also be a factor in the position of Malta, whose population is heavily Christian, and in that of the Holy See.[4]

4. In the case of other countries that had neither signed nor ratified, the extent to which religion and custom is a factor cannot be assessed, although it is probable that there is some relationship in many of them. The category included numerous countries in Sub-Saharan Africa (Botswana, Central African Republic, Mozambique, Sao Tome and Principe, South Africa, Swaziland, Seychelles, and Zimbabwe). It also included countries in mainland Asia (Bhutan, Burma, Cambodia, Democratic People's Republic of Korea, Maldives, Nepal, and Singapore) and the Pacific Islands (Fiji, Kiribati, Papua New Guinea, Samoa, Solomon Islands, Tonga and Vanuatu). There were only two countries in Latin America and the Caribbean (Bahamas and Suriname) that were not parties to the Convention.[5]

5. Some countries had ratified or acceded to the Convention with reservations or declarations, based on religious laws or cultural tradition. While the specific reservations vary from country to country, among the articles that the States may not consider as binding upon them are Articles 2, 9, 15, and 16 which are taken to conflict with national laws or customs. Countries making reservations on one or more of these articles include Bangladesh,

Brazil, Cyprus, Egypt, Iraq, Jamaica, Republic of Korea, Libyan Arab Jamahiriya, Malawi, Mauritius, Thailand, Tunisia, and Turkey.[6]

The articles on which one or several of these reservations have been entered are those that obligate the States Parties to combat prevailing discrimination against women actively, that is, through establishing legal protection of equal rights of women, including enforcement mechanisms; abolishing existing discriminatory regulations, customs and practices (Article 2); equality of rights with men with regard to nationality of women and their children (Article 9); equality before the law in civil matters, in terms of legal capacity, including administration of property, conclusion of contracts, freedom to choose residence or domicile (Article 15); elimination of all forms of discrimination in matters relating to marriage and family relations, such as the same free choice of a spouse, the same responsibilities during marriage, and as parents the same rights to decide on the number and spacing of children, their adoption or guardianship; the same rights as husband and wife, including the right to choose a family name, or a profession (Article 16).

It should be noted that the articles in question constitute the essence of the Convention and touch upon crucial areas of the discrimination of women in many parts of the world. Many other States Parties have stated that these reservations "are incompatible with the object and purpose of the Convention." Under a procedure in which other States Parties can enter objections to reservations, it was stated that "... the reservations in question, if put into practice, would inevitably result in discrimination against women on the basis of race, which is contrary to everything the Convention stands for ... " (objection by the Federal Republic of Germany to a reservation) and that "the reason why reservations incompatible with the object and purpose of a treaty are not acceptable is precisely that otherwise they would render a basic international obligation of a contractual nature meaningless. Incompatible reservations, made in respect of the Convention on the Elimination of All Forms of Discrimination Against Women do not only cast doubts on the commitments of the reserving States to the objects and purpose of the Convention, but moreover, contribute to undermine the basis of international contractual law. It is in common interest of States that treaties to which they have chosen to become parties are also respected, as to object and purpose, by other parties" (Sweden).

The reasons for non-ratification and for reservations are sufficiently clear: the status of the Convention for a given country is a broad proxy indicator of the possible effect of culture and religion on a country's legal structure relating to equality between women and men. This legal status measure is thus used as a main variable for examining women's advancement.

Economic and Social Equality and the Convention

Measurement of women's *de facto* situation relative to men is now possible through the use of international statistics. A consequence of the United Nations Decade for Women has been the development of these statistics. These have been assembled by the United Nations Statistical Office in its Women's Indicators and Statistics Data Base. A number of indicators have been seen as particularly useful in measuring women's economic and social participation because of their content and the fact that they are available for most countries. These include education measures such as women's literacy by age and ratios of girls to boys in school enrollment at the primary and secondary levels. They also include measures of economic participation such as the ratio of women to men in different sectors of the economy.

The extent to which a legal commitment to equality is reflected in practice can be seen in terms of the different indicators. Differences in these indicators among groups of countries classified according to the status of the Convention can suggest the relationship between *de jure* and *de facto* status of women and, depending on which groups of countries have the greatest differences, the broad effects of religious and cultural norms.

Literacy

Female illiteracy is a function of age and reflects, in large measure, past lack of access to education by women, as well as the existence of programs to promote literacy among adult women. On a global basis in the most recent (1980) census rounds, it has been found that on average 30 percent of women between the ages of 15-24 were illiterate, 44 percent between ages 25-44, 60 percent between 45-64, and 71 percent of women 65 years of age and over. For each of these groups, the average illiteracy of countries that had ratified the Convention without cultural reservations was lower than that of countries that had ratified with reservations, had signed but not ratified or had done nothing.

Enrollment in School

The ratio of girls to boys in enrollment is an indicator of the extent to which equality in access to education has been achieved. A ratio of 1.0 would reflect equality. In terms of primary (or first-level) education, the average ratio worldwide is 0.84, indicating that girls have slightly less access to education than boys. In this, however, there are no differences among countries in terms of whether and how they have ratified the Convention.

However, for secondary education, there is a different pattern. The worldwide average ratio of girls to boys in enrollment in second-level education is 0.80. As can be seen from Table 21.1, countries that have ratified the Convention without reservation have the highest ratio, followed closely by countries that signed but not ratified. Much lower ratios are found in those countries that have not fully accepted the international norms set out in the Convention. Secondary education is where intellectual values are instilled as well as skills that permit persons to compete in the labor force. Denial of equal opportunity has a long-term effect on future possibilities of economic and political participation.

Economic Activity

An indicator of equality in women's economic participation is the ratio of women to men in specific economic sectors. This measure is independent of the level of development, but does show the extent to which women have the same access to economic activity as men. Figures are available in terms of the whole economically active population as well as for the main economic sectors: agriculture, industry, and services.

Those countries who, by ratifying without reservation or by signing, have indicated full acceptance of the principles of the Convention, also provide greater access for women to economic activity, as can be seen from Table 21.2. For economically active population as a whole, as well as for the industrial and service sectors, the ratios of women to men are higher for these countries than for those that have ratified with reservations or have neither signed nor ratified. The exception is in agriculture, the most traditional sector of the economy, where there are no differences among types of country.

TABLE 21.1 Ratios of Girls to Boys in Enrollment in Second Level Education, by Relationship to the Convention on the Elimination of All Forms of Discrimination Against Women, 1989

Status of Convention	Girls/Boys
Ratified	0.86
Ratified, with reservations	0.71
Signed but not ratified	0.82
Neither signed nor ratified	0.70
ALL COUNTRIES	0.80

Source: *Women's Indicators and Statistics* (WISTAT) (New York: United Nations Statistical Office, 1989).

TABLE 21.2 Ratios of Women to Men in Measures of Economic Participation in 1980, by Status of the Convention in 1989

Status of Convention	Active Population	Agriculture	Industry	Services
Ratified	0.6	0.5	0.3	0.7
Ratified, with reservations	0.4	0.5	0.2	0.4
Signed but not ratified	0.6	0.5	0.3	0.5
Neither signed nor ratified	0.4	0.5	0.2	0.4
ALL COUNTRIES	0.5	0.5	0.3	0.6

Source: As in Table 21.1.

Political Power

The extent to which women are actively involved in the political process of their countries is indicated by their representation in parliaments and in the higher levels of public decision-making. In general, women's participation in political decision-making is low, but, as Table 21.3 shows, it is particularly low in countries that have either ratified the Convention with reservations or not signed nor ratified it. Both the Convention and the Strategies emphasize that women must have access to decision-making if they are to achieve equality in other areas. It is clear that in countries that have not accepted the international norms of equality, women are denied that access.

TABLE 21.3   Percentage of Women in Decision-Making Positions, by Status of the Convention in 1989

Status of Convention	*In Parliament* %	*Ministers* %	*In Top Government Levels* %
Ratified	10.6	4.9	5.6
Ratified, with reservations	5.8	1.8	2.3
Signed but not ratified	8.9	4.7	5.1
Neither signed nor ratified	5.8	0.7	2.4
ALL COUNTRIES	8.8	4.4	3.4

Source: Interparliamentary Union (Parliaments), Division for the Advancement of Women (Ministers and top four levels).

Conclusions

Sexual equality and religious freedom are not contradictory and are consistent with international norms. Thus, if religious fundamentalism, both in its theory and its practice, respects these norms it can not be considered discriminatory to anyone, including women. However, if certain religious practices and interpretations having provisions discriminatory to women *de jure* or *de facto* are incorporated into civil law, they are obviously incompatible with international legal norms.

If these religious practices prevail, they can lead to the creation of social, economic and political structures that oppress women at all levels: in the family, in the community and in society. As has been shown empirically, they lead to lesser equality in social opportunities as reflected in access to education, to reduced economic opportunities and to reduced participation in decision-making. In that sense, they maintain inequitable power relationships and may systematically reduce the possibility of women to contribute to development, whether of the women as individuals or of the society as a whole.

Where the level of discrimination leads to legalized or sanctioned persecution of women who are unwilling to conform, the issue may become one of human rights. There is beginning to be a sense, at the international level, that in some cases this persecution may have reached a level that it must be acknowledged. For example, the expert group meeting on refugee and displaced women and children organized by the United Nations Division for the Advancement of Women and the United Nations High Commissioner for Refugees in July 1990 was of the view that systematic persecution on the basis of sex should constitute "a well-founded fear of persecution ..." on the basis of social group membership that could be used to claim refugee status.

The issue of the discrimination of women is one of the key problems of modern societies. Like other global problems, such as the environment or armed conflict, it should be systemically addressed by the international community at all levels: national, regional and international. If discrimination is not addressed, women will remain, in practice, second class citizens, viewed as vulnerable members of society who must be protected and assisted rather than as creative contributors to social progress, economic development and change.

While changes in the underlying values and attitudes, including those reflected in some interpretations of religious belief, have already been recommended in such international statements as the Nairobi Strategies, this has not proved to be easy. As a minimum, however, national laws that conflict with international norms (such as civil law vis-à-vis religious law, constitutions vis-à-vis civil codes and family codes) should be reviewed and amended.

Notes

1. See, for example, Eric Hobsbawm's classic study *Primitive Rebels* (New York: W.W. Norton, 1965).

2. Subsequent to the preparation of this study, the Netherlands acceded to the Convention and has become a State Party.

3. Subsequently, Israel and Jordan signed the Convention, but with reservations.

4. Since 1990, Namibia has signed the Convention, as has Malta. Following the break-up of the Soviet Union, the newly-independent states have not yet completed the procedure for accession to the Convention.

5. Of the countries in this category, new signatories are Central African Republic, Zimbabwe, Bhutan, Nepal, and Samoa. Burma is now known as Myanmar.

6. Israel and Jordan have since joined this category of States Parties.

Glossary

Aggadah	Judaic tradition
alamaniyya	Arabic word for secularism. Alamaniyya bila din is secularism without region.
andaruni	Persian word for inner section of a house (to which women were once confined)
arusak-i farangi	European dolls; derogatory Persian term for unveiled and westernized Iranian women
Ashkenazi	Israeli Jews of European descent
azadi	Persian word for freedom (n., azad)
Ba'al teshuva	Contemporary orthodox Jewish revival in the United States
Ba'alot teshuvah	Newly orthodox Jewish women in the United States
Bad-hijabi	Persian word for mal-veiling
Beruni	Persian word for outer house
Bharat Mata	Mother India
Brahmins	Upper caste in India
burqa	Pushtu word for tent-like veil for Afghani women and among Pushtus (Pathans) in Pakistan
chador	Persian word for a kind of cloak worn by Iranian (and some urban Afghan) women
Code du Status Personnel	Personal Status Code, in North African countries, based on Muslim family law (itself derived from the Sharia). Concerns marriage, divorce, child custody, inherit-ance.
Dalit	"Untouchables," in India
dars	Urdu word for religious instruction, in Pakistan
das Weib	Derogatory German word for woman
dawa	Muslim proselytizer
deeni madrassah	Religious school or seminary, in Pakistan
dopatta	Part of the traditional Pakistani dress for women, a two-meter-long cotton or silk cloth loosely wrapped around head and body

El Mounquid	Algerian newspaper of the now-banned FIS
Farang/Farangistan	Persian word denoting Europe
Farangi	European, or foreigner
fassad	Arabic and Persian term for decay
fatwa	Religious edict in Islam
fitna	Arabic word for moral decay or turmoil
Front Islamique du Salut	Fundamentalist movement in Algeria, banned by the government in 1992
Führer	German word for leader
gharbzadegi	Persian term denoting "westoxication," or excessive westernization (adj., gharbza-deh; Urdu, maghrebzad)
Halakha	Jewish canon law
Halutziot	Pioneering ideology of the Zionist Labor Movement in Palestine
Haredi	Ultra-Orthodox Jews
Hasidim	Ultra-Orthodox Jews
hijab	Arabic term for Islamic modest dress for women (Persian, hejab)
Hindu Rashtra	Hindu nation (goal of religio-national chauvinists in India)
Hudood Ordinances	Quranically derived criminal laws intro-duced in Pakistan
Hudud	Islamic criminal punishments
idda	Required period of sexual abstinence, such as following the dissolution of a marri-age, in Islam
ijtihad	Individual inquiry into religion, in Islam
Ikhwan	Muslim Brotherhood
imam	Senior religious leader, in Islam
Intifada	The Palestinian uprising against Israeli occupation of the West Bank and Gaza, begun in 1987
Jahilia	Pre-Islamic "era of ignorance" in Arabia
Jamaat-e Islami	Ruling party of most of the 1980s in Pakistan, which introduced Islamic laws
jati	Birth distinctions based on local systems of ranked, hereditary, and mainly endogam-ous groups, in India
jihad	Arabic word for Islamic holy war
Kashrut	Jewish dietary laws
kibbutz	Collective farm or settlement in Israel

kulle	Nigerian word for seclusion
lathi	Long stick wielded by police, in India
Lebensborn	"Well of Life" Organization, Nazi Germany
Maguzawa	Nigerian word for non-Muslim Hausa
manzel	Persian word for home
mardana	Persian word for men's quarters in a house
Mashruahkhvah/ Mashrutahkhvah	Opposing ideological camps, respectively Islamist and secular-nationalist, during Iran's Constitution Revolution of 1905-1909
maulvis	Clerics in Pakistan
millat	Turkish and Persian word for nation
Mitzvot	Judaic commandments
Mizrachi	Israeli Jews from North Africa and the Middle East
mleccha	"Unclean people," Indian Brahmin word for lower castes and tribals
Moharem	Arabic term for chaperone
Mojahedin	Iranian left-Islamic opposition group that fought the Shah in the late 1970s and the Islamic Republic of Iran during the 1980s
Moudjahidates	Algerian women liberation fighters
moutahajiba/muhajjabat	Arabic term for a woman who wears hijab
mufti	Religious scholars in Pakistan
Mujahedeen	Afghan tribal-Islamist opposition group based in Peshawar, Pakistan, that fought the government in Kabul during the 1980s
Munaqqabat	Arabic word for one who wears a face veil
mut'a	Arabic term for temporary marriage (see Sigheh)
Neo-Destour	Ruling social democratic party of Tunisia
niddah	Jewish laws pertaining to menstruation
nikah	Arabic term for permanent marriage
niqab	Arabic word for face veil
Nun	An Egyptian women's magazine launched by the AWSA
patrivrata	Hindu term for a faithful wife
purdah	Urdu word for seclusion, segregation, and veiling of women in South Asian Muslim communities
Quran	Muslim holy book
Ramayana	The Hindu saga of the god Ram
Rassenpolitisches Amt	Bureau for Race Policy, Nazi Germany

rath yatra	Massive marches and parades in India to evoke Hindu religious sentiment
sari	Traditional Indian women's dress
sati, sati-daha	Hindi word for ritual self-immolation of Hindu widow
Sephardi	Originally, Jews from Spain and Spanish Jews who fled for safety to Ottoman Istanbul
shakhas	Hindu brotherhood units
shaman	North American indigenous medicine men (and sometimes women)
Sharia	Islamic canon law, derived from the Quran (Muslim holy book revealed to Prophet Muhammad) and Hadith (sayings of the Prophet as recorded by his disciples). Islamic law is interpreted by different schools: Hanafi, Hambali, Maliki, and Sha'afi.
Shia Islam	The branch of Islam predominant in Iran. A Shia or Shi'ite is a member of that branch.
sigheh	Temporary marriage, permitted for Shia Muslims
Sufism	Mystical branch of Islam
sunna	Arabic word for tradition (of the Prophet)
Sunni Islam	The largest branch of Islam. A Sunni is a member of that branch.
sura	Quranic verse
Taggamu Party	Egyptian socialist party
Taharat hamishpacha	Judaic family purity laws, such as required two-week sexual abstinence around menstruation
talakawa	Nigerian word for "common people"
talaq	Islamic divorce
Talmud	Commentary on the Torah
tobe	Traditional dress worn by northern Sudan-ese women, a thin, cotton, full-body wraparound
Torah	Hebrew Bible
ulama	Muslim senior clergy
umma	Arabic word for Islamic community
Upanishad	One of a class of Vedic treatises dealing with broad philosophical questions
varna	Indian caste system, which divides society into four orders: Brahmin (priestly cate-gory), Kshatriya (warrior group), Vaishya (traders or agriculturalists), and Shudra (people performing menial work). These are said to

	be birth distinctions (jati).
Veda	Any of four canonical collections of hymns, prayers, and liturgical formulas that comprise the earliest Hindu sacred writings
Volk	German word for People
vrata	Special ritual fasts and worship in Hindu-ism
wali	Matrimonial tutor or guardian in Muslim marriages
yeshiva	Jewish religious school
zaar	Sudanese term for spirit possession cult
zakat	Islamic alms tax (tithe)
zanana	Persian word for women's quarters in a house
zananigi/mardanigi	Persian words denoting femininity and masculinity, respectively
zina	Arabic word for fornication
Zuchtanstalt	"Stud farm" for the SS in Nazi Germany

About the Contributors

Margot Badran is an Oxford-educated historian, who divides her time between the Middle East and the United States.

Alya Baffoun, Ph.D., Sorbonne, teaches social psychology at the University of Tunis.

Cherifa Bouatta and **Doria Cherifati-Merabtine** both teach social psychology at the University of Algiers, and are active in the women's and democratic movements.

The Division for the Advancement of Women is part of the United Nations and monitors the Convention on the Elimination of All Forms of Discrimination Against Women.

Shahin Gerami is associate professor of sociology at Southwest Missouri State University in Springfield, Missouri.

Sondra Hale is an anthropologist and longtime scholar of Sudan, who is based in Women's Studies and the Center for the Study of Women, UCLA, and directs Women's Studies at California State University, Northridge.

Marie-Aimée Hélie-Lucas, Algerian sociologist, taught methodology and epistemology at Algiers University for 12 years. She is founder and coordinator of the international network Women Living Under Muslim Laws, based in France.

Ayesha M. Imam teaches sociology at Ahmadu Bello University in Zaria, Nigeria, and is active in the women's movement. She is currently at AFRAS, University of Sussex, Brighton, United Kingdom.

Debra Renee Kaufman is associate professor of sociology at Northeastern University in Boston.

Rebecca E. Klatch is associate professor of sociology at the University of California, San Diego.

Radha Kumar is an historian, and was for many years active in the women's movement in India. She is now Executive Director of the Helsinki Citizens' Assembly, in Prague.

Sucheta Mazumdar teaches history at the University of New York, Albany, and is an editor of *South Asia Bulletin*.

Silva Meznaric is a sociologist who teaches at the University of Ljubljana and heads a research project on violence and forced migration at the University of Zagreb.

Valentine M. Moghadam is Senior Research Fellow and Coordinator of the Research Programme on Women and Development at the World Institute for Development Economics Research (UNU/WIDER), in Helsinki, Finland.

Khawar Mumtaz is with Shirkat Gah Women's Resource Centre in Lahore, Pakistan.

Hanna Papanek is with the anthropology department of Boston University, and has long specialized in south and southeast Asian societies.

Joan Smith is Professor of Sociology at the University of Vermont, Burlington.

Mohamad Tavakoli-Targhi teaches Middle Eastern history at Illinois State University, Normal.

Binnaz Toprak teaches political science at Bogazici University in Istanbul, Turkey.

Madeleine Tress teaches political science at New York University in New York City.

Nira Yuval-Davis is Reader in Ethnic and Gender Studies in the Sociology Division of Thames Polytechnic in London.

About the Book

Identity politics refers to discourses and movements organized around questions of religious, ethnic, and national identity. This volume focuses on political-cultural movements that are making a bid for state power, for fundamental juridical change, or for cultural hegemony. In particular, the contributors explore the relations of culture, identity, and women, providing vivid illustrations from around the world of the compelling nature of Woman as cultural symbol and Woman as political pawn in male-directed power struggles. The discussions also provide evidence of women as active participants and as active opponents of such movements. Taken together, the chapters provide answers to some pressing questions about these political-cultural movements: What are their causes? Who are the participants and social groups that support them? What are their objectives? Why are they preoccupied with gender and the control of women?

The first section of the book offers theoretical, comparative, and historical approaches to the study of identity politics. A second section consists of thirteen case studies spanning Muslim, Christian, Jewish, and Hindu countries and communities. In the final section, contributors discuss dilemmas posed by identity politics and the strategies designed in response.

Index

447